ARCHIBALD THOMPSON DAVISON

ESSAYS ON MUSIC

in honor of

ARCHIBALD THOMPSON DAVISON

by his Associates

Department of Music, Harvard University
Cambridge, Massachusetts
1957

ARCHIBALDO THOMPSON DAVISON

UNIV. HARV. A.B. MDCCCCVI, A.M. MDCCCCVII, PH.D. MDCCCCVIII;
MUS. D.
COLL. WILL. MDCCCCXXXIII, UNIV. OXON. MDCCCCXXXIIII,
UNIV. HARV. MDCCCCXXXXVIII;
LITT. D. UNIV. WASH. MDCCCCLIII;

MUSICO, STUDIOSO, ORGANICO, PHONASCO, SCRIPTORI;

RATIONUM MUSICARUM INTERPRETI,
QUI DISCIPULIS OMNES EXERCITATIONES ITA PROBAVIT
UT ARTEM MUSICAM AMPLIUS INHAURIRENT;

HISTORIÆ MUSICÆ EXPLICATORI,
QUI HOC STUDIUM QUASI PEREGRINATIONEM CONTINUAM
NOVAS IN ARTIS PERCEPTIONES VERSAM REDDIDIT;

CHORORUM MODULATORI,
QUI MUSICAM SACRAM ELATIONE AC REVERENTIA
MUSICAM PROFANAM FERVORE AC VIGORE
CARMINA NUDISSIMA SIMPLICITATE AC SUAVITATE EXORNAVIT;

QUI DENIQUE,
A SUMMA ARTE NULLO MODO, NULLO TEMPORE DECLINANS,
CANTUM CHORALEM PATRIÆ SUÆ ANIMO CANORO PENITUS EXCOLUIT;

HUNC LIBRUM
ANNO DOMINO MDCCCCLIII ET ÆTATIS EIUS SEPTUAGESIMO,
NATALICIIS A.D. V IDUS OCT. CONCELEBRATIS,
DISCIPULI REVERENTES, COLLEGÆ ADMIRANTES, AMICI DEVOTI
SUMMO CUM AMORE

D.D.D.

TO

ARCHIBALD THOMPSON DAVISON

A.B. HARVARD 1906, A.M. 1907, PH.D. 1908
MUS.D. WILLIAMS COLLEGE 1933, OXFORD UNIVERSITY 1934, HARVARD 1948
LITT.D. WASHINGTON UNIVERSITY 1953

MUSICIAN, SCHOLAR, ORGANIST, CONDUCTOR, AUTHOR

TEACHER OF THEORY
WHO HAS MADE EVERY EXERCISE
AN EXPERIENCE IN MUSICAL ART

TEACHER OF THE HISTORY OF MUSIC
WHO HAS MADE IT
AN UNENDING VOYAGE OF DISCOVERY

CONDUCTOR WHO HAS BROUGHT
TO SACRED MUSIC REVERENCE AND RAPTURE
TO SECULAR MUSIC WARMTH AND VIGOR
AND TO THE SIMPLEST TUNE SIMPLICITY AND DELIGHT

AND WHO, WITH UNSWERVING DEVOTION TO QUALITY
TRANSFORMED THE CHORAL SINGING OF THE NATION
BY HIS SINGING SOUL

THIS BOOK IS AFFECTIONATELY DEDICATED
ON HIS SEVENTIETH BIRTHDAY
BY HIS
REVERING STUDENTS, ADMIRING COLLEAGUES
AND DEVOTED FRIENDS

Contents

FOREWORD
Randall Thompson

I ANTIQUITY

MUSES AND SCALES   3
Curt Sachs, New York University

II THE MIDDLE AGES

AN INTRODUCTION TO THE PRE-HISTORY OF POLYPHONY   11
Lincoln Bunce Spiess, Washington University (St. Louis)

GIRALDUS CAMBRENSIS ON WELSH POPULAR SINGING   17
Lloyd Hibberd, North Texas State College

IMITATION IN THE THIRTEENTH AND FOURTEENTH
    CENTURIES   25
Willi Apel, Indiana University

III THE FIFTEENTH AND SIXTEENTH
CENTURIES

A FIFTEENTH-CENTURY "CHRISTMAS ORATORIO"   41
Richard H. Hoppin, University of Texas

ABOUT ORGAN PLAYING IN THE DIVINE SERVICE, CIRCA 1500   51
Otto Gombosi, Harvard University

A STUDY IN PROPORTIONS   69
Helen Hewitt, North Texas State College

A CURIOUS USE OF COLORATION IN THE PIXÉRÉCOURT
    CODEX   83
Carl Parrish, Vassar College

A CHANSON SEQUENCE BY FEVIN   91
A. Tillman Merritt, Harvard University

EQUAL VOICES IN THE A CAPPELLA PERIOD   101
Otto Kinkeldey, Cornell University

MODAL HARMONY IN THE MUSIC OF PALESTRINA   111
Andrew C. Haigh, College of William and Mary

PUEBLA'S REQUIEM CHOIRBOOK 121
Steven Barwick, Western Kentucky State Teachers College

TEXTURE VERSUS MASS IN THE MUSIC OF GIOVANNI GABRIELI 129
G. W. Woodworth, Harvard University

IRRATIONAL DISSONANCE IN THE ENGLISH MADRIGAL 139
Henry G. Mishkin, Amherst College

WATERMARKS IN CERTAIN MANUSCRIPT COLLECTIONS OF ENGLISH KEYBOARD MUSIC 147
Stephen D. Tuttle, Harvard University

IV THE SEVENTEENTH AND EIGHTEENTH CENTURIES

THE "AUTHENTIC" PERFORMANCE OF BAROQUE MUSIC 161
Putnam Aldrich, Leland Stanford University

BIFOCAL TONALITY: AN EXPLANATION FOR AMBIGUOUS BAROQUE CADENCES 173
Jan La Rue, Wellesley College

DYNAMICS IN SEVENTEENTH- AND EIGHTEENTH-CENTURY MUSIC 185
David D. Boyden, University of California

NOTES ON THE SIGNIFICANCE OF SEVENTEENTH- AND EIGHTEENTH-CENTURY MUSIC CRITICISM 195
Gordon A. Sutherland, University of Michigan

CARROUSEL MUSIC AT THE COURT OF LOUIS XIV 205
Caldwell Titcomb, Brandeis University

MOLL DAVIES, FIRST LADY OF ENGLISH OPERA 215
Henry Leland Clarke, University of California (Los Angeles)

MUSICAL SYMBOLISM IN THE VOCAL WORKS OF JOHANN PACHELBEL 225
Henry Woodward, Carleton College

THE RITORNELLO FORMS IN BACH'S CATECHISM CHORALE PRELUDES 235
Robert S. Tangeman, Union Theological Seminary

DOMENICO SCARLATTI'S CHORAL MUSIC 243
Ralph Kirkpatrick, Yale University

SOME WORKS FALSELY ASCRIBED TO FRIEDEMANN BACH   247
  George Benson Weston, Harvard University

A NEGLECTED WORK IN BEETHOVEN'S CHORAL MUSIC:
    THE FUNERAL CANTATA   253
  Elliot Forbes, Princeton University

V THE TWENTIETH CENTURY

HINDEMITH'S "FRAU MUSICA": THE VERSIONS OF 1928
    AND 1943 COMPARED   265
  William Austin, Cornell University

THOUGHTS ON THE CHORDAL CONCEPT   273
  Walter Piston, Harvard University

PROBLEMS OF CHORAL TEXTURE IN THE TWENTIETH
    CENTURY   279
  Harold C. Schmidt, Leland Stanford University

OPERA IS NOT WHAT IT SHOULD BE   293
  Robert E. Middleton, Vassar College

MUSIC VIA TELEVISION   303
  Norma Bertolami Sapp, Cambridge, Massachusetts

THE RECORD REVIEW: CONTENT AND PURPOSE   313
  Allen Sapp, Harvard University

CHURCH MUSIC   325
  Lowell P. Beveridge, Virginia Theological Seminary

CHURCH MUSIC   331
  Willard L. Sperry, Harvard University

SCHOLAR-MUSICIAN AS TEACHER   337
  David Stone, Temple University

ON HISTORICAL AUTHENTICITY IN THE PERFORMANCE OF
    OLD MUSIC   341
  Donald Jay Grout, Cornell University

VI BIBLIOGRAPHY

A BIBLIOGRAPHY OF ARCHIBALD THOMPSON DAVISON'S
    WORKS   351
  J. M. Coopersmith, Library of Congress

ARCHIBALD THOMPSON DAVISON became Professor Emeritus of Music at Harvard at the close of the academic year 1953–1954. He had taught there for forty-one years with undiminished vigor. On October 11, 1953, his seventieth birthday was celebrated. This volume of essays was written in homage to him on that occasion.

The year before, the Music Department had undertaken to sponsor such a volume and invitations had been sent out for the voluntary contribution of essays. It was not easy to decide which among Dr Davison's friends might most appropriately be asked to contribute. In the end, to keep the volume to reasonable size, the list had to be confined to his past and present musical colleagues at Harvard and to those who had received advanced degrees under his instruction. A few who were invited were prevented by circumstances from accepting. Many more would gladly have contributed. Those who were able to contribute have done so *con amore*.

The authors were given complete freedom in the choice of subject. The wide variety of topics chosen and of periods of musical history treated is testimony to the breadth of Dr Davison's taste and to the sweep of his interests. With regard to those of the authors who studied under him, the marked variety of treatment testifies also to the freedom of his teaching and to his assiduous avoidance of anything approaching Procrustean methodology in musicological matters.

The variety of topics which the authors chose made it not altogether easy to determine the order in which the essays might best be arranged. The chronological grouping by principal epochs seemed logical and convenient. This arrangement of the essays also shows that, while certain epochs have received more attention than others, many important phases of musical history are touched upon.

To ensure all possible accuracy, both the texts of the essays and the musical examples accompanying them were resubmitted to the authors in proof, and final corrections were duly entered. Consistency in editorial usage has been sought in general matters but care has been taken to respect the personal editorial style of the individual contributor.

It would have been a happy thing for all concerned if the volume could have been published nearer to the day which it was written to celebrate. The publication committee consisted of Professor Otto J. Gombosi, Associate Professor Stephen D. Tuttle and the undersigned. Professor Tuttle died on April 9, 1954, and Professor Gombosi on February 17, 1955. The tragic death of each in turn was a severe setback. In addition to the essays which they had contributed, most of the labor of planning and assembling the volume had been theirs. The volume's debt to them is here recorded in gratitude.

The Dedication was originally written in English. In view of Dr Davison's enthusiasm for the Classics, a Latin version seemed clearly indicated. Our colleague Professor Mason Hammond, of the Classics Department, provided it with gusto. To him and to his collaborator, Assistant Professor Philip Levine, we offer our sincere gratitude for an inscription worthy of the Age of Augustus. With them and with Dr Davison, we can only bewail the passing of the days when teachers of Music did such things themselves, unaided.

At the kind suggestion of Mr Thomas J. Wilson, Director of the Harvard University Press, Mr Burton L. Stratton designed the volume and supervised its production. For his skill and imagination, Mr Stratton's liberal assistance is acknowledged with grateful thanks. The difficult and often highly specialized task of proofreading has been carried out by his wife, E. Naomi Stratton. The book owes much to them both, individually and as a team.

Mr Gordon Mapes, of Princeton, New Jersey, prepared the reproduction copy from which the numerous musical examples were made.

To the authors themselves, whose separate labors have created this combined tribute, is extended the warm appreciation of the entire Department of Music. Beneath the surface of their words lie the admiration and affection which we all feel for a great teacher, true musician, ageless friend.

RANDALL THOMPSON

Music Building
Harvard University
September, 1956

PART ONE
Antiquity

Curt Sachs

Myth, the mirror of national thought and memory, is partial to the so-called arts of time, to epics, lyrics, and drama, to music and dancing. It has ignored as lowly, despicable handicraft the arts of space: architecture, painting, and sculpture. Gods and demigods are in charge of the former arts; the latter ones are seldom present in the pantheon. Even in the far-off North the poet and singer Bragi is the son of Odin, father in Asgard; but to build the castle of Valhalla the Nordic gods must hire (and cheat) the rugged, clumsy giants whom they despise. The Indian heaven, devoid of plastic arts, resounds with music: Siva dances, Vishnu crashes the cymbals, Krishna plays the flute to his lovely nine shepherdesses, and many divinities in distress blow the eerie, powerful conch trumpet; Brahma himself invents the drum, and the first to strike it is Ganesha, the god with an elephant's head, but above them as a musician stands Narada: born of the goddess of learning and eloquence, he is himself inventor of the harp and the god of law and astronomy.

In creating Narada, Indian myth displays the momentous connection of music with thought and science. The same idea recurs in other oriental cultures. In Egypt, Bes, the jolly god of pleasure, plays a few instruments to entertain his fellow divinities. But he does not personify music in as far as it reaches beyond entertainment. As an object of understanding and study, that is, as a liberal art, music is taken care of by Thoth, the ibis-headed god of wisdom and knowledge, inventor of numbers and script and author of some forty books including music, acoustics, and, once more, astronomy. Music on the Nile as well as in India rose to the highest rank of an art established on scientific research and worthy of scholarly interest.

This lofty attitude reappears much later beyond the Mediterranean in Greece. Athena, the goddess of knowledge and wisdom, has learned to strum the lyre and gives the exciting pipes at least a trial; and Apollo, god of wisdom as well, plays the lyre and leads the Muses, who have given their name to music.

Begotten by Zeus himself and by Mnemosyne, the incarnation of mindful memory, the Muses were immortal maidens (although a few versions of their myth do not exactly corroborate this noun). Their title meant originally the contemplative ones, thus, oddly enough, drawing near to the English word musing, which despite its similar sound and meaning has a different pedigree.

Generally speaking, the Muses were much less the ideal performers of music and poetry than protectors, inspirers, and personified allegories of these arts. Specifically, however, neither their names nor their numbers, tasks, and attributes were consistent in Grecian times and lands. In every age since Homer and Hesiod, in all the regions of Hellas they differed. Only in the century of Aristotle, the fourth B.C., a turn to neat, consistent classification in the arts and sciences gave the nine Muses, too, a certain stability and overall pattern:

Erato, for lyrics and erotic singing;
Euterpe, for lyrical singing;
Kalliope, for epical poetry;
Klio, for history;
Melpomene, for tragedy;
Polyhymnia, for lyrical singing;
Terpsichore, for dancing and choral singing;
Thalia, for pastoral poetry and for comedy;
Urania, for astronomy.

This is a bewildering array. There are no less than three lyrical Muses — possibly in order to fill the sacred number of nine, or three times three, which is in Greece the number of Cybele's corybantes and in India that of Krishna's shepherdesses. More bewildering is the fact that seven of them stand for the musical arts in the proper sense of the word, that is, for the various branches of poetry, singing, and dancing, and two for fields of knowledge: astronomy and history. The presence of history is not hard to explain: in the times when the myth of the Muses took shape, history was not yet the strict, objective prose description of national customs and events that it became in the age of Herodotos, but existed only in the artistic form of epical poetry such as Homer's Iliad. The case of Urania is less conspicuous. Astronomy might have had a justification for appearing in the circle of the musical arts in the age-old oriental (and Grecian) concept of the so-called harmony of the spheres. But this line of contact is rather short, and the more so, as the sounding stars are a late misunderstanding of an entirely non-sounding ratio common to musical intervals and the orbits of planets. There is so far no fully satisfactory answer except the fact that again and again the lore of music and the lore of the stars are found in closest relation. Narada in India and Thoth in Egypt were astronomers, and the schools of music connected with Sumerian temples seem to have had astronomy, too, as a field of learning. In this context, the historian of music will think of Peter the Venerable, abbot of Cluny, *musicus* and *astrologus* (twelfth century), and, above all, of the greatest among the earlier English masters, John Dunstable, who died in 1453 as "an astrologian, a mathematician, a musi*t*ian, and what not?"

In dealing with the changing number of Muses in various regions and times, historians have suggested that in the earliest ages there might have been one single Muse. Their main reason was that in the first verses of both the Iliad and the Odyssey the poet invokes *Mousa* in the singular. This is not convincing. Even among the complete Nine, only the one Kalliope was duly qualified for epic poetry; Homer could not very well appeal to the Muses of lyrics, astronomy, or the dance.

Still, we, as historians of music, are interested at least in one of the various numbers in which the Muses appear: in the number three. Plutarch, well informed if late (d. 120 A.D.), tells us that at Delphi the three Muses stood for the notes *nētē*, *mesē*, *hypátē*. These notes had indeed a particular significance. They were doubtless the oldest names of notes in Hellas; their later neighbors in the scale, *paranētē* as well as *paramesē* and *parhypátē*, have clearly the stamp of derived terms (*para* meaning "next to"); and the seventh note, *lichanós*, literally "index finger," adds an entirely foreign concept to the triad of spatial terms as are the just mentioned "nether," "central," and "upper." We know from another passage in Plutarch that the oldest lyre of the country had altogether only three strings, and that these strings were tuned to exactly the same pitches covered by the three original terms. We know furthermore from a number of vase paintings that such archaic lyres were actually used in the ninth and eighth centuries B.C. The author of this paper has shown that with the help of a stopping finger the three strings were sufficient to produce the obviously oldest, "enharmonic" scale of Greece:

Ex.1

This direct connection of the Muses with a musical scale seems not to be unique. One other case shows, or at least suggests, that at times even the Nine had a scale relationship. Though mentioned as early as the eighth century in Hesiod's Theogony (and in a spurious passage of the Odyssey), the Nine are not depicted and identified before the sixth century B.C. This earliest representation is painted on the beautiful archaic François Vase of the Archaeological Museum in Florence. In the center of her sisters, Kalliope, the leader of the Nine, is, as the only one, holding an instrument, and an unusual instrument at that: a rectangular *syrinx* or set of panpipes. And the number of pipes is nine. This is very strange. Nine, the number of the Muses, recurs in the pipes although the latter had, as a rule, only seven tubes. And how can the Muse of epic poetry perform on a wind instrument, which, requiring the perpetual action of the mouth, is incompatible both with singing and with reciting?

An explanation might come from the Far East. Such an explanation could seem far-fetched and thus inadmissible. But there are innumerable musical parallels between East Asia and Greece — so many, in fact, that there appears to be a common prehistoric source midways in Central Asia. The very scale that we printed in the last but one paragraph is with all its derivations the national gamut of modern Japan as it was the national gamut of ancient Greece; the lyres of Hellas were tuned in the same minor-third and whole-tone pentatonics as are the zithers of China, Korea, and Japan; the connotation of music with the planets, human characters, and education in the interest of the State appear at first in Confucian China and subsequently in Platonic Greece. Panpipes were rare in Hellas as in all the West; they are indispensable in the East, whence they have spread across the Pacific to the American Indians. But it would be wrong to fancy that the ancient Orientals devised this instrument for the easy performance of melodies by shifting the proper pipes to the mouth. From a good many evidences we know that they rather were bundled pitch pipes, to be blown one at a time as standards for singers and players.

It is tempting, indeed imperative, to interpret Kalliope's nine-tubed panpipes, too, as tuned to a scale providing individual pitches for each of the Muses.

Which scale could this have been? Where do we find nine notes in a set?

There seem to be two possibilities. One comes from a list that Aristides Quintilianus gives of the scales that — as he says — "the very oldest" musicians used. It is in his terminology a "Dorian" and has nine notes. This could be what we are looking for. But then, Aristides lived rather late, in the second century A.D., and he makes us believe more than we can accept: all these "very oldest" scales are "enharmonic," with major thirds, and have the semitones cleft into two microtones each, which according to everything that we know is a considerably later development.

It is much safer to follow the other traditions, which all agree upon the fact that Terpander, greatest poet-musician of the seventh century B.C., created the earliest octave by adding a high *e'* to an older heptad. This would mean that the original diatonic scale of the Greeks had been

that is, a heptad out of two conjunct Dorian tetrachords, similar to the later Mixolydian. If Terpander had just repeated the lowest note *e* as *e'* to achieve an octave, his feat would hardly have been worth remembering over nine hundred years. Rather, the new scale attributed to Terpander was the Dorian proper out of two disjunct Dorian tetrachords:

This oldest couple of diatonic scales in Greece required the latter's eight notes plus the $b\flat$ of the former mode. It had the nine notes that would in the seventh and the sixth century make sense on Kalliope's pitchpipes for the Muses.

But we still need an explanation for the concept, so foreign to modern ideas, that a group of demigods are associated with individual notes each, which in turn form an accepted scale. This strange connotation is an integral part of oriental cosmology. Indian legend tells us how one of the gods, very proud of his voice, was taken to the abode of the Seven Notes embodied in seven lovely nymphs, and how, whenever the god sang a note incorrectly, one of the nymphs swayed and fell dead. Whereupon a greater god had to interfere and, playing the notes correctly, revive the victims of amateurish vanity. Somewhat weakened, the personification of notes lived on in ancient Greece and still exists in European astrology. Eager to see in the universe a supreme organism, cosmologists coördinated the various part organizations that the human mind experienced: the spheres of the planets with the gods for whom they were named, the seasons, the cardinal points, the gamut of basic colors, the musical scale. Mercury, Jupiter, Saturn, Venus, and Mars were brought into proper relation with a musical scale and each corresponded to one of its notes. The Muses, united in a definite set, were they not apt to a similar scale organization — they who were *ex definitione* musical?

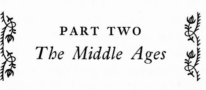

PART TWO

The Middle Ages

AN INTRODUCTION TO THE PRE-HISTORY

OF POLYPHONY [1]

Lincoln Bunce Spiess

THE ultimate origin of polyphony has been the subject of some research and theorizing in recent years. The publication which has attempted to deal with this subject from the most monumental point of view is Marius Schneider's *Geschichte der Mehrstimmigkeit* (2 vols., 1935–36). According to Schneider, the organum of the ninth century is the culmination of a development in which aboriginal polyphony (such as, for instance, still exists today in certain parts of Africa) is the earliest stage, and in which Greek heterophony was an intermediate development. The theory is logical, but there is perhaps room for speculation as regards the alleged "purity" of the aboriginal tribes from which stem the musical examples of Schneider's hypothetical first stage. An investigation of this problem is outside the scope of this brief study, but it does seem that during the one thousand years that polyphony has definitely known to have been in existence (exclusive of the heterophony of classical antiquity) some influence, however indirect, may have reached such aboriginal nations and tribes as referred to by Schneider.

More tangible in the pre-history of polyphony is the heterophony of Greek antiquity. Here scholars have worked on more solid ground due to the existence of the Aristotelian work, the so-called "Problems of Aristotle." [2] (The *Problems* are now generally accepted as the work of a follower of Aristotle; for our purposes, however, they are still valuable source material for the musical practices of antiquity.) In Book XIX, "Problems connected with Harmony," [3] several problems contain clear references to simultaneity (#12, 13, 16, 17, 18, 19, 34, 35, 39, 41, 49), and three in particular refer specifically to heterophonic instrumental accompaniment (#12, 16, 49). Problem 17 also mentions *singing* in fifths but this is apparently spurious, or else the reference is purely theoretical, because the next following problem asks: "Why is the octave consonance alone used in singing?"

With the problem of simultaneity in the early Middle Ages we are not so fortunate as with antiquity. There are three major references on which the arguments for a polyphony in the early Middle Ages are usually based. All three are, however, of decidedly questionable scientific value.

The most important of these references is the mention of para-phonistae and archiparaphonistae (cantors singing at the fourth or fifth from the cantus firmus) in the *Ordo Romanus I*.[4] The main body of this work dates from the time of Gregory the Great (pope 590–604); the reference to paraphonistae, however, occurs *only* in the Appendix to the *Ordo Romanus I*,[5] and the Appendix, according to no less inaccessible a source than the *Catholic Encyclopedia* (article: *Ordines Romani*), is at least of ninth century origin.

The second reference to early simultaneity occurs in the *Sententiae ad Braulionem* of St. Isidorus Hispalensis (c. 560–636) which Gerbert published in the *Scriptores*.[6] Unfortunately the Gerbert *Sententiae* is from a thirteenth century manuscript (Vienna, Staatsbibliothek), and the very passage which is most important for our present subject, the *Excerptum de rhythmimachia* (Gerbert, I, 25), is absent from the *Opera omnia*.[7] The editor of the complete works, moreover, remarks that this *Excerptum* in Gerbert is of doubtful authenticity.[8]

The third reference for the pre-history of polyphony is a passage from Giraldus Cambrensis's *Descriptio Kambriae* describing polyphonic folk singing in Wales. Giraldus lived in the late twelfth century (1147–c. 1220) and it is of some moment whether evidence of such late date is of value in showing the existence of any kind of polyphony in the early Middle Ages.

There are, in addition to the above three questionable references for a pre-history of polyphony, two passages which are more authentic, but here again it is doubtful whether anything decisive can be based on them. The first of these is by a "Monk of Angoulême" who says that the "Roman cantors taught the French cantors in the 'ars organandi.' " [9] This passage occurs, however, in Angoulême's *Another Life of Charlemagne* (*Karoli Magni . . . vita alia*); the title alone of this work is enough evidence that the writer was living well into the ninth century and we know definitely that organum was already in existence in that century, so that this does little more than confirm something already known.

The second one of this group of passages uses two terms which, in the ninth century, are associated with polyphony, namely: "diafonia" and "organica modulatio." This reference occurs in the works of Bishop Aldelmus (639?–709) [10] and is as follows: [11]

Unde ergo ista diversitas et veluti inconveniens *diafonia* nascatur, cum in praedictis X pedibus aequo divisionis exagio trutinatis, quasi quaedam [Handschin has "quadam"] organicae modulationis melodia, ita concors temporum armonia teneatur?

Whence, therefore, arises that diversity, and truly just like the inconsonant diaphony, when, in the aforesaid ten poetical-feet, balanced by the equal weight of the phrase, like the melody of a certain "organica modulatio," a common harmony of the measures is thus kept.

Unfortunately, "organica modulatio" in the seventh century commonly means "instrumental melody" (see Isidorus: *Etymologiae, Liber III, Caput XXI*); [12] and "diaphonia," or "diafonia" as Aldelmus has it, means "dissonance" (Isidorus: *Etymologiae, Liber III, Caput XX*). [13]

The use of the term "dissonance" implies, in a backhanded way, the existence or at least the knowledge of "consonance," and the question arises whether in the authentic writings of Isidorus himself, who provides us with our definitions, there is any intimation of simultaneity. The answer is that in his definition of "symphonia," and there only, he seems to show a *theoretical* knowledge of simultaneity. This definition of "symphonia" is as follows: [14]

Symphonia est modulationis temperamentum ex gravi, et acuto concordantibus sonis, sive in voce, sive in flatu, sive in pulsu. Per hanc quippe voces acutiores, gravioresque concordant, ita ut quisquis ab ea dissonuerit, sensum auditus offendat. Cuius contraria est *diaphonia*, id est, voces discrepantes, vel dissonae. [15]

Symphonia is the constitution of a melody, by means of notes which are concordant above and below either in the voice, in breathing, or in accent. [16] By means of this, to be sure, higher and lower tones are concordant in such a way that should any one note disagree in sound with this, it offends the sense of hearing. The opposite of this is *diaphonia*, that is, notes which disagree, or are dissonant.[17]

Isidorus was quite familiar with the essential theories of Greek music and these definitions reflect Greek theory. The term "symphonia" was used by the Greeks, incidentally, in connection with heterophonic accompaniment (as well as having other meanings) and in that sense it was in contradistinction to "antiphonos," or a performance in octaves (Aristotle: *Problems*, Problem 16).

On the basis of available evidence it is not possible to show satisfactorily the existence of a continuous practice of polyphony before the ninth century works which have sometimes been attributed to Hucbald. If we except theoretical references (which do not necessarily point to a contemporary polyphonic practice) and the heterophony of Greek antiquity, there is no scientific evidence extant to prove beyond question that there was a rudimentary polyphonic practice before the organum of the ninth century.

1. We use the term "polyphony" in its widest sense, namely in contradistinction to "monophony."

2. The available editions are the following:

a. Gevaert et Vollgraf: *Les problemes musicaux d'Aristote*. Gand, A. Hoste, 1903.

b. Aristotle: *Problems*, Books I–XXI, W. S. Hett, translator (Loeb Classical Library). Cambridge, Harvard University Press, 1936.

c. Forster, E. S.: *Problemata* (*The Works of Aristotle*, W. D. Ross, ed., Vol. VII). Oxford, Clarendon Press, 1927.

The Loeb translation, as well as the Gevaert edition have the original and the translation on opposite pages, and the Gevaert edition has the additional advantage of indicating the supposed spurious passages by smaller type.

3. "Harmony" in the classical sense refers to music in general.

4. *Patrologiae latinae cursus completus*, Vol. 78, col. 937 ff.

5. *Ibid.*, col. 965.

6. Gerbert: *Scriptores ecclesiastici de musica*, I, 20.

7. The section in the *Opera omnia* entitled *De musica* (Isidori. . . *Opera omnia*, Arevalus ed., Vol. III, p. 132 ff.) is identical, except for a few minor variants, with the *Sententiae* up to, but not including, the *Excerptum*.

8. *Ibid.*, Vol. I (*Isidoriana*), p. 451.

9. "Similiter erudierunt Romani cantores supradictos cantores Francorum in arte organandi." (Du Chesne: *Historiae Francorum Scriptores*, II, p. 75.)

10. *Monumenta Germaniae historica, Auctorum antiquissorum, Tomus XV*.

11. *Ibid.*, p. 189. This passage was first pointed out by Handschin in ZfMW, VIII, p. 323 (in the article: *Zur Geschichte der Lehre vom Organum*).

12. *Opera omnia*, Vol. III, p. 136.

13. *Ibid.*, p. 135.

14. *Loc. cit.*

15. This same definition of "symphonia" is given more or less verbatim (as far as it goes) somewhat earlier by Cassiodorus.

16. Perhaps better: " . . . in singing, on wind instruments, or on (string and) percussion instruments."

17. This meaning of "diaphonia" should not be confused with its later meaning (from the ninth century on) when it came to be synonymous with organum at the fourth or fifth. In the twelfth century the term "discantus" appears as a more or less literal translation of "diaphonia" and at the same time "organum" takes on a different meaning from discant and diaphony, the two latter continuing to refer to the note-against-note style while organum begins to refer to the more elaborate style which culminated in the Notre Dame organa. This change of meaning of these three terms is mentioned so that the reader will understand that key terms have undergone major change of meaning in the medieval period and that one cannot necessarily use a later definition of a term as evidence for an earlier period. This is of course a basic truism for research generally.

GIRALDUS CAMBRENSIS ON

WELSH POPULAR SINGING

Lloyd Hibberd

THE Welsh polyhistor Giraldus Cambrensis (c. 1146–c. 1223) is the author of a passage, in his *Descriptio Cambriae* (c. 1188),[1] about popular singing in Wales that has long been, and continues to be, taken as referring to part singing in some form of organum, or even canon. It seems at least as likely, however, that Giraldus is speaking of heterophony, an interpretation not, to the present writer's knowledge, previously advanced.

The passage in question occurs in Chapter III which is entitled "Concerning their symphonic song (*symphonicis cantibus*) and 'organic cantilenas' (*cantilenis organicis*)." It may as well be stated at the outset that it is impossible to tell what differences, if any, are implied in the names *cantus, canticum, cantilena,* and *carmen,* all of which are used by Gerald and all of which usually mean merely "song." It is equally impossible to tell whether the adjective *organicus* here has to do with any type of organum as known to us from other and more technical sources, or is a generic name for music other than at the unison. And there are several other ambiguous terms whose rendition in the following translation will be explained later:

"As to their musical euphony (*modulamine*), they do not sing uniformly (*uniformiter*) as is done elsewhere, but diversely (*multipliciter*) with many rhythms and tunes [or intervals?: *modulis*] so that in a crowd of singers, such as is the custom among these people, you will hear as many different songs and differentiations of the voices as you see heads, and hear the organic melody (*organica melodia*) coming together in one consonance with the smooth sweetness of B flat.

"Moreover, in the northern part of Great Britain, that is across the

Humber and on the borders of Yorkshire, the English people who inhabit those parts employ the same kind of symphonious harmony (*symphonica harmonia*) in singing, but in only two parts [literally differences of tones and varieties of voices]: one murmuring below and the other in a like manner softly and pleasantly above. Both nations have acquired this peculiarity not by art but by long usage which has made it, as it were, natural. Moreover it prevails in both countries and is now so deeply rooted there that nothing musical (*melice*) is performed simply, but only diversely among the former people and in two parts among the latter. And what is more remarkable children scarcely beyond infancy, when their wails have barely turned into songs (*cantus*) observe the same musical performance (*modulationem*).

"Since the English in general do not employ this method of musical performances (*modulationibus*) but only the northerners, I believe that it was from the Danes and Norwegians, by whom these parts of the island were more frequently invaded and held longer, that they contracted this peculiarity of singing as well as their manner of speaking." [2]

In examining the key words, italicized above, upon whose interpretation the meaning of the passage as a whole largely depends, it must be remarked that in practice Latin is not quite the precise and unchanging language it is sometimes reputed to be; for not only does it vary with the period and country but also the degree of education — sometimes, as here, even the technical education — of the user.[3]

Henry Owen states that Gerald "prided himself on his classic style, and although he uses many Low-Latin words . . . his Latinity is of a higher type than that of most of his contemporaries; the language had not yet been debased by the barbarous jargon of the school-men." [4]

We may assume then that Gerald's meanings correspond to those of classical usage save where the latter make no sense or are contrary to known facts, and that he is consistent in his terminology. Unfortunately Du Cange [5] offers no aid and recourse must be made to the Lewis and Short revision of *Harper's Latin dictionary*. For *modulamen*, whose usual meanings are "melody, euphony," the latter has been chosen because *melodia* occurs in the same passage. *Uniformiter* may mean "in unison," and *multipliciter* may mean "in parts," but these meanings are not given in Lewis and Short, and it has seemed safer to translate them as above. For *modus* Lewis and Short give "measurement of tones, measure, rhythm, melody, harmony, time." Among these the best seems to be "rhythm," not only because "melody" and "harmony" are covered by *melodia* and *harmonia*, but because *modus* is primarily a non-musical term having to do with measurement of size or quantity, and therefore more properly concerns rhythm, while "measure" and "time" are too closely associated with metrical music of a later period. *Modulus* can mean "rhythmical measure, rhythm, music, time, metre, mode [in the sense of 'scale'], melody." The translation "music" sheds no light, and, since we do not know that this music was measured, it is best to reject "rhythmical measure," as well as its occasional equivalent "time." And we already have *modus* for "rhythm."

The choice of a translation for *modulus* is admittedly difficult. If we seek elsewhere in Gerald for modifiers or contexts as clues, we find that a few pages earlier in the *Descriptio* he mentions guests being entertained by *cithararum modulis*, which must mean melodies on, or songs to, the harp.[6] And there is a reference to the *moduli* of the sirens.[7] And finally the term occurs three times in his famous passage on Irish instrumental music:[8] once modified by *crispatus* (originally "curled" but by transference "uneven, variegated"); again as the object of *intrant* and *exeunt* (probably best translated here as "begin" and "end"); and thirdly where he speaks of the Scotch and Welsh as trying to imitate the Irish in their *modulis*. Unless we assume that Gerald is inconsistent, the translation should be one that satisfies all passages, especially one to which *crispatus*[9] might apply. "Melody" would do except that the stricter term *melodia* occurs in the same passage.[10] One might employ the medieval meaning "melodic interval" were it not for the passages concerning the reception of guests, the *moduli* of the sirens, etc. It is, of course, possible that *melodia* means melody in a general sense (Gerald does not use that term in the plural), and then *moduli* may mean specific melodies, or perhaps as we should say "tunes." One is, in fact, left with the choice between "melodies" (tunes) or "intervals," neither of which quite satisfies all the passages.

A difficulty occurs with *organica melodia* similar to that with *cantilenis organicis* above: whether the adjective refers to some kind of organum already known to us, or merely to music other than at the unison.[11] *Symphonicus* [*recte* "symphoniacus"] originally meant merely an agreement of sounds, and does not, in itself, imply those intervals traditionally regarded as consonances. *Melice* and *cantus* require no particular comment, and we are left with *modulatio*, whose classical meanings are: "a regular measure . . . a marching to time . . . a rhythmical measure, modulation; [12] hence singing and playing, melody." For the reasons given above in connection with *modulus* we may discard "melody" and those meanings that suggest "measures" in the modern sense; and there is no connection with marching here. From the nature of the passage *modulatio* seems to mean singing or playing in general, i.e. musical performance.[13]

As for the phrase about "coming together with the sweet smoothness of B flat," we shall probably never know what is meant. Perhaps they really did end on their note equivalent to B flat; perhaps it merely means that they used some sort of scale similar to those portions of the hexachord system that employed a B flat — an F-f scale with B flat, for example, equivalent to the Ionian mode or modern major, which was not usual in ecclesiastical music (Gerald was a priest in the train of Baldwin Archbishop of Canterbury, at the time of his *Descriptio*) and therefore would be worthy of mention. Or it is possible that Gerald is trying to say that they always avoided the tritone by the use of B flat whatever the scale.[14]

F. Ludwig, in Adler's *Handbuch der Musikgeschichte*,[15] sees a connection between this passage and early polyphony "wohl in Terzen," as does Reese,[16] both of whom cite the hymn *Nobilis, humilis* as evidence, with its predominance of parallel thirds,[17] whose manuscript dates from the late thirteenth century but whose text celebrates St. Magnus (d. 1115). Now it is quite possible that singing in thirds was practiced that early and was known in Gerald's time and place, since the Orkney Islands, whence this hymn comes, had been, like Wales, subjected to the influences of Scandinavian culture. However, no actual connection between such a practice and the reference in Gerald can be established, and Gerald nowhere mentions thirds.

When we consider the two types of music, Welsh and Northumbrian, here described, we find that the former, especially in the use of the adjectives *symphonicus* and *organicus*, does seem to imply part music of some kind. However, we must remember that these words may be very indefinite in meaning, particularly when used by a non-professional like Gerald, and cannot be taken with certainty to mean more than two or more sounds (at indeterminable intervals) heard at the same time.

The real difficulty in accepting Gerald's description of Welsh singing as denoting part music in the usual sense is that he clearly states that "you will hear as many different songs and differentiations of the voices as you see heads" ("*quot videas capita tot audias carmina discriminaque vocum varia*"), which could be true of genuine polyphony (conceived as different voices progressing in organized relationship to each other in respect to intervals) only of a relatively small group; otherwise the parts, even at as small an interval as the third, would cover a wider range than is possible within the compass of human voices. But Gerald speaks of a *turba canentium*, or *crowd* of singers, presumably a rather large number.

Unless *turba* is an exaggeration, a more likely interpretation is that this Welsh practice was really heterophony, i.e. the simultaneous variation of a melody. In heterophony it would be quite easy for each singer, however untrained — even the children mentioned by Gerald — to perform his version, as of a familiar tune, against the independent variations of his fellows, so that together they produced a sort of "symphonious song" with "as many songs and differentiations of the voices as . . . heads." The two part Yorkshire singing, with its upper and lower voices, may have been the same thing, or possibly a melody above a drone bass. Both practices occur in primitive music [18] and probably preceded polyphony in the usual sense of the term. At any rate, the theory that Gerald's reference is to heterophony seems at least tenable and deserves consideration. Unfortunately no additional evidence is to be found in Gerald's writings, or, to this writer's knowledge, anywhere else.

1. With the exception of *De instructione principum*, which was published incompletely, under the editorship of J. S. Brewer, by the Anglia-Christiana Society in 1846 (not available for the present study), the works of Giraldus appear in eight volumes, edited by Brewer, J. F. Dimock, and G. F. Warner, as part of the Rolls series, *Rerum Britannicarum medii aevi scriptores*, London: Longmans, Green, 1861–91. In addition the *Itinerarium Cambriae* and the *Descriptio Cambriae*, as translated by Sir Richard Colt Hoare, have been republished in *Everyman's Library*.

2. "In musico modulamine, non uniformiter, ut alibi, sed multipliciter, multisque modis et modulis, cantilenas emittunt. Adeo ut in turba canentium, sicut huic gente mos est, quot videas capita, tot audias carmina discriminaque vocum varia, in unam denique sub B mollis dulcedine blanda consonantiam, et organicam convenientia melodiam.

"In borealibus quoque majoris Britanniae partibus, trans Humbriam scilicet, Eboraci finibus, Anglorum populi, qui partes illas inhabitant, simili canendo symphonica utuntur harmonia; binis tamen solummodo tonorum differentiis, et vocum modulando varietatibus; una inferius submurmurante, altera vero superne demulcente pariter et delectante. Nec arte tamen, sed usu longaevo, et quasi in naturam mora diutina jam converso, haec vel illa sibi gens hanc specialitatem comparavit. Qui adeo apud utramque invaluit, et altas jam radices posuit, ut nihil simpliciter, nihil nisi multipliciter ut apud priores, vel saltem dupliciter ut apud sequentes, melice proferri consueverit: pueris etiam, quod magis admirandum, et fere infantibus, cum primum a fletibus in cantus erumpunt, eandem modulationem observantibus.

"Angli vero, quoniam non generaliter omnes, sed boreales solum, hujusmodi vocum utuntur modulationibus, credo quod a Dacis et Norwagiensibus, qui partes illas insulae frequentius occupare, ac diutius obtinere solebant, sicut loquendo affinitatem, sic et canendi proprietatem contraxerunt" (*Descriptio Cambriae*, Capitulum XIII, Rolls VI, 189).

3. For generous assistance in rendering the Latin herein, the present writer is indebted to Professor J. F. Cronin of Southern Methodist University.

4. *Gerald the Welshman*, London: Whiting & Co., 1889, 26–27.

5. *Glossarium mediae et infimae latinitatis . . . cum supplementis integris D. P. Carpenterii*, ed. G. A. L. Henschel, Niort: L. Favre, 1883.

6. "Qui matutinis autem horis adveniunt, puellarum affatibus et cithararum modulis usque ad vesperam delectantur." Rolls VI, 183.

7. "In cantu resonant lyra, tibia, tympana, plusquam Sirenum modulos organa vocis habent," *Symbolum electorum*, Rolls I, 351. In addition there are two passages where *modulus* seems to refer to that kind of melody found in plainchant: "puer quidam extra parietem domus hunc sermonem quasi sub cantus modulo ingeminabat" (*De jure et statu Menevensis ecclesiae*, Rolls III, 309–10); and "sonoritate vocali moduloque jocundo pariter ac laetabundo tantum emiserunt antiphonam Salve Regina" (*Speculum ecclesiae*, Rolls IV, 144).

8. Full quotation of this passage is impossible here (but see excerpts in footnotes 11, 13, 14 below) not only because it is too long but because it is controversial and deserves its own treatment elsewhere. It must suffice here to point out that, since it speaks of thicker and thinner strings ("grossioris chordae . . . et gracilium chordarum"), it cannot, as at least one recent writer would have it, concern organ music. The reader will find the original Latin in the *Topographia Hibernica*, Rolls V, 153–55.

9. See footnote 11 below.

10. See footnote 11 below.

11. That *organum* does not refer exclusively to vocal music is shown in Gerald's reference, in the passage on Irish instrumental music, to "organa . . . multipliciter intricata" where "it is remarkable that, with such a rapid snatching of the fingers, the musical proportion is preserved, and, with art unimpaired, in spite of everything, the melody is finished and remains agreeable with such smooth rapidity, such unequal equality, such discordant concord, throughout the varied *moduli* and the many intricacies of the organa." ("*Mirum quod in tanta tam praecipiti digitorum rapacitate, musica servatur proportio; et arte pro omnia indemni, inter crispatos modulos, organaque multipliciter intricata, tam suave velocitate, tam dispari paritate, tam discordi concordia, consona redditur et compleatur melodia,*" Rolls V, 153.) See also the use of *organum* for the organ of the human voice in footnote 7 above.

12. In the sense of vocal inflection rather than in the modern technical meaning of a change of tonal center.

13. So also in the following from Gerald's *Vita S. Hugonis* where he speaks of a singer who "beginning at once the introit in a loud voice, continued with a musical and suitable performance" ("*introitum statim alta voce incipiens, cum*

melice debitaque modulatione protraxit," Rolls VII, 100). And again, this time with an implication of tempo, in the passage on Irish instrumental music: "Among them, the musical performance is not slow and solemn, as on English instruments to which we are accustomed, but rapid and lively, though the sound is soft and pleasant." (*"Non enim in his, sicut in Britannicis quibus assueti sumus instrumentis, tarda et morosa est modulatio, verum velox et praeceps, suavis tamen et jocunda sonoritas,"* Rolls V, 153). On the other hand, where he is describing a Welsh orgy of penitential dances, *modulatio* seems actually to mean the song itself, specifically a work song: "You will see this man put his hand to the plough, and that one as if goading on the oxen, both mitigating, as it were, their labor by uttering the usual crude work songs." (*"Videas hunc aratro manus aptare, illum quasi stimulo boves excitare; et utrumque quasi laborem mitigando solitas barbarae modulationis voces effere." Itinerarium Cambriae,* Rolls VI, 32.)

14. Nor do we get help from the reference, in the passage on Irish instrumental music, to the fact that "whether the strings sound in 4ths or 5ths, they always start from B flat and return to it so that everything ends with the charm of a pleasant sonority." (*Seu diatesseron, seu diapente chordae concrepent, semper tamen a B molli incipiunt, et in idem redeunt, ut cuncta sub jocundae sonoritatis dulcedine compleantur,* Rolls V, 153-54.)

15. P. 166.

16. *Music in the middle ages,* 387-88.

17. Transcribed in the Adler *Handbuch,* 167.

18. See Curt Sachs, *Rise of music in the ancient world,* 48, 60.

IMITATION IN THE THIRTEENTH
AND FOURTEENTH CENTURIES

Willi Apel

Ever since first encountering them, I have intensely disliked the terms caccia-motet and caccia-mass. Particularly the "caccia-mass" struck me as being a rather preposterous lingoism, with its suggestion of an unholy alliance between the occupation of hunting and the celebration of the Mass. Naturally, no such connotation was ever intended. The words were introduced, by F. Ludwig, as purely technical terms for Masses and motets of the late fourteenth and early fifteenth centuries showing the use of imitation, a device which is of basic importance in the caccia. Simultaneously he coined terms such as *Balladenmesse* and *Conductusmesse* for Mass pieces of the same period written in a style similar to that of the fourteenth-century ballade, or of the thirteenth-century conductus. These word formations have found their way into most books and articles dealing with the period around 1400, and it was not until recently that misgivings about the two last-mentioned terms were expressed, by Professor Handschin.[1] Judging from the tenor of his remarks, I am rather certain that he looks with no more favor at the others. I like to join him in his efforts to rid musical terminology of these ill-chosen and, in the case of the "caccia"-hybrids, actually misleading vocables. That these are misleading, will be shown subsequently. Before turning to this demonstration, however, it may not be amiss to say that, generally speaking, word formations of this type are open to objection from the point of view of what modern philosophers (if I understand them correctly) call semantics. They imply or give the impression that musical development resulted from the activity, not of men, but of forms. No doubt, there is a good deal of justification in this "morphologic" approach to music history. More than any other art, music presents the picture of an organic development resulting from the birth, growth, and death of fairly well defined forms, and musical historiography would be reduced to its former status of anecdote telling if we were to renounce interpreting and describing music history as the development of organum, motet, suite, or sonata. However, even good things can be carried too far. Converting tools into autonomous beings is always a dangerous thing to do, and it seems to me that danger is clearly present when, in addition to the caccia and the Mass, the caccia-mass is admitted to the rank of musicological deities. Admitting for the time being that there exists historical evidence for an interaction of these two types, why couldn't this be referred to by speaking of a "Mass composition showing the influence of the caccia?" To those who insist that this is exactly what the term caccia-mass means, I can only reply: *c'est le ton qui fait la musique.*

Let this be enough of what some readers may think is mere quibbling about words. Actually, there is more involved than this, namely, the theory that the imitative methods which gradually emerged during the fifteenth century had their origin in the caccia or, in other words, in the canon technique of the fourteenth century. That this is the view generally held, appears from the subsequent quotations, all taken from relatively recent publications. H. Besseler, in his article on "Ars Nova," [2] speaks of "die aus der Caccia stammende Anfangsimitation," and in the article "Ciconia" [3] he says that Ciconia's motet *O felix templum* "beginnt mit einem zehntaktigen Triplum-abschnitt, der vom Motetus genau wiederholt wird. . . . Da auch im weiteren Verlauf immer wieder kurze Triplumabschnitte im Motetus wiederkehren, haben wir hier eine 'Cacciamotette' vor uns." E. Dannemann, in *Die spätgotische Musiktradition in Frankreich und Burgund* (1936) says that Baude Cordier's *Belle bonne* "die Satzanlage der Caccia zeigt" (p. 19f). Van den Borren, in his *Études sur le XVe siècle musical* (1941) speaks (p. 98) about a Gloria by Pycard as being "conçu dans le style de caccia" (p. 98). Finally, G. Reany in his contribution to the article "Chanson" in *MGG* makes the following statement: "Vom Kanon, sicherlich aber nicht von der Imitationstechnik in andern französischen Werken leitet sich der Aufstieg des imitierenden Kontrapunkts im 15. Jahrhundert her" (vol. II, col. 1041).

Of all these statements only one, that by Mr. van den Borren, refers to a real canon. The others show that the caccia is considered responsible not only for the relatively few examples of canon that occur in Mass pieces and motets of our period, but also, and primarily, for the much more common and much more important device of normal imitation, that is, of short imitating passages inserted within in otherwise free contrapuntal texture. This indicates a tendency to consider canon and imitation as merely two different aspects of one and the same technique, a view that prevails in modern theory where the canon is treated as one of the higher devices of imitative counterpoint, alongside of invertible counterpoint, double counterpoint, etc.[4] Without questioning the propriety and advisability of this procedure as far as present-day instruction is concerned, it is hardly possible that matters appeared in a similar light to a musician of the fourteenth, fifteenth, or even sixteenth century. Canons (usually called *fuga*) were considered a subspecies, not of imitation, but of *canon* in the medieval sense of the word, that is (as Tinctoris explains it) "a rule showing the intention of the composer in some obscure manner." In fact, canons were nearly always written in an obscure manner, by notating only one part and indicating by a sign (*signum congruentiae*) the place where the second voice should start with the same melody. It is almost superfluous to point out that, from the point of view of composition technique as well, the canon poses an entirely different problem from imitation plain and simple. The difference is particularly striking in the case of the *caccias* (as well as the French *chaces*), since their canons usually start at the distance of eight or more measures, thus making the canonic procedure a purely structural and practically inaudible device, much in contrast to the striking effect produced by the immediate restatement of a short phrase.

All these considerations show that it would be a difficult feat to make a plausible case for the theory or line of thought represented by the terms caccia-motet or caccia-mass. Nor is it necessary to have recourse to the caccia as the protagonist in the "Prelude to the History of Imitation." Actually, the history of imitation proper cannot only be traced back to the beginning of the thirteenth century (as has long been known), but also continues throughout the fourteenth century (as will be shown). True enough, the

emerging picture is one strikingly lacking the trait of steady
growth that we would expect to attend the discovery of such an
important device as imitation. However, such an erratic course is
still present in the fifteenth century which, by general consent,
represents "Act I" of the spectacle.[5]

The history of imitation starts with Perotinus, that is, with the
very first composer to develop a musical style involving the basic
premise of imitation, equivalence of two voice-parts. His *Viderunt
omnes* has long been noted for its various devices of repeat technique (*color*, in thirteenth-century terminology), some of which
are true examples of imitation, particularly the passage reproduced
in Example 1.[6]

Ex.1

Here the imitation is carried to such length that, from the modern
point of view, it could be called a canon. However, the technique
of composition involved is quite different from that of the "long-
distance canons" of the fourteenth-century caccias and chaces.
It is not difficult to find other examples of imitation in compositions
from the same period, e.g., in the conductus *Pater noster* (Example
2, *a*), *Dum sigillum* (*b*), and in the organum triplum *Descendit*
(*c*, *d*).[7] Considering the small number of works available in modern
publications, the yield is rather high, and it may be assumed that a
thorough examination of the entire repertory would bring to light
a considerable number of additional instances.[8]

A similar search through the repertory of the middle and late
thirteenth century, most of which is available in the publications
of motets (*Montpellier*, *Bamberg*, *Huelgas*), proves, by comparison, disappointing, thus indicating something like a retreat
right after the first step had been taken. This is partly due to the
fact that large portions of the motet repertory are incapable of
imitation, e.g., all the two-voice motets (and, for that matter,
clausulae) and most of the three-voice motets of the late thirteenth

century whose triplum contrasts rhythmically with the motetus (Petronian motets). There still remains a considerable number of three-voice motets from the mid-thirteenth century (Franconian motets) which are potential candidates but which so far have yielded only a few instances of imitations. These, however, are of particular interest, because they involve also a restatement of the text — a very remarkable and striking phenomenon in composi-

tions predicated upon polytextuality. Three motets have been found [9] whose upper parts, as usual, have different texts, but these have one or two sentences in common, and it is exactly in connection with these identical words, which appear in slightly shifted positions, that identical music is introduced. The motet *Riens ne puet* (*Mo*, no. 105) contains three such passages, one of which is shown in Example 3. Another example is the passage "Et le rosignol chanter, A donc fine amors . . ." in the motet *En non diu* (*Mo*, no. 104), remarkable for its close imitation at the shortest possible distance of one perfection (⅜-group in the modern edition). It is interesting to note that in this example the imitation extends exactly as far as the words are the same in both parts, but ceases right in

the middle of the poetic line (after "amors") where the upper part continues "me prie," the lower, "m'envie." Easily the most ingenious example of thirteenth-century imitation is the motet *S'on me regarde* (*Mo*, no. 325) with its numerous references, musical and textual, between the two upper parts. Somewhat less striking, but also interesting is the motet *Jam nubes- Jam novum- [Solem]* (*Mo*, no. 275), whose musical syntax is characterized by constantly overlapping phrases, all starting with the word "Jam." In two places (meas. 18–24 and 28–33) this results in imitation, because the same melody is employed for two neighboring phrases.

In turning now to the fourteenth century, we come to the main part of the present study. As regards France, the situation can be summed up in the statement that imitation practically disappears. This is all the more surprising since the motet, with its characteristic duet of the upper parts, could well have proved a favorable medium for the continuation and development of this technique. An early-fourteenth-century motet such as *Nulla pestis*,[10] with its numerous overlapping phrases separated by whole-measure rests, presents such ideal opportunities for imitations that their absence seems almost deliberate. As far as I have been able to ascertain, none of the motets by (or commonly ascribed to) Philippe de Vitry contains a convincing example of imitation. A few instances can be found in the motets of Machaut, but actually these are due to the omnipresence of elementary rhythmic-melodic patterns which occasionally appear in close succession.[11] Nor is the situation much different in Machaut's secular works. Here the main device of constructive integration is the use of one or two motives (more individually designed than in the motets) which recur sporadically throughout the composition.[12] In a few instances such a motive occurs in two neighboring measures, resulting in what amounts to imitation, but actually is the incidental by-product of a different technique.[13] Only one composition, the rondeau *Dame mon cuer* from the *Remède de Fortune* (ed. Ludwig, p. 103), shows short motives in imitative position to a sufficient extent to be considered as intentional. (*Cf.* superius and tenor, meas. 4–5; 8–9; 17–18; 26–27; 29–30; 34–35; 39–40.)

A perusal of the Codex Ivrea[14] reveals practically nothing in addition to the single example of initial imitation quoted by Besseler with the remark that "the upper parts are connected through imitation after the model of the caccia."[15] Similarly, in the Codex Apt I have found, aside from two or three cases of what may be called chance imitation, only one instance of sufficient interest to be mentioned here, that is, the passage from Guymont's *Kyrie* shown in Example 4.[16] A somewhat different situation exists in the works

Ex4

of French composers represented in my *French Secular Music of the Late Fourteenth Century*. True enough, the majority of these compositions, particularly those of the "manneristic style," show no trace of imitation. Such traces do appear, however, in some of the "realistic virelais," always in connection with realistic words set to fanfare motives, e.g., "cocu" (Senleches, *En ce gracieux temps*; p. 83*, meas. 41–44), "oci" (Borlet, *Ma trédol rosignol*; p. 112*, meas. 4), "alarme" (Grimace, *Alarme alarme*; p. 122*, meas. 1–3), "restoés" (*Restoés restoés*; p. 124*, meas. 1–2, 6–7, 10–11), or "tirés a li" (*ibid.*, p. 125*, meas. 31–32). Imitation of a fanfare motive, set to the words "qui fu de Rome neis" and "toudis en loialté," occurs in the anonymous ballade *Martucius qui fu* (p. 85*, meas. 13–14 and 38–39). The ballade *Amour me fait* (p. 86*) begins with a triple stretto imitation of the motive c'-bb-a-g-f. The most impressive example of imitation, perhaps the only one fully deserving of this name, occurs in the anonymous ballade *Ne celle amour* (p. 88*) which, because of its unsophisticated charm and folk-like simplicity, I am inclined to consider, together with the realistic virelais, as a product of the Northern-French school. Here two full lines of the text, the first and the last, are imitated, words and music, in the middle part which, aside from these two passages, is instrumental (meas. 1–4; 33–34). Very likely, the performer of this part switched from his instrument to his voice, thus introducing an effective element of liveliness and surprise. In summary, we may say that practically all the examples of imitation occur in the Northern-French repertory of our collection, and that they have an unmistakably realistic effect. This statement is made in disregard of the works of the Frenchified Italian Matheus de Perusio whose late works (characterized in my book as the most typical examples of the Modern style) "indicate the beginning of that fusion of French and Italian elements which reached its consummation in Dufay" (p. 20). As far as his use of imitation is concerned, Matheus must be considered in connection with the development in Italy, to which our attention now turns.

The basic texture of early Italian music is a vocal duet whose parts proceed in what may be termed ornamented conductus style (the ornamentating figures being in the upper part), with simultaneous pronunciation of the syllables of the text. In its pure form, this style is not conducive to — in fact, not capable of — imitation. Not a few works of this period, however, show an occasional deviation from the principle of simultaneous placement of syllables, snatches of the text appearing in one part ahead of the other. It is in connection with this practice that imitation makes its appearance in Italian music. The earliest source of Italian polyphony, the

Codex Rossi 215 of the Vatican Library, includes an anonymous madrigal, *Cum altre ucele*, which contains three imitative passages, shown in Example 5. Using this remarkable piece as a point of

departure for the history of imitation in Italy, one cannot help noticing a somewhat retrogressive tendency in the works of early composers such as Giovanni da Cascia and Magister Piero (born c. 1300?), each of whom is represented in the *Codex Rossi* by one piece.[17] Imitation, as we understand it here, is practically absent in their compositions, although canon technique is fully represented, either by caccias or by madrigals having a canon for the stanza or for the ritornello. Imitation reappears in the works of Jacopo da Bologna who, very likely, belongs to the generation of Francesco Landini (1325–97). In contrast to Giovanni and Piero, Jacopo quite frequently introduces portions of the text in shifted positions,[18] and there are perhaps half a dozen of cases in which, owing to the use of identical music, this leads to imitation (see Example 6). Also of interest are a few instances of "rhythmic imitation," that is, the immediate restatement of a textual phrase in identical rhythm, though with a different melodic design. This device occurs more frequently, and in a more definite manner, in the works of Donato da Cascia, a particularly interesting example

(a) and (b): *Fenice fu*; (c) *Sotto l'imperio*.

(from the madrigal *L'aspido sordo*) being shown in Example 7. No less interesting is an example of inverted imitation in Donato's madrigal *Dal cielo*, in which the words "che n'e radice e ra[ma]" occur, at the distance of one measure, with the melodies e′-c′-c′-d′-d′-e′ and a-c′-c′-b-b-a. Altogether I have found eleven instances of imitation (including rhythmic imitation) in the sixteen known compositions by Donato, a fairly substantial number for the period we are dealing with.

A perusal of the collected works of Francesco Landini gives a yield which, proportionally, is considerably smaller, namely, about twenty instances in 152 compositions.[19] The previously mentioned technique of introducing portions of the text in shifted positions is not at all rare in Landini, and a motive technique similar to that found in the secular works of Machaut is very characteristic of the

Ex.7 (Sa-) tum' e Mar-te die - ne lor la for- (ça) ·

(Sa-) tum' e Mar-te die - ne lor la

Italian master, perhaps even more so than of his French contemporary. Both methods are potential factors of imitation, the one for snatches of the text, the other for purely musical patterns. Actually, there are only a few instances in which the shifted words appear with identical music, as in the passage "el me gli' è di te qui[vi]" in *Muort' orama* (Ellinwood, p. 242), or with the words "Theb' avanç'el chiudent' Enfi[one]" and "fecto à'l contrario del Gor-[gone]" near the end of *Si dolce non sonò* (p. 33f; see also *HAM*, no. 54). More frequent are examples entailing the restatement of a short melodic formula (e.g., at the end of the stanza of *Si dolce*) which, however, is usually not identical with the basic motive of the composition (if it has one).

Fourteenth-century imitation reaches a culmination in the works of Lorenzo da Firenze (Lorenzo Masini) and Paolo Tenorista. Of the former, ten madrigals are known,[20] and six of these contain snatches of imitation, some of them to a degree approximating the standards of the early fifteenth century. The most fully imitative piece is *Dà dà a chi avareggia*, which starts out with a four-fold imitation (more correctly, perhaps, alternation, because of the intervening rests) of a melodic figure set to the words "dà, dà, dà," and continues with three imitative passages each involving the immediate restatement of a textual phrase in parlando style. One of these is shown in Example 8, *a*. The ritornello opens with an imitation (or shall we say, canon?) of eight measures, continues with a particularly interesting example of inverted imitation (word painting?) shown in Example 8, *b*, and closes with a vocalization during which the same (or nearly the same) melodic figure recurs six times in immediate imitation (alternation). One cannot help feeling that here imitation has already reached the stage of virtuosity, an impression confirmed by the examples in Lorenzo's *Dolgomi a voi* (Example 8, *c*), *l' credo, Ita se n'era* (imitative sequence), *Come in sul fonte*, and *Sovra la riva*.

Among the compositions by Paolo Tenorista,[21] the madrigal *Tra verdi frondi* stands out for its extended use of imitation, including two instances of text repetition ("verdi frondi 'n isolan sul fon[te]" and "vidi un orsa c'odorav' un' fio[re]") and an interesting imitative sequence, shown in Example 9. Two other imitative sequences occur in *Una fera* and in *Lena virtù*, a triple imitation of a one-measure motive in *Chi vol vedere*, and an imitation at the lower seventh (in connection with "Danno di Pisa 'l tuo popol' victo[ria]") at the end of *Godi, godi Firenze*. As regards other composers active in the last quarter of the fourteenth century, the scarcity of available transcriptions prevents us from making specific statements. Several of the published pieces, however, contain imitative passages, e.g., *Ita se n'era star* by Vincentius de Arimino,[22] *Non dispregiar* by Nicolaus Praepositus,[23] Bartholino de Padua's *Patrem*,[24] an anonymous *Benedicamus Domino*,[25] etc. We close this

long list of Italian fourteenth-century imitation with a reference to the compositions of Matheus de Perusio. To the various examples found in his French pieces [26] may be added the passage from his ballata *Sera quel giorno* [27] shown in Example 10.

We have come to the point where it was possible for Ciconia to make his further, and much more definitive, contributions to the development of imitation, and to its establishment as a fundamental device of composition. Returning to our opening argument, we believe that it is neither necessary nor admissible to conjure up the spectre of a caccia-ballade or caccia-motet as antecedents of the imitative methods of the fifteenth century. Not only the special device of canon, but also, and even more so, the fundamental method of imitation has a prehistory of two centuries in which Italy played the leading role.

1. *Revue Belge de Musicologie*, i (1946), p. 94ff. This reference should not be construed to imply that I agree with all the details of Mr. Handschin's argumentation.

2. *Musik in Geschichte und Gegenwart*, vol. I, col. 723.

3. *Ibid.*, vol. II, col. 1428.

4. For the sake of clarification I should like to say that the term canon is used here invariably to denote a composition (or, at least, a self-contained section of a composition) in which two (or more) parts have the same melody throughout,

starting at different points. In modern theory the term canon or canon technique is often used for what is more clearly indicated by stretto or close imitation. It may be noticed that the caccias are usually just the opposite of close imitation.

5. See E. H. Sparks, "Some Uses of Imitation in Sacred Music of the 15th Century" [*JAMS* v (1952), p. 269]: "its development followed a twisting — or even what may be called a spiral — path."

6. Regarding imitation in this and other compositions of the early thirteenth century, see J. M. Müller-Blattau, *Grundzüge einer Geschichte der Fuge* (1923, 1930), p. 6ff; Adler, *Handbuch der Musikgeschichte*, i, p. 229; H. Schmidt, *Die 3- und 4-stimmigen Organa* (1933), p. 54. Here and elsewhere imitation is treated on par with *Stimmtausch*, a common thirteenth-century device which is excluded from our study.

7. See *Oxford History of Music*, vol. i (1901), p. 254; *ibid.*, p. 290; W. Apel, *Notation of Polyphonic Music* (4th edition, 1949), Facsimile 47. Our example (d) is one of those elusive *copulae* which can be transcribed in many different ways. In any transcription of this passage, however, the imitation, clearly noticeable in the original notation, should be present. None of the three versions given in the Appendix (Transcriptions), No. 33 (g) fulfills this requirement completely.

8. See, e.g., the conductus *O gloriosa* in the Codex *Huelgas* (edition by Anglès, vol. iii, p. 332, meas. 24-35, and p. 336, meas. 118-25).

9. Müller-Blattau (see fn. 4), p. 13; F. Gennrich, *Formenlehre des mittelalterlichen Liedes* (1932), p. 92f. For some rather obscure reason Müller-Blattau denies the character of imitation to these examples as well as to all the other instances of thirteenth-century *color*. This attitude is justified, it seems to me, only for the *Stimmtausch*, a device which differs from real imitation no less than does the canon technique of the caccia.

10. *Roman de Fauvel*; see J. Wolf, *Handbuch der Notationskunde*, i, p. 282.

11. Cf. Ludwig's edition, vol. iii, pp. 6, meas. 33-34; 62, 13-16; 79f, 31-32 and 103-104; 82ff, 11, 39-42, 46-50. See also G. Reese, *Music in the Middle Ages*, p. 355. I have been unable to find the "somewhat more effective imitation" in *Bone pastor*.

12. See G. Perle, "Integrative Devices in the Music of Machaut" (*MQ* xxxiv, p. 169).

13. See, e.g., Ludwig's edition, pp. 22, meas. 6-7; 25, 7; 34, 50-52; 36, 49-51; 87, 11-12.

14. Based on a transcription made by Miss Mildred Johnson in preparation of a doctoral dissertation on the Ivrea MS.

15. *Musik des Mittelalters und der Renaissance*, p. 168.

16. See Gastoué's edition, p. 32.

17. The subsequent study is largely based on J. R. White, *Music of the Early Italian Ars Nova, 1325-1375* (typescript dissertation, Indiana University, 1952).

18. See, e.g., the examples in *HAM*, nos. 49, 50.

19. In order to facilitate a check, I give here the pages in Ellinwood's edition: pp. 3, 7, 17 (twice), 20, 34, 39, 57, 184, 190, 193, 198, 212, 221, 227, 236, 242 (twice), 245. Probably a careful scrutiny will bring a few more examples to light.

20. In addition, there is a caccia, *A poste messe* (published in Marrocco's *Fourteenth-Century Italian Cacce*), five monophonic ballatas, and a *Sanctus* (published in de Van, *Les Monuments de l'Ars Nova*, i, p. 13).

21. Thirty-two in number, of which nineteen have been available for this study.

22. J. Wolf, *Geschichte der Mensuralnotation*, iii, p. 123.

23. *Ibid.*, p. 129.

24. G. de Van, *Les Monuments de l'Ars Nova*, i, p. 9, "Et ascendit."

25. *Ibid.*, p. 18, beginning.

26. Cf. W. Apel, *French Secular Music*, pp. 8*, meas. 83-85; 16*, 1-2; 17*, 29; 20*, 11-12 and 31-32; 25*, 24-27.

27. Ms. Modena, Bibl. Est. *Lat. 568*, f. 47^v/48^r.

PART THREE
*The Fifteenth
and
Sixteenth Centuries*

A FIFTEENTH-CENTURY

"CHRISTMAS ORATORIO"

Richard H. Hoppin

In 1734, Johann Sebastian Bach used the title *Christmas Oratorio* for a series of six cantatas based on the Gospel narrative — with lyrical commentary — of the Saviour's birth and the events following immediately thereafter. Bach thus emphasized the textual and spiritual unity of these works whose performance took place on six different days between Christmas 1734 and Epiphany 1735.[1] Somewhat more than three centuries earlier, another set of Christmas pieces was composed, and presumably performed, at the court of Cyprus. Naturally, these pieces bear no relation to the form and style of the eighteenth-century oratorio or cantata; they are, indeed, characteristic examples of the French isorhythmic motet of the early fifteenth century. But their composition as a musical and textual unit and the probability that they were performed on successive days from December 17 to Christmas may perhaps be considered sufficient justification for calling them a fifteenth-century "Christmas Oratorio."

Although completely anonymous, the large collection of Cypriot music now in the *Biblioteca Nazionale* of Turin (Ms. J. II. 9.) is obviously the product of French or of French-trained musicians.[2] The compilation of the manuscript can be placed with some assurance between the years 1413 and 1434,[3] and in all probability the years 1410–1425 saw the composition of most of the music.[4] In clearly defined sections, the manuscript presents the major types of early fifteenth-century music: plainchant Offices and Masses; polyphonic settings of Gloria and Credo; motets; French secular songs, *ballades, rondeaux* and *virelais*.

The third section of the manuscript contains thirty-three Latin and eight French motets. Forty of these are isorhythmic, and all are written in the discant-duet style with two differently texted upper voices over instrumental tenor and contratenor parts.[5] Our "Oratorio" comprises the series of pieces beginning with M 23, *O Sapientia — Nos demoramur*, and ending with the Christmas motet *Hodie puer nascitur — Homo mortalis firmiter* (M 31). Actually this last motet stands outside the series proper. But it is obviously related by virtue of the poetic forms of its texts, its position in the manuscript and most of all by its celebration of the climactic event which the preceding eight motets have been anticipating. The essential feature unifying these eight motets is the relation of their texts to the great *O* antiphons for Advent. There is one motet for each antiphon whose text is elaborately troped by both texts of the motet. This being so, it is with the texts that our consideration of these pieces must begin.

The origin of the seven *O* antiphons is shrouded in the darkness of the Dark Ages, but their great age and widespread use is attested to by the Anglo-Saxon paraphrases of them to be found (c. 800) in Cynewulf's *Christ*.[6] The original seven were undoubtedly written as a unit: each begins by describing some attribute of the Saviour and ends with a plea for His coming. Furthermore, they are arranged so that their first words, read backwards, form the acrostic *Ero cras*.[7] (See Table 1.) This reverse arrangement of the acrostic is evidently connected with the practice of performing one antiphon a day at Vespers, beginning with *O Sapientia* on December 17, and ending with *O Emmanuel* on December 23. This practice — going back at least to the twelfth and thirteenth centuries [8] — is still observed in the performance of the *O* antiphons at the Vesper hour as the antiphons to the Magnificat in the ferial Offices of the seven days preceding the vigil of Christmas.[9]

To the original seven *O* antiphons, the Middle Ages added several others, the most common and perhaps the oldest being *O Virgo virginum*.[10] Since the performance of the *O* antiphons in conjunction with the Magnificat already emphasizes the role of the Virgin Mary as the instrument of Christ's coming, the addition of a special antiphon in Her honor is not surprising. In many older antiphonaries *O Virgo virginum* follows immediately after the original seven,[11] although it is now performed on December 18 as the proper antiphon to the Magnificat in the second Vespers of the feast, *Expec-*

tatio Partus B.M.V. The prayer of the feast is followed by the antiphon *O Adonai.*[12] In the Middle Ages, however, the addition of one or more antiphons often meant that the series began earlier.[13] It is possible, therefore, that the performance of the motets in Cyprus began on the sixteenth rather than the seventeenth of December.

As the following table shows, the eight motets in the Cyprus manuscript follow the normal order of the *O* antiphons, and it may be assumed that the motet replaced one of the two or three performances of the antiphon. (By exception to the rule for ferial Offices, the *O* antiphons are now sung complete both before and after the Magnificat [14] and in earlier times were apparently sung three times during the service.[15])

TABLE 1

Motets in *Turin, B.N., J.II.9.*	*O Antiphons* *
M 23. O Sapientia incarnata Nos demoramur benigne rector	O Sapientia, quae ex ore . . .
M 24. O Adonay domus Israel Pictor eterne syderum	O Adonai, et Dux domus Israel, . . .
M 25. O radix Yesse splendida Cunti fundent precamina	O Radix Jesse, . . .
M 26. O clavis David aurea Quis igitur aperiet	O Clavis David, et sceptrum domus Israel: . . .
M 27. Lucis eterne splendor Veni splendor mirabilis	O Oriens, splendor lucis aeternae, . . .
M 28. O rex virtutum gloria Quis possit dign[e] exprimere	O Rex gentium, . . .
M 29. O Emanuel rex noster Magne virtutum conditor	O Emmanuel, Rex et legifer noster, . . .
M 30. O sacra virgo virginum Tu nati nata suscipe	O Virgo virginum, . . .
M 31. Hodie puer nascitur Homo mortalis firmiter	— — — — — — — — —

* The complete texts of the first seven may be found in *Liber Usualis*, pp. 340–42. For *O Virgo*, see Callewaert, *op. cit.*, p. 407. Also, F. Cabrol, *The Year's Liturgy* (London, 1938), I, 40.

From no more than the first lines of these motet texts it is evident that it is primarily the *triplum* texts which expand and paraphrase the original antiphons. However, the *duplum* texts are not unrelated. They all contain prayers for Christ's coming, and they frequently refer — usually in the last stanza — to the opening words of the antiphon.

This relationship between the motet texts and the O antiphons is in itself sufficient reason for supposing that the tropes were written as a unit, and the supposition becomes a certainty when we examine the poetic forms of these tropes. The basic form of the *triplum* texts consists of six four-line stanzas with eight syllables to a line, plus one added line at the close. By their rhymes these stanzas are grouped in pairs, rhyming *abababab*, with the added line included in the rhyme-scheme of the last two stanzas. In the *duplum*, the basic poetic form employs only five stanzas of four eight-syllable lines with the first four stanzas again grouped in pairs by their rhymes, leaving the fifth stanza standing alone.

In a few cases the necessity for beginning with the words of the prose antiphon brought about some departures from these basic forms. Thus in Motets 23 and 24, the *triplum* texts consist of five stanzas of four ten-syllable lines, and M 23 also uses this form in the *duplum* but with only four stanzas. (It may be noted that the ten-syllable lines use a different rhyme-scheme: all four lines of a stanza end with the same rhyme, and there is also internal rhyme, usually the same throughout a stanza.) Another exception is found in the *triplum* of M 27, whose first two stanzas alternate seven- and nine-syllable lines, returning thereafter to lines of normal length. This is the more remarkable as M 27 is the sole motet whose first line does not begin with O. Despite these variations from the basic poetic forms — and they are worthy of note for this reason — each of the *triplum* texts has a total of 200 syllables, while all the *duplum* texts, with one exception, have 160 syllables. (In M 26, the *duplum* lacks the last two lines of its fifth stanza, a fact which makes this part unusually melismatic.) This striking regularity of the texts with regard to length presents a sharp contrast with an equally striking disparity in the lengths of the musical settings. (See Table 2.) Here may be seen quite clearly one facet of that absolute independence of words and music so characteristic of the motet in the fourteenth and early fifteenth centuries.

Although it too departs in some measure from the basic poetic forms used in the preceding eight motets, it is by the forms as well as the subject of its texts that the Christmas motet (31) reveals its relationship to the tropes of the *O* antiphons. The *duplum* text uses the standard form, except that each of its five stanzas has its own rhymes. The *triplum*, too, adheres to the basic form for this voice, but has two added lines instead of one at the close. However, the Christmas subject seems to have inspired a tour de force in the matter of rhyme: the syllables *-itur* are used in lines one and three of the first and last two stanzas and in all four lines of stanzas three and four. These divergences — chiefly of rhyme-schemes rather than of poetic forms — are so slight that the texts of M 31 must be regarded as the intended culmination and climax of the whole series.

On the other hand, the Christmas motet is set apart from the musical organization which makes of the preceding eight motets an entity obviously conceived and composed as a unified whole. The methods of achieving this musical organization are twofold: mensural and modal. In other words, these eight motets exhibit a planned sequence of mensurations, or meters, and a planned sequence of modes. With characteristic medieval ingenuity, these two sequences organize the eight motets in two different, if not opposing, ways. According to mode, the motets are grouped in pairs in the succession: Dorian (23 and 24), Lydian (25, 26), Hypolydian (27, 28) and Hypomixolydian (29, 30). In the sequence of mensurations, however, the motets are arranged in two groups of four. Each of the four basic mensurations of the period is allotted to one motet in each group in the order: 9/8 (⊙), Motets 23 and 27; 3/4 (O), 24 and 28; 6/8 (₵), 25 and 29; 2/4 (C), 26 and 30. In these two sequences of mode and mensuration lies the proof that the tropes of the *O* antiphons were composed as a musical, as well as a textual, unit.

Beyond their use as a method of organization, there is nothing particularly unusual about the modes themselves. Thirty-one of the forty-one motets are in either the Dorian or Lydian mode (twelve and nineteen respectively), and three motets in addition to Nos. 27 and 28 are Hypolydian. Only Hypomixolydian is not to be found in any other motets in the collection. It should be noted that, in every case, mode has been determined by the range of the tenor and its final, which, being always the lowest note, determines the final chord.

The equal use of all four mensurations is of somewhat larger significance than the choice of modes. As might be expected in a collection dating from before 1430, 6/8 meter is the most common, although it is found in only nineteen of the forty-one motets. Twelve are in 3/4, five in 2/4 and four in 9/8. One more motet (36) is basically in 3/4, but the upper parts frequently change mensuration, using all four mensural signs in rapid succession and in polymetric combinations. If the number of motets in 3/4 seems unusually large, the proportionate use of the different mensurations is about what one would expect in a manuscript from the latter half of the transitional period between 1400 and 1430.[16] That all four mensurations are used equally in our "Christmas Oratorio" may serve as a warning, however, that one must be extremely cautious about dating a composition on the basis of the mensuration it employs. For the sake of completeness, be it noted that, in all of the motets under consideration, the *modus* is perfect in tenor and contratenor, as it is in all but three motets in the entire collection.

With regard both to mode and mensuration the Christmas motet stands outside the musical unit formed by the tropes of the Advent antiphons. M 31 returns to the Dorian mode and is in 6/8 mensuration, used by Dufay even after 1430 for particularly ceremonious occasions.[17] Thus is recognized and made manifest, not only the unity of the Advent antiphons, but the separateness of the Nativity as the climactic culmination of the previous days of prayerful anticipation.

The separateness of the Christmas motet is further emphasized by its use of an isorhythmic form that is both more complex and more traditional than the forms used for the Advent tropes. Curiously enough, this increasing complexity of form begins with the motet troping *O Virgo virginum*. Are we to see in this an indication that *O Virgo virginum* was recognized as an addition to the original seven antiphons? Such a conjecture is tempting and perhaps not unwarrantably subtle in view of medieval thinking habits.

An unusual aspect of the entire collection of Cypriot motets is their repudiation of pre-existing *cantus firmi*. Only three of the forty-one tenors are identified in the manuscript as being taken from the plainchant repertory.[18] The rest are merely labeled *Tenor* and must be considered original melodies, written expressly for the motet to which they belong. Along with Gregorian tenors, the Cypriot motets generally repudiate the use of melodic repetition in the tenor, either in the original note values or in diminution. As a result, the most frequently used form in these motets — found in twenty-two of the forty — consists of three identical statements of an isorhythmic period. It is this form which is used for the first seven motets in the group under consideration. (See Table 2.) M 30

TABLE 2

Motet	Mode	Mensuration	Length of iso-rhythmic period *	No. of periods
M 23	Dorian	⊙	$\frac{39}{13}$	3
M 24	Dorian	O	$\frac{45}{15}$	3
M 25	Lydian	ℭ	$\frac{46}{15\,1/3}$ **	3
M 26	Lydian	C	$\frac{57}{19}$	3
M 27	Hypolydian	⊙	$\frac{48}{16}$	3
M 28	Hypolydian	O	$\frac{51}{17}$	3
M 29	Hypomixo-lydian	ℭ	$\frac{36}{12}$	3
M 30	Hypomixo-lydian	C	$\frac{96}{16}$	$\frac{2}{4}$
M 31	Dorian	ℭ	$\frac{66 > 33}{22 > 22}$ ⊙	2 > 2

* The figures above the line give the number of breves (bars) in the vocal parts. The figures below the line give the number of perfections of *modus* in Tenor and Contratenor.
** The *modus* is perfect, but the period has an extra breve.

is only slightly more complicated in form. The tenor states its forty-eight-bar period four times while the three other parts have two statements of a period ninety-six bars in length. However, the endings of the tenor periods are marked by such strong cadences — two full perfections of *modus* with one chord for each perfection — that the upper parts give an impression, not of one long period stated twice, but rather of two different periods alternating in an A B A B pattern.

The Christmas motet is one of the few in the entire collection that does make use of melodic repetition in the tenor. A *color* comprising two statements of a *talea* is repeated in diminution according to the canon: *Tenor. Primo dicitur perfecte. 2º per semi de primo.* As the upper parts reproduce the plan of the tenor — but without diminution in the second part — the overall form of the motet may be indicated by the letters A A B B. It is curious that this method of construction, so frequently used throughout the history of the isorhythmic motet, should be found in only one other instance (M 40) in the Cyprus collection.

For the sake of convenience, Table 2 assembles in one place the pertinent facts concerning the musical organization of our "Christmas Oratorio." Further discussion of the musical style of these motets cannot here be undertaken in detail. It must suffice to say that — despite the different mensurations — these pieces are generally representative of that "Engschrittgang" style described by Besseler and regarded by him as characteristic of late-Gothic French music.[19]

It is in their isorhythmic structure that the chief interest of these motets lies. In all of them all four parts are isorhythmic,[20] and they all follow the "new fashion" observed by Dannemann in Nicolas Grenon's motet *Nova vobis*.[21] After a normal opening with the vocal parts moving in *tempus* and prolation, while tenor and contratenor are primarily in *modus* and *tempus*, the isorhythmic period rises to a climax in which the lower parts — through the use of shorter note values — become completely intermeshed with the voices in complicated patterns of rhythmic imitation and sequence. As a rule, this rhythmic climax leads directly to a strong cadence marking the end of the period by an almost complete cessation of all rhythmic activity for the duration of a full perfection of *modus*. Thus the isorhythmic period becomes an easily recognizable musical entity, and the structure of the motet stands forth in almost classical simplicity.

In view of the notable repudiation of Gregorian tenors in all the Cypriot motets, we need not be surprised to find that the motets based on the *O* antiphons show no musical relationship to the plainchant settings of the original texts. In fact, the modal scheme alone of our "Christmas Oratorio" makes any such relationship almost impossible, as adaptations of the same plainchant are used for all

the O antiphons. What we have here is a group of completely original pieces — unique in their time — related by their texts and
organized by musical means into a unified whole, although their
performance extended over a period of at least eight or nine days.

There is no more probability that we shall ever know the occasion for the composition of this group of Christmas pieces than that
we shall discover by whom they were written. Yet we may perhaps
be permitted the assertion that this fifteenth-century "Christmas
Oratorio" compares worthily with the later Christmas work of
Johann Sebastian Bach as a monument of human ingenuity, as an
artistic achievement within the most rigid formal confines and as a
consummation of an epoch.

1. C. S. Terry, *The Music of Bach* (London, 1933), p. 72.

2. H. Besseler, "Studien zur Musik des Mittelalters, I," *Archiv für Musikwissen-schaft (AfMW)*, VII (1925), 209–17, describes the manuscript and catalogues its contents.

3. *Ibid.*, pp. 209–10.

4. Cf. M. Bukofzer, *Studies in Medieval and Renaissance Music* (New York, 1950), pp. 76 and 219.

5. Three motets (Nos. 11, 12 and 14) lack a contratenor.

6. *Catholic Encyclopedia*, articles on *Cynewulf* and *O Antiphons*.

7. Cf. C. Callewaert, "De groote Adventsantifonen O," *Sacris Erudiri* (Steen-brugge, 1940), p. 409.

8. *Ibid.*, p. 413 and notes 54 and 55.

9. *Cath. Encyc.*, *O Antiphons*.

10. It is found in a ninth-century antiphonary. Cf. Callewaert, *op. cit.*, pp. 411–12.

11. *Ibid.* See also W. H. Frere, *Antiphonale Sarisburiense*, p. 42.

12. *Cath. Encyc.*, *O. Antiphons*.

13. Cf. Callewaert, *op. cit.*, p. 411, and *Cath. Encyc.*, *O Antiphóns*.

14. Cf. *Liber Usualis*, p. 339.

15. Callewaert, *op. cit.*, pp. 417–18.

16. Cf. H. Besseler, *Bourdon und Fauxbourdon* (Leipzig, 1950), Chapter VII and the Table on p. 124.

17. *Ibid.*, p. 126.

18. Nos. 1, 12 and 16. None in the group 23–31.

19. Besseler, *Bourdon und Fauxbourdon*, pp. 127–38.

20. This is true of twenty-nine of the forty isorhythmic motets. (Nos. 1–5, 8 and 19–41.)

21. E. Dannemann, *Die spätgotische Musiktradition in Frankreich und Burgund vor dem Auftreten Dufays* (Strassburg, 1936), p. 74. The motet is published in J. Marix, *Les Musiciens de la Cour de Bourgogne* (Paris, 1937), pp. 233 ff.

ABOUT ORGAN PLAYING IN

THE DIVINE SERVICE,

CIRCA 1500

Otto Gombosi

Aᴌᴛᴇʀɴᴀᴛɪᴍ participation of the organ in the liturgy is considered today to have been the standard practice of the fifteenth-sixteenth centuries. In view of the overwhelming evidence from practically all over Western Europe the essential correctness of this assumption cannot be doubted. Yet, on second thought, certain points seem to be in need of further elucidation.

It remains to be seen, for instance, whether the alternatim practice has always been uniformly enforced by tradition and prescriptions or whether a certain latitude of arrangement has been left in the hands of the responsible participants, the celebrant, the choirmaster, and the organist.

The second point to be raised refers to the other factors in the alternation. It seems that the majority of scholars assumes that the alternation took place between the organ and Gregorian singing or between polyphonic singing and Gregorian chant. Yet alternation between organ and polyphonic choir, or even between all three factors — organ, Gregorian singing and polyphonic choir — cannot be dismissed without careful checking of all available data.

To propose a thorough investigation of these two points within the space available here would be presumptuous, indeed. Thus the following considerations should be taken for what they are: a bouquet of random flowers gathered along the ways and byways that for many years have lured the steps of this writer across the centuries.

It seems to be practical, in further limitation of the scope of this investigation, to omit references to the Ordinary of the Mass and, for specific reasons, also to the Sequence. The little that could be added here would not substantially change the picture.

Let us limit ourselves at this time to specific forms of the liturgy as used at a few places and let us see first whether the alternatim practice as applied to them shows the rigidity usually assumed to have prevailed or, rather, a flexibility according to place, time, and conditions. In view of the material at our disposal it seems advisable to limit ourselves mainly (1) to Responsoria, and especially to the last Responsory of the major holidays, and (2) to the Introits, whereby a glance will be cast at other antiphonal forms.

The Responsoria of the Matins of the highest holidays were, during the period under consideration, among the musically most elaborate items of the liturgy, a place of concerted effort toward adornment of the service, and among the principal forms entrusted to the organ. Nativity, Easter, Ascension, Pentecost, Trinity, Corpus Christi, with Epiphany, Purification, and the Feast of Dedication of the particular church — in other words, the holidays of the *duplex major* class — stand out in this respect. In Exeter[1] for instance, the participation of the organ — *as an alternative to organum singing* — was prescribed, in the fourteenth century, for the last Responsory of each of the three Nocturns, i.e., the third, the sixth, and the ninth Responsory of the Matins. Hereby Psalm-Verse and Doxology were reserved for choral performance, presumably Gregorian. On the numerous holidays of the *duplex minor* class only the ninth Responsory was performed in such solemn manner. The *"De ordo psallendi et modulandi discantandi aut organizandi"* prescribes this *organizare cum vocibus vel organis*. The role of the organ is considerable throughout the Exonian rite and it is regulated with unusual rigor.[2]

At other places, the ninth Responsory is still the musical highpoint of the Matins (its only competitor being the solemn *Te Deum*), but the manner of participation of the organ is more varied. Few places refrain from using the organ at this point, as does Notre Dame of Paris at the beginning of the fifteenth century. Thus the Esztergom rite,[3] at the see of the primate of Hungary, the last Responsory of Christmas, *Verbum caro*, "solemniter cantetur in organo," around 1500, while the Versus and the Doxology were reserved "canendo toto choro" (according to Ms. 73). Evidently the

Repetenda between Verse and Doxology, and after the latter, remained in the realm of the organ, and thus the alternation was regular. Thus also at St. Anne in Augsburg.[4] In the Matins of Easter, however, the ninth Responsory, *Dum transisset*, shows a richer apparatus in Esztergom. While the Eger rite [5] — to call in the evidence of the other Hungarian see for which we possess data — prescribes only in a summary fashion "tangitur in organo," the Strigonian rite specifies organ for the Responsory, "choratores" for the Verse, and "chorus" for the Repetenda. A third possibility is recommended for the Gradual-Responsory *Haec dies* as sung in the second Vespers of the same holiday. It is begun by the "choratores" with the "chorus" following, obviously either from the point at the end of the intonation or from where later the Repetenda is to be started (i.e., the place marked in modern editions by an asterisk). The Verse *Confitemini* "tangitur in organo." The Augsburg organ book contains the same direction (Söhner 10): "In Vesperis [of Easter] primo organista incipit Kyrie paschale, post hoc super psalmos organista repetit antiphonam; qua finita chorus cantat graduale haec dies, organista versum [sc. *Confitemini*]; post hoc chorus cantat alleluja cum verso; quo finito organista incipit sequentiam victimae paschali; qua finita sequitur Magnificat 3ii toni bbgbag." In Augsburg, the same regulation prevailed for the Gradual of Easter Mass — this in direct defiance of more orthodox customs.

Yet with these examples the variety of performance practices is still not exhausted. The Responsory *Vidi aquam* of Saturday of the Holy Week, performed in Eger "tangendo in organo vel cantando" — note the free choice! — is divided in Esztergom. It starts "cum organo," its Verse is sung by the "choratores," and the organ plays the Doxology *Gloria patri*. The manner of performing the Repetenda is not specified.

The following Responsory, *Christus resurgens*, is also started "in organo," while the canons ("Domini"), "choratores," "pueri vociferati" and "alii volentes" join in singing the Verse *Dicant nunc*. In this case the Doxology is specifically omitted and immediately the organ plays the final Repetenda. This latter is explicitly given to the organ by a rubric, combining the abbreviation "org" with the

sign ℟ calling for the Repetenda: ℟⁰, on fol. 61 of the Sarum Processionale, Brit. Mus. Harl. 2945. ᵍ

While such Responsoria as used in Vespers and Processions possibly show an irregular sequence of their constituent parts, strict alternation of choir and organ is indicated for the Procession-Responsory *O crux gloriosa* in a Ms of the University Library of Erlangen.[6] Of course, *O crux gloriosa* is, originally, an Antiphon and is designed as such in Esztergom: "Antiphona *O crux gloriosa*; et repetitur antiphona in organo si est. Si non: a choro. Et mox incipitur a choratore Versus scilicet *Arbor amara nimis* usque finem." But, of course, the liturgical situation is different here, since the Antiphon serves to the *Magnificat*.

Another rather anomalous situation is encountered in Eger for the Non-Responsory of Ascension, *Ascendo ad Patrem*, which has to be sung "in mensuris 4 or 5 vocum." Yet this clarity of purpose which puts a feather in the cap of partisans of *à cappella* performance is rather exceptional.[7]

To quote only one more instance showing the freedom and variety of performance of processional Responsoria, let us quote *Ite in orbem* of the same holiday, used in Halle,[8] 1532, as regular Responsory of the Matins. It is started by "pueri" and sung by organ and choir, while Erlangen mentions only choir and organ. But Meissen,[9] 1520, gives more details for its use in the procession: "Cantatur in organis R/ *Ite in orbem*, et fit processio . . . Chorus cantat Repetitionem R[esponsorii]. Item versus cantetur in organis; et non plus." Here, the Repetenda after the Verse (and obviously also the Doxology) is explicitly omitted — a highly irregular procedure admissible only for processional use of Responsories.

It could be a most welcome corroboration of this changing picture of performance practices if the extant organ books of the time would offer more examples. Yet they are strangely void of responsorial forms. Thus, with two exceptions, neither of the three great Polish tablatures [10] contain any Responsoria, since their liturgical repertoire pertains, for the most part, to the Mass and to the Vespers. Of the two exceptional pieces, *Surge Petre-Angelus Domini* in the Cracow Tablature is an intavolated polyphonic motet of the "refrain" type, to be dealt with presently. The unique organ Responsory is *Verbum caro* in the Leopolita Tablature, consisting of the first section *Verbum caro* and the Repetenda *Plenum gratia*, the latter in two versions. Hans Buchner's Fundamentum [11] offers only two Responsoria: *Quae est ista* with Repetenda *Et universae* for

Assumption, and *Judea et Hierusalem* with Repetenda *Cras egre-mini* for the Vigil of Nativity. Significantly, these Responsories are not through-composed: the Verse and Doxology are lacking. The bisection of the Responsory permits the organ-performance (a) of both parts before the Verse and (b) of the Repetenda after the Verse and/or after the Doxology, or (c) a change of medium in the middle of the first rendering of the Responsory. Thus a certain latitude of the performance practice is, at least, not excluded.

Turning now to the Introit of the Mass, we find in it the role of the organ well established by the latter part of the fifteenth century, although Notre Dame of Paris in 1415 [12] or Bourges in 1407 [12a] do not make any provisions for it. It is prescribed, for instance, at St. Anne in Augsburg for all duplex holidays but those of Advent, Lent, the six Sundays after Epiphany and the twenty-four Sundays after Pentecost. Exeter follows a similar rule; on duplex holidays (major and minor) the "Officium," i.e., the Introit, is performed with the organ participating, while "triplex" holidays, i.e., those with only three Responsories in the Matins, limit its use, within the Mass, to Kyrie, Sequence, Sanctus, and Agnus. Richer is the task of the organ, around the middle of the sixteenth century, in Monreale (Sicily) [13] where practically all days in the calendar are celebrated by the organ playing in the Mass, beginning with the Introit. Among the specifically exempt days are the Feast of Innocent Martyrs and the Vigil of Epiphany if not falling on a Sunday.

By these descriptions of, and prescriptions for, the use of the organ the extra-liturgical playing before and after the service is not touched upon. This was taken for granted, although sometimes referred to, e.g., in Halle: ". . . et sub ingressu Organista ludet tamdiu in organis, donec omnes personae ecclesiae reperent se ad medium ecclesiae, ab Stationem." Or, referring to the beginning of Vespers: "Organista ludet tamdiu in organis, donec cessandi signum illi nola in choro pulsata detur."

Well established as the participation of the organ in the Introit may be, the sources already quoted offer a few rather specific directives. Thus, while the Ordinarius Agriensis leaves open the manner of performance of the Introit In Cena Domini: "in organo vel per choratores incipitur Introitus missae videlicet *Nos autem gloriari* cum *Gloria patri* solemniter," the Ordinarius Strigoniensis strictly prescribes both the use of the organ and the omission of the

Doxology: "Interim [i.e., by the end of the procession] in organo incipitur missa solemniter *Nos autem gloriari* sine *Gloria.*" Similarly, the Introits for both Resurrection and Ascension (*Resurrexi et adhuc* and *Viri Galilei*) are to be started by the organ. No organ is, however, mentioned for the Introit of the Saturday of the Holy Week or for that of the Vigil of Pentecost. In the first instance, the *Kyrie pascale* is started out by the organ, in the second, "in organo vel a choratoribus, intrando ad chorum."

In the case of the Introit, the organ tablatures contain some valuable supplementary information. Thus the organ book of John of Lublin offers five Introits (*Gaudeamus omnes* in three versions, *Resurrexi* for Easter, and *Benedicta sit* for Trinity) with the Doxology attached. The Psalm-Verse, however, is omitted. One of the two versions of the Corpus Christi Introit *Cibavit eos* (fol. 29v) is followed by a "Versus" without identifying text incipit. The Psalm-Verse is unequivocally indicated in only two cases. The Introit de beata Virgine *Salve sancta parens* is followed by the Verse *Sentiant omnes*, and the Verse *Caeli enarrant* is attached to the Advent-Introit *Rorate caeli* in one of the two versions. In these cases, however, the Doxology (or reference to the repetition of the music of the Verse for the Doxology) is lacking. As to *Rorate*, organ playing was generally speaking prohibited during Advent;[14] this rule was, at some places, suspended for the Sundays. Both the Versus and the Doxology are absent from the four other Introits (for Christmas, Pentecost, Corpus Christi, and de uno Martyre *Protexisti*) of the main body of the manuscript.

Richest in Introits is the Leopolita tablature. Of its seventy liturgical compositions not less than forty-seven are of this category, with three variants added. In twenty-three Introits the full Antiphon is composed without Verse or Doxology. Four more contain only incomplete Antiphons, yet in two of these the final cadence is indicated in a note. On the other hand, in five cases (three of which have the full Antiphon, one the unfinished Antiphon, and one the Intonation) the tone of the Versus (i.e., Doxology) is indicated. Thirteen Antiphons have the full Doxology attached. To one incomplete Antiphon the first half of the Doxology is added. Only one of the two versions of the Antiphon *Rorate caeli* is followed by the Verse *Caeli enarrant* — exactly as in John of Lublin's book.

Buchner's Fundamentum attaches the Doxology to the Introits of Christmas (p. 133) and Easter (p. 142), but omits it from those for Christmas (p. 27), Assumption (pp. 111 and 114) and Pentecost (p. 124). An isolated Introit-Antiphon *Resurrexi* for organ occurs, without Verse or Doxology, in a Breslau manuscript.[15] Let us add that Clemens Hör [16] in his additions (of 1553) to Isaac's Missa Paschalis refers to both the beginning of the Introit-Antiphon and of the Doxology as originally intended for the organ and continuing with polyphonic singing.

In this light, the omission of the intonation of both the Antiphon and the Verse, and the total omission of the Doxology which, however, could follow the music of the Verse, from many a polyphonic Introit-composition takes on a new meaning.[17] Instead of the generally assumed choral intonation in *cantus planus*, organ beginning may be substituted.[18] While, as in the Introits of Lent, the manuscripts often notate the Gregorian incipit, this alone does not categorically exclude organ performance. German sources of the mid-sixteenth century, especially, abound in such incomplete polyphonic Introits by masters such as Finck, Isaac, Stoltzer, Rener, etc. We shall take a glance at some of these sources presently.

First let us return, for a moment, to John of Lublin. He prefaces his manuscript with an introductory instruction on improvised playing on a choral cantus firmus. Since the manuscript is the topic of a dissertation in progress, detailed analysis of this highly important document can be omitted here. The little treatise systematically explains and documents by examples different techniques, such as

I. Simultaneous beginning in all parts
    (a) with the c.f. in the Discant
    (b)   ”   ” ” ” ” Tenor
    (c)   ”   ” ” ” ” Bass
II. Successive (imitative) beginning
    1) Imitation in the octave
        (a, b, c,) as above
    2) Imitation in the fifth
        (a, b, c,) as above
    3) Imitation in the fourth
        (a, b, c,) as above.

Among the practical examples we find, together with Hymns, Antiphons, Responsories, Sequences, etc., a number of Introit-

Intonations such as *Benedicta sit* (Trinity), *Salve sancta parens* (de beata Virgine), *Gaudeamus omnes* (Assumption), *Resurrexi* (Easter), [*Protexisti me*] (St. Stanislas), *Laus tibi Christe* (Mary Magdalene), *Sapientiam sanctorum* (de pluribus Martyribus), *Mihi autem nimis* (de Apostolis), *Cibavit eos* (Corpus Christi), *Statuit ei Dominus* (de Confessore Pontifice), *Loquebar de testimoniis* (de Virgine et Martyre), *Os justi* (de Confessore non Pontifice), and *Intret in conspectu* (de pluribus Martyribus). Beyond doubt, the accomplished organist of the time was able to improvise such organ intonations. Thus, as pointed out above, the omission of the intonation from polyphonic compositions does not necessarily mean that such intonation was to be sung choraliter. It could have been, and often was, played by the organ.[19] In optimal cases, it took the form of sophisticated imitative playing. When and what the organist was supposed to play depended, obviously, on local conditions and on the special occasion. The above mentioned Augsburg organ book definitely assigns the end of the Doxology with the Psalm-Difference and the repetition of the Antiphon to the organ. This practice, not born out by our Ordinaria for the Introit, seems to have been more widely used in other antiphonal forms such as the Psalm-Antiphons of Laudes and Vespers, and in the Antiphons to the Cantica.

Again, a great diversity of practice can be observed. General regulations, e.g., in Exeter or Monreale, leave open the possibility of rendering the initium by the organ, although it was left, more often, to the cantor. More regularly, the repetition of the Antiphon after the Psalm was entrusted — partly or wholly — to the organ. The latitude is well illustrated by the Esztergom rubric for Feria tertia post Pentecosten: "in secundis Vesperis antiphona de laudibus in organo tangitur, sed iam antiphonae non duplicantur. Si vis autem duplicare, potes hodie." A few specific rubrics, from widely separated areas, may be cited here.

Usually, e.g., in Monreale, the last of the five Psalm-Antiphons of Vespers, Laudes, and Tertia, and those to the Cantica were performed, the season permitting, with the participation of the organ. But on some holidays all Antiphons were adorned with organ playing. Thus those of the second Vespers of St. Andrew, Conceptio, St. Maurus, St. Matthew, etc. — also those of the first Vespers of St. Andrew and of the second Vespers of Innocent

Martyrs, if falling on a Sunday. All Antiphons of the Vespers of "organ days" were played, after the psalm, in Augsburg.

The repetition of the Antiphon after the Psalm was given to the organ, e.g., in Halle, in the Vespers of the Saturday of Holy Week: "Senior dextri chori incipiet Antiphonam *Alleluja* quam chorus totam complebit. Cantor incipit psalmum *Laudate dominum omnes gentes*. Chorus *Laudate eum omnes populi*. Repetent antiphonam. Sequitur *Quoniam confirmata est super nos misericordia ejus: et veritas domini manet in eternum*. Tunc cantabit ille in organo Antiphonam *Alleluja*." This practice prevailed also in Augsburg, or in Constanz. In the same office, alternation is prescribed in Halle for the Canticum, but not for its Antiphon, while no mention is made of the repetition of the latter: "Interim duo seniores Canonici inponentes ibunt ad Cantorem et Rectores ad incipiendam Antiphonam *Vesperae autem Sabbati*, quam chorus complebit. Tunc Cantor cum Rectoribus incipiet solemniter *Magnificat*. Quod similiter [!] in choro et organo alternantis vicibus cantabitur." The repetition of the Antiphon of the Magnificat is expressedly prohibited for Easter Vespers in Augsburg. Again, in Halle, in the Compleat of Annuntiation, the organ is strictly excluded even from the Canticum: "Antiphona super *Nunc dimittis, Haec est dies*. Quam etiam domini praelati et chorus prosequuntur alternatim, et non in organis."

If, when, and where only the intonation of the Antiphon was required before the Psalm or Canticum, and the latter was to be played by the organ, straight alternation resulted. Thus in Esztergom. Also, because the Hymn often was to be performed in alternation, this order of performance frequently extended over a long part of the office. Thus, in the Laudes of Corpus Christi: ". . . choratores incipiunt laudes. Chorus prosequitur et post quemlibet psalmum antiphona in organo perficitur. . . . Mox incipitur hymnus in organo *Pange lingua*. ℣ *Posuit fines tuos alleluja*. Antiphona [*Ego sum panis vivus*] incipitur per choratores et chorus prosequitur. Finita antiphona mox incipitur psalmus *Benedictus* in organo. Finito psalmo resumitur in organo antiphona."

Another Esztergom rubric contradicts the above quoted Halle regulation for the Compleat of Annuntiation: ". . . finitis psalmis resumitur antiphona *Laus tibi do*[*mine*]. Statim organum incipit hymnum *Lux mundi beatissima*. Antiphona *Dilectus*. Psalmus *Nunc dimittis incipitur* in organo." Again, no repetition of the Antiphon is mentioned, and the Oratio follows immediately. Yet in similar situations both the repetition and the instrument may be called for, as shown above.

For special reasons, such as extended liturgical action or procession, the duration of the Antiphon may be drawn out by alternating repetition. Thus in the Laudes of Ascension in Meissen: ". . . hymnus *Festum nunc celebre* incipiatur in organis et cantetur totius. Quo finito, provisores incipiant antiphonam *Ascendo ad patrem.* Tunc in organis cantetur *Benedictus,* primus versus tantum. Chorus: *Gloria patri.* In organis: *Sicut erat.* Tunc chorus cantat totam antiphonam, et tunc incipiunt qui ordinati sunt paulatim et morose sursum trahere ymaginem ascensionis. Item in organis cantetur tota antiphona *Ascendo.* Chorus iterum cantet eadem antiphonam totam. . . ." The Halle regulations for the same part of the office are even more explicit and provide for additional splendor: "Cantor incipiet Antiphonam *Ascendo ad patrem meum* et non ultra. Tunc statim succentor solemniter incipiet *Benedictus:* quod in organo et choro usque ad finem alternatim cantatur. Post *Benedictus* decanus et cantor . . . cantantes *Ascendo ad patrem meum et patrem vestrum.* Et respondebit chorus *Deum meum et deum vestrum, alleluja.* Tubicines vel fistulatores Civitatis, super testudinem personabunt canticum aliquid artificialiter compositum . . . [procession] . . . Deinde iterum praedicti Prelati cantabunt *Ascendo ad patrem meum,* respondente choro *Deum meum* etc. Iterum tubicines vel fistulatores cantabunt . . . [procession] . . . Deinde iterum praedicti prelati tertio cantabunt *Ascendo,* respondente choro *Deum meum,* tubicinibus vel fistulatoribus iterum canentibus dum circumfertur tertia vice imago salvatoris. Qui facto debent modulari donec Prelati, Canonici, et Vicarij in cappis imaginem salvatoris fuerint osculati. . . ." The participation of instruments in the liturgy is highly interesting and adds significantly to the data published by Norlind, Handschin, Moser, Rokseth, etc.[20] More of it shall be said at another occasion.

The special case of the Magnificat-Antiphon *O crux gloriosa* in the Esztergom liturgy has been mentioned before in connection with its use as a processional Responsory in the Erlangen manuscript.

From our point of view two rather interesting practices have been demonstrated to have existed. They deserve closer documentation. The first is the *ad libitum* duplication of Antiphons by the organ, depending on the wish of the celebrant or the choir master; the second is the multiple repetition of Antiphons.

As to the first point, the Esztergom rubric for the second Vespers of Easter may be quoted: "Prius canitur *Kirie*. Et per illud secunda vespera usque feriam sextam inclusive semper incipitur sicut in missa solet cantari, sed prius dicitur in organis illis tribus diebus. Si autem vis, manda ut tangitur in organo per totam octavam, tam in vesperis quam etiam in missis. Si autem vis in aliis sequentibus diebus ferialibus usque octavam, quod non tangatur in organis, sed choratores incipiant *Kirieleison*, chorus autem persequatur." It is hardly probable that this practice was limited either to the Easter Week or to the specific case of the *Kyrie*.

As to the singing or performing certain verses more than once, the intonation of the Gloria was called for five times in the third Mass of Christmas in Halle: ". . . *Gloria in excelsis* quinquies cantabitur. Primo Praepositus solus cantabit illud pressa voce. Secundo omnes ministri altaris levata voce et solemniter illud cantabunt. Tertio Cantor et Rectores. Quarto ille in organis. Quinto totus chorus cantabit illud vertendo se ad altare. Deinde Cantor et Rectores subiungunt alta voce *Et in terra*. Ita servabitur etiam ad sequentes duos dies proximos. Similiter si festum Innotentium dominica die evenerit." Another case in point is the Sequence. It may suffice here to state that three presentations of the same verse by different media is often specifically called for. The widely used vocalized repetition of each verse may also have been done by singers and repeated by the organ. More about this shall be said at another occasion.

Quite unique seems to be the regulation in a document of Constanz, 1502, published by Söhner, inasmuch as it seems to require the repetition of the whole *Magnificat*, first by the Choir alone, then by alternating with the organ: "in primis vesperis *Magnificat* quae duplicatur, primo per chorum decantetur et ea completa *Magnificat* in organis incipiatur decanteturque versus pro versu." The closing Antiphon is to be played by the organist.

Our sources, both the organ tablatures and the liturgical auxiliary books and marginal rubrics, confirm our first hypothesis. The alternation of the organ with other means of performance was, in the fifteenth-sixteenth centuries, far from being rigidly and uniformly regulated. It is safe to say that this was the case not only with the liturgical forms taken up in the present paper, but quite generally over the whole field of church music. Local customs and regulations show a wide range of deviations and sufficient leeway for the active participants to divide up the task between themselves according to their own light.

In some respects the tradition of "vocal" music confirms this observation. If we knew more about the specific localities for which certain works were written, valuable conclusions could be drawn from a comparison of their specific features with the locally prevailing practices. Future research may, in this respect, clarify many a mysterious point.

For the present, let us return to our specific task. It will be well to remember, in this connection, the change in formal organization that took place at the beginning of the sixteenth century in the motettic Responsory. Its classic formulation was aptly pointed out by Oliver Strunk [21] as that of the so-called "Refrain-Motette." This typical sixteenth-century Responsory is a two-section Motet, the sections of which end with the identical (or only slightly changed) "refrain" of text and music. The "refrain" extends to about one half or one third of the section. Strunk showed that the apparent A plus B / C plus B "form" is not so much the result of musical shaping as that of the liturgical cast, namely of the Responsory. Part one, comprising A plus B is nothing but the Responsory proper, up to the Verse. Part two, consisting of C plus B, contains the Verse followed by the Repetenda. Probably the singers could substitute the text of the Doxology for that of the Verse, if the total Responsory was to be performed by polyphonic choir, but we have no positive indications to go by. Be this as it may, the sixteenth-century Responsory, through-composed and without any break between A and B or between C and B (as a matter of fact, the points of imitation often overlap), was obviously created for an unified performance by an uniform body of sound — that of the à cappella ensemble, whatever the true meaning of the term may have been.[22] No change in this body of sound, in the means of performance, no alternation of any kind is a priori contemplated or counted on.

The earlier type of the Responsory, on the contrary, sectionalizes the form. Responsories of the fifteenth century and those of German composers (or composers working in Germany) of the early sixteenth century, such as Isaac, Finck, Stoltzer, Rener, etc., consists normally of three well defined sections marked by final Long, double bar, and occasionally a choral intonation for the first and third sections. If the Doxology is set polyphonically, the number of sections is increased to five. The three principal sections correspond to (1) the Responsory up to the asterisk, (2) the Repetenda, and (3) the Verse. This arrangement provides for a variety of possibilities such as (a) taking up again the Repetenda after the Verse, (b) omitting any section if it was to be performed by a different medium — be it the organ or the plainchant — and (c) applying the music of the Verse to the text of the Doxology and repeating the appropriate section of the Responsory after it, if any of these constituent parts were to be sung by the polyphonic choir. Within the great oeuvre of Thomas Stoltzer, for instance, there is only one Responsory, the especially festive *Verbum caro*,[23] that approaches a through-composed form by re-composing the Repetenda and adding a separate Doxology. Thus this Responsory consists of five well defined sections:

℞	*Verbum caro*
Rep.	*Plenum gratia*
℣	*In principio*
Rep.	*Plenum gratia*
Dox.	*Gloria superno*

and even here no provision has been made for a Repetenda after the Doxology. Probably local custom required the repetition of the whole Responsory (the first two sections). The re-composition of the Repetenda is quite exceptional. Even in Responsories with attached Doxology, such as Leonhard Paminger's *Verbum caro* (Breslau, Ms. 12, No. 25–26)

℞	*Verbum caro*
Rep.	*Plenum gratia*
℣	*In principio*
Dox.	*Gloria patri*

the Repetenda appears only once.

Contrary to this exceptional fuller form, some responsorial compositions of the time take care of only one or two sections. Thus, to mention only one instance, the Dresden manuscript 265 contains the Repetenda *Plenum gratia* as composed by Johann Walther, while another, anonymous, setting includes also the Verse *In principio*.[24] The beginning, *Verbum caro*, is lacking in both instances.

As to antiphonal compositions of the same period, reference has been made above to the Introits, some of which include the whole text (and Gregorian material), while others omit the intonation of both the Antiphon and the Verse. In some cases the plainchant intonation is explicitly marked in the source. The combination of evidences shows a flexibility of practice that includes, potentially, all available media of performance.

There is, in addition, a peculiar group of sources that seem to have been adjusted to specific local conditions and to fit into the picture gained from liturgical and instrumental sources. Dresden Ms. 265, cited above, belongs to this category. More explicit is the reorganization of Introits and Mass-Allelujas in the same source and in related Mss in Dresden,[25] Zwickau,[26] and Breslau,[27] to name only a few outstanding examples. These particular Mss, containing for the most part compositions of the Introit of the Mass followed by parts of the Ordinary, the Alleluja and the Sequence for the principal holidays, uniformly invert the liturgical order of sections of the Introit inasmuch as the Antiphon — with or without Incipit — follows rather than precedes the Psalm-Verse the first half of which is also sometimes omitted. This is the shape of the Pentecost-Introit in Dresden 266, of the Introits for the fourth Advent Sunday (Stoltzer), Christmas (Stoltzer), Epiphany (Stoltzer), and Purification (Isaac) in Zwickau C'4, or of those for Christmas (Isaac), Epiphany (Rener), Purification (Isaac), Easter (Galliculus), Ascension, Pentecost, Trinity (Isaac) and St. John Baptist in Breslau 92.

Since many of these compositions are known, in perfectly normal shape and form, from other sources (e.g., from Georg Rhaw's printed editions), their re-arrangement must be due to local regulations and conditions of performance practice. The initial Antiphon and the first half of the Verse, if omitted, are omitted obviously because they were to be performed by another medium (or by other media) than the one for which these sources were written and to which the conclusion of the Verse and the following rendering of the Antiphon (complete or without intonation) were assigned, i.e., the polyphonic choir, *à cappella* or otherwise. Before deciding that the missing parts were supplied by Gregorian singing, it well behooves us to remember that both the Ordinarium Strigoniense and the organ tablatures occasionally provide for the performance of the initial Antiphon, or of its intonation, by the organ. The well-nigh unlimited freedom and variety of local customs is illustrated by the uniform and unique assignment to the organ of the end of the Doxology with the Psalm-Difference and of the repetition of the Antiphon in the Augsburg organ book.[28]

The attitude of the above mentioned Mss sources is further corroborated by the inverted order of the sections of the Mass-Alleluja. Thus Dresden 265 (Nativity, Epiphany, Purification, Trinity), Breslau 92 (Nativity [Rener], Epiphany [Rener], Purification [Isaac], Easter [Conrad Rein], Ascension, Pentecost, Trinity, St. John Baptist) and Zwickau C'4 (Advent, Christmas [Stoltzer], Epiphany) offer the Verse at the first place and have it followed by the Alleluja. The initial Alleluja, here omitted, and probably not performed in full, obviously calls for another medium. As in the case of such inverted Introits, it is impossible to assume that the respective piece, standing at second place, would have been performed twice by the choir: once before the Verse, and once after the Verse where these sources place it. Just as in the case of the Introit, organ performance of the first Alleluja has to be taken into account, along with Gregorian singing, although in the case of the Alleluja neither the liturgical books nor the tablatures give us any hint to this effect.

Let us finally mention that the only Responsory preserved in these sources, Balthasar Resinarius' *Verbum caro* in Breslau 92 (A 17) is also written down in inverted order:

Ꝟ *In principio*
ꝶ *Verbum caro*
Rep. *Plenum gratia*

and seems to imply (1) the performance of the Responsory before the Verse by a different medium (or different media), and (2) the repetition of the full Responsory, after the Verse, by the polyphonic choir.

We may arrest our preliminary report at this point. Our sources show

(1) the *rich variety* of performance practices of liturgical music,

differing from place to place, from holiday to holiday, and giving ample elbow room to those responsible for an orderly and ornate liturgy,[29] and

(2) the probable extent of *free alternation* of organ playing, polyphonic singing, and Gregorian chant.[30]

Indeed, richness and freedom were the qualities of liturgical music-making in the Renaissance. No doubt, more thorough research will only confirm our results. While the liturgist may speak of decadence and decay, and regret the low standards and the liturgical anarchy of pre-Tridentine times, the historian of music must disagree. Rigid alternation of media was alien to the musical life; the high quality, the great number of masterpieces, the stylistic variety of music could come about only in the atmosphere of co-creativeness of the performer, of artistic freedom, of lack of any rigidity. Only by keeping this in mind — and by continual searching for additional evidence — can we escape such booby-traps of half-truth as "Orgelmesse" and "*à cappella* practice."

1. Ordinale Exon., ed. J. N. Dalton, Publications of the Henry Bradshaw Society, vols. 37–38 and 63, London, 1909–1926.

2. "Inhibemus eciam ne in choro discantetur vel organizetur nisi in temporibus infrascriptis" (p. 19). The conspicuous transition from organum singing to organ playing should be investigated. Besides the Exeter rite several others will have to be taken into account, e.g., The Ordinal and Customary of the Abbey of St. Mary, York, ed. the Abbess of Stanbrook and J. L. B. Tolhurst, Publications of the Henry Bradshaw Society, vols. 73, 75 (third vol. in preparation), London, 1936–1937.

3. Ordinarium Strigoniense, Nürnberg, 1496, (Lyon, 1510) Ordinarius Strigoniensis, Venice (1505), 1509, 1520 "Incipit Rubrica Strigoniensis" fragm. Ms. 73, University Library, Budapest. (I have not examined the editions indicated in parentheses.)

4. München, University Library, Cod. Ms. 2°, 153. Cfr. P. Leo Söhner OSB, Die Geschichte der Begleitung des gregorianischen Chorals in Deutschland, Augsburg, 1931. The Ms., written in 1510–1511 for the Carmelite Church of St. Anne in Augsburg, was at one time in the hands of Paul Hofhaimer.

5. Ordinarius secundum veram notulam sive rubricam almae ecclesiae Agriensis . . . (Cracow, 1509), Venice, 1514.

6. Erlangen, University Library, Mss. 416–17. Cfr. Carl Lange, Die lateinischen Osterfeiern, München, 1887, 127; Jacques Handschin, Review of the Festschrift für Johannes Wolf, ZfMw 16, 417ff. I am indebted to Professor Handschin for further information given by letter of April 10, 1934. The Mss, obviously of German origin, have not been more accurately localized. In the eighteenth century they formed part of the library of the Markgrave of Bayreuth. Of the original four volumes only two are still extant.

7. While "figural" singing is often mentioned in chronicles and related sources, specific indications are rather rare. One instance of singing mensural music by schoolchildren, mentioned in the accounts of the Hungarian court, April 26, 1495, is worth being quoted: "Item eodem die succentori de beata Virgine cum

suis consodalibus et pueris, qui cecinerunt in mensuris coram Regia Maiestate, ad co[missi]onem Domini Regis dati sunt [fl] 2." Cfr. J. Ch. Engel, Geschichte des ungarischen Reichs, Halle 1797, I, 17–181.

8. Bamberg, Stadtbibliothek, Cod. Ms. Ed VI. 3 = Liturg. 119. "Breviarius gloriose et prestantissime ecclesie Collegiate Sanctorum Mauritij et Marie Magdalene, Hallis ad Sudarium Domini, 1532." Curt Sachs has used a related source for his Geschichte der Musik und Oper am kurbrandenburgischen Hofe, Leipzig, 1910.

9. Breviarius denuo revisus et emendatus ceremonias ritum canendi ceterasque consuetudines in choro insignis et ingenue Misnensis Ecclesie observandas compendiose explicans. Leipzig, 1520.

10. (1) Organbook of John of Lublin, Cracow, Academy of Sciences Ms 1716. Cfr. Adolf Chybinski, Polnische Musik und Musikkultur des 16. Jahrhunderts in ihren Beziehungen zu Deutschland, SIMG 13, 1911–1912, 463 ff.

(2) Organbook of the Holy Ghost Monastery in Cracow. Cfr. Zdislaw Jachimecki in ZfMw 2, 1919, 206.

(3) Organbook of Martinus Leopolita. Cfr. the unpublished dissertation (Lemberg) of Melania Grafczynska.

Photostat copies of all three tablatures and of the dissertation referred to above are to be found in the Isham Memorial Library, Harvard University.

11. Zürich, Zentralbibliothek, Cod. 248, and its copy, Basel, University Library, F I. 8a. Cfr. Carl Paesler, Hans von Constanz . . . , VfMw 5, 1889.

12. Cfr. Yvonne Rokseth, La musique d'orgue au XVᵉ siècle, Paris, 1930, 160, note 1.

13. Rome, Biblioteca Casanatense Ms 896: Rituale Ecclesiae Archiepiscopalis Montis Regali (1559, passim).

14. Also during Lent. Cfr., for instance, the strict prohibition of organ playing in the Ordinarius Missarum secundum Majorem Ecclesiam Coloniensem, Coloniae 1486 (1505): aiij: "Nota etiam quod per totum adventum non luditur in organis nonobstante aliquo festo qualecumque etiam fuerit, nisi forte fuerit dedicatio alicuius ecclesie . . . ," and bIVᵛ: "Nota etiam quod a LXX usque pasce non luditur in organis cuius quumque etiam festum agatur."

15. Breslau, Stadtbibliothek Ms. 102, fol 45v (no XIX).

16. Zürich, Zentralbibliothek Ms. Car. V. 169 a–d. Hör states that he is supplementing the passages that were supposed to be "choral organisiert," "damit es gantz werd." Cfr. G. Eisenring, Die Ostermesse eines Schweizerkomponisten des 16. Jahrhunderts, Witt's Musica Sacra 46, 1913, 63 ff., and Arnold Geering, Die Vokalmusik in der Schweiz zur Zeit der Reformation, SchwJbfMw 6, 1933, 194 ff, 237 ff.

17. J. Georg Eisenring, Zur Geschichte des mehrstimmigen Proprium Missae bis um 1560. Veröffentlichungen der Gregorianischen Akademie 7, Freiburg (Schweiz), 1913.

18. Cfr. Söhner, loc. cit., quoting Arnold Schlick. Cfr. also the conflicting indications of the Barberini Lupus Mss, St. Gallen, Stiftsbibliothek 542–543, Eisenring, op. cit., 179 ff.

19. Cfr. Söhner, op. cit. Of course, Pater Söhner's concept of unaccompanied playing of Gregorian passages on the organ is quite untenable. Hör's expression "choral organisiert" refers, in my opinion, to the choral content of the more or less improvised polyphonic organ music.

20. Tobias Norlind, Die schwedische Hofkapelle in der Reformationszeit, Festschrift für Johannes Wolf, Berlin, 1929, 148 ff.; Jacques Handschin, loc. cit.; Yvonne Rokseth, Instruments a l'église au XVe siècle, RdM 14, 1933, 206 ff.; Yvonne Rokseth, op. cit., 161 (quoting Philippe de Vigneulles about musicians playing to the Offertory in Metz, 1510); "Trompettes et clairons" also play "durant l'allée et revenue" to the Offertory, and also to the exclamation "Vivat

Rex" in the coronation ceremony of the Kings and Queens of France (cfr Godefroy) and at similar festive occasions such as a solemn *TeDeum* (e.g. Augsburg, 1518) and High Mass (e.g. Augsburg, 1530).

21. Oliver Strunk, Some Motet Types of the 16th century, in: Papers read at the International Congress of Musicology held at New York, 1939, American Musicological Society [1944], 155–60.

22. Cfr. Acta Musicologica 7, 109.

23. Zwickau, Ratsschulbibliothek, Ms. 73, part V, No. 20.

24. Dresden, Sächsische Landesbibliothek Ms. 265, five partbooks of the mid-sixteenth century:

No 8: Walther, ℞ Plenum gratia

No 20–30: anon., ℞ in Nativitate Domini Plenum gratia — In principio erat.

Similar cases e.g. in Ms. 34 of the University Library, Jena. Cfr. the thematic index by Rödiger.

25. Dresden, Sächsische Landesbibliothek Ms. 266, six partbooks of the mid-sixteenth century.

26. Zwickau, Ratsschulbibliothek, Ms. C'4, bass partbook, containing two distinct collections of which we are interested in the first one, fol. 1–18v, at this time.

27. Breslau, Stadtbibliothek, Ms. 92, written 1562.

28. Polyphonic psalm compositions of the early sixteenth century sometimes include (cfr. Rhaw 1540, with psalms by Isaac, Rener, Stoltzer, Walther, etc.), sometimes omit de Doxology. On the other hand, the initial Antiphon opens the composition of the psalm in Stoltzer's Nisi tu Domine — Nisi Dominus (DDT 65, 114).

29. A local confirmation of this view is contained, e.g., in the Frankfurt "Schulordnung" of 1425, published by J. Müller, Vor- und frühreformatorische Schulordnungen, Zschoppau 1885, 47, and referred to by Söhner, l. c., 11. (School-master and organist should agree in order to avoid confusion.)

30. An exhaustive bibliography obviously cannot be included here. Let us mention only a few items, such as G. Rietschel, Die Aufgabe der Orgel im Gottes-dienste bis ins 18. Jahrhundert, Leipzig, 1893, G. Frotscher, Geschichte des Orgelspiels, 1935; Rokseth, op. cit.; Ursprung, Die katholische Kirchenmusik; Wagner, Geschichte der Messe; Moser, Paul Hofhaimer; the studies by Sigl, Marxer and Eisenring in the Veröffentlichungen der Gregorianischen Akademie, A. Pirro, Orgues and organistes de Haguenau, RdM 17, 1933; J. Handschin, l. c.; L. Schrade in AfMf 2, 1936; Kroyer and Fellerer in the Peter Wagner Festschrift; Anglès, Leichsenring, K. Schmidt, Bauch, Valentin (Musikgeschichte der Stadt Frankfurt), etc.

A STUDY IN PROPORTIONS

Helen Hewitt

"*Philomathes*: What is Proportion?

Master: It is *the comparing of numbers placed perpendicularly one ouer another.*

Phi.: This I knewe before, but what is that to Musicke?

Ma.: In deede wee doe not in Musicke consider the numbers by themselves, but set them for a signe to signifie the altering of our notes in the time."

THOMAS MORLEY, *A Plaine and Easie*
Introduction to Practicall Musicke

I N A little two-part setting of the *Regina celi* by Jacobus Hobrecht found in the Segovia Ms.[1] one finds an employment of proportions which merits the attention of even the student already well versed in the various meter signatures and the proportions of fifteenth-century mensural notation.

A correct transcription might result from the employment of empirical means, but only by thinking along with the composer as he spins this intricate web of subtly intermingled metrical and proportional signs does one gain fresh insight into the operation of the fifteenth-century musico-mathematical mind.

The *Duo* may have been written for the purpose either of instructing the student in the science of proportions, or, which is the more probable, of examining him in various aspects of this complex subject. A third possibility suggests itself: that Obrecht contrived this little work to demonstrate the feasibility of using three numbers, rather than the customary two, for the indication of proportions which follow a meter signature which in itself constitutes one type of proportion.

JACOBUS HOBRECHT

The *Duo* shows the melody of the *Regina celi* [2] lying in the *tenor*, its notes moving in slow, simple, rhythmical patterns. The *superius*, on the other hand, consists of a counterpoint whose quicker notes appear in the guise of one proportion after another. The work divides naturally into two sections at the point where both voices change from triple to duple meter. The first section deals with an adaptation of the Gregorian setting of the verse "Regina caeli laetare" with the melody of the chant now simplified, now embellished, as it suited the purpose of the composer. The closing section treats the second melodic phrase of the same antiphon, whose text, here absent, reads "Quia quem meruisti portare."

The composition opens with both voices showing the sign for *tempus imperfectum cum prolatione perfecta*. There is no indication within the sign itself as to whether the notes should be performed in their *integer valor* (when the *semibrevis*, S, represents the *tactus*, t), or whether the sign should be taken to mean one of the four varieties of augmentation current in the fifteenth century. Of the latter the one used most commonly was triple augmentation; this was known as *prolatio perfecta*, and under its sign the *minima*, M, represented the *tactus*.

A glance at the transcription shows that triple augmentation was intended, and that the M has the value of one *tactus*.[3] Since both voices open in *prolatio perfecta*, a disagreement with Morley's teaching (at the end of the sixteenth century) is apparent, for he states that "*augmentation proceedeth of setting the signe of the more prolation in one parte of the songe onely, and not in others.*" [4] Assuming that the performer was not told in advance the intended meaning of the sign, and assuming that the five possible interpretations of the sign were all known to him, let us follow his reasoning to determine the speed at which the written notes must be performed.

The *superius* provides several hints that augmentation of values must take place. The profusion of *fusae* near the beginning of this voice offers one hint, for, as Sachs puts it, musicians of this period had a "*horror fusae*," [5] and as Apel comments, normally *fusae* were "used only in groups of two as a quick 'cadential mordent.' " [6]

It is equally noticeable that the *semiminima* appears in this opening passage not as a blackened *minima* but as a white *minima* with one flag or tail. In connection with his explanation of the meaning of *proportio dupla* Tinctoris describes other relationships to which the term *dupla* is applied. A hundred years later Morley inveighs against one of these, saying, "I cannot imagine how the teachers (which these 30, or 40, years past haue taught) should so farre haue strayed from the truth, as for no reason to call that common sort of Musick, which is in the time vnperfect of the lesse prolation *dupla*, or that it is in *dupla* proportion, except they would say, that any two to one is *dupla*: which none (at least who is in his right wits) will affirme. For when proportion is, then must the things compared be of one kind." [7] In another place he says, "But by the way you must note that time out of minde we haue tearmed that dupla where we set two Minymes to the Semibriefe, which if it were trew, there should be few songs but you should haue dupla, quadrupla and octupla in it, and then by consequent must cease to be dupla." [8]

Although the description of Tinctoris is not so clear as that of Morley, it is interesting for its description of our "white *minima* with tail." He says: "And for the reason that it is not always signed by figures in respect to the minima, because if 2 minimae are referred to 1, or 4 to 2, or 6 to 3, in place of a sign they are filled with some color, of course now generally black ink, or, minimae of this type of dupla are bent back at their summits by a little line obliquely from the right side, and on these no final law is imposed, which minimae, of course, like the others can be filled and, moreover, made duple, but more frequently we use the former in the minor prolation, the latter in the major." [9]

In the present connection it is necessary only to note that Tinctoris connects the "white *minima* with tail" with the major prolation, although since "no final law" controls this, one may not find perfect consistency. Although the example given by Tinctoris appears to mean the *integer valor* of the notes, elsewhere in the *Proportionale* he employs the "white *minima* with tail" when proportionate values are intended. It is probable that Obrecht also was using this special note-shape "as a sign" that the *superius* was not opening in *integer valor*; if so, the performer would have found in the *semiminimae* a second hint.

A third hint may be obtained from the first proportion that appears in this voice, *sesquitertia*. This is the Latin name applied to the ratio 4:3, and it means here that 4 M of the proportion (if following *prolatio perfecta*) or 4 S (if following *integer valor*) shall have the same temporal value as 3 M or 3 S respectively of the opening meter. Since the lowest common multiple of the two terms of this ratio (4 and 3) is 12, one M (or S) of the proportion would be equal to 1/4 of 12 or 3 of that denomination of note of which one M (or S) of the basic meter, ℂ, would equal 1/3 of 12 or 4. Now, in ℂ one M equals 4 *fusae*, but one S equals either 3 M, 6 Sm, or 12 *fusae*; it is clear, then, that the proportion *sesquitertia* is not a relationship of S to S, but of M to M, and that either 4 M's of the proportion or 3 M's of ℂ will have the temporal value of 12 *fusae* of ℂ. The sign ℂ does not here indicate *integer valor* of the notes, but augmentation of values with one *minima* having the value of one *tactus*.

The composer has supplied not only the term *sesquitertia* but the numerical indication $\frac{12}{4}$ as well. The two lower figures are the numerical indication of *sesquitertia*; the "12" stands for the 12 *fusae* contained in 3 *minimae* and at the same time functions as the necessary link with *integer valor* to which all proportions must

ultimately relate; in *integer valor* 12 *fusae* are the equivalent of 3 M or 1 S, and one S has the value of one *tactus*, so that 1 M = 1/3 t. In a proportion the denominator refers to the note representing the *tactus*, here the M. In 4:3, then, 3 M = 3 t, whence 1 M = 1 t. The M of the augmentation is thus related to the M of *integer valor* as 3:1; augmentation is not only present, but is shown to be triple augmentation. Obrecht has used this sign, then, as a *prolatio perfecta* and shown his meaning very concisely and efficiently by the indication $\frac{12}{4}$.
$$\frac{3}{}$$

With it now established that the value of the M is 1 t, and, conversely, that the *tactus* is represented by the M, succeeding proportions may assume their proper meanings, and proportional notes their correct values. It has been observed that the composer employs three numbers rather than the usual two in presenting these proportions. This device is a clever one, for it enables him to convey a great deal of useful information to the performer. Obrecht's formula is as follows.

Although the external shape of the M is the same in *integer valor*, in *prolatio perfecta*, or in any of the proportions, its temporal value is different in each. Since the *tactus* (or "beat" in modern terminology) is the one fixed and unchangeable factor in the composition, each new value of the M must be shown in terms of this *tactus*. This is done indirectly, however, for a "proportion" indicates the number of M of the proportion which must have the same temporal value collectively as an indicated number of M (= t) of the original meter. It is then computed from this ratio what proportion of the *tactus* shall be allotted to the new M.

In the "three-number" proportions of the *Duo* we have, then, an equation of numbers of M's in three *tempi* as follows:

the first (top) number refers to the proportion in question;
the second (middle) number refers to the next-preceding proportion;
the third (bottom) number refers to the opening *prolatio perfecta*.

Let us test, as an example, the third proportion 5:6:3. This means that 5 M of the passage in 5:6:3 equal (i.e., have the same temporal value collectively as) 6 M of the preceding proportion which is numbered 6:4:3. This relationship is a "proportion" in one sense of the term, but in itself does not relate the "5 M" either to *prolatio perfecta* or to *integer valor*; the figure 3 is placed at the bottom to equate the 5 M of the proportion with 3 M of *prolatio perfecta* (= 3 t). It is obvious that this scheme could have been extended to include every preceding proportion; e.g., 5:6:3 could have read 5:6:4:3. Similarly, the next proportion could have read 8:5:6:4:3. However, such a scheme would not only have been cumbersome — surely unnecessary and perhaps even confusing to the performer — but, more important, it would have obscured the composer's purpose.

His purpose was to relate each proportion accurately to the next-preceding proportion and to the basic *prolatio perfecta*. At any change in the value of the M these three speeds, and these only, needed to be known; hence, three numbers were sufficient. To the initiated performer the presence of "three-number proportions" would doubtless have brought instant recognition of *prolatio perfecta* as the meaning of the sign C. Since the number 3 is present as the bottom number of each ratio, it seems also to be stressing the fact that the *tactus*-note of *integer valor*, the S, is here worth 3 *tactus*.

With sets of three numbers available, the performer had two courses open to him: (1) he could relate the M of any proportion to the M of the next-preceding proportion by observing top and middle numbers only; or (2) he could relate the M of the proportion directly to the M of *prolatio perfecta* by using top and bottom figures only.

The effect of the former ratios is cumulative; i.e., each depends on the preceding for the value of its notes. For example, to discover the value of the M of the last proportion, 18:16:3, in relation to the *tactus* (= M of *prolatio perfecta*) the fractions composed of the top and middle numbers of each proportion may be multiplied as follows:

$$\frac{4}{3}\times\frac{6}{4}\times\frac{5}{6}\times\frac{8}{5}\times\frac{9}{8}\times\frac{12}{9}\times\frac{16}{12}\times\frac{18}{16}=\frac{18}{3}$$

This same process can be applied to any one of the proportions, and the product will always turn out to be a fraction whose numerator is the top figure of the proportion, its denominator the bottom figure.

Thus we see that in using three figures the composer could provide the "solution" (relation to *tactus*, shown by top and bottom numbers) as well as set the "problem" (relation to preceding proportion, shown by top and middle numbers). The performer having difficulty with any one proportion could easily resume singing at the next proportion by relating his new M to that of *prolatio perfecta*; i.e., by measuring it directly by the *tactus*.

To relate the value of the M of 18:16:3 back to *integer valor* would require only one additional step, *viz.*, to multiply by 1/3, the fraction representing the triple augmentation of *prolatio perfecta*: $1/3 \times 18/3 = 18/9$, which in turn equals 2/1, the ratio indicating *proportio dupla*. The term *dupla*, found at this point in the *Duo*, is therefore relating the value of the M of 18:16:3 to the M of *integer valor*, not, as one might have expected, the M of the proportion in question to the M of the next-preceding proportion.

This seemingly curious manner of naming a 9:8 (18:16) proportion invites an investigation of the correlation between the numerical proportions and the Latin terms accompanying them. It has already been pointed out that the first proportion, 4:3, was relating the M of 4:3 and the M of *prolatio perfecta*, and was thus correctly labeled *sesquitertia*. The remaining proportions of this first section of the *Duo*, as the reader may verify for himself, also apply the Latin term to the relation between the proportion in question and *prolatio perfecta*; i.e., name the ratio of top number to bottom number. For example, the second proportion composed of top and bottom numbers, 6:3, is named *dupla*.

There exists here, then, an established procedure from which the naming of the final 18:16:3 departs. The logic behind this seeming inconsistency is based on the application of a name which will assist the singer in achieving the proper value of the M in question in the easiest possible manner. Surely to suggest that the M of 18:16:3 should be allotted just 1/2 its *integer valor* is to help a performer who might otherwise attempt to measure 16/18 of a M which itself is related to the M of *prolatio perfecta* as 16:3.

At measure 37 a new meter signature, C, destroys the effect of ¢. The proportions interspersed among measures of C are represented by only two numbers: 5:4, 3:2, 9:4, or 9:8. Since the notes of C have their *integer valor*, only two speeds need to be related. One may conclude, then, that for Obrecht this rule obtains: "two speeds, two numbers; three speeds, three numbers." This confirms once again that C̵ is not used at the beginning as a sign of *integer valor*.

In these proportions following C the numerator states the number of S of the proportion to be equated with the number of S of C indicated by the denominator; i.e., the number of *tactus*, for in C, S = t. This is quite in line with Morley's "general rule" which states that *"in all proportions the vpper number signifieth the semibriefe, and the lower number the stroke, so that as the vpper number is to the lower, so is the semibriefe to the stroke."* [10] Each of the proportions following C is named for the relationship between the S of the proportion and the S of the basic meter, C, with the exception of 9:8 to be discussed below. It might be called to attention that where two proportions stand next to each other (5:4 is followed directly by 3:2) their effect is not cumulative; i.e., the proportion 3:2 does not depend on 5:4 but relates the S of 3:2 directly to the S of C.

Another interesting irregularity occurs at the end of the *Duo* where a seemingly simple *sesquioctava*, 9:8, appears in the *superius*. Nine S appear in this passage, and one would normally expect the equation 9 S of 9:8 = 8 S of C. However, this ratio proves not to be the one intended.

In the *tenor* at this point appears a *maxima* in ¢ 2; i.e., a note equalling 2 *tactus*; 8 S of C, however, would have the value of 8 *tactus*. Since 9 S of the proportion must equal 2 t, the ratio of S of the proportion to S of C would be 9:2, but this is not the ratio indicated by the name *sesquioctava*. The meaning of 9:8 here is as follows. Considering the difficulty of thinking the intended rhythm in relation to the notes of the preceding passage in this voice, it seemed more practical to relate the notes of the proportion to the single *maxima* of the *tenor*, a note equalling 8 S. Tinctoris states explicitly that proportions are indicated in two different ways, "either when we refer following notes immediately to the preceding in one and the same part . . . or when the notes of one part are referred directly to the notes of another against which they are composed." [11]

The theorist's amplification of this statement is so apt at this point, where one is inclined to inquire how the performer might know that he was suddenly to measure his S by the lower part, that it will be given in full. Tinctoris continues: "But since it has been planned doubly, as it were, there should be a manner of indicating the proportions, whether it is in the first manner of setting forth proportions of any song according to signs that they be written (that is, through the relation to the preceding number in one and the same part) or in the second manner (that is, through the relation to the notes of the other part) that is recognized by no singer unless by divining or by inspecting the counterpoint; whence it comes about that a hestitation or doubt arises in the singing, which must by all means be avoided; for when compositions are in the middle they ought to be performed continuously without any hesitation. Therefore, I should advise, nevertheless, that a simple manner be assumed, and, of course, that the proportions should be indicated according to the relation to the other part, unless it should be a hindrance that in the other manner (of course, through the relation to the preceding notes in one and the same part) many proportions be singable which would not be otherwise." [12]

Obrecht has, then, in this *Duo* followed the advice of Tinctoris in its fundamental meaning, *viz.*, to indicate any proportion in the manner easiest for the performer to calculate. In fact, all four proportions of the second section of the *Duo* are written so that they could be thought in relation to the *tenor*.

A brief summary of the meters and proportions used in the *Duo* will show the enormous variety of temporal values attached to the same note-shape (♪ or ◊) that Obrecht contrived to combine in one short composition.

Meter Signatures

c	(*tempus imperfectum*; notes in *integer valor*)	$S = t$
¢	(*tempus imperfectum diminutum*; all values halved)	$S = 1/2\, t$
¢ 2	*quadrupla* (all values quartered)	$S = 1/4\, t$
C	(*prolatio perfecta*; all values tripled)	$M = t$
¢	(*prolatio perfecta diminuta*; values of *prolatio perfecta* halved, not reduced to *integer valor*, in which M would equal 1/3 t)	$M = 1/2\, t$

Numerical Proportions

(Terms used in the *Duo* represent relation between M of the proportion and M of *prolatio perfecta* or between S of the proportion and S of *tempus imperfectum*. The proportions are classified here within the 5 *genera* recognized by contemporary theory.)

I. *Genus multiplex*

    1. *dupla*   2:1 (or 6:3 as in 6:4:3)   M = 1/2 t
    2. *tripla*   3:1 (or 9:3 as in 9:8:3)   M = 1/3 t
    3. *quadrupla* 4:1 (or 12:3 as in 12:9:3)   M = 1/4 t

II. *Genus superparticulare*

    1. *sesquialtera* 3:2   S = 2/3 t
    2. *sesquitertia* 4:3 (in 12:4:3)   M = 3/4 t
    3. *sesquiquarta* 5:4   S = 4/5 t
    4. *sesquioctava* 9:8 $\left\{\begin{array}{l} \text{S} = 2/9 \text{ t} \\ \textit{or} \quad = 8/9 \text{ S of } ¢ 2 \end{array}\right.$

III. *Genus superpartiens*

    1. *superbipartiens* (here *superbipartiente tertias*) 5:3 (in 5:6:3)   M = 3/5 t

IV. *Genus multiplex superparticulare*

    1. *quindupla sesquitertia* 16:3 (in 16:12:9:3)   M = 3/16 t
    2. *dupla sesquiquarta*   9:4   S = 4/9 t

V. *Genus multiplex superpartiens*

    1. *dupla superbipartiens* 8:3 (in 8:5:3)   M = 3/8 t

An inspection of the notation of the various proportions now reveals its simplicity. Since 3 M of the original notation make one measure of 3/4 meter of the transcription, it will be seen that Obrecht sets, in turn, 4 M, 6 M, 5 M, 8 M, 9 M, 12 M, 16 M, and 18 M in the place of 3 M of the original notation or one measure of the transcription. Odd and even numbers alternate, so that the performer must always think a fractional part of the preceding M.[13] As the number of M set against 3 M gradually increases, multiples of 3 appear (6, 9, 12, 18). One understands now why *dupla, tripla, quadrupla*, and *sextupla* cannot always be represented by the simpler ratios having 1 as denominator: it depends on what they follow. For example, here the ratio 2:1 must be written 6:3, for 6 M must replace 4 M of the preceding proportion, which in turn replace 3 M of *prolatio perfecta*; therefore, 6:3 is the required ratio.

It is also interesting to observe how the same rhythm of three triplets in one measure of the transcription appears in the original notation in two different ways. First, it appears as true *"tripla"* when 9 M (following 8 M) are related to 3 M of *prolatio perfecta* (= 3:1). Second, it appears labeled *"dupla"* at the point where 18 M (following 16 M) replace 3 M of *prolatio perfecta*. This rhythm is of course only *dupla* in relation to the values in *integer valor*, as mentioned above; it is actually *sextupla* in relation to *prolatio perfecta* (18:3 = 6:1). It will be observed that the passage is written in black notation, in which 3 black S or 6 black M must be sung in the time of 1 M of ℂ. This was the customary manner of writing *sextupla* in Morley's time, apparently, for he says, "But if we consider rightlie, that which we call *sextupla* is but true *tripla* prickt in black notes." [14]

Of *tripla* Morley says "This is the common hackney horse of all the Composers, which is of so manie kindes as there be maners of pricking, sometimes al in blacke notes, sometimes all in white notes, sometimes mingled, sometimes in briefes, sometimes in semibriefes, and yet all one measure. . . . true *tripla* maketh three Semibriefes or their value in other notes to the time of one semibriefe." [15]

Sesquitertia (four quarter-notes to one measure of 3/4 meter in the transcription) also appears not only as true *sesquitertia*, 4:3, in the first proportion, but later as *dupla superbipartiens*, 8:5:3, and again as *quindupla sesquitertia*, 16:12:9:3. The insertion of the extra number, 9, in this last proportion is irregular and actually unnecessary. It appears to be referring the singer more forcibly to "12:9:3," the *quadrupla* proportion immediately preceding, as a reminder of the quadruple speed at which this *"sesquitertia"* must progress; no such reference was deemed necessary in the *"sesquitertia"* at duple speed (8:5:3) for the name of this proportion contained in itself a sufficient hint: *"dupla" super bipartiens*. It will be observed that although each of these three proportions transcribes as quadruplets of quarter-notes, the ancient notation requires *minimae* for the opening *sesquitertia* (4:3), *semibreves* for 8:3 (following *dupla*) and *breves* for 16:3 (following *quadrupla*).

Quadrupla also appears in two different notations, although resulting in two different rhythms since appearing under two different meters. In ℂ, *quadrupla* is expressed by 12:9:3, since 12 M must replace 9 M of the preceding proportion, and those in turn replace 3 M of *prolatio perfecta*. In C, *quadrupla* is represented by the meter signature ¢ 2 which indicates performing the notes at 1/4 their value in C.

Dupla is also represented both by numerical proportions (6:3 and 18:16:3, discussed above) under the sign C, as well as by meter signatures. In duple meter we find *dupla* represented by ₵ (*tempus imperfectum diminutum*) which means to "diminish" the notes, or, to perform them at half their *integer valor*. In triple meter *dupla* appears as ₵ (*prolatio perfecta diminuta*) with the same general meaning; however, it is an interesting fact that this sign does not restore the notes back to their *integer valor*, for M under this sign = 1/2 t, while the M of *integer valor* = 1/3 t.

Possibly this whole matter is best summed up in the words of Philomathes, spoken after the Master had shown him a madrigal of Giulio Renaldi (c. 1500–c. 1570) involving various meters and proportions. Philomathes comments: "This hath been a mightie musicall furie, which hath caused him to shewe such diversitie in so small bounds." [16]

1. A fifteenth-century manuscript without library number belonging to the Cathedral of Segovia, Spain. The *Duo* is found complete on folio 200 *verso*.

2. *Liber Usualis*, p. 241.

3. The transcription conforms with Willi Apel's judgment that the modern quarter-note most suitably represents the *tactus* of fifteenth-century music. (Willi Apel, *The Notation of Polyphonic Music, 900–1600*, 4th ed., Cambridge, Mass., The Mediaeval Academy of America, 1949, p. 97.)

4. Thomas Morley, *A Plaine and Easie Introduction to Practicall Musicke* (London, 1597), p. 24. Other theorists who agree with Morley are Adam of Fulda, Ornithoparchus, and Glareanus. Consult Curt Sachs, *Rhythm and Tempo: a Study in Music History* (New York: W. W. Norton & Co., Inc., 1953), p. 213.

5. Sachs, *op. cit.*, p. 214.

6. Apel, *op. cit.*, p. 191.

7. Morley, *op. cit.*, "*The Annotations*" to "*Pag. 27. vers. 40. Dupla.*"

8. Morley, *op. cit.*, p. 27 where the word "*Dupla*" stands in the margin.

9. Johannes Tinctoris, "Proportionale Musices," *Scriptores de Musica Medii Aevi*, ed. E. de Coussemaker (4 vols., Paris, 1876), IV, 157.

10. Morley, *op. cit.*, pp. 27–28.

11. Tinctoris, *op. cit.*, p. 155.

12. Tinctoris, *op. cit.*, p. 155.

13. Although 4 and 6 are both even numbers, the ratio reduced to its lowest terms is 3:2; similarly, 16:12 = 4:3, and 18:16 = 9:8.

14. Morley, *op. cit.*, p. 54.

15. Morley, *op. cit.*, "*The Annotations*" to "*Pag. 29. vers. 3. Tripla.*"

16. Morley, *op. cit.*, p. 35.

A CURIOUS USE OF COLORATION

IN THE PIXÉRÉCOURT CODEX

Carl Parrish

T HE codex f. fr. 15123 is one of the brightest jewels in the rich treasury of musical manuscripts in the *Cabinet des Manuscrits* of the Paris Bibliothèque Nationale. It is commonly referred to as the Pixérécourt Codex, after the name of its donor, René Charles Guilbert de Pixérécourt, who was a successful operetta librettist, and director of the Opera-Comique at Paris from 1824 to 1827. As this valuable manuscript has not yet been made the object of a special study except in part, a brief description of it may be in order before turning to the particular feature of it with which this article will deal.[1]

Written in the late fifteenth century in an elegant French hand — and apparently by the same hand throughout — the attractive appearance of the codex fittingly reflects the character of its musical contents. Its 198 parchment folios contain 178 complete pieces, the parts of which are disposed in the usual manner of the period, the Superius being on the upper half of the left-hand page, facing the Contra on the opposite page, while the Tenor occupies the lower lines of the left-hand page and continues on the lower staves of the opposite page. In the case of a four-part piece the Cantus and Tenor are on the left-hand page, opposite the two Contra parts.

The codex has suffered certain mutilations during its existence. Folio 83 has been cut out completely, so that parts of two chansons are lacking, and at one time a brutally careless bookbinder has trimmed the margins of the volume down to the present page size of 180 × 120 milimeters, in such a way that many of the composer's names which occur at the top of the pieces have been lopped off, either completely or just enough to prevent their identification. In many cases only a tiny part of the downward flourish of a single letter of a name remains. About one out of every five pieces is identifiable by name, and it is possible, considering the great care with which the manuscript was put together, that at one time each of the pieces carried the name of its composer.

The names that remain in the volume include Busnois, with 22 pieces, Caron, with 11, Ockeghem, 3, Dufay, 2, and the following, each of whose names occurs but once — Compère, Ycart, Morton, and Cornago. Since the time of its discovery several of the pieces in this codex have been found in other Renaissance chansonniers (e.g., the *Odhecaton* contains ten of the Pixérécourt pieces), and the composers of a good many other pieces in it have been identified. The list includes Philippe Basiron, Bedingham, Dunstable, Hayne van Gizeghem, J. Legrant, Johannes Martini, Gilles Mureau, Tinctoris, Joannes Tourout, Juan Urrede, and Vincinet.

The vast majority of pieces in the book are settings of French texts. Some are in Italian (although these are outnumbered by the French texts by about six to one), Latin is used in 3, and Flemish in one. Fourteen of the pieces have only text incipits, while three compositions do not even bear incipits. About one fifth of the compositions are in three voices, the remainder consisting of four-part compositions.

The great significance of this manuscript was realized soon after it came to light in the library of its donor. A striking testimonial to this fact is the existence of a nine-page document by F.-J. Fétis, dated February 12, 1826, which is pasted in the back of the volume. It bears the title: "Notice sur quelques compositeurs du quinzième siècle, dont les ouvrages se trouvent dans un manuscrit précieux appartenant à Monsieur Guilbert de Pixérécourt, par M. Fétis." The "Notice" is in Fétis' own handwriting, and is an interesting peripheral feature of the codex for the light it throws on the state of knowledge about, and attitude toward, Medieval and Renaissance music that obtained in France about a century and a quarter ago. According to Fétis the music written before the time of the composers in the Pixérécourt manuscript was "of a sort of harmony that would today put to flight the most ardent devotees, and tear the ears of the least trained." The oldest polyphonic music that he knew was the Machaut Mass, which he had put in score, he says, "as an historical curiosity." The true "patriarchs of harmony" were those mentioned by Tinctoris in his *Liber de natura et proprietate tonorum* — namely, Dunstable, Dufay, Binchois, Ockeghem, Regis, Busnois, Caron, and Faugues.

The actual music of these masters was practically unknown at the time of the discovery of the Pixérécourt Codex, and Fétis realized the manuscript's importance even before he had any actual acquaintance with its musical contents; as he says, it "fills an immense gap in the succession of great musicians, and one which enables us to bring together some facts which, without its help, would remain isolated. No doubt the transcription of these various pieces would uncover some interesting and hitherto unknown principles which guided these first musicians in their works." The uncovering of these principles has been a major concern of musicologists for the past half century and more, and it would surely amaze Fétis to realize how deeply the roots of this art lay in the music he considered to be of merely historical curiosity.

The progressive characteristics of the compositions in this manuscript are emphasized by Fernando Liuzzi in his study of its pieces with Italian texts, to which reference has already been made. Liuzzi points out the forward-looking features of form and spirit that they manifest, such as the sonnet settings which anticipate in their formal outlines those of the sixteenth-century madrigal, the descriptive pieces such as the spirited *Alla Battaglia*, and *Alla Caccia*, and the programmatic character of certain textless pieces such as *La Martinella*, which imitates the bells of the Palazzo Vecchio at Florence. From the standpoint of technique, these pieces are also remarkable for their definite bent toward a homophonic character, conserving imitative resources for textual illustration, and also for a melodic simplicity and precision that is in strong contrast to the Northern melismatic ostentation of the previous period. Similar traits are evident in the Franco-Flemish compositions in this collection, which, it should be recalled, greatly outnumber the Italian pieces. However, it is not with such considerations that the present article will now deal, but rather with an unusual notational detail found in one of the compositions.

The pieces in the Pixérécourt manuscript present no special notational difficulties. White notation is employed throughout, and the formation of the semibreves and all notes smaller than it display the characteristic roundish shape of the latter fifteenth century. The meter signs employed are the complete circle, the number "3," the broken circle, and the broken circle with a vertical line through it. Proportional changes are very rarely employed. One piece (*Sirica fu labadessa*, fol. 108ᵛ–109, the "secunda pars" of *Orudite il buono horare*) has exceptionally a section in sesquialtera in the middle. Several pieces have a change from duple to triple meter in the second part.

There is a notational peculiarity in one piece of the collection (*Vostre senture*, fol. 80ᵛ–81, the "secunda pars" of *Et hola, hola, ho, fist elle*, fol. 79ᵛ–80) that deserves consideration, as it concerns a certain eccentric use of coloration that presents something of a mystery. Coloration, in the sense of blackening the prevalent white notes to produce a change of note values, occurs freely throughout the volume. In three pieces (*Plaisant houlete*, fol. 42ᵛ–43, *Faites de moy tout qu'il vous plaira*, fol. 132ᵛ–133, and *Departe nous*, fol. 133ᵛ–134), coloration is introduced simultaneously in all voices in the last section and continued until the end, to produce a change from duple to triple meter. This is a perfectly natural and logical extension of the coloration principle, although it might be noted that in other pieces in the collection where the same metrical change occurs, this end is accomplished by simply introducing the numeral "3."

However, in *Vostre senture*, coloration is applied in a most unusual manner. (The piece is appended in transcription at the end of this essay.) The "prima pars" (*Et hola, hola*) bears the meter sign of the broken circle with a vertical line through it, and is in this duple meter throughout. At the beginning of *Vostre senture* all parts change to triple meter ("3," meaning □=◊◊◊) except the Superius, which changes to "black notation," in which it remains throughout (with the insignificant exception of the last note, and one note in the middle — the breve of bar twelve). Black notation in this case is actually coloration, of course, since this brings about the desired equivalence of note-values (♦♦♦ in ₵ = ◊◊◊ in 3).

It should be added that the change from duple to triple meter in the three lower parts does not occur simultaneously, as the following transcription of the last few bars of *Et hola, hola* illustrates:

It will be noted, too, that the change to triple meter is not written in the Contratenor-bassus until after *Vostre senture* has already begun (see bar four of the transcription of *Vostre senture*).

The mystery lies in the use of coloration throughout the Superius to produce triple rhythm while the other parts change from duple to triple meter through the use of the meter sign. This is all the more puzzling in that the Tenor part is in canon with the Superius through the first half of *Vostre senture*, and has the same melodic character as it throughout the piece. Neither of these parts has any metrical change within itself that is brought about by the usual function of coloration, i.e., to produce hemiola rhythm, or what is sometimes called "courante rhythm," although a few passages of normal coloration of this kind occur in both Contra parts, as the transcription indicates.

Aside from this curious discrepancy in the Superius, *Vostre senture* has a few other notational inconsistencies, such as the syncopation in bar seven (Tenor), which is produced by alteration, even though the same rhythmic figure in bars fifteen and eighteen is written out as semibreve-breve; such details are not at all unusual in other fifteenth-century manuscripts, however.

The mysterious use of coloration in the Superius invites speculation as to the motive for its use. There is the possibility that it was a mere whim on the part of the composer or scribe, although this is a very unsatisfactory answer. If the text were not so nonsensical one might assume a certain symbolical use of black notes here, such as Josquin des Pres employed for his *Deploration de Johan. Oke-*

ghem, but one seeks in vain for any such suggestion in the verse of either the first or second part of the piece.[2] Another surmise would be that the scribe forgot to put in the triple meter sign for the Superius, and found it simpler to blacken all the notes rather than try to squeeze in a "3" of the proper size. This, too, seems unlikely, as does the possibility that the blackening might have been a device to indicate that only the Superius was to be sung in the "secunda pars," since the text is completely and carefully written in throughout the Tenor, indicating a performance by two solo voices, with instruments carrying the Contra parts.

There remains the fascinating possibility that the composer intended an effect of cross-rhythm throughout the whole of the second part of the composition. Since coloration within a triple meter always indicates imperfect meter, it is possible that the Superius ought really to be transcribed in duple meter, thus creating a rhythmically sophisticated effect in which the two principal lines of the piece (and the only parts with words) sing in free canon, but one in the accentuation of duple meter against triple meter in the other. Enhancing this rhythmical effect would be the free shifting of the two Contra parts from triple to duple meter in their passages of coloration.

Ex.2

Against this theory is the fact that a triple meter sign has not been added to the Superius for *Vostre senture*, and that a strict observance of notational rules would demand triple rhythm in the coloration

Paris, Bibl. Nat.,
fr. 15123, fol. 80ᵛ–81

Ex.3   VOSTRE SENTURE

passage. But this is more than a passage, it is a large part of the entire composition; furthermore it is operating within the triple-meter framework that has been set up in all the other parts. Under these circumstances it might be the natural reaction of a singer reading a part in black notes to perform it in duple meter, and this is what might have been expected of him in this case.

The very beginning of *Et hola, hola* shows a somewhat similar rhythmical effect, where one and the same motive is carried on in two different rhythmical characters. The accentuation of the first two bars of the Contratenor-altus is shifted by means of coloration. This situation differs from the other, of course, in that the two voices are carrying on the same motive simultaneously in different speeds.

This is not offered as corroborative evidence in support of the explanation suggested for the black notation in *Vostre senture*, but it is "in character," appearing as it does in the same piece. A similar rhythmical effect of two-against-three is seen at the end of the previously quoted example of *Et hola, hola*, where the Contratenor-altus announces the opening figure of *Vostre senture* two measures before the double bar, thus serving as an anticipation of the main canon between Superius and Tenor.

The point raised in the discussion of this unusual notational feature of the Pixérécourt Codex admittedly does not involve a principle of any consequence, but its rarity in the notation of the Renaissance gives it a claim to consideration. If there is any validity to the interpretation suggested above, the piece might be regarded as an experiment on the part of the composer, and one that would be enchanting indeed if brought off with the rhythmical subtlety that it appears to suggest through its curious manner of notation.

1. Fernando Liuzzi discussed the Italian pieces of this manuscript in a paper entitled "Notes sur les *Barzelette* et les *Canzoni a ballo* du Quattrocento Italien, d'après des Documents Inedits" (printed in "Papers read at the International Congress of Musicology . . . Sept. 11–16, 1939," American Musicological Society, New York, 1944). Liuzzi's projected large study of the manuscript was not completed before his untimely death.

2. The text of the Superius in the "prima pars" reads:

> Et hola, hola, ho, fist elle,
> Ne voullies elle que le fous du val
> Aprontes vous pouriens trouves la vaiselle.

A CHANSON SEQUENCE

BY FEVIN

A. Tillman Merritt

SAMUEL PEPYS was a man of remarkably wide interests, and one of his hobbies was collecting books. His object in making a collection was not simply to amass more and more tomes; he was of the opinion that a private library should "comprehend in fewest books and least room the greatest diversity of subjects, stiles, and languages its owner's reading will bear," and that it should be for the "self-entertainment only of a solitary, confined enquirer into books." It should contrast with "the more extensive, pompous, and stationary libraries of Princes, Universities, and Colleges." Yet, when he had done with his collection he bequeathed "what I can hope to leave most valuable in the world, my books" to the college where he had been an undergraduate, Magdalene College at the University of Cambridge. And in Magdalene College his library stands today, housed in a special room, the books arranged in the very cases which he had provided for them originally and in the exact position which they had occupied in these cases during his lifetime.

In the company of books and manuscripts dealing with a considerable number of fields — the humanities as well as the sciences — are to be found several musical manuscripts of more than common interest. One of them, *Pepys 1760*, seems to have maintained an elusive existence in musical circles, although on account of its contents and its beauty it deserves wider acquaintance. The table of contents was listed by Barclay Squire and published in the Library catalogue thirty years ago.[1] And yet, Bukofzer[2] speaks of it as a "little-known manuscript," while Kahmann[3] in his excellent study of Antoine de Fevin obviously knows it only by hearsay. Bukofzer speaks of it as being an excellent source, especially for the works of Fevin, which it is. But in his bibliography of Fevin Kahmann lists only two motets, out of eight contained in *Pepys 1760*, presumably because these two were also published by Petrucci. And he lists only four chansons as being known, although he suspects that there are more. There are fifteen chansons attributed to Fevin in this collection alone.

Like many manuscripts of the late fifteenth and early sixteenth centuries *Pepys 1760* contains both sacred and secular compositions in almost equal number, but not intermingled. The first half of the collection consists of polyphonic pieces with Latin texts, often of Marian significance, and the second half consists of French chansons, but ends with Prioris' *Consomno la vita mya.*[4]

The names of the composers to whom the various compositions are attributed are not invariably in agreement in the *tabula* at the beginning and in the body of the manuscript. Even so, Fevin is the composer chiefly represented, and Gascongne comes second with ten pieces. Other composers with more than one composition each are Josquin, Mouton, Prioris and Richafort. On account of its musical contents, as well as other things such as the coat of arms, *Pepys 1760* may prove helpful in throwing more light on some of the composers and upon their creative activities. Two of the canons at the beginning of the collection are mutilated by the cutting out of a miniature said to have been of the "then Prince of Wales," Arthur, son of Henry VII, to whom the manuscript belonged and presumably for whom it was made. One of the motets, *Sufficiebat nobis*, uses for its upper voice the tenor of Ghizeghem's chanson *Mon souvenir*. Other compositions, notably those by Josquin and Obrecht, are well known.

*   *   *

One of the most interesting treasures in *Pepys 1760* is a sequence of seven chansons attributed to Fevin, numbers 31–37 of the collection. They are clearly related to each other; in effect they seem here to constitute almost a cycle. The subject of the poems is the jealous husband. The texts run as follows:

1. (No 31) On a mal dit de mon amy don jay le cuer triste et marry, mays que ont il affaire ou syl est beau or sil est lait puisquil est bien a mon plaisir.

2. (No 32) Tres doulce dame debonnaire, ouvrez moy votre huys, votre amour est si necessaire quavoir ne puys ung seul repos.

3. (No 33) Mauditz soient ces marys jaleux qui sur leur femmes font le guet, Il font au poures amoureux souvent endurer chaut et fret. Mais jalousie et le caquet des envyeux ou maint apointement se font Tant qui nen valent de riens mieulx.

4. (No 34) Helas je suys mary helas de ces marys jaloux qui ont sur moy si grande fantasie. Leur femmes nont bonne heure ne demye helas, Il leur sambloit que jen fusse amoureux.

5. (No 35) Je le laire puys qui my bat, he dieu helas. Et lort vilain mal engrogne qui dessus moy a controuve que jestois allez a lesbat, he dieu helas, je le leray puys qui my bat.

6. (No 36) Chacun mauditz ces jaleux. Mais je ne les mauditz mye, car il nest pas vray amoureux qui nest jaleux de sa mye. Lautre jour jouer maloye tout alentours dung vert buisson Je trouvay la ma mignonne qui parloit a ung compagnon. Mais je ne scay qui luy disoit, le jeu ne me plaisoit mye don jeu le cuer triste et mary. Et entre en jalousie.

7. (No 37) En amours na sinon qui bien ne mal qui ne ly pence. Amours font faire maints tours et mainte contenance. Je le dis pour mon amy qui est coinct et bien joli Je le congnoys danfance. Il mayme aussy faige luy Dieu gard de meschance.

A certain number of the poems are unquestionably expressions of the lady's sentiments — sometimes annoyed, sometimes philosophical — and it is possible to interpret nearly all of them as being hers. Nevertheless, all except one of the chansons are for three men's voices. *Tres doulce dame*, the only one for three high voices, could even be considered as a representation of the mocking or falsetto-like voice which she employs in repeating the persuasive tones of the lover of whom her husband is so jealous. All voices are provided with texts throughout.

Musically, the forms of all the chansons are most concise and show remarkable variety.[5] The last two of them consist of two *partes*, and sections of the first *pars* are in both cases repeated literally in the second. With the exception of *Je le laire*, which gives the middle voice the character of a cantus — even though the upper and lower voices participate in imitating and embroidering it — these chansons are all constructed in sections based on a characteristic rhythmic and melodic motive which is treated imitatively by the voices in succession. Only *Helas je suys mary* does not begin with such imitation. Generally each chanson consists of three or four sections, and in all seven of them at least one section, usually the first, is repeated later on in the piece either literally or with slight variation. In *On a mal dit* this first section is repeated immediately; in *Je le laire* the first section is repeated toward the end after intervening sections; in *Mauditz soient* the first two sections are repeated immediately.

The "key signatures" in themselves do not provide any reason for believing that these seven chansons are related musically. All except the last have one flat in the signature of each voice, and in *En amours* B demands to be flatted often by its position in the melodic line. But this is common in many other pieces as well. The cadential notes are no more significant, since there is considerable variety: number 2 cadences on A, number 3 on F, number 7 on D, and the other four on G. Moreover, the imitative technique which Fevin employs here is no more pronounced than it is in many of his other chansons.

The fact which seems to relate the "jealous husband" chansons is the actual themes themselves. The melodic turns which the initial motives exhibit in the various sections are not dissimilar to many individual themes of other composers; and it is seldom that themes are transferred literally from one chanson in the group to another. However, with all the variations which they show, there is a resemblance which gives an impression of close relationship which cannot be ignored, and which can hardly be purely accidental. One of the motives most used begins with an upward leap of a fourth or a third followed by descending movement stepwise. (The numeral at the beginning of each illustration indicates the number of the chanson, the letter the section in which the motive is used.)

Closely related to this motive is the one beginning with an upward leap, followed by continued rising motion:

Another motive begins with a twice repeated note, followed by an upward leap of a third, sometimes a descending third, or even a fourth, and sometimes by stepwise movement:

An added characteristic of most of this set of chansons is the final cadence and the way it is prepared. About two measures before the end the upper voice in particular begins from a low point to ascend scalewise in semiminums to a point as high as, if not higher than, any point reached in the course of the whole piece, from which it descends by way of two or three suspensions to the cadential note, which itself is often rather high. The exception among the seven pieces is again *Je le laire*, which has a relatively low cadence. These final cadences call attention to themselves mostly by the fact that no comparable amount of semiminum movement usually has

taken place up to this time. Since the final cadential notes differ
as often as they do the point to which the upper voice rises also
differs: *On a mal dit* reaches B flat; *Helas je suys mary* and *Chacun
mauditz* reach A; *Tres doulce dame, Mauditz soient* and *En amours*
all reach only G.

These charming chansons, along with others by Fevin and his
confreres in *Pepys 1760*, deserve to be studied at greater length.
Their present significance is that they seem to belong together and
are the work of a composer who is relatively little known even to
polyphonic enthusiasts.

Table of Contents of *Pepys 1760*

[Names of composers in parentheses are those given in the Tabula]

1.	Ave Maria (Canon)		Jo. Bortel	folio	1r
2.	Que est ista (Canon)		A. de Fevin		1r
3.	Ista est speciosa (Canon)		M. Gascongne		1v
4.	Dulcis amica dei	3 voc.	Prioris		2r
5.	Dei genitrix	4 voc.	"		2v–3r
6.	Verbum bonum	4 voc.	P. de Therache (Fevin)		3v–5r
7.	Suscipe verbum	4 voc.	(Bontemps)		5v–7r
8.	O admirabile commercium	4 voc.	Josquin des prez		7v–9r
9.	Quando natus est	4 voc.	"		9v–11r
10.	Rubum quem viderat	4 voc.	"		11v–12r
11.	Germinavit radix Jesse	4 voc.	"		12v–13r
12.	Ecce Maria	4 voc.	"		13v–15r
13.	Ave Maria	4 voc.	Jo. Mouton		15v–16r
14.	Ecce Maria	4 voc.	"		16v–17r
15.	Sub tuum presidium	4 voc.	A. Brumel		17v–19r
16.	Sancta trinitas	4 voc.	A. de Fevin		19v–21r
17.	Nobilis progenie	4 voc.	"		21v–23r
18.	Adiutorium nostrum	4 voc.	"		23v–25r
19.	Lectio prima: Aleph	4 voc.	" (Ro. de Fevin)		25v–28r
20.	Lectio secunda: Gimel	3 voc.	" (Ro. de Fevin)		28v–32r
21.	Lectio tertia: Zay	4 voc.	A. de Fevin		32v–33r
22.	Quam pulchra es	4 voc.	Prioris		33v–34r
23.	Benedicite; Agimus tibi	4 voc.	Jo. Mouton		34v–36r
24.	Sufficiebat nobis (Mon souvenir)	4 voc.	Jo. Richafort		36v–38r
25.	O preclara stella maris	3 voc.	A. de Fevin		38v–39r
26.	Dulcis mater	3 voc.	M. Gascongne		39v–41r
27.	Ave Maria	3 voc.	Prioris		41v–42r
28.	Inclita pura	3 voc.	A. de Fevin		42v–43r

29.	Nigra sum	3 voc. M. Gascongne	43v–46r
30.	Parce Domine	3 voc. (Obrecht)	46v–47r
31.	On a mal dit	3 voc. A. de Fevin	47v–48r
32.	Tres doulce dame	3 voc. "	48v–49r
33.	Mauditz soient	3 voc. "	49v–51r
34.	Helas je suys mary	3 voc. "	51v–52r
35.	Je le laire	3 voc. "	52v–53r
36.	Chacun maudit	3 voc. "	53v–55r
37.	En amours	3 voc. "	55v–57r
38.	Petite camusette (text-less)	3 voc. "	57v–58r
39.	Fors seulement	3 voc. "	58v–60r
40.	Il faict bon ayme	3 voc. "	60v–62r
41.	Jayme bien mon amy	3 voc. N. le Petit (Fevin)	62v–63r
42.	Adieu solas	3 voc. A. de Fevin	63v–64r
43.	Faulte dargent	3 voc. (A. de Fevin)	64v–65r
44.	Jay veu la beaute	3 voc. A. de Fevin	65v–67r
45.	Il mest advis	3 voc. Hyllayre (Perrichon)	67v–68r
46.	Dieu gard de mal	3 voc. Jo. Mouton	68v–70r
47.	Jay mys mon cuer	3 voc. M. Gascongne	70v–72r
48.	Je voys je viens	3 voc. "	72v–73r
49.	Pastourelle dieu te doint joye	3 voc. "	73v–74r
50.	Pour avoir faict	3 voc. "	74v–76r
51.	En ce joly temps	3 voc. "	76v–78r
52.	Celle quy ma demande	3 voc. "	78v–79r
53.	Hellas madame	3 voc. Jo. Brunet	79v–81r
54.	Jaymes james une villaine	4 voc. A. de Fevin	81v–83r
55.	Damours je suys desheritee	5 voc. Jo. Richafort	83v–84r
56.	Sy jeusse marion	4 voc. M. Gascongne	84v–86r
57.	Consommo la vita mya	4 voc. Prioris	86v

1. M. R. James, *A Descriptive Catalogue of the Library of Samuel Pepys, Part III, Mediaeval Manuscripts*, 1923, pp. 36–38.

2. Manfred F. Bukofzer, *Studies in Medieval and Renaissance Music*, 1950, p. 210.

3. B. Kahmann, *Antoine de Fevin — Part II, A Bibliography* in *Musica Disciplina*, V, 1951, pp. 146 and 148.

4. Bukofzer, *op. cit.*, p. 211.

5. Mlle Paule Chaillon, in her article on *Le Chansonnier de Françoise*, in La Revue de Musicologie, July, 1953, which appeared after the completion of the present paper, discusses at greater length the poetical forms of the chansons in *MS. Harley 5242* in the British Museum. This source has a considerable number of chansons in common with *Pepys 1760*. Both of them exhibit in polyphonic settings a number of the chansons contained in monophonic guise, and with a greater number of stanzas each, in *MSS. Fr. 9346* and *Fr. 12744* in the Bibliothèque Nationale in Paris.

EQUAL VOICES IN THE

A CAPPELLA PERIOD

Otto Kinkeldey

Cᴏɴᴅᴜᴄᴛᴏʀs of choral groups of women as well as of men, especially directors of college glee clubs or choral societies, are often, when their interests run beyond the conventional classical, romantic and modern repertoire, faced with the question of the use of such special groups in the compositions of the a cappella period. So far as I know, no thorough study of this question has yet been made. The following pages are by no means a complete study; but a few notes and observations will indicate the lines which such a study might take.

That the composers of the period in question, even in the fifteenth century, were well aware of the effect, in a mixed choir, of the contrast between a group of low voices and a group of high voices, is evident from their works. But these composers also, for aesthetic or for purely practical reasons, sometimes wrote for groups whose tonal limits were narrower than those of the mixed choir. The normal compass for mixed voices was a little more than three octaves from G (often F, rarely E) in the Bass to a″ (rarely b-flat″) in the Cantus or Soprano.[1] It must be remembered in this connection, that there was no standard pitch in the Renaissance. Choirmasters took a higher or a lower pitch within wide limits, to suit the convenience of their choirs. The normal compass of our modern men's choruses is hardly more than two octaves, G (F) to a′. For women's choruses the same compass, one octave higher, would seem theoretically proper. But few of our women singers, at any rate among the amateurs, are well enough trained in the artistic use of the chest register to provide a really effective alto part between f and c'. In the a cappella period the alto part in church singing and often in secular music was sung by men. By training their falsetto register they could render with ease, clarity and volume long passages in the upper notes of the alto clef. English cathedral and college choirs use male altos up to the present day. The counter tenor of the late eighteenth and early nineteenth century English glees was really a male alto.

Renaissance composers chose the limited compass for the sake of tone color and expression, or for the sake of contrast and relief in single movements of longer works of a cyclic nature, like a mass or a Magnificat setting or the Lamentations. As a technical indication of the limited compass they used the words *voces aequales* or *voces pares*. Where a distinction is made between works for a full mixed chorus and for equal voices, the expression for the former is *voces communes* or *impares*, or, in Italian, *à voce piena*. It may be mentioned here that the majority of pieces for equal voices that I have seen, are written in the higher clefs (g-clef, soprano-clef, mezzo-soprano-clef and alto-clef). Pieces in the lower clefs (alto, tenor, baritone and bass) are in the minority. But many of the pieces in higher clefs could easily be, and doubtless often were, transposed an octave downward to be sung by a men's chorus.

The music publishers of the sixteenth century printed many anthologies or miscellaneous collections, both of sacred and of secular music. They seem to have been profitable financial ventures. Robert Eitner's invaluable catalog of these anthologies, *Bibliographie der Musiksammelwerke*, enables us to answer the question as to how much attention was paid to anthologies for equal voices. They are not very numerous as compared with the great numbers of anthologies for mixed voices, but there are enough of them to show that works for equal voices were in some demand. Sacred music for low voices, including alto and sometimes even mezzo-soprano, was probably often used in monasteries where the monks had no choir school to provide them with singing boys; and sacred music for high voices was much used in convents, in some of which the nuns often reached a high level of performance.[2]

A number of the titles listed in Eitner's *Bibliographie* will give us an idea of the kinds of compositions for equal voices which seem to have been in demand. The famous Paris music printer and publisher, Pierre Attaingnant, entered the field fairly early.

1534 *Missarum musicalium ad quatuor voces pares, liber secundus.*
It contains two masses by Claudin, one by Allaire, one by Moulin.

1534 *Liber quartus XXIX quatuor vel quinque parium vocum modulos habet.*
Here we have twenty-nine motets by Consilium, Courtoys, Gombert, Josquin des Prez, Verdelot, Willaert and others.

Italy follows with:

1542 *Missae cum quatuor vocibus paribus decantandae, Moralis Hispani ac aliorum authorum in hac scientia non vulgarium.* Venice: Hieronymus Scotus.
Two masses by Morales, one by Jachet, one by Ruffo, and two anonymous.

1543 *Moralis et reliquorum Musica, vocum quatuor, cujus pars est aequali voci, reliqua impari decantanda.* Venice: Hieron. Scotus.

1543 *Musica quinque vocum: Motetta materna lingua vocata, ab optimis & variis authoribus elaborata, paribus vocibus decantanda.* Venice: Hieron. Scotus.
Twenty-three anonymous pieces.

1544 *Liber quartus missarum quinque cum quatuor vocibus.* Venice: Antonio Gardano.
Five masses by Morales, Jachet, Ruffo, Charles (Argentil?) and one anonymous. Gaspari's Catalog of the Library of the Bologna Liceo Musicale (II, 31) says that these are composed for four tenors! But only Tenor I is preserved at Bologna. No complete copy seems to be recorded.

1549 *Musica quatuor vocum, quae materna lingua Moteta vocantur, ab optimis & variis authoribus elaborata, paribus vocibus decantanda.* Venice: Hieron. Scotus.
Motets by Consilium (20), Dom. Finot (4), Jehan Gero (6), Gombert (2), Jachet, Morales, Yvo, Verdelot and Willaert (2). This must have been a popular collection, for in the same year, Scotto's rival publisher, Antonio Gardano in Venice, brought out his own edition with the same title and the same works. Gardano also published in this year:

1549 *Musica quinque vocum, quae materna lingua moteta vocantur ab optimis et variis authoribus elaborata, paribus vocibus.* Venice: Antonius Gardanus.
It contains twenty-five motets. Six are by Arcadelt, Arnold (Bruck), Finot and Pierrison. The others are anonymous.

1560 *Variarum linguarum Tricinia a praestantissimis musicis ad voces*

fere aequales composita. Tomus secundus. Nuremberg: Johann
Berg and Ulrich Neuber.
> This is a collection for three *almost* equal voices. The compo-
> sitions are by Clemens non Papa, Verdelot, Claudin, Crequil-
> lon, Gombert, Jannequin, Morales and others.

It will be observed that our list thus far includes only sacred
music. It is a striking fact that anthologies of madrigals for equal
voices seem never to have been published, although they are numerous for mixed voices. Perhaps the social entertainment nature of
the madrigal and of madrigal singing, in which women had a much
larger share than they did in church music, may account for this.
But madrigals for equal voices were not entirely unknown. The
Venetian music publisher, Girolamo Scotto (Hieronymus Scotus)
who was responsible for most of the sacred works in the preceding
list, also offered his customers:

> 1539 *Tertio libro de i madrigali di Archadelt et di altri eccellentissimi
> authori. Con la gionta de alcuni madrigali a voci mutate bellissimi
> a quattro voci.* Venice: Girolamo Scotto.
> > Forty-eight madrigals by Arcadelt and Costanzo Porta.
> > Twelve of them are *à voce mutata.* That this expression actu-
> > ally means "for changed voices," that is, for men's voices, we
> > may surmise from the fact that Eitner's Bibliography remarks
> > that the expression *à voci pari* is also used in connection with
> > them.

The publisher of this work was also a composer in his own right. To
him we owe:

> 1542 *Madrigali a quatro voce* [sic] *di Girolamo Scotto con alcuni a
> la misure breve et altri a voce pari.* Venice: apud ipsum authorem.
> > There are thirty-seven pieces in all, four of which are by
> > Willaert.[3]

But many of the pieces in ordinary collections of secular music,
though not specifically marked "for equal voices," are limited in
compass and lend themselves easily to performance by men's voices.
Some could be sung by women's voices. Such pieces may be found,
for example, among the charming French chansons in folk-song
style for three and for four voices by Arcadelt. They have been
edited by Everett Helm in the Smith College Music Archives, No.
V. And equally attractive and really delightful folk-song imitations
for two, three and four voices are contained in the unusual collec-

tion of fifty-four Spanish Villancicos, published by Scotto in Venice in 1556. They have been printed in a modern edition under the title: *Cancionero de Upsala* (Mexico City, Colegio de Mexico, 1944, edited by Jesus Bal y Gay, with a study on *El Villancico Polifonico* by Isabel Pope).

The anthologies for equal voices seem to have been less popular after 1560; but enough compositions of this kind are scattered among the later publications of individual composers to prove that interest in such music had not died out. Even as far back as the fifteenth century single movements of this kind were written. Ockeghem, for example, has, in the *Missa sine nomine* (Vol. 1 of the Plamenac edition, p. 15) a Kyrie à 3 ($\flat$AA) [4] with a compass of f to g''. The piece could easily be transposed a seventh or an octave lower to be sung by men's voices. An *Agnus Dei* (30 measures) in the same Mass (p. 96) is actually written for four lower voices (MTTT) from c to c''. It could be transposed a third or a fourth downward. The threefold *Kyrie* of Ockeghem's *Missa Mi-mi* (vol. 2, p. 1) is written for MTTB with a compass from G to a'.

Obrecht's *Missa Malheur me bat* (Wolf's edition of the WERKEN, vol. I, pp. 142, 161, 177) contains three movements à 3, *Christe eleison*, *Crucifixus* and *Benedictus*, all for ATB, compass A to a'. In the Obrecht *Missa de Sancto Martino* (Vol. II, p. 118) we find: *Christe eleison* (13 measures) ATT, from c to b-flat'; *Domine fili unigeniti* (84 measures) for ATB, from B-flat to c''. *Et resurrexit* (56 measures) TTB, from G to f'. Also in the *Missa O quam suavis* (Vol. III, p. 43) *Et incarnatus* (43 measures) ATB, from F to d'. And in a *Missa sine nomine* (Vol. IV, p. 43) *Christe eleison* à 4, ATTB, from G to a'.

Josquin des Prez has bequeathed to us a beautiful setting of that loveliest of Marian antiphons: *Alma Redemptoris Mater* (Smijer's edition of the Werken, Motetten, Bundel VIII, p. 77) in two movements (55 and 63 measures) for AAAB, from A to g'. Josquin's Mass *Mater Patris* (Missen, Bundel XII) is written entirely for low voices (five, four, three and two voices) from Mezzo to Bass. The Bass goes down to G. The Mezzo, used only in the *Sanctus* and the first *Agnus*, occasionally touches b-flat''. The third *Agnus*, the only movement for five voices, four Tenors and a Bass, has the compass G to a'.

Pedrell's edition of the works of Vittoria provides us with a number of motets actually designated *cum paribus vocibus*, as for example,

Vol. 1,	p.	29	*O Regem coeli* (62 meas.) ♭ ♭ MA,	f to a″
	p.	34	*O sacrum convivium* (34 meas.) CCCA,	f to d″
	p.	35	secunda pars, *Mens infletur* (38 meas.)	f to d″
	p.	36	*Duo seraphim clamabant* (36 meas.) CCAA	d to d″
	p.	37	sec. pars, *Tres sunt* (44 meas.)	d to d″
	p.	39	*Domine non sum dignus* (58 meas.) CAAT	c to c″
			sec. pars, *Miserere mei* (27 meas.)	c to c″

All of these can be transposed to an easy range for men. Among the masses of Vittoria we find:

Missa Quam pulchri sunt

Vol. 2,	p.	52	*Benedictus* (30 meas.) ATB	F to f′
	p.	41	*Domine Deus, Agnus Dei* (22 meas.) ATB	F to f′
	p.	46	*Crucifixus* (52 meas.) CAT	c to c″

Missa de Beata Maria

| | | | *Benedictus* (24 meas.) ♭ CAA | f to d″ |

Missa Ascendens Christus

| | p. | 170 | *Crucifixus* (35 meas.) ♭ ♭ CA | g to g″ |

There are many other pieces by Vittoria for three or four equal voices, including verses from *Magnificat* settings, and the third verse of his *Salve Regina* à 6:

| Vol. 7, | p. | 116 | *Et Jesum, benedictum fructum* ♭ ♭ CC | g to g″ |

The works of Lassus also offer us a number of such compositions. There is, for example, a psalm setting, *Beatus vir, qui timet*, in eleven separate sections or movements for ATTB, from F to g′, with a final movement, *Sicut erat* from the *Gloria Patri* for ATTBB with the same compass.

In the thirty-odd volumes of Palestrina's works there are more than two hundred pieces for equal voices. The great majority are written in the high clefs, but, as usual, many can be satisfactorily transposed for men. They are to be found in every form except one cultivated by the Princeps Musices — in masses, among the motets, in hymn settings, Lamentations, litanies, Magnificats. But there is no actual madrigal by Palestrina for equal voices. There are only two canzonets for three voices (♭ CA) f to f″ (Vol. 28, pp. 135, 136).

The masses of the great composer are a perfect treasury of short pieces for equal voices. Like most of his predecessors and contemporaries Palestrina very often set in a smaller compass for three or four voices certain portions of a mass written for four to six mixed voices. The great majority of *Crucifixus* and *Benedictus* movements are so treated. Among these the choirmaster or glee club director, who cares to search, may find some of the tenderest, most deeply expressive, and at the same time contrapuntally interesting pieces in the whole Palestrina dispensation. The pieces for three voices are as fine as those for four. The *Pleni sunt coeli* in the *Gloria* is also sometimes set in this fashion.[5]

One of Palestrina's publications, 1581, . . . *Motettorum quatuor vocibus, partim plena voce, et partim paribus vocibus, liber secundus.* Venice: Angelus Gardanus (Works, vol. 5) went through five editions. Most of the equal voice motets in this book are written in higher clefs. A number of them are published in modern clefs for men's voices in R. Casimiri's *Anthologia Polyphonica*, to which we shall refer later. Some of Palestrina's motets for four voices actually written in lower clefs, are:

Vol. 5, p. 177 *Surrexit pastor bonus* (75 meas.) ATTB, F to g′

Vol. 7, p. 55 *Ascendens Christus in altum* (68 meas.) AAAT, c to a′

    p. 57 *Domine secundum actum meum* (65 meas.) AAAT, c to a′

    p. 60 *Ne recorderis peccata mea* (70 meas.) for funeral services AAAT, c to a′

    p. 62 *Ecce nunc, benedicite Dominum* (59 meas.) AAAT, c to a′

This seems to have been a favorite voice combination with Palestrina. The four pieces just named are included in Casimiri's collection, transposed a fourth lower.

Vol. 7, p. 64 *Deus, qui animae famuli tui* (53 meas.) for the Feast of St. Gregory TTTB, G to e′

Among Palestrina's sometimes elaborate settings of Latin hymn tunes we often find special verses set for equal voices, most of them, again, in high clefs. But a number of them could be sung by men's voices just as the composer wrote them.

Vol. 8, p. 31 *Tu nobis dona fontem lacrymarum* (41 meas.)
　　　　　Verse 4 of the hymn *Ad preces nostras*
　　　　　à 3, MABar A to a′

p. 54 *Hostem repellas longius* (47 meas.)
　　　　　Verse 3 of the hymn *Veni Creator spiritus*
　　　　　à 4, MAABar c to g′

p. 103 *Tristes erant apostoli* (28 meas.)
　　　　　Verse 2 of the hymn *Illae dum pergunt*
　　　　　à 3, MABar c to a′

p. 114 *Hi prote furias* (36 meas.)
　　　　　Verse 2 of the hymn *Sanctorum meritis*
　　　　　à 3, ATB A to g′

p. 128 *Quocunque pergis virgines* (36 meas.)
　　　　　Verse 2 of the hymn *Jesu corona virginum*
　　　　　à 4, AABarBar c to f′

Among the Lamentations for the successive days of Holy Week those in Book 2 (Vol. 25, pp. 37–53) for Maundy Thursday and Good Friday, from three to five voices, are for low voices, although the Mezzo-soprano, used in only one movement, touches b-flat′. The Bass sometimes descends to F. In Book 3 of the Lamentations (Vol. 25, pp. 153–204) the music for the three days, Thursday, Friday and Saturday, for five and six voices, runs from A to c″. It could be transposed a third downward.

One of Palestrina's successors as a leader of the Roman school, Giovanni Matteo Asola (c. 1560–1609) whose style is more homophone than Palestrina's, seems to have been a specialist in compositions for equal voices. Between 1574 and the end of the century he published masses, vesper-psalms, Requiems and music for Compline, *à voce pari*. Sometimes there are compositions *à voce piena* in the same books. One of his Requiems for four voices (ATTB) was published complete in C. Proske's *Musica Divina* (Annus I, Tomus I, pp. 259–86) in the original pitch, F to g′. It was published more recently in Casimiri's collection transposed one tone higher.

Carl Proske's *Musica Divina*, which ran to four volumes (1853–1863) was followed by a second series of four volumes edited by Joseph Schrems and F. X. Haberl (1864–1869). It uses the three old c-clefs for C, A and T. In this collection are included compositions for four men's voices by G. Croce, Handl, Hassler, Rudolph Lassus, G. M. Nanini, Porta, Ruffo and Zoilo.

But the richest modern source for music of this kind, so far as men's voices are concerned, is the *Anthologia Polyphonica auctorum saeculi XVI paribus vocibus* in two volumes published in Rome: Edizioni Psalterium, 1924, 1932, by that energetic and industrious Palestrina enthusiast, the choirmaster of St. Johns Lateran, the late Raffaele Casimiri. The edition uses modern clefs. Many of its pieces are transpositions from high clefs. The two volumes together contain 128 pieces by about sixteen composers. Among them are Palestrina (32 pieces), Lassus (21), Vittoria (8), Gio. Croce (2), Viadana (2), Francesco Suriano (13), Jac. Gallus (Handl) (8), G. M. Asola (13), G. F. Anerio (5). Jacob de Kerle († 1583) is represented by a complete Mass, *Regina Coeli* at the end of vol. 2 (pp. 207–45).

Even this incomplete survey must have made it evident that the a cappella period was not barren of works for equal voices, and that every one of the great masters contributed his share to the repertoire.

1. We use the conventional designations in c-Octaves for the names of the notes. Below the c in the second space of the bass staff the names are capital letters. From this c to the b above the bass staff they are lower case letters. Middle c is written c'. The tenor's high c is c'' and the soprano's high c is c'''.

2. See: Kathi Meyer, *Der chorische Gesang der Frauen mit besonderer Bezugnahme seiner Beteiligung auf geistlichem Gebiet.* 1917.

3. It is quite probable that single, isolated pieces for equal voices could be found scattered among the hundreds of volumes of Italian madrigals for mixed voices. There is the well-known experiment in chromatic melody by Cipriano de Rore, the setting of a Latin (not Italian) ode, *Calami sonum ferentes*, for four bass voices. It has been reprinted by Burney, Franz Commer and more recently by Joseph Musiol. Beside this Einstein (The Italian Madrigal) cites de Rore's *I mi vivea di mia sorte contento* for five low voices, TTBB and low Bass; Baldisserra Donato's *I' vo piangendo i miei passati tempi* for five low voices, TT Bar B and low Bass; and Francesco Corteccia's *Quel foco ch'io pensai che fusse spento* for five low voices, TTTTB.

4. The single voices are indicated according to the clefs in which they are written. The g-clef occurs often. C (Cantus), A (Alto), T (Tenor) and B (Bass) are the usual c- or f-clefs associated with these parts. M stands for Mezzo-soprano with the c-clef on the second line of the staff; and Bar stands for Baritone, f-clef on the third line.

5. Professor Knud Jeppesen has recently unearthed a number of unpublished Palestrina masses, written for the choir of Duke Guglielmo Gonzaga at Mantua about 1568 to 1578. See Acta Musicolog. vol. 22 (1950), pp. 36–47 and vol. 25 (1953), pp. 137–179. Among them is a simple rather homophone Missa sine nomine, related in style to the Marcellus Mass. It is written for AAAT and it is the only Palestrina mass now known composed throughout for equal voices.

MODAL HARMONY IN THE

MUSIC OF PALESTRINA

Andrew C. Haigh

THIS paper is about something which, according to R. O. Morris, has never existed.

"As various text-books express a pious hope that the student is familiar with what is called 'Modal Harmony,' it may be as well to explain in conclusion, that *such a thing has never existed.*[1] 'Modality' is properly a term of melodic definition; it is only in a derivative sense that harmony can be described as 'modal.' In that sense you might say that modal harmony is harmony formed strictly from the diatonic series of notes constituting the mode in which the melody of any given piece is written. . . . Such harmony is to all intents and purposes our diatonic major and minor harmony in its simplest form, except that tonality in the modern harmonic sense did not yet exist, whilst modulation . . . did not mean quite the same thing for Palestrina as it means for us."[2]

Anyone who has perused many student exercises in sixteenth-century counterpoint — exercises which may be technically flawless as to contrapuntal procedure — must have wondered, as has the present writer, why they did not sound like sixteenth-century music. Could the harmonic scheme have anything to do with it? "Such [sixteenth century] harmony is to all intents and purposes our diatonic major and minor harmony in its simplest form . . ." Can we accept this statement at its face value — even with the exceptions attached?

Morris and Jeppesen,[3] whose contributions to the understanding of sixteenth-century music merit the gratitude of every student in the field, are scholars of erudition, painstaking thoroughness, and caution. Though they treat contrapuntal procedures in detail, they appear to minimize the importance of harmony as a formative element in sixteenth-century music. By their reticence on the subject, they seem to give tacit assent to what I believe to be two widely held and fundamentally erroneous views.

One of these is the view that the modes are indistinguishable harmonically, except by the final cadence. If the piece cadences on G, it is mixolydian; if on D, dorian, and so on. That which precedes the final cadence is just our diatonic major and minor harmony in its simplest form.

The other is the view that sixteenth-century harmony "just happens," as a secondary result of contrapuntal exigencies — that Palestrina's music has no systematic harmonic organization of its own.[4]

The questions raised above prompted the writer to embark on a research into the harmonic organization of Palestrina's music.[5] It was his conviction that dependable conclusions could be reached only on the basis of facts established through a minute statistical analysis of a fairly large representative sample of Palestrina's complete works — that intuitions, even though based on a thorough familiarity with Palestrina's music, might be untrustworthy. He therefore set about sampling, and collecting facts. The contents of some 22,000 measures (about 20% of the complete works of Palestrina) were scrutinized from about a dozen points of view, and the results tabulated and percentaged. The present essay summarizes the conclusions about only one aspect of Palestrina's harmonic style: that of its relation to the modes. The facts supporting these conclusions are presented in a series of tables and graphs to which the interested reader is referred.[6]

Morris is right, of course, in saying that modality is *properly* a term of melodic definition. I should also accept the statement that modal harmony is harmony formed strictly from the diatonic series of notes, if I were permitted to delete the word *strictly*. In the sample analyzed, all the chromatic tones were found, excepting only D flat, G flat, and A sharp. Palestrina's tonal material, then, consists of the 'modal' tones (white keys of the piano), plus C sharp, D sharp, E flat, F sharp, G sharp, A flat, and B flat.

What harmonies does Palestrina form out of this tonal material? The smallest number of harmonies found in any piece was six: these being, as might be expected, the triads (with their inversions) on C, d, e, F, G, and a.[7] This minimal assortment is possible only in the 'major' modes, and in mixolydian only if it is willing to get along without authentic cadences.

What we might call the normal assortment of harmonies consists of the six mentioned above, plus D, E, A, g, and B flat. Almost exactly a third of the sample contained just these eleven harmonies, and many more pieces contained ten, or nine harmonies. The harmony on b (only as chord of the sixth) appeared on rare occasions.

Added to these are six extremely rare harmonies, namely, c, E flat, f, f sharp, A flat, and B. These harmonies appeared in only five pieces: three madrigals, *Vox dilecti* from the *Song of Songs*, and one other motet — a total of twelve occurrences. The employment of these unusual harmonies seems to be chiefly a characteristic of the secular style, in which they are used mostly for expressive purposes.

In regard to chord forms, it is customary to say that Palestrina used only triads and chords of the sixth, with possibly a few six-fours. However, it is not difficult to find other forms, including most of those used in the classical period. Augmented and diminished triads, sevenths of four types (major seventh with major third, minor seventh with minor third, minor seventh with major third, and 'seventh on the leading tone'), and most of the six-fives, four-threes, and chords of the second corresponding to the four varieties of sevenths occur, though many of them are extremely rare. I have called them independent chord forms because in most cases their roots are different from the roots of the chords preceding and following them. In all cases the dissonating tone is prepared and resolved in the usual manner.

We come now to the modes, and to the question of their relationship to Palestrina's harmony. Does Palestrina exhibit a preference for one mode or another? Do pieces in the various modes show characteristic and distinctive harmonic patterns? Do they show distinctive patterns of modal cadences (i.e., cadences classified according to the location of their final harmony)? Of cadence forms (i.e., authentic, plagal, etc.)? The answer to all these questions is an unequivocal affirmative. Let us review briefly the harmonic and cadential facts revealed in the sample, and then see if we can find plausible explanations of them.

Palestrina uses the modes in the following rough proportions: dorian, 30%; mixolydian, 25%; ionian, 20%; aeolian, 15%; phrygian, 10%; lydian, one-tenth of one per cent. Pieces in the 'minor' modes preponderate slightly over those in the 'major,' in the ratio of about five to four; but major harmonies are slightly in excess of minor harmonies. However, if we compare the harmonies *normally* major — B flat, C, F, and G(g) — with those *normally* minor — d(D), e(E), and a(A) — the proportion is almost exactly 50–50. Pure chance, or mathematically contrived by Palestrina? Neither hypothesis seems tenable. Rather I should see in these facts evidence of the composer's fine musical instinct and sense of harmonic proportion.

In order to show harmonic relationships more clearly, the writer drew a series of graphs, in which the various components were arranged in a cycle of fifths: for the modes, and the modal cadences, the order was lydian, ionian, mixolydian, dorian, aeolian, phrygian; for the harmonies, B flat, F, C, G(g), d(D), a(A), e(E), and b. The first set of graphs represented the complete sample, i.e., contained a mixture of all the modes. These graphs showed, as might be expected from the modal percentages already given, a normal and fairly regular distribution curve. The graphs for harmonies and for modal cadences resembled each other strikingly, and showed even more symmetrical curves.

Now when the modes were separated, and graphs drawn for samples that were exclusively ionian, dorian, etc., pronounced individual differences appeared. Each mode had its characteristic pattern of distribution of harmonies and cadences, which differed from all the rest. Let us take them in order, and note the most striking facts.

The lydian graph is the most irregular of all, and this is taken to be the result of individual variation, in a very small sample, represented by only one piece of 52 measures. It is therefore impossible to describe Palestrina's normal or average use of the lydian, since he wrote only a handful of pieces in this mode.

The ionian mode has a numerically strong 'tonic' C, and a 'dominant' G(g) which is almost equally strong. The 'subdominant' F, however, is only about half as strong as the 'dominant.' Next in strength is the 'submediant' a(A).

In the mixolydian, on the other hand, the 'dominant' d(D) is much weaker than the 'subdominant' C. D harmonies are, however, more frequent in the mixolydian than in any other mode. In both ionian and mixolydian, B flat harmonies are insignificant. They are much stronger in dorian, aeolian, and lydian.

The dorian presents the interesting spectacle of a mode whose 'dominant' a(A) is stronger than its 'tonic.' Its 'subdominant' G(g) is rather weak, its 'mediant' F relatively strong. As might be guessed, dorian has the largest proportion of A harmonies of any mode.

Aeolian has the strongest 'tonic' of all the modes, slightly exceeding the mixolydian in this respect. It also has the largest proportion of minor harmonies. It leans heavily on its 'subdominant' d(D), its 'dominant' e(E) being very weak. Its 'submediant' F is fairly strong, exceeding its 'mediant' C.

The phrygian, at the end of the cycle of fifths, has a pattern which differs most strikingly from all the others (except possibly lydian). It has a very weak 'tonic,' with a 'subdominant' a(A) greatly in excess. It has no proper 'dominant' b(B), but it might be permissible to consider d(D) its 'dominant,' in view of the special form of "phrygian" cadence. d(D) harmonies prove to be about on a level with e(E) harmonies, as are also those of the 'submediant' C.

The pattern of the modal cadences in the various modes corroborates in a striking way the pattern of their harmonies. In all cases except the phrygian, the cadences on the modal 'tonic' are greatly in excess of any of the others (about 48% to 67% of totals). In the phrygian mode, cadences on e(E) represent only about 25% of the total, being exceeded slightly by cadences on a(A). Furthermore, those modes which show a preference for 'dominant' harmonies (ionian, dorian), show an even more decided preference for cadences on the 'dominant'; the modes showing a preference for 'subdominant' harmonies (aeolian, mixolydian), show a similar preference for cadences on the 'subdominant.' The authentic ('V–I') form of cadence is most prevalent in all the modes; but the plagal ('IV–I') form reaches the highest percentage in aeolian, mixolydian, and phrygian.

It should be emphasized that these results are averages obtained from fairly large modal samples. Within these samples, a respectable range of individual variation was found. The writer believes, however, that these patterns, so distinctive for each of the modes, could not have happened by chance or by purely random choice. The operation of pure chance, he believes, would have reduced the harmonic and cadence patterns to a much greater uniformity — as is implied by the author quoted at the beginning of this essay.

It would be very difficult to maintain, on the other hand, that Palestrina deliberately and arbitrarily set a harmonic pattern for each of the modes, and on the average adhered to it. What, then, is the explanation? The writer offers a theory of modal harmonic gravitation.

The idea of the attraction of harmonies to a tonic or key center is of course nothing new; it can be found in almost any textbook on harmony. Dominant and subdominant are attracted strongly to the tonic; second dominants, and farther outlying harmonies are attracted less strongly, and normally through the closer harmonies. But the theory of *modal* harmonic gravitation here advanced is quite at variance with this idea: harmonies are attracted, not toward the modal 'tonic,' but *toward the center of the total harmonic sphere*, in which the modal 'tonics' occupy varying positions. This would account for several odd facts noted in the discussion above: the fact that the modal 'tonic' harmonies are in some cases not the strongest numerically; the fact that the 'tonic' leans in some cases toward the 'dominant,' in other cases toward the 'subdominant.'

At this point it may be objected that, by my arbitrary arrangement of modes, harmonies, and cadences in a cycle of fifths, I have artificially produced the results which I claim to have discovered as indigenous characteristics of the Palestrina style. In rebuttal I would call attention to the following points: (1) any arrangement (e.g., a diatonic one) would show the same numerical relationships of harmonies, etc., as presented in the preceding paragraphs; (2) in the music of Palestrina, root progressions by fifths (or fourths) are greatly in excess of root progressions by seconds or by thirds — roughly in the proportions 5:3:2 — and these proportions are not substantially altered, no matter how we divide the sample (by class of composition, by mode, etc.); (3) the arrangement in a cycle of fifths always results in a curve which approaches the form of the normal distribution curve. (2) and (3) would seem to indicate that the arrangement chosen corresponds to some inherent properties of Palestrina's music.

To return to modal harmonic gravitation: why should it operate as described? Presumably not to please the analyst, who may like to see normal distribution curves emerge. I am not sure that I can give a complete answer; but two circumstances seem to point to influences which may have affected the composer's choice, whether consciously or unconsciously, and whether restrictively or effectively.

1. Many writers have noted that the impulse toward the tonic was weaker in the music of the sixteenth century than in that of our era. In the Gregorian melodies, the 'final' can hardly be described as a tonic, in our sense. The 'dominant' or reciting note probably approaches this function more closely. In most sixteenth century music, the final harmony is properly described as a 'tonic,' though sometimes a weak one, by our standards. The 'leading tone' was normally used in final cadences, even in those modes (mixolydian, dorian) where it would appear to vitiate the strict modal canon. But there was not the same compelling impulse to return to the tonic, or to imply or refer to it constantly. This relatively weak pull toward the tonic would leave the field open to other forces or attractions, which might in some cases be away from the modal 'tonic.'

2. The range of Palestrina's harmonies, though wider than commonly supposed, was narrow as compared to that of the eighteenth and nineteenth centuries. Thus there was in the harmonic sphere a certain constriction or pressure, limiting complete freedom of harmonic motion. This limitation was greatest at the peripheries of the sphere. If we take F and e(E) as the extremes of the cycle of fifths (since B flat and b were so rarely used), we note that these peripheral harmonies can proceed, by the normal root progression of a fifth, in one direction only — inward toward the center of the series. And we find that their frequency of occurrence amounts to only about 12% and 9% respectively — roughly half the frequency of the other harmonies. The next in the series (reading inward), C and a(A), can proceed only one degree outward, and then are forced to return toward the center. This restriction is apparently not very serious, since their frequencies are only slightly below those of the inner harmonies. The peripheral pressure of the series of harmonies, then, would suggest a reason for the preponderance of harmonies at the center of the sphere.

If the forces and restraints noted above were quite unhampered in their operation, we might expect to see, in the whole sample, completely symmetrical distribution curves for harmonies and modal cadences, when these are arranged in a cycle of fifths. But such is not the case. The center of the total harmonic sphere would be equally shared by G(g) and d(D) harmonies, or by mixolydian and dorian. However, d(D) harmonies and dorian cadences, in the complete (mixed) sample, are slightly in excess of G(g) harmonies and mixolydian cadences (20.6% to 19.4% for harmonies; 23.6% to 22.7% for cadences). The next pair, C and a(A), or ionian and aeolian, are almost equally balanced, and very little inferior to the central pair. Then there is a big drop to F and e(E) harmonies (11.5% and 8.4%), and an even bigger drop to lydian and phrygian cadences (4.7% and 4.2%). Finally the curve approaches zero at the B flat and b harmonies (1.6% and .04%).

In the samples separated by mode, our theory of attraction to the center of the harmonic sphere accounts for the preference of some modes for 'dominant' harmonies, of others for 'subdominants,' but not completely. It breaks down (though slightly) in the mixolydian and dorian, where the preferences are reversed. If we are to presume that the theory represents a fundamental 'law' or uniformity, an explanation must be found for the exceptions. Two related facts of the music of Palestrina's time suggest themselves for consideration: the developing feeling for "tonicity," and *musica ficta*.

It has been noted by many writers that the feeling for tonicity in the sixteenth century, while weaker than in nineteenth-century music, was growing, and was in the process of obscuring modal differences, and reducing all the modes to two types — major and minor. The use of the modes had largely disappeared by the middle of the eighteenth century. The feeling for tonicity demanded a leading tone, and we find that in Palestrina's music the penultimate harmony in authentic final cadences is almost without exception major. *Musica ficta*, of course, served other purposes as well — melodic ones, as in the well-known rules: "mi contra fa, diabolus in musica" and "una nota super la, semper est canendum fa." But it is impossible to say how rigorously these rules were applied. Indeed it is not hard to find situations where they could not be applied, because the use of musica ficta would contravene some other, more stringent rule. I think we can assume a certain reticence in the use of *musica ficta*, where a solution of a problem which did not require *musica ficta* suited the composer's purposes just as well.

Now in the dorian final *plagal* cadence, the penultimate harmony is always minor, which requires the note b flat. Similarly in the mixolydian, the final authentic cadence requires f sharp. Mixolydian has a perfectly acceptable *plagal* cadence not requiring *musica ficta*; and although the dorian authentic cadence involves c sharp, it is the required leading tone. It should be noted, however, that mixolydian contains more D harmonies, and dorian more g harmonies, than any of the other modes. Thus the comparative freedom of motion of the inner harmonies would leave room for other forces — in this case the pull of the tonic and reticence in the use of *musica ficta* — to operate.

One other pronounced effect of the modes can be seen in the *form* of the cadences. Authentic cadences are greatly in excess in all the modes (56.7% to 75.6%) except in phrygian, where they drop to 44.5%. Phrygian, naturally, has by far the largest percentage of "phrygian form" cadences (12.9%). It also has a large proportion of *plagal* cadences (17.2%), being slightly exceeded only by aeolian (17.8%). "2–1" cadences (e.g., d-f-b to c-e-c) are most numerous in phrygian (16.8%), being closely approached only by ionian (14.5%).

The picture presented here is that of a struggle between two opposing forces: the modes, traditional, backward looking, and the major-minor system of tonality. That the modal influence on the harmonies was still strong is evidenced by the distinctive modal harmonic patterns; that these patterns show certain slight unexplained irregularities seems to me evidence of the pull of tonality. This conflict may explain why the curves are not in all cases just what the theory of modal gravitation would lead us to anticipate; however, their chief import, that of modal influence on harmonic distribution, seems to me incontestable.

There is one other influence, perhaps the most important in the stylistic picture, which I have not considered, because it is not amenable to statistical treatment. It is the composer's creative genius, which is subject to no restrictions save his artistic probity. There is no reason why a sixteenth-century composer should not have written polytonal music if he chose — as in one remarkable instance [8] he came close to doing. In many of Palestrina's pieces the patterns diverge rather widely from the norms given above (see the secular madrigals, particularly "Placide l'acq'" and "La cruda mia nemica"). Palestrina was not a slave to the musical conventions of his time, though he chose to work within them, for the most part. Neither was he insensitive to the newer developments of his era, as is shown in the remarkably modern sounding madrigals mentioned above. Here is one more bit of evidence (if further evidence were needed) that Palestrina is among those musical great who, like Bach and Brahms, represent the summation and culmination of their times, rather than the exploration, pioneering, and revolution of a new age.

1. Present writer's italics.

2. Morris, R. O., *Contrapuntal Technique in the Sixteenth Century*, London, Clarendon Press, 1922, pp. 43, 44.

3. Jeppesen, Knud, *The Style of Palestrina and the Dissonance*, translated by Margaret Hamerik, London, Oxford University Press, 1937.

4. Read the passage (too long for quotation here) in Jeppesen, *The Style of Palestrina and the Dissonance*, p. 76. See also Shirlaw, Matthew, *The Theory of Harmony*, London, Novello and Co., New York, W. H. Gray, pp. 4, 6.

5. The results of this research are to be found in Andrew C. Haigh, *The Harmony of Palestrina* [Thesis, Ph.D.], Harvard University (1945).

6. *Ibid.*

7. Capital letters indicate major harmonies; lower case letters indicate minor harmonies.

8. "Der Juden Tanz," by Hans Neusiedler, in Davison, Archibald T. and Willi Apel, *Historical Anthology of Music*, Harvard University Press (1946), p. 108.

PUEBLA'S REQUIEM CHOIRBOOK

Steven Barwick

PROBABLY one of the most interesting of the eighteen choir-books of polyphony preserved in the archives of the Cathedral of Puebla, Mexico, is *libro de coro number three*, a volume devoted entirely to music for the Requiem and offices for the dead. The book's contents indicate that it must date from the middle or second half of the seventeenth century, for composers represented include the Spaniards Morales and Guerrero, the Neo-Hispanic Fernando Franco and Juan de Padilla, and the unknown Saldaña and Tabares. In addition, a number of anonymous or unidentified compositions complete the ninety-eight folios of the manuscript which consists of paper pages bound in leather-covered boards measuring about fifteen by twenty-one inches. Apart from being a valuable source of some Neo-Hispanic music of the sixteenth and seventeenth centuries, the volume remains a testimony of the sort of polyphony mid-seventeenth-century Puebla church musicians were using in their funeral services, and it is even possible that this particular choirbook was one used in special ceremonies performed in Mexico to commemorate the deaths of certain Spanish sovereigns.

In her article "Music in the Cathedral of Mexico in the Sixteenth Century"[1] Lota M. Spell refers to the sixteenth-century New World chronicler Francisco Cervantes de Salazar's *Túmulo Imperial* (1560) and its account of the services in Mexico City commemorating the death of Charles V. These ceremonies took place in 1559, a year after the emperor's death, and music played a prominent part throughout. The service as it is described was a version of the first nocturn of matins or the vigil, and two choirs were used for antiphonal singing. To begin, one choir sang *Circumdederunt me* in a polyphonic setting of Morales, and the other sang the psalm

Exultemus, also of Morales. Additional polyphony to which explicit reference is made included the psalm *Domine ne in furore* which was performed in an alternation of plainchant with a four-voice setting of Lázaro del Álamo (chapelmaster of the Mexico City Cathedral from 1556 to 1570), and a Morales setting of *Parce mihi*. Specific composers are not named for other polyphonic settings which are cited, such as the response *Qui Lazarum*.

Quite possibly the Puebla *libro number three* represents a handing-down of at least some of the material mentioned in Cervantes de Salazar's account. At any rate, the Morales four-part psalm setting *Venite exultemus*, an unidentified *Circumdederunt me*, and four different settings of *Parce mihi*, two of which remain unidentified, are included in the choirbook. There is furthermore the possibility that the polyphonic setting of the response *Qui Lazarum*, cited above, may have been the setting of Fernando Franco contained in the Puebla *libro*. Although the Puebla volume probably was not used for the first colonial commemorative ceremony in 1559, it is more likely that it was employed in later seventeenth century occasions, inasmuch as such ceremonies were performed in Mexico after the deaths of the Spanish rulers who followed Charles V. However, a final word on this point must wait until the necessary descriptive printed accounts of these ceremonies become available.[2]

If at present we are unable to say definitely whether the Puebla volume figured in such commemorative services, we can be certain, by all means, that it was used a great deal, for it shows signs of heavy wear. Many of the pages are badly frayed, while others are even partially destroyed. An additional suggestion of the book's popularity with the Puebla church musicians comes from its music, if one can consider the presence of many compositions of unknown authorship an indication that the works were particularly well known at the time they were used regularly. The quantity of anonymous compositions plus the signs of heavy wear would seem to indicate either that the composers were so well known that their names did not have to appear on the manuscript, or, on the other hand, that if they were *unknown* their music was accepted and performed. The first of these theories, of course, can be supported easily by evidence available from other sources about various composers' renown and popularity in early colonial Mexico, while the latter premise must simply depend upon the condition of the choir-book for substantiation.

Because there is still much to be learned about music in sixteenth- and seventeenth-century Mexico, investigators are inclined to indulge in a great deal of speculation on many points in the hope that more facts may be uncovered. Some theorizing in the nature of the above, for example, helped to identify some of the unlabeled compositions in the Puebla *libro number three*. Fernando Franco was found to be the composer of the psalm *Domine ne in furore*, one of the settings of the lesson *Parce mihi*, and the response *Qui Lazarum*, while Guerrero was identified as the composer whose requiem mass, including the introit (*Requiem aeternam*), *Kyrie*, gradual (*Requiem aeternam*), tract (*Absolve Domine*), offertory (*Domine Jesu Christe*), *Sanctus*, *Benedictus*, and *Agnus Dei*, occupies over a dozen folios of the manuscript. Although these composers' names do not appear in the book, their authorship was discerned upon comparison of the music of the choirbook with that of some well-labeled part books found in another section of the Cathedral Archives. Naturally, one can rather easily identify music which is known in another source, and, eventually, stylistic analysis and a comparison of styles will lead to probable attributions. But these methods will be helpful only in a process of elimination when it comes to the hope of finding music of composers such as the above-mentioned Lázaro del Álamo or other obscure early Mexican chapelmasters or churchmen who wrote music but are known to us by name only. Furthermore, while the better-known Neo-Hispanic composers Fernando Franco, Pedro Bermúdez, Francisco López y Capilla, and Juan de Padilla have left a quantity of music sizable enough to make stylistic comparisons possible, there are lesser figures such as Pedro Hernández and Fructos del Castillo, known only by one short motet apiece, for whom stylistic analysis remains impractical. Indeed, the Puebla volume under discussion affords ample material for more research, as it still contains some twenty hymns, psalms, motets, and mass movements of unknown authorship.

Of the works of known composers which are found in the choir-book the Neo-Hispanic or Mexican compositions are of especial interest, for they are still among the more unfamiliar literature of the period. Fernando Franco,[3] whose contributions to this volume have been listed above, and Juan de Padilla,[4] whose sole example here, an eight-part *Dies irae*, occupies five folios, were respectively sixteenth- and seventeenth-century Neo-Hispanic composers known to have been born in Spain, but both Saldaña and Tabares (or Tobares — both spellings occur in the book) remain completely obscure at present. Although a Manuel de Tavares is listed in the famous catalogue of John IV of Portugal, no relationship between him and the Tabares of the Mexican manuscript has been established. Judging from the music of Tabares and Saldaña, both composers were active around the middle of the seventeenth century. Tabares is represented by one piece — a seven-part setting of the *Parce mihi* — although he, Saldaña, and Padilla probably wrote some of the volume's unidentified works for six, seven, and eight voices. Saldaña's name is listed for four works: a four-part offertory, *Domine Jesu Christe*, a five-part motet "defunctorum" which is the response *Domine secundum actum meum*, the requiem introit set for two four-voice choirs, and a *Kyrie*, also for two four-voice choirs. In the manuscript, the *Kyrie* directly follows the introit which begins with the words *requiem aeternam* appearing only in the bass part of the first choir in plainsong.

The polychoric activity in mid-seventeenth-century Puebla is known through the music for two and three choirs by the composers Juan de Padilla, Saldaña, and Bernardo de Peralta. While Padilla [5] was perhaps the most prolific of all Neo-Hispanic composers and has left numerous works, including masses, of the *cori spezzati* genre, Saldaña is known only by his few pieces in Puebla's *libro number three*, and Peralta, only by his three-choir *Magnificat* [6] which is preserved elsewhere in the Puebla Cathedral Archives. The following brief remarks about Saldaña's music are offered merely as a description of what the composer left in the volume under discussion.

Saldaña seems to be at his best in the two double chorus compositions which are for the most part chordal in style and are made up of phrases alternating between the two choirs. At the close of each principal section of the music the choirs are combined for a climactic effect. If this describes the structure of Saldaña's tripartite *Kyrie*, his eight-voice requiem introit, though sectional, follows a plan which produces a highly colorful piece of music. Here the element of contrast is used beautifully for dramatic effect and expressivity of the text. Following the basses' chant on the words *requiem aeternam* which begins the piece, the two choirs answer one another with two simple statements each of the words *dona eis Domine*. This is interrupted by the rhythmic note-against-note setting of *et lux perpetua* using the following pattern: ♩ ♪ ♫ ♫ | ♩. After this is sung alternately by both choirs, the setting of *luceat eis* offers the most brilliant writing in the work. This bright period of several measures, where both choirs are climactically combined, is a fine example of colorful text setting, for the character of the music here seems to suggest light — both from the use of the two choirs together and from a use of some higher notes in the soprano parts. Creating an intensely dramatic moment immediately after this section in the composition is the contrasting setting of *te decet hymnus Deus in Sion* which is scored for only the soprano, alto, and tenor of the first choir. The work concludes with the conventionality with which it began, and the soprano parts draw freely from the plainsong sources.

In his four-part offertory Saldaña makes clear use of Gregorian melody, although his adaptation is by no means literal if it can be compared to the chant melody in the *Liber Usualis*. After an invocatory opening of the words *Domine Jesu Christe Rex Gloriae*, notated as plainsong in the soprano part alone, the soprano continues with a version of the chant melody for the entire motet, while the remaining voices are given a sort of figured harmony background making use of free imitation. This chant melody is intentionally a solo-type part, for it is written in long note values which make it stand out against the faster-moving accompanying voices.

Space here can permit only a few comments about a selection of the music contained in the Puebla *libro number three*, but surely in conclusion some mention should be made of the representation of Fernando Franco who was the most outstanding church composer in Mexico during the last quarter of the sixteenth century. Although the place of his birth has been established (La Serena, Spain), practically no more definite information seems to be available about him until around 1575 when he became chapelmaster of the Mexico City Cathedral. While the date of his birth remains a conjecture, and even the time of his arrival in the New World is uncertain, Franco yet retains the unique position of being the first Neo-His-

panic composer known by his music, and this makes him a particularly important figure in the cultural history of Mexico. If it is true
that he spent some twenty years in Guatemala [7] before the ten-year
period as chapelmaster in Mexico which ended his life, information
about his age and musical training before he left Spain must still be

Example 1

discovered. Franco's music has been preserved in six different
sources in Mexico, not the least important of which is the Puebla
volume under discussion. This source is of value not for the number
of his works which it contains (the Franco Codex in the Mexico
City Cathedral Archives contains seven twelve-movement Mag-

nificats), but rather especially for one motet of unusual beauty which is included. This motet, a four-part setting of *Parce mihi Domine*, is perhaps one of Franco's finest single works known to date, as it is a profoundly expressive piece written principally in a chordal style. An arrangement of Job's sorrowful lament, it shows highly sensitive text setting, a richness of modulation (in the sixteenth-century sense of placing cadence chords on varying scale degrees), and a use of the somber colorings which can be associated with sixteenth-century Spanish composers. These qualities are shown clearly in the accompanying excerpt [8] which illustrates some melodic lines particularly effective for the expression of the text on the setting of the word *peccavi* (I have sinned).

And so it can be seen from the short discussion in the preceding paragraphs that the Puebla *libro number three* is a valuable component of the Cathedral's collection of eighteen choirbooks of polyphonic music. Furthermore, it has been demonstrated, though not exhaustively by any means, that the volume's worth is not limited to its historical interest alone. On the contrary, the music it contains has intrinsic value, and it is becoming known not only to musical scholars but also to performing musicians. While fine colonial religious music of Mexico is not confined to this particular source, the *libro number three* has been singled out for special attention at this time largely because of its unusual features. It remains the only volume in all the colonial collections in Mexico that consists solely of music for the requiem and offices for the dead, and, paradoxically, it is surely one of the most interesting of the choirbooks from the point of view of its varied contents.

1. *The Hispanic American Historical Review*, August, 1946, pp. 305–6.
2. Robert Stevenson has pointed out in his *Music in Mexico* (New York: Crowell, 1952, p. 90) that these records are preserved in the Biblioteca Nacional in Madrid.
3. Spell, *op. cit.*, p. 313.
4. Stevenson, *op. cit.*, p. 168.
5. Padilla's music has been treated thoroughly in the doctoral dissertation of Alice Ray of the University of Southern California.
6. A transcription of Peralta's *Magnificat* appears in the supplementary volume of the Harvard dissertation of 1949 *Sacred Vocal Polyphony in Early Colonial Mexico*, by Steven Barwick.
7. Stevenson, *op. cit.*, p. 105.
8. The motet has been published in a modern edition by the Peer International Corporation, Southern Music Publishing Company, New York, as one in a series of seven "Motets from Mexican Archives," under the joint editorship of Steven Barwick and Hugh Ross.

TEXTURE VERSUS MASS IN THE MUSIC OF

GIOVANNI GABRIELI

G. W. Woodworth

I

THE famous antiphonal choirs of the Church of St. Mark, celebrated since the sixteenth century as a Venetian specialty, have, I think, been commonly misunderstood. The simple opposition of two choruses, echoing each other across the church, from gallery to gallery, was no more than the most primitive manifestation of Venetian antiphonal technique. The culmination of that technique in the works of Giovanni Gabrieli reveals the mature synthesis of two great traditions: one, the rich polyphonic texture so well known as the common practice technique of the sixteenth century; the other, the simple harmonic style dramatized in the opposition of antiphonal choirs.

The former is recognized as the "international" style of the Renaissance; the latter is commonly associated with Venice, and especially with the name of Giovanni Gabrieli. The older view of Gabrieli's style, which emphasized mass rather than texture, may be summed up in the remark of H. E. Wooldridge, reprinted in the second and revised edition of the Oxford History of Music (1932):

"In contrast to the contrapuntal complexity of his predecessors, his music is conceived in a simpler, more harmonic idiom, and aims at bold effects rather than delicacy of texture." [1]

Bukofzer, in "Music in the Baroque Era" (1947), penetrates more deeply into the heart of Gabrieli's style when he stresses the writing for "real voices, interwoven in infinite variety," and recognizes Gabrieli as "a consummate master of the magical effects of many-voiced texture." [2]

The common error is partly the result of repeated publication and performance of a few simple pieces. An outstanding example is the *Sonata Pian e Forte*, an *echo* piece, exploiting the monotonous contrast of a loud and a soft choir of instruments. This is a delight-ful but simple stunt, to be found in hundreds of echo pieces for chorus, instruments, harpsichord and organ all through the Renaissance. But Gabrieli's works for instruments alone, and for instruments and voices, are full of examples of a much more advanced and interesting manifestation of this technique of the opposition of masses. He is, as a matter of fact, rarely concerned with contrasting or echoing two equally balanced choirs, but rather with the far more complicated strategy of playing off against each other masses of unequal and varying weight, ranging from a single voice to the extraordinary richness of 7, 8, 10, 12, 14, 15 and 16-part writing for voices and instruments.[3]

The primitive double chorus technique antedated Giovanni Gabrieli by at least two generations. Bukofzer has pointed out that it was "brought to fame (not invented)" by Willaert.[4] It became the chief exportable commodity of the Venetian school, and spread northward into Germany and southward toward Rome. Palestrina, classic master of polyphony though he was, recognized the effec-tiveness of masses set over against each other in a simple harmonic style, as opposed to the more usual and far more complicated texture of interweaving strands. Of the 32 volumes of the works of Pales-trina, the equivalent of one full volume is devoted to music for double or triple chorus, of which the Stabat Mater for Two Choirs is well known, and that for Three Choirs almost never performed. Hassler, Praetorius, and Lassus provide other superb examples.

In 1607, five years before the death of Giovanni Gabrieli, Michael Praetorius published Part V of his *Musae Sionae*. The frontispiece of the Tenor part gives us a superb illustration of antiphonal choirs, labeled and diagrammed with the accuracy of an architect's draw-ing.[5] There are three choirs: "1 Chor" in the left balcony, "z(zweite) Chor" in the right balcony, and "3 Chor" on the floor below. Any conductor, choral singer or instrumentalist who has ever participated in the hazardous operations of antiphonal per-formance will observe with mixed amusement and concern how the conductors of "1" and "z" have turned their backs on their choirs and devoted themselves exclusively to the job of synchronizing their beat!

André Maugars, French viol player, reporting on the musical fashions in Italy in the early years of the seventeenth century, gives the following account of antiphonal singing raised to a high power of showmanship.

". . . this fairly long and spacious church had two great organs erected on both sides of the main altar with room for choirs around them. Along the nave there were eight more choir lofts, four on each side, elevated on scaffolding eight or nine feet high, and separated by the same distance but facing each other. . . . The master composer beat the principal measure at the head of the first choir. . . . In every one of the other choirs there was a man whose only duty was to keep his eyes on the original beat given by the chief maestro in order to conform the measure of his choir to it. Thus all choirs sang in the same measure without dragging the movement." [6]

What dull music it must have been!

The essential ingredients of the simple but monumental style which came to be known as "Venetian" were as follows:

(1) the dramatic contrast of equal antiphonal choirs, of high and low voices, of forte and piano, of voices and instruments, and of solo voice and full chorus (the "solus" and "omnes" mentioned in the *Syntagma* of Praetorius).

(2) a love of sonority, sound for the sake of the sheer splendor of sound, to match the sheer splendor of color in the Venetian scene. (See Gentile Bellini's painting "Processione in Piazza San Marco.")

(3) mass effects and the opposition of masses, at first simple, but later so grand and powerful that Professor Lang has referred to them as "the towering tone clusters of Gabrieli's double and multiple choirs." [7]

(4) a melodic style dictated by the instruments rather than the voices.

(5) short, clipped phrases, designed to fit into harmonic blocks; the predominance of colorful chord progressions over independent linear parts.

(6) text underlaying in short phrases, equal and vertical in all parts, emphasizing the block harmony.

(7) a simple, strong unmistakable rhythm — look once more at the conductors in the frontispiece of Praetorius!

(8) a formal structure of dull simplicity, consisting of the antiphonal repetition of very short spans, with no imitative counterpoint, no "points of imitation," and a minimum of contrapuntal elaboration even in the final cadences.

In contrast to this "Venetian" style, consider the basic principles of structure and texture, the fundamental technique of composition which was developed early in the Renaissance and became the common and universal practice of the sixteenth century. This technique applies equally to vocal and instrumental music. It is the form of the vast literature of the ricercare, canzona, and fantasia, as well as the mass, motet, and madrigal.

(1) The text is broken up into short phrases, each of which is treated successively, so that the whole composition falls into a series of spans, like the great arches of a bridge, or the bays of a cathedral.

(2) The opening phrase is often announced in four or five part harmony, the simple chordal setting of the *stile familiare*.

(3) The succeeding phrases are likely to open with a theme announced in one voice, followed by the other voices successively, in the endless variety of "points of imitation."

(4) The phrases close with cadences, frequently marked by an extra flow of melody on the syllables of the last word, with suspensions, dissonances, and a final resolution on consonance.

(5) There is the greatest variety in the treatment of the joints between the spans. Sometimes there is a complete stop and a new start; more often the new theme or subject gets started in the midst of the tapering off of the cadence, so that the spans are actually interlocked, and the ear is carried on from span to span, just as the eye follows naturally the succession of arches in the nave of a cathedral.

It was the unique achievement of Giovanni Gabrieli to unite the two opposing styles which had been developing throughout the Renaissance — the special Venetian technique of the antiphonal masses of sound, and the international technique of the interwoven strands. He inherited and assimilated both traditions, he resolved their conflicts, and in the *Symphoniae Sacrae* of 1597 and especially of 1615, he pushed on over the bridge-head separating Renaissance and Baroque, and penetrated far into the new territory.

II

The experience of conductors and performers often point up and reaffirm the deductions of historians and analysts. The sounds themselves offer their own evidence to qualify or to illuminate the printed page. The following reflections come from the practical experiences of repeated rehearsals and performances of Gabrieli's music by the Harvard Glee Club and the Radcliffe Choral Society over a period of a quarter of a century. Recordings of three motets from the *Symphoniae Sacrae* of 1597 and 1615 were made in 1940 and issued by Victor under the title *Processional and Ceremonial Music*.[8] In 1953 the Harvard-Radcliffe Choruses with members of the brass choir of the Boston Symphony Orchestra made a second recording of the same pieces, plus the *Benedictus* for Three Choirs.[9]

In the first place, it is clear that most of the music cannot be performed with "separated choirs" (cori spezzati). The *Benedictus* is an exception. Our performances of this work (in Sanders Theatre, Cambridge, and in the rotunda of the Museum of Fine Arts in Boston) allowed for the separation of the choirs exactly in the manner of the frontispiece of *Musae Sionae*, with three conductors, one on the floor, two in the galleries above. It is a real question whether the spectacular effect was worth the trouble; the recording, made with all three choirs together on the stage of Symphony Hall, was quite as satisfactory from the musical point of view. Moreover, the enthusiasm of the public, in contrast to the boredom of the singers, who had not found the rehearsals interesting, is proof that this is a spectacular but musically elementary style, offering more to the eye than to the ear.

In contrast to the *Benedictus*, most of the motets in *Symphoniae Sacrae* involve such freedom of texture and diversity of antiphonal combinations, that the entire body of singers and instrumentalists must perforce be located together, not in opposite galleries. A study of the instrumental canzoni and sonate in *Istituzione e Monumenti dell'Arte Musicale Italiana*, vol. 2,[10] will reveal two styles. In one there is the simple antiphonal effect of *Sonata Pian e Forte* and the *Benedictus*; in the other the instrumental choir is split into the most varied combinations, similar to the majority of the motets.

Gabrieli's "grand plan" for *In Ecclesiis* (*Symphoniae Sacrae*, Liber II, 1615) [11] is a superb example of the extension of the antiphonal technique far beyond the simple antiphony of equal choirs. The text of *In Ecclesiis* illustrates the independence of the St. Mark's ritual and suggests by its nonliturgical and episodic structure that it may have been especially arranged for a grand ceremonial occasion in the Piazza and the Church of San Marco. There are five verses, each concluding with an identical refrain or ritornello on the word "Alleluia," set in the quick triple rhythm of Renaissance jubilation. There are eight voice parts, divided into Coro I and Coro II, and there are six instruments, making a total of fourteen parts in all. This total mass of fourteen is never divided seven against seven, and never in evenly balanced choirs of instruments against voices, nor are the voices divided four against four despite the labels *Coro I* and *Coro II*. Only once, and then for only four bars at the opening of the final Alleluia, are the two choruses balanced against each other on equal terms. Following is the lay-out:

Verse I — A single voice, or unison Sopranos.
Alleluia — Antiphonal, between one Soprano and Chorus of four parts.

Verse 2 — Single voice, or unison Tenors.
Second Alleluia — Same as the first one, interrupted with overpowering effect by a Sinfonia for the six instruments alone.

Verse 3 — Duet of Altos and Tenors with six instruments, divided three against three, four against two, one against five and combined with the two voices in a constantly shifting texture.
Third Alleluia — Chorus I Altos and Tenors against Chorus II, SATB, with instruments in six parts.

Verse 4 — Duet for Soprano and Tenor, preferably solo voices.
Fourth Alleluia — Chorus I Sopranos and Tenors against Chorus II, SATB, without instruments.

Verse 5 — Chorus in eight parts, instruments in six parts, split into all sorts of combinations.
Final Alleluia — Two choruses of four parts each, plus all instruments, and a triple repetition of the culminating Alleluia.

Beside the complicated strategy of *In Ecclesiis*, the renowned echoes of *Sonata Pian e Forte* are obvious and elementary.

A further practical consideration is the size of the performing forces. If "masses of sound . . . ultimately welded into gigantic tuttis" [12] were the paramount element in style, a large chorus would serve best. That was the specification for the Harvard-Radcliffe performance of 1940. The writer feels that the small choir used for performances and recording in 1953, and the resulting concentration on flexibility and expressiveness of individual lines, revealed to the ear itself the infinite variety of texture and the vitality of the individual lines. The powerful effect of the tuttis, and the oppositions of equal masses do not require forces of the magnitude of *Ninth Symphony*. In a similar way this writer has found the dynamic effects in *Messiah* more impressive and the climaxes more stunning when he used a small choir and Handel's original orchestration, than with a large choir and the "powerful" orchestra of Mozart and Franz. Handel's orchestration allows for gradations of dynamics and combinations of texture involving continuo alone, string concertino and string tutti, a wind choir of oboes and bassoons, and a very sparing use of trumpets and drums. This concept of dynamics is the direct descendant of the dynamic strategy of Gabrieli. In a word, the dynamic impact of both *Messiah* and the *Symphoniae Sacrae* comes not at all from sheer power of numbers, but from clarity of texture. The same is true of the music of Bach, whether it be the organ fugue in G minor or *Cum sancto spiritu* from the *Mass*.

Possibly the most complicated, difficult, equivocal — and at the same time the most beautiful example of Gabrieli's style — is *O Jesu mi dulcissime* from *Symphoniae Sacrae*, Liber II, 1615.[13]

Gabrieli died in 1612. During the last decade of his life, Venice, more than any other spot in Europe, was the turbulent crossroads between the waning Renaissance and the new Baroque. The extraordinary style of this piece is a complex of conflicting forces — on the one hand, the survivals from the common practice of the Renaissance, and on the other, the new experimental technique of the Baroque. *O Jesu mi dulcissime* is at once a motet for double chorus, a Sacred Symphony with basso continuo, and a chromatic madrigal with a sacred text. The term *madrigale cromatico* refers strictly to a madrigal using many black notes — minima, semi-minima, fusa or croma, semi-fusa or semi-croma, 8ths, 16ths, 32nds, all black, hence chromatic. But it was no accident that in this black or "chromatic" music there were many sharps and flats, the chromatics of modern terminology. Both these phenomena, quick passages in black notes, and strange chromatic harmonies, were part of something far more fundamental than musical technique. They were the first intimations of the new world of the Baroque, of a new aesthetic ideal, the ideal of the *affections*, the drawing out of *affects* in the listener, through the unmistakably expressive qualities of the music.

The extraordinary juxtapositions of very long and very short notes produce phrases of an intimate expressiveness far more vivid than the common practice counterpoint of the international style, yet we are still dealing with a highly personal manifestation of linear texture. The stream of superb cross relations, e.g., F-natural, F-sharp, E-flat, E-natural, in the last beat of the opening measure, the B-flat–B-natural in m. 95–96; the bold harmonies, half modal, half modern, e.g., *O Christe*, m. 28–30, and *Adoramus Te*, m. 34–36, the plagal cadence at the end with F-A against E flat-G of the chord of C minor, so characteristic of Giovanni Gabrieli — all these and many other purple splashes of harmonic color, reveal the ultra-progressive in Gabrieli. Above all, the text underlaying and the exquisitely sensitive text setting command our wonder and admiration. We are dealing here not with a liturgical or Biblical text but with madrigal poetry. To be sure, it is sacred, not secular, the love of Christ, not the love of woman. But it is none the less akin to the exaggerated tenderness and passion of the Monteverdi madrigals. Observe the superlatives — *dulcissime, dilectissime, piissime* — and the poetic antithesis of human and divine in the Christmas mystery:

> in feno cubantem,
> in coelo fulgentem
>
> datus est a patre,
> natus est de virgine matre.

And yet, notwithstanding the evidence of advanced technique, this piece has examples of the simple and primitive double chorus method. Both choirs are uniformly low and they are approximately equal in range. The normal SATB chorus must be reassigned to achieve an equality between the two choirs and between the four parts of each choir. The monotonous series of antiphonal phrases *ut veneremur*, m. 68–93, is characteristic of the Venetian double chorus technique in its least attractive form. Such a passage would come to life if the two choruses could actually be separated in performance, but it is hard to see how this could have been possible even in the choir galleries of San Marco, since there are so many adjacent passages requiring the utmost intimacy of madrigalian performance.

In *Jubilate Deo* (*Symphoniae Sacrae*, Liber I, 1597),[14] there is no suggestion that the eight parts (SSAATTBB) be divided into Coro I and Coro II. On the contrary, each part is constantly shifting its position in a kaleidoscopic texture of duets, trios, quartets, quintets, and sextets. The simple opposition of Coro I and Coro II, "decani" and "cantori," high and low, loud and soft, is left far behind in the incredibly rich tapestry of sound. A sensitive performance requires that *each singer* keep his place in the shifting texture, that he join first one and then another part in duets and trios. Yet the antiphonal style is part of the form and fabric of the piece. The grouping and regrouping of forces for the four evenly matched antiphonal shouts — *Deus, Deus*, m. 26–27 and the thrice repeated *In laetitia*, m. 126– 130, 137–141, 148–151 — offer an excitement akin to that of the marshalling of forces in a military assault. The composition of the opposing groups is never the same, but the impact of the overlapping shouts is all the greater. Points of imitation, suggestions of familiar style, the grand plan of the classical Renaissance motet, all the apparatus of polyphonic common practice are here welded into the antiphonal style of opposing choirs. Moreover, the new unified fabric of sound is caught up and whirled along at a speed hitherto unknown, with a prophetic sense of motion, power and climax. Here in 1597 is the complete assimilation of the great streams of Venetian and Roman art, and a reconciliation of mass and texture.

Giovanni Gabrieli remains, to date, the least known of the great figures of the Renaissance in music. No complete edition of his music exists, and Carl von Winterfeld's "Johannes Gabrieli und sein Zeitalter," published in 1834, one of the earliest monuments of nineteenth-century musicology, is still the most comprehensive and authoritative study of his works and style. Practical performing editions of separate works have been few and repetitive, and recordings are similarly limited. Scholars and performers should join forces to recover, analyze, and bring to life in real sound the music of the most complex, most experimental, and most imaginative of the Venetians.

1. *The Oxford History of Music*, Vol. II, Second Edition, Oxford University Press, London, 1932, p. 428.
2. Manfred F. Bukofzer, *Music in the Baroque Era*, W. W. Norton & Co., New York, 1947, p. 22.
3. Cf. Gabrieli's title page: *Sacrae Symphoniae . . . senis 7, 8, 10, 12, 14, 15, & 16, Tam Vocibus Quam Instrumentis . . . Editio Nova*, Venetiis, M.D. XCVII, reprinted in *Istituzioni e Monumenti dell'Arte Musicale Italiana*, Vol. 2, Ricordi, Milan, 1932.
4. *Op. cit.*, p. 20.
5. Reprinted as frontispiece for Praetorius-*Werke*, Bd. 5, Kallmeyer, Wolfenbüttel, 1937.
6. André Maugars, "Response Faite à un Curieux Sur le Sentiment de La Musique

d'Italie," reprinted in Paul H. Lang, *Music in Western Civilization*, W. W. Norton, New York, 1941, p. 362.

7. Paul H. Lang, *ibid.*, p. 237.

8. G. Gabrieli, Processional and Ceremonial Music, Harvard Glee Club, Radcliffe Choral Society, Boston Symphony Orchestra Brass Choir, Victor Album 78RPM, No. DM798.

9. G. Gabrieli, Symphoniae Sacrae, Harvard Glee Club, Radcliffe Choral Society, Boston Symphony Orchestra Brass Choir, Cambridge Records LP, No. CRS-201

10. *Op. cit.*, Canzoni e Sonate . . . contenute nelle Sacrae Symphoniae del 1597.

11. Harvard-Radcliffe Choral Music, G. Schirmer, New York, 1952, No. 10121.

12. Henry Prunières, tr. E. Lockspeiser, *A New History of Music*, MacMillan, New York, 1943, p. 125.

13. Harvard-Radcliffe Choral Music, G. Schirmer, New York, 1950, No. 9898.

14. Harvard-Radcliffe Choral Music, G. Schirmer, New York, 1950, No. 9881.

IRRATIONAL DISSONANCE IN THE

ENGLISH MADRIGAL

Henry G. Mishkin

THE aberrations from common practice in the contrapuntal procedure of the English madrigal composers of the Elizabethan Age have evoked many diverse comments from music historians. At one pole is Charles Burney's censure of certain "offensive combinations" which lead him to say, "Taste, rhythm, accent, and grace must not be sought for in this kind of music; indeed we might as well censure the ancient Greeks for not writing in English as the composers of the sixteenth century for their deficiency in these particulars."[1] And at the other pole is the more usual and tolerant comment of recent historians expressed by E. H. Fellowes who, in writing of the unusual practices in the contrapuntal technique of William Byrd,[2] uses such phrases as "remarkable originality," "ripeness and maturity," and "independence of orthodoxy."

The fact that there are certain recurring aberrations in English technique has long been recognized and commented upon by historians. The recognized divergences have been listed in detail by Fellowes in his study of the style of Byrd.[2] Although he claims them as special evidence of Byrd's originality and enterprise, actually these same procedures can be found in the music of most of the other madrigalists and can serve here as an enumeration of the usual divergences, the most common of the uncommon practices, of the Elizabethan composers: (1) cross relations, usually as a result of voice leading; (2) consecutive octaves and fifths, usually by contrary motion, less frequently in similar motion; (3) leaping in the same direction from a passing seventh; (4) the seventh freely introduced as a cambiata; (5) sounding of the note of resolution against the suspension of the same note; (6) the entrance of a voice on a dissonance.

It is not, however, with such practices, the recognized and catalogued aberrations, that one need be involved at this late date. Although they are infrequent, and, indeed, derive their strength from their very infrequency, they are frequent enough to be recognized as consistent and "rational" deviations from common practice, rational because they normally result from a reasonable melodic movement within a texture of imitative counterpoint, a context in which a linear justification for unorthodox treatment of contrapuntal dissonance can usually be supplied.

There remain, however, in addition to these familiar exceptions, certain "irrational" and even capricious procedures, certain extreme instances of unorthodoxy in whose behalf there has not been a progressive accumulation of justification. The basis for a critical justification of contrapuntal unorthodoxy may be very broad: it may be and often is melodic, the logical movement of independent voices in a contrapuntal fabric; it may occasionally be pictorial, as the use of cross relation to illustrate such words as "bitter" or "sting"; or it may even be the contrapuntal result of exuberant harmonic or tonal experimentation. But there are other instances of unorthodoxy that do not come under these categories, broad as they are. There are passages that seem deliberately to practice the irrational, passages for which a reasonable explanation based upon the common sixteenth-century procedure or the recognized aberrations therefrom is difficult to apply.

Let us examine a few of these aberrations. Those passages in which the note of resolution in one voice sounds against the suspension in another are, in a sense, legitimatized by the sheer frequency of the practice. But an added violence is introduced when the resolution of the suspension is a minor second and involves a cross relation as well, as in the following examples by Richard Carlton.[3]

Ex.1

The usual uncommon leap from a dissonance is from a passing 7th which leaps in the same direction,[4] sometimes returning, as in the double auxiliary, to the note of resolution, but often continuing downward by step. But in the following cadence from Michael Cavendish the tenor leaps from "c," a 4th (11th) above the bass.[5]

Or here Greaves leaps from a 9th.[6]

and Vautor, in the following passage, resolves the cadential 6/4 in the upper two voices while the tenor leaps to the nonharmonic "g" and then back to the 7th.[7]

Robert Jones leaps from a suspension twice within three measures.[8]

There are also cases where the cross relation occurs not as a result of voice leading but in spite of it. In Example 6 a B-natural is
sounded by the bass. The tenor, even though ascending, sounds
the B-flat against the suspension in the soprano which in turn
resolves to B-natural.[9]

And in the following passage, even though both voices are
ascending, the F-natural in the bass pointlessly contradicts the
F-sharp in the alto.[10]

Even these few examples seem to indicate that there are actually
two levels of unorthodoxy, two degrees to what R. O. Morris calls
"the peculiarities of English sixteenth century craftsmanship." [11]
The extreme level is illustrated by the contrapuntal procedures of
the radicals, of such men as Greaves, Cavendish, Jones, and Carlton,
in comparison with which the uncommon practices on the moderate
level of Byrd, Weelkes, East and Wilbye are relatively conservative.

It is possible, of course, to contemplate this stylistic discrepancy
within unorthodoxy as a purely musical phenomenon. And, in
judging these two levels of uncommon practice, it is possible to
return to either of the two critical positions represented by Burney
and Fellowes from which the unorthodoxy is evidence either of the
technical deficiency of this "second class of English masters of the
sixteenth century" [12] or of a refreshing enterprise and originality.
We could choose to stop here and establish a preference for either
position. But it is tempting to move outside music and entertain
the idea that at least part of the explanation for this stylistic dichot-

omy is extra-musical, that the English madrigalists, flourishing toward the end of the polyphonic era, were susceptible to the positive pressures of the new philosophic thought of the seventeenth century.

The madrigal was firmly linked to the past, to a poetic convention and a musical convention that were parts of the sixteenth century's inheritance of the mental discipline culture historians call scholasticism. Is it possible that the extreme musical unorthodoxy of certain madrigalists is the beginning of a breakdown, from within, of the orderly rational structure of the scholastic contrapuntal system, influenced by a similar breakdown in the scholastic philosophic system? Is this evidence of a growing lack of conviction in the assumptions of the contrapuntal rational structure that not only accounted for the radical deviations within the system but also for the withering of the creative impulse among the madrigalists who in many cases outlived the school itself? [13] Are we already in the presence of that mood of anti-intellectualism that was beginning to pervade English letters and thought in the seventeenth century? Are these irrational tendencies in contrapuntal practice, this intolerance with dogma, with a set of contrapuntal rules, a manifestation of the same reaction against rationalism, against the "Gothic," which gave rise to the empirical philosophies of Bacon and Hobbes for which the age is best known in intellectual history?

Basil Willey points out Bacon's campaign against excessive rationalism, his distrust of the "meddling intellect," the important "anti-rational tendencies of his program." [14] Bacon stated, "The understanding, left to itself, ought always to be suspected . . . Logic . . . by no means reaches the subtilty of nature." [15] Lamprecht says of the political philosopher Hobbes "his distrust of human reason was excessive . . . And because men are not sufficiently reasonable (a fact which can be abundantly confirmed empirically) Hobbes refused any proper play to reason in human affairs." [16] And, in analyzing the poetry of the seventeenth century, Ruth Wallerstein finds "the distrust in the power of reason," "the strong sense of the wickedness of endeavoring to compel thought," and the "general mood of the limitation of reason" dominant forces in the literary thought of the seventeenth century poets. [17]

Are these contemporary tendencies responsible, even in a slight degree, for the extreme unorthodoxy of the English composers of the seventeenth century? One cannot assert positively that a purely technical phenomenon, such as a discrepancy in the application of a firmly entrenched stylistic procedure, is the result of an inclusive impulse which caused similar discrepancies in other manifestations of English thought and letters in the seventeenth century. One cannot assert positively that an "irrational" treatment of dissonance is comparable to other "anti-rational" elements of the empirical point of view. But it is of value to appreciate the strength of the movement that Willey calls "the rejection of scholasticism" and to realize that in the invigorating intellectual atmosphere of the English seventeenth century, "the century of genius," it was difficult for a musical technique rooted in the scholastic past to preserve its stylistic unity or conviction.

The departures from common practice in the works of the "radical" madrigalists were extreme. The compulsion to interpret this fact, either as evidence of a lack of skill, an excess of enterprise, or a sensitivity to a general mood of anti-intellectualism, perhaps fulfills the worthy function of reminding us again to what a degree the madrigal school is "the strangest phenomenon in the history of English music." Fellowes sums up the magnitude of mystery left by the unsolved problems of his intensive study of the school:

"Nothing is more astonishing in the whole history of music than the story of the English school of madrigal composers. The long delay of its appearance, lagging behind the Italian school by no less than half a century; the suddenness of its development; the extent of the output; the variety and originality as well as the fine quality of the work; the brevity of its endurance and the completeness with which it finally collapsed; all these features combine to distinguish the madrigal school as the strangest phenomenon in the history of English music." [18]

1. Charles Burney, *A General History of Music*, London, 1789, Vol. III, p. 144.
2. E. H. Fellowes, *William Byrd* (London, 1936), new edition London, 1948; see Chapter XV, "Some Features of Byrd's Vocal Technique."
3. Richard Carlton, *Madrigals to Five Voices* (1601), English Madrigal School, Vol. XXVII, pp. 121, 148.
4. See examples in Fellowes, *op. cit.*, pp. 226–27.
5. Michael Cavendish, *Madrigals to Five Voices* (1598), E.M.S., Vol. XXXVI, p. 55.
6. Thomas Greaves, *Madrigals for Five Voices* (1604), E.M.S., XXXVI, p. 17.
7. Thomas Vautor, *Songs of Divers Airs and Natures* (1619), E.M.S., XXXIV, p. 60.
8. Robert Jones, *First Set of Madrigals* (1607), E.M.S., XXXV, p. 68.
9. Thomas Greaves, *Songes of Sundrie Kindes* (1604), E.M.S., XXXVI, p. 4.
10. Robert Jones, *op. cit.*, p. 48. Compare the Jones procedure to a more usual treatment by Weelkes, E.M.S., XI, p. 20, in a similar passage.

11. R. O. Morris, *Contrapuntal Technique in the Sixteenth Century*, Oxford, 1922, p. 64.

12. Burney, *op. cit.*, p. 13.

13. "Wilbye produced his second book of madrigals in 1609, and although he lived for nearly thirty years after that date he seems to have written nothing further except two short 'hymns' or anthems for Leighton's collection in 1614. Weelkes, as far as is known, wrote but one madrigal of first rate importance in the last twenty-three years of his comparatively short life. Tomkins lived for thirty-four years after his book of *Songs* or madrigals was published in 1622, and wrote no more of this class of work. It is remarkable, too, that Orlando Gibbon's set of madrigals was issued before he was thirty years old, and that he never wrote any others, as far as is known." E. H. Fellowes, *Orlando Gibbons*, Oxford, 1951 (second edition), p. 76.

14. Basil Willey, *The Seventeenth Century Background*, London, 1934, pp. 36–37.

15. Preface to *De Augmentis*, quoted by Willey, p. 25.

16. Thomas Hobbes, *De Cive*, edited with an introduction by Sterling Lamprecht, New York, 1949, p. xxix.

17. Ruth Wallerstein, *Studies in Seventeenth Century Poetic*, Madison, 1950, pp. 184, 233.

18. E. H. Fellowes, *Orlando Gibbons*, Oxford, 1951, p. 74.

WATERMARKS IN CERTAIN MANUSCRIPT COLLECTIONS

OF ENGLISH KEYBOARD MUSIC

Stephen D. Tuttle

It is highly improbable that scholars three hundred years
hence will spend much time examining the paper upon which twentieth-century composers wrote their music. The lives and works of
even the most unassuming of contemporary composers are so well
documented that an examination of the music paper on which they
wrote would yield nothing to the investigator which he could not
more easily find elsewhere. It is, moreover, improbable that scholars
will be able to spend time in such a study even if they wish to do so
for the greater part of the music paper in use today will almost
certainly have disintegrated before three centuries have elapsed.

For the scholar who today studies the music of three hundred
years ago an investigation of something even so remotely connected
with music as the watermarks in the music paper may, however,
prove valuable. Like an archeologist, sifting the earth which contains relics of an ancient civilization, he may discover fragments
which will fill in details of the history of music in periods when
the lives and works of even the greatest composers were documented
sparsely, if at all.

Few composers today give much thought to the music paper on
which they write. If the size of the sheets, the ruling and the quality
of the surface are satisfactory little more is demanded. Matters like
the rag or acid-content of the paper, or its durability, are rarely
considered. Should a watermark exist in the paper it will, if it is
noticed, be correctly taken for an assumption of elegance or a
gesture to tradition rather than as an indication of quality or size.

In the sixteenth and seventeenth centuries the composer's atti-

tude toward the material to which he was entrusting his most profound, or most inconsequential, creations was undoubtedly little
different from that of his modern counterpart. If he were sufficiently egocentric to believe that his work could interest posterity
he may have hoped that the paper would last for some time. This
would be particularly the case if he happened to be writing keyboard music for he would know that its chances of being printed
or engraved were slight. The composer was, however, often more
fortunate than he realized, or than he sometimes deserved, for he
could not foresee the astonishing permanence of the fragile handmade sheets, so susceptible to destruction, upon which he wrote.

The contents of the manuscript collections of sixteenth and
seventeenth century English keyboard music have been described
in greater or less degree and are relatively well known. The material
composition of the manuscripts has, however, been somewhat
neglected. As little is known of the compilers, the exact dates, and
the circumstances of the compilation of many of these collections
an investigation of any details of the manuscripts may produce an
occasional fragment of useful knowledge.

It was with the hope of finding some fragments of information
that these tentative notes on watermarks in certain of the collections
were made. They must be considered as little more than a preliminary study of an aspect of the manuscripts which has been almost
completely ignored.

The paper of which the manuscripts are composed is of course
handmade and of quality excellent enough to have withstood the
aging effects of some three hundred years, if not always the de-
structive effect of the acid content in certain of the inks. It is mostly,
if not altogether, paper of European origin and the greater amount
of it undoubtedly came from northern France. It is of varying sizes
and is almost without exception watermarked.

The watermark in a sheet of handmade paper was, and still is,
formed by a pattern made of wire shaped into the required design
and fastened with fine wire to the mould. This pattern, lying above
the chain and laid wires of the mould, produced an impression in
the paper. Two moulds were generally used for each size of sheet,
both having the same watermark design. These designs were frequently formed so skillfully by the makers that the watermarks
which they produced in the paper often appear to be identical.[1] If

one of the designs was less well formed or became damaged through wear the use of two moulds becomes clearly apparent to even the unpracticed eye.

One of the oldest existing collections of English keyboard music is the manuscript *Royal Appendix 56* in the British Museum. This is a small oblong volume containing thirty-two folios. There is only one watermark,[2] a hand surmounted by star (or conventionalized flower or rose of bliss) approximately 8×2.5 centimeters in size. (Ex. 1.) The sheets were cut in half to produce the desired oblong shape with the result that the watermark is divided, the upper part appearing at the bottom of certain folios, the lower part at the top of others. It has not been identified.[3] *Royal Appendix 58* has a similar watermark.

Example 1

Some light is thrown on the compilation of the most famous of the collections, *The Fitzwilliam Virginal Book*, in the Fitzwilliam Museum at Cambridge, by the watermark. It is generally accepted that this manuscript was copied by the younger Tregian during the some ten years when he was imprisoned in The Fleet. The large number of compositions in the collection and the meticulous care with which they are copied are evidence that the compilation must have extended over a period of time.

Two hundred and twenty folios of paper 33.7×22.5 centimeters in size constitute a large volume. It would be reasonable to suppose that under the circumstances Tregian had obtained the music paper in small quantities as the size of the project grew and not all at one time. The uniformity of the paper, the ruling and particularly the single watermark suggest, however, that all the paper was obtained at one time and that Tregian planned the manuscript on a large scale.

The watermark is one of the numerous forms of the crozier of Basel. This does not necessarily mean, as Fuller Maitland and Barclay Squire surmise, that the paper is Swiss in origin.[4] The *crosse de Bâle* is not infrequently found in paper manufactured in other parts of Europe. This particular form has not been identified.

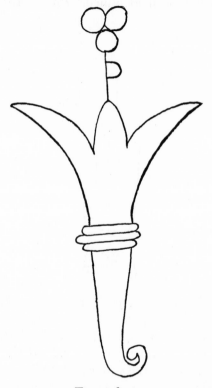

Example 2

Of the manuscripts examined only *Royal Appendix 56*, *Royal Appendix 58*, the *Fitzwilliam Book* and *Additional Manuscript 31392* in the British Museum have a single watermark. This last is a fine manuscript but a tantalizing one as much of the volume was left blank and as twenty or more folios were at some time cut out. It was clearly designed to be a collection of music for virginals, lute and bandora. After each group of pieces there is left a series of blank folios which the compiler did not fill up. The virginal music consists of four pavans and galliards by Byrd, the beginning of the first pavan being incomplete as the folio on which it was written was cut out. It can be seen from the stubs that at least some others of the cut-out folios also contained music. What this may have been is a matter for conjecture, but it was quite possibly more keyboard music by Byrd. The contemporary binding is one of the most handsome of all the virginal manuscripts.

The single watermark is a version of the Strassburg bend and lily. It has not been identified, but it is near *Heawood 141*. As the volume is oblong (21×27.5 centimeters) the sheets have been cut in half and the watermark is consequently divided.

It is much more customary to find in both manuscripts and printed books a uniform size paper with a variety of watermarks than with a single one. Various explanations have been advanced for the occurrence of a multiplicity of watermarks in a book or manuscript, but no general agreement has been reached.

Both *Will Forster's Virginal Book* and *Benjamin Cosyn's Virginal Book* [5] are composed of paper which appears at first to be uniform but is shown by the variety of watermarks to have come from more than one paper mill.

Will Forster's Book contains four watermarks. The first, found only on folio 2, is a fleur de lys. The others are three versions of the flagon-like "pot watermark." (See Ex. 3.) This type is extremely common in sixteenth- and seventeenth-century paper and exists in hundreds of forms. The variety which the mould makers obtained and the variations which they evolved out of two more or less basic designs, the single-handled and the double-handled pot, are remarkable as is the skill with which the frequently intricate patterns were formed. It is true that the watermarks sometimes appear so lopsided and ill-formed that if one were not aware of the distorting effect of wear on the wire design one might be led to suppose that the *formaires* who made the designs were more influenced by the contents of their models than by their shapes. A distortion frequently reveals clearly the "twin" aspect of the watermarks as will be seen in *Additional Manuscript 30485*.

The three versions of the pot watermark in *Forster's Book* are well formed although not particularly elaborate. All bear letters, the second, of which no drawing is given, having the letters on the lower part of the bowl. None of these watermarks has been identified.

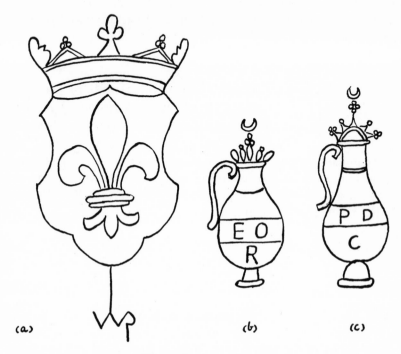

Example 3   a, b, c

The paper in *Benjamin Cosyn's Book* also contains four watermarks. Three of these appear between folios 1 and 112 which form that part of the volume which contains keyboard music. The fourth watermark appears between folios 113 and the end of the manuscript.

It is by no means always easy to distinguish a watermark clearly. The light available in the library in which the manuscript is being examined and the degree of skill of the examiner may be partly responsible. But the quality of the paper is also a factor for if it is long fibered the watermark will probably be less distinct. As Hunter explains, "The strength of the paper is usually sacrificed if a well defined and sharp watermark is desired." [6]

In music manuscripts the ruling, the heaviness of the writing and the quality of the ink often obscure a watermark which might otherwise be clearly visible. This is true of the first and third watermarks in the folios examined in *Cosyn*. (See Ex. 4.) The first is for the most part clear but the third, apparently a coat of arms measuring 7 × 3 centimeters, is quite difficult to distinguish. It is not reproduced here.

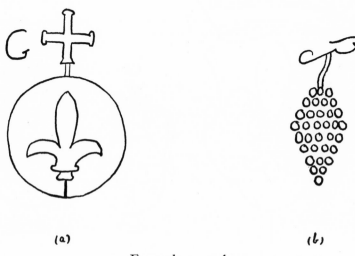

(a)   (b)

Example 4 a, b

The design of the fourth watermark is large, bold and handsome. It consists of a double-headed eagle with spread wings surrounded by a laurel wreath, the whole surmounted by a large crown. It measures 15.5 × 9.5 centimeters and resembles *Heawood 1240*. The paper on which this mark is found is rather lighter in quality than the rest of the manuscript and may represent a second manuscript bound in with the first.

The variety of the contents of British Museum *Additional Manuscript 29996* sets it apart from many of the other collections. It is an extensive volume of some 219 folios containing music by composers from Preston and Redford to Thomas Tomkins and Carleton. It belonged at one time to Tomkins whose many annotations add greatly to the interest of the manuscript.

The variety of hands and the diversity of the contents make the volume appear to be a composite of several manuscripts bound together. An examination of the paper and watermarks shows that it is more probably a composite of only two. Folios 5–68 are composed of a heavy paper which bears no watermark. These folios constitute the earlier manuscript. Folios 69–219 make up a later manuscript. The paper is lighter in quality and bears a single watermark. (See Ex. 5.) This is an amusing design used by one of the two or more papermakers who bore the name Jehan Nivelle.

Example 5

Although it is not identical this bears striking resemblances to *Briquet 3639.* Of the watermarks examined this is the only one which suggests a musical connotation although the suggestion is illusory for, as Briquet writes,

"La première fois que nous vîmes ce filigrane nous pensâmes au 'chien de Jean de Nivelle qui fuit quand on l'appelle.' On se demand s'il y a quelque rapport entre ce filigrane et le héros de la chanson. . . . Notre filigrane n'a pas une origine aussi illustre. Le Jean Nivelle qui accompagne le chien est le nom d'un papetier de Troyes que l'on trouve souvent filigrané. . . . Peut-être etait-ce ce Jean Nyvelle 'l'esné' Marchand demeurant à Troyes qui en 1621 vendit à Nicolas Denise les deux moulins à papiers de Sancy près de Troyes. Il y a du avoir au moins deux papetiers du nom de Jean Nivelle car ce nom est filigrané, sous une fleur de lis déja en 1540." [7]

Much of the music written on these watermarked folios is in Tomkins' hand and the last piece in the volume, the *Pavan: Lord Canterbury* is dated by him *1647.* If Briquet's suggestion that the maker who used this type of watermark may be the seventeenth-century Jean Nyvelle "l'esné" it is quite possible that the paper may have come from his mill.

There is more variety and interest of design in the watermarks which occur in *Additional Manuscript 23623* than in those found in many of the manuscripts. This particular collection, which contains for the most part music by John Bull, was probably compiled in the Netherlands. It would be interesting if the watermarks were to show that the paper was manufactured in the Netherlands, but they offer no conclusive proof.

Three watermarks are found, one of which has a countermark. Two (a and b) are found on folios 2–92. (See Ex. 6.) The first is one of the types which Briquet classifies as "Lettres assembles" and his explanation of its origin increases the interest of a design which is attractive in itself. He writes,

"Les deux C opposés embrassant la croix de Lorraine couronnée constituent un filigrane qui denote sa provenance et sa date originaire. Ce sont la les insignes de Charles III, duc de Lorraine et de sa femme Claude de France. Cette marque que l'on voit dès son origine en 1578 accompagnée d'un second filigrane aux letters F A est devenue rapidement banale en Lorraine et on la trouve très vite accompagnée d'autres contremarques." [8]

Between folios 93–94 and 97–108 there appears the third watermark (c) together with the first. The second watermark and the countermark to the first do not appear. None of the watermarks has been identified.

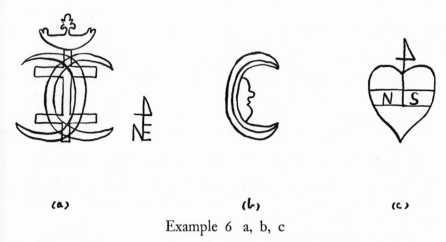

(a) (b) (c)

Example 6 a, b, c

Other manuscripts may be distinguished by having only one watermark or a variety of watermarks but *Additional Manuscript*

30485 in the British Museum has four versions of one type, the pot watermark, all bearing letters. The last of these resembles the second of the three pot watermarks in *Will Forster's Book*. None has been identified. (See Ex. 7.)

The "twin" aspect of the watermarks is clearly shown by the two forms of watermark (b) which occur between folios 8 and 24. The watermark design is the same but in one of the moulds the pattern has become distorted.

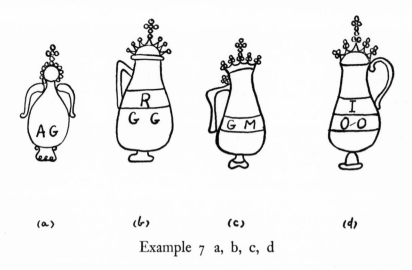

(a)   (b)   (c)   (d)

Example 7 a, b, c, d

The Thomas Tomkins autograph manuscript in the Paris Conservatoire, *Réserve 1122*, is made up of paper which has six watermarks. The first is a cutlass, or dagger, 10.5 centimeters in length; the second a pot bearing the letters A B; the third is an example of posts approximately 6 × 4 centimeters; the fourth another example of posts of approximately the same size but bearing the letters R P; the fifth, another example of the pot watermark with the letters $\genfrac{(}{)}{0pt}{}{B}{H\,[?]}$; the sixth, grapes surmounted by a crown. Although the quality of the paper varies somewhat there is no reason to doubt that the manuscript was put together at one time except for the final page, 189, which was added later.

Susanna van Soldt's Book (British Museum *Additional Manuscript 29485*) contains three versions of the pot watermark. Two of these although differing in size and in details of the shape bear the same letters. (See Ex. 8.) The third of the marks bears the letters E O.

(a)   (b)

Example 8 a, b

Elizabeth Rogers' Virginal Book (British Museum *Additional Manuscript 10337*) contains two watermarks, one an example of the pot, the other a cardinal's hat.

A more detailed study of the watermarks in these manuscripts might well be made. It should include a careful examination and comparison of each pair of twin watermarks and should be illustrated with photographs. These would not only reproduce exactly the size and details of the watermark but would show its position in relation to the chain and laid lines. This cannot be done satisfactorily with even the most careful tracing and cannot be done at all with "eye drawings" such as those included here. When these drawings were made it was not possible to trace nor to photograph the watermarks. Libraries are properly reluctant to allow tracings to be made. Photographs, although not easy to make, do no harm to the manuscripts and are far more satisfactory for the student.

The entire field of music manuscripts offers rich and almost untouched material to the music historian and to the *filigranist* as well.

1. Allan H. Stevenson, "Watermarks are Twins," *Studies in Bibliography: Papers of the Bibliographical Society of the University of Virginia*, IV (1951–52), p. 64.

2. Only the watermarks in the paper which constitutes the original manuscripts are considered. Frequently when manuscripts have been rebound or their bindings have been repaired additional fly leaves of more modern paper have been added. The watermarks appearing in these are disregarded.

3. The drawings of the watermarks are all "eye drawings" made with as much accuracy as circumstances permitted. The ideal method of reproducing watermarks is by means of photography, but this was not possible at the time.

In attempting to identify the watermarks the following works have been consulted:

Charles-Moïse Briquet, *Les Filigranes, Dictionnaire historique des marques du papier*. . . . (1907), 4 v.

Edward Heawood, *Watermarks* (1950).

W. A. Churchill, *Watermarks in Paper in Holland, England, France etc. in the XVII and XVIII centuries*. . . . (1935).

4. J. A. Fuller Maitland and W. Barclay Squire, *The Fitzwilliam Virginal Book* (1894–99), 2 v., p. v.

5. In the British Museum, The Queen's Music Library; manuscripts *R.M. 24.d.3* and *R.M. 23.1.4*.

6. Dard Hunter, *Papermaking*, 2nd ed. (1947), p. 268.

7. Briquet, *Filigranes*, pp. 233–34.

8. Briquet, *Filigranes*, p. 493.

[*Editor's Note*: The reproductions of the watermarks appearing in this article were made directly from admittedly rough sketches and tracings prepared by Stephen D. Tuttle. No attempt was made to perfect them. Mr. Tuttle's time during the last few weeks of his short life was spent in large measure in assembling and perfecting the materials submitted by the other contributors to this volume. By favoring the work of his associates rather than his own, he demonstrated that fine native characteristic that endeared him to so many.]

PART FOUR

*The Seventeenth
and
Eighteenth Centuries*

THE "AUTHENTIC" PERFORMANCE OF

BAROQUE MUSIC

Putnam Aldrich

THE quest for authenticity in musical revivals is a strictly twentieth-century phenomenon. When the members of the Florentine Camerata attempted to revive the music of the Ancient Greeks, they had nothing to go on but vague descriptions, and they came out with something entirely different — opera. When Mendelssohn revived Bach's *St. Matthew Passion* in 1839, he was not concerned with how it had sounded in Leipzig one hundred years before. The resurgence of Baroque music which occurred early in this century first took the form of transcriptions or arrangements that frankly adapted Baroque works to modern practice and taste. The music was used as a vehicle for exploiting concert resources — the symphony orchestra, the grand piano, gigantic choral forces — and the criterion of excellence lay in its appeal to large audiences. The current crusade for authenticity came as a reaction against these falsifications of the music. It is based on the wholly valid assumption that an adequate understanding, appreciation or evaluation of a musical composition can only be attained through hearing it performed (or at least imagining it as performed) in an authentic manner; that is, the way the composer expected it to sound.

This standpoint has been aided and abetted by great advances in scholarly research and by the development of that branch of musicology known as *Aufführungspraxis*, which deals with the manner in which early music was performed at the time of its origin. The first steps toward authenticity were taken by the scholars who prepared critical and historical editions that reproduced the original musical texts. When performers began to have recourse to the

editions published by the Bach-Gesellschaft, the Händel-Gesell-
schaft, the Purcell Society, the German and Austrian Denkmäler,
there was at least some assurance that the notes written down by
the composers would be heard. Research in *Aufführungspraxis* revealed, however, that strict adherence to the composers' texts by
no means assures authentic performances. Quite the reverse, indeed, for it transpired that Baroque musicians did not write what
they performed or perform what they wrote. Further investigations
have disclosed Baroque standards of timbre, tuning, techniques of
performance and interpretation which differ strikingly from those
that prevail in the musical world today. Each new scholarly contribution adds to our accumulated knowledge and, at the same time,
exposes a sphere of hitherto unsuspected ignorance.

This may be as good a time as any to take stock of our knowledge
and potentialities in this field; at the same time it may be well to
explore the boundaries of our ignorance. The following survey of
the basic problems encountered by the performer of Baroque music
makes no pretense to completeness of detail, but rather aims to
examine, in general terms, the following questions:

(1) To what extent is authenticity in the performance of Baroque
music attainable?

(2) Insofar as it is attainable, what degree of authenticity is desirable and suitable for present-day concerts?

The problem of timbre, depending as it does upon the physical
properties of sound, should be the most amenable to the modern
scientific approach. The sound ideal of the Baroque period was not
the full, rich, vibrant sonority that is cultivated by modern instrumentalists and singers. It was a thin, clear, somewhat piercing tone.
This quality is inherent in most of the instruments of the period —
the viols, recorders, cornetti, high trumpets, harpsichord, the stops
of the Baroque organ, and even the seventeenth-century violins
(which have had to be structurally altered to make them conform
to modern demands of volume and sonority). Some aspects of the
Baroque sound-ideal can therefore be recaptured through the use
of old or reconstructed instruments. Others, however, are wholly
dependent on playing and singing techniques. The gamba-player,
for instance, who treats his instrument like a 'cello, using modern
bowing techniques and a pervading vibrato, minimizes the timbre

inherent in the instrument and creates a quality of sound quite different from that formerly produced by the Baroque player. And so with the human voice; its timbre varies enormously according to the technique of voice production that is used. Modern voice training places much emphasis upon the fullness and vibrancy of sustained tone. In the Baroque period, on the other hand, emphasis was upon agility and the clear execution of graces, trills and rapid scale passages. The beauty of an individual sustained note was scarcely appreciated at all, since the appearance of a long, held note in the score was almost invariably an invitation to embellish it with some sort of ornament. I have yet to hear a singer attempt the ornate version of *Possente Spirto* in Act III of Monteverdi's *Orfeo* (1608). A glance at a single phrase of this aria may (or may not!) help the reader to imagine the quality of voice that would be compatible with the clear execution of these notes.[1]

Yet this is by no means an isolated case; a similar kind of technique and tone quality (though couched in a different musical idiom) was still required a century-and-a-half later for the proper rendition of Handel's operas.[2] Evidently the performer who wishes to meet Baroque standards of timbre must have specialized technical training. Existing symphony orchestras or choral groups can scarcely be expected to satisfy this criterion. From this point of view, then, any approach to authenticity must be renounced by all but soloists or small groups, each member of which has had individual training.

Closely allied to problems of timbre, in that they are concerned with physical sound, are those of tuning and pitch. During the period from 1600 to 1750 many different systems of tuning were used, both simultaneously and successively. The legend that J. S. Bach brought about the triumph of equal temperament with his *Well Tempered Clavier*, and its corollary that equal temperament is an authentic tuning for the music of Bach and his contemporaries, has been proved false.[3] The most prevalent tunings throughout the entire period were varieties of mean tone temperament. Now the characteristic of all mean tone temperaments is the fact that while the chords of certain keys sound almost perfectly in tune, those of more remote keys sound progressively more and more dissonant. Thus, the concept of "key character," which in equal tempered music is either purely imaginary or based on some psychological pitch-association had, in the Baroque period, a material, acoustical reality. I once had the experience of hearing Bach's F-sharp Minor Toccata played twice; first on an instrument tuned to equal temperament, then on a mean tone instrument.[4] The passage just before the change to 6/8 meter, in which Bach repeats a one-measure progression twenty-two times in succession in different transpositions, sounded the first time incredibly dull, in spite of variations in dynamics which attempted to give some shape to the period. The second hearing was a revelation, in that each successive repetition of the figure actually sounded differently, owing to the greater or less dissonance of its component chords. The harmonic tensions and relaxations brought out the form of the passage with no need for dynamic change to relieve the monotony. Is it not possible that many of the frequent rosalias and sequences in Baroque music were calculated expressly to make use of the dissonances inherent in mean tone temperament? This is a field that remains to be explored.

Another instance of the musical importance of mean tone temperament is its probable effect upon performance. It is known that in Baroque performance-practice the exact values of certain notes

— especially appoggiaturas and ornamental tones — were variable according to their context. The relative duration of such tones was often correlated to their dissonant or consonant quality. This being the case, would not, for example, an appoggiatura to a dissonant chord have a different duration than an appoggiatura to a more consonant chord? The performer would therefore base his decision as to whether to play a quick or a slow note upon its status in the mean tone temperament used. Another field for exploration! The whole problem is complicated, it is true, by the fact that in practice temperaments were often accommodated to the particular music to be played by retuning the instrument.[5]

But the greatest obstacle to the introduction of old systems of tuning lies in audience reaction. So imbued have we become with the sounds emanating from equal-tempered instruments that any deviation therefrom results in the impression of hearing something out of tune. It is doubtful whether even an audience made up of musicians could sit through a concert given in a Baroque tuning without being more conscious of the "out-of-tuneness" of the music than of the music itself. Only after a lengthy exposure to these sounds would one be able to judge impartially — so to speak — the musical effect of the temperament.[6]

The problem of interpreting a Baroque score places the modern performer face to face with imponderables. He must first be prepared to make a drastic change in his attitude. He expects the musical score to be set up in such a way that every detail of execution is clearly indicated — not only what note to play, but just how fast to play it, how long to hold it, how loud to play it, what expression to give it, etc. But this type of score is a modern product, an achievement of the last 150 years, and is specifically associated with concert hall music. It has certain advantages: it insures a performance that corresponds approximately to the composer's intention, and makes it possible for people with no musical imagination to become professional musicians. The Baroque musician, however, would have considered it excessively dictatorial. It does not permit the performer to collaborate in the creation of the music or to satisfy his needs for spontaneous expression. Rather than allowing for a variety of interpretations for a given piece, it aims at a single, crystallized version. The musical score of the Baroque is the opposite in almost every respect. The bass line, for instance, is to be played by the "fundamental" instruments, which, in addition to rendering the written notes, must provide a complete harmonic background for the piece. The other parts, for the "ornamental" instruments, or soloists, contain numerous stenographic signs denoting ornaments. It is up to the performer to interpret these appropriately, often in different manners at various occurrences of the same sign. Additional extended improvisation was expected at certain places, especially the breaking up into faster movement of melodies which appear in the score as long notes. Thus, the performer must first of all think of himself in the role of a creator, collaborating with the composer; he must not only supply the details of execution, but must in many ways complete the thought outlined by the composer.

The modern performer who wants to render authentically a Baroque score can best approach these improvisational elements through the numerous contemporary treatises on performance, most of which devote far more space to *ex tempore* additions to the score than to actual instrumental or vocal technique. But even here, he has to be on the alert for discrepancies between what was written down and what was actually performed. In the field of figured bass realization, for instance, the student of the time was mainly interested in learning how to provide the correct harmonies to the bass. Consequently, instruction books are full of rules about intervals, spacing and voice-leading. It is more than likely, however, that the written-out realizations given as examples do *not* correspond to what was actually played, but are schematic condensations contrived to illustrate the points under discussion. The background provided by the fundamental instruments had a rhythmic as well as a harmonic function. Under the standard procedure of allotting one chord to each bass note or figure, the rhythmic function often remains unfulfilled. These basic harmonies need elaboration in performance. The occasional examples of such elaboration in contemporary instruction books are likewise schematic.[7] To illustrate, may I ask the reader to compare the two realizations from Corelli's Sonata Opus 5, No. 1. (Example 2 a and b.) Both are "correct" according to rule. The second is probably a closer approximation of actual Baroque practice, but far be it from me to claim that any eighteenth-century harpsichordist ever played it *exactly* like that! Authenticity may lie at the end of a trip along roads from which the signposts have been largely removed.

In the field of ornamentation an analogous situation obtains. The stenographic signs which stand for trills, turns, mordents, etc., denote ornaments that have a stereotyped melodic form but a free rhythm. The realizations given in the numerous instruction books and prefaces are necessarily schematic. That is, each realization represents the *approximate* note-values of the given ornament as it is interpreted *under certain conditions*. Actually, Baroque ornaments cannot be translated into exact note-values at all. They are expressive, and therefore "irrational." The preparation of an ade-

quate "manual" of ornamentation for the otherwise uninitiated performer is an impossibility, as I found out to my sorrow after publishing one.[8]

I have alluded to the Baroque practice of enlivening what appear in the score to be slow-moving passages, through more or less extensive improvisation in faster note-values. This is, of course, a soloistic procedure and does not apply to thickly scored choral or orchestral movements. Nor does it apply, in general, to the works of J. S. Bach, who, to the disgust of some of his contemporaries, insisted on "writing out in exact notes everything that is ordinarily taken for granted in the method of performance." [9] In all other Baroque music some such improvisation was expected of every instrumental or vocal soloist. Indeed, the reputation of performers was often based rather upon their imagination and invention in completing and varying the composers' ideas than upon their technical proficiency. Models for such improvisation may be found in a few pieces that have been fully written out for instructive purposes. Corelli left us one such model, two measures of which are shown in Example 2b.[10] Other valuable sources are Bach's transcriptions of works by other composers and some of his own slow movements in which the underlying basic structure can be detected beneath the florid elaboration.[11] It must be admitted that modern performers who can train themselves to improvise in seventeenth- or eighteenth-century styles are few and far between. The alternative is the preparation of carefully-worked-out versions along the lines of the models preserved to us. The working-out itself is, of course, a denial of the spontaneous character of the original improvisation, but it is the closest approximation to authenticity available to most of us.

Elements of expression — such as tempo, bowing, phrasing, and dynamics — are rarely indicated in Baroque scores; they must be deduced from the character of the individual piece, with the aid of a few general instructions furnished by the treatises of the time. To these must be added a factor that is not customarily regarded as an aspect of expression; namely, the variability of written note-values. A dotted note did not always last one-and-a-half times as long as an undotted note, but was sometimes longer and sometimes shorter. A succession of even eighth notes or sixteenth notes was not always played evenly.[12] To determine the relative length of notes as well as other expressive factors, the performer must be aware of stylistic distinctions, such as whether the composer intended the French or Italian style to be dominant at a given moment.

In deciding such matters, extra-musical considerations must also be taken into account. The music of the Baroque period was not written for a concert audience. The general public did not gather together, as they do today, for the specific purpose of listening to music. Each musical composition was written for a definite function; usually for some particular occasion in a church, in a theater, or in an aristocratic drawing room. A different code of performance applied to church music than to theater music or drawing-room music. Furthermore, the meaning the music had for the listener and musician of the time naturally influenced its manner of performance. The musical symbolism of the Baroque period was dominated by the so-called "doctrine of the affections," according to which certain more or less stereotyped musical figures or processes were supposed to express or correspond to definite *affections*; that is, emotions or states of mind.[13] These were exploited systematically by composers. Indeed, the formal principle of late Baroque musical composition can be reduced to the statement of a basic affection in a musical motive, and its subsequent elaboration by continuous expansion. Some knowledge of the doctrine of the affections is indispensable to the performer to enable him to determine the intended character and expression of the music.

The final problem, and certainly the most baffling of all, which confronts the performer of Baroque music is that of communication. He finds that what he needs most in his struggle toward authenticity is the ability to equip his audience with Baroque ears. For if the music communicates nothing, or the wrong thing, to the listener, of what use is the authentic performance? The conventions and associations that give psychological content to combinations and progressions of musical tones are conditioned by the experience and environment of the listener. It is impossible that the most authentic performance of a Baroque composition should reach the modern audience on anything like the same terms that it once reached the Baroque audience. If, for instance, an old tuning is used, the music will inevitably sound strange and out of tune; the attention of the listener will be directed strongly toward something the Baroque audience didn't hear at all. The same is true, to a lesser degree, of the tone of any unfamiliar instrument. If stringed instruments are played without vibrato, they will seem cold and inexpressive. Nor will the warmth and expressiveness that to Baroque ears were furnished by the ornaments replace the vibrato, because the modern audience is not accustomed to associate ornaments with warmth and expressiveness. The improvised or carefully worked out additions to the score will be interpreted by the audience in the same way as the crystallized performances of concert hall music, and if there are any present who are familiar with the work, one will be accused of playing wrong notes or of being "unfaithful to the composer." The possibility of communicating the original meaning of the music, as determined by the doctrine of the affections, is practically non-existant. The subject is too long and involved for program notes; any intelligible elucidation would require a lecture and demonstration for each type of piece, which is out of the question except at an educational gathering.

What conclusions may be drawn from the foregoing discussion? In the first place, true authenticity is obviously a chimera. Too much guesswork is involved in all points of intepretation to admit the possibility of reconstructing a Baroque work with anything like scientific accuracy. The degree of approximation to accuracy will necessarily vary according to available physical resources and according to the knowledge, skill, and musical imagination of the performers. Secondly, if the music is to fulfill its proper function, the participation of the audience must be regarded as part of the performance. Consequently, there must be some willingness to compromise on points of too great perceptual difficulty. Will this line of action lead us back to bombastic Stokowskian transcriptions? Not necessarily. While there is no use browbeating the audience with sounds beyond its scope of receptivity, there is also no need to cater to its whims and preconceptions or to underestimate its capabilities. In other words, the type of performance should be adjusted to the occasion.

It may be that the all-out, high-pressure attack, using old or reconstructed instruments, old techniques of playing, old tunings, etc., had best be restricted to something like laboratory experiments at which the audience, if any, is composed of musicians, scholars, students, and other enthusiasts who come primarily motivated by a desire to learn. At more normal occasions the performer-scholar (and who else is going to venture into this thorny realm?) must let his artistic conscience be his guide. My own can be induced to connive at an occasional bit of trickery, such as the use of unauthentic means to produce a more authentic effect. If this paradox seems to need elucidation, let us consider, for instance, the case of a Bach fugue for harpsichord, or any other piece with a complex polyphonic texture. Now there is no doubt that an eighteenth-century audience had a far greater facility in following the individual lines of a polyphonic web than does any modern audience. Therefore, I would not hesitate to use a registration that, for mechanical reasons, could *not* have been used on Bach's harpsichord, if by so doing I could help to clarify the texture for modern ears. Again, many Baroque works were built on motives or themes — such as the celebrated *Romanesca* — that were widely known at the time and would have been recognized instantly, however carefully the composer had concealed them. I feel that any sort of emphasis in performance that would bring such elements to the attention of the listener would be justified aesthetically, even though not intended by the composer.

Such examples could be multiplied. But enough has been said, I think, to suggest that while the "authentic performance" must stand as an ideal — the only possible ideal, if we wish to approach a true understanding of the music of the past — nevertheless the blind pursuit of authenticity at all costs has its dangers as well as its virtues. If allowed to become a fetish, it may succeed in a detail and at the same time cause the totality of a musical event to fail in its purpose.

1. Cf. facsimile from the original edition in Leo Schrade's *Monteverdi*. Norton, New York, 1950, p. 97.

2. Cf. Donald J. Grout, *A Short History of Opera*. Norton, New York, 1947, p. 192 ff.

3. Cf. J. Murray Barbour: *Bach and the Art of Temperament*, in The Musical Quarterly, XXXIII, 1947, p. 64 ff.

4. By Wesley Kuhnle of Los Angeles.

5. *Loc. cit.* Cf. also the same author's *Tuning and Temperament*, Michigan State College Press, 1951, p. 191.

6. Mr. Barbour's method of determining the tuning from the internal evidence of the music does not seem justified, since it is based on the premise that composers would not have written combinations that "fail to satisfy the ear" (*op. cit.*). Whose ear? (*Bach and the Art of Temperament*, p. 88.)

7. E.g., the examples in Gasparini's *L'Armonico practico al cimbalo* (Venice, 1683), Cap. IX, which are given in indeterminate note-values.

8. *Ornamentation in Bach's Organ Works*. Coleman-Ross, New York, 1951.

9. J. A. Scheibe: *Der critischer Musikus*. Leipzig, 1745, p. 62.

10. From P. Mortier's edition of Corelli's Opus 5, Amsterdam, 1700.

11. Cf. P. Aldrich: *Bach's Technique of Transcription*, in The Musical Quarterly, XXXV, 1949, p. 26 ff.

12. Cf. Sol Babitz: *A Problem of Rhythm in Baroque Music*, in The Musical Quarterly, XXXVIII, 1952, p. 533 ff.

13. Athanasius Kircher, for instance, lists the following affections: love, sorrow, lamentation, joy, exultation, fury, indignation, pity, fear, affliction, presumption, audacity, admiration, and gives appropriate musical illustrations. (*Musurgia Universalis*, Rome, 1650, I, p. 598.)

BIFOCAL TONALITY: AN EXPLANATION FOR

AMBIGUOUS BAROQUE CADENCES

Jan La Rue

Many harmonic curiosities of the baroque period may be dismissed as isolated experiments, since they produce neither positive musical results nor later influences. Now and again, however, some unusual feature attains a distribution wide enough to challenge us to find its meaning. One small but intriguing question of this sort concerns the final cadences of slow movements in sonatas and concertos. In many cases these movements reach completion in a

ABBREVIATIONS

BCM	*Collegium Musicum*, ed. Riemann et al., Breitkopf & Haertel
CE	Collected Edition
DdT	*Denkmaeler deutscher Tonkunst*
DTB	*Denkmaeler der Tonkunst in Bayern*
DTOe	*Denkmaeler der Tonkunst in Oesterreich*
HAM	*Historical Anthology of Music*, ed. Davison & Apel
MB	*Musikgeschichte in Beispielen*, ed. Riemann
MKS	*Kammersonaten des 17. und 18. Jahrhunderts*, ed. Moffat
MMB	*Monumenta Musicae Belgicae*
MMfR	*Monuments de la Musique française au Temps de la Renaissance*, ed. Expert
NMA	Nagels *Musik-Archiv*
OCM	*Old Chamber Music*, ed. Riemann (Augener)
PSfM	*Publications de la Société française de Musicologie*
VfM	*Vierteljahrsschrift fuer Musikwissenschaft*
WE	*Wellesley Edition*
WIS	*Instrumentalsaetze vom 16. bis zum Ende des 17. Jahrhunderts*, ed. Wasielewski

full cadence or connect by means of a half-cadence on the dominant to a following movement. In both situations the intention of the composer is entirely clear: the full cadence creates an independent movement, while the half-cadence forges a strong link of harmonic tendency between two movements. Ambiguity arises, however, in the case of the not inconsiderable number of slow movements, particularly interior movements, which close upon a dominant other than that of the following movement. Does the composer intend completion or connection?

The situation distilled to its very essence may be seen in the Bach *Brandenburg Concerto No. 3*, where two fast movements in G major are separated by the following enigmatic cadence:

Bach: *Concerto* (CE XIX: 59)

In the instrumental works of Bach, the *V of vi* slow movement close, usually with the phrygian half-tone descent in the bass, occurs too commonly to be considered by any means extraordinary. A good example of the phrygian type can be seen in the *Sonata in A major* for violin and harpsichord. The third movement of this sonata is in the relative minor, ending on its dominant (*V of vi* in the original major tonality): [1]

Bach: *Sonata* (CE IX: p. 84)

When the initial key is minor, with interior slow movements typically in the relative major, the *V of vi* close produces a stronger
tonal feeling for our modern, dominant-conscious ears. Thus in
the *Concerto in F minor* for harpsichord, the slow movement in
A♭ closes on *C*, leading back very naturally to the original minor
tonic in the final movement: [2]

Bach: *Concerto* (CE XVII: p. 135)

As a check on Bach's procedures, we turn naturally to Handel's
sonatas and concertos, finding there a much greater standardization
of practice. The phrygian cadence terminates a larger number of
interior slow movements, occurring just as in the Bach examples
on *V of vi* in the two relationships described above.[3] An interesting
third pattern emerges in Handel: some sonatas initially in minor
tonality employ the submediant for the interior slow movement,
yet still close on the original dominant: [4]

Handel: *Sonata* (CE XXVII, p. 9)

The following table presents in schematic form these three main
types of cadence relationships:

	Original Key	Interior Key	Cadence	Following Key
Type I	C	a		C
Type II	a	C		a
Type III	a	F		a

The probable source for both Bach and Handel lies in the works of Corelli. Numerous Corelli sonatas and concertos employ phrygian closes for interior slow movements, most frequently of Type I. This practice is already clear in the *Trio Sonatas* opus I (1683),[5] and increases in frequency with later works. In the relatively rare works in minor mode, Corelli employs only the Type III relationship, establishing a precedent for Handel.[6] The connection with Handel is particularly direct in other ways as well: where Bach absorbed merely a principle, applying it rather freely in his own way, Handel sometimes borrowed a good deal of the actual practice, especially in regard to melodic line.[7]

Apart from Corelli, Bach, and Handel, the wide distribution of the *V of vi* cadence among baroque composers may be seen from the following sampling:

J. P. Krieger, *Trio Sonata* (NMA no. 135)
Stoelzel, *Trio Sonata* (NMA no. 133)
——, *Concerto* (DdT XXX: 252)
Buxtehude, *Sonata a Due* op. I no. 7 (DdT XI: 73)
Telemann, *Quatuor* (Tafelmusik I, DdT LXI–LXII: 33)
——, *Conclusion* (Tafelmusik II, DdT LXI–LXII: 172)
——, *Concert* — (Tafelmusik III, DdT LXI–LXII: 214)
Bella, *Sonata* (NMA no. 83)
A. Scarlatti, *Concerto Grosso* (HAM no. 260)
Mascitti, *Sonata* (MKS no. 7)
Marcello, *Cello Sonata in G* (Schott)
Abaco, *Sonatas* op. I nos. 6, 11 (DTB I: 30, 46)
——, *Sonatas* op. I nos. 1, 10 (DTB IX/1: 7, 41)
——, *Trio Sonata* op. III no. 1 (DTB IX/1: 112)
Vivaldi, *Concerto* (CE no. 6)
Porpora, *Sinfonia da Camera* op. II no. 4 (BCM no. 23)
Senaillé, *Sonata* (MKS no. 11)
Leclair, *Trio Sonata in B♭* (Lengnick)

The absence of Purcell from this list may come as a slight surprise. Although Italian models were available to Purcell, we must not underestimate the strong polyphonic survivals in the English tradition, maintained by composers such as Jenkins and Locke. Perhaps because of this background, Purcell's approach to harmony seems to be more linear than structural; and his daring modulations within the course of a given movement are balanced by a notable reluctance to venture away from the original tonic in arranging the fundamental key sequence of movements in a sonata. As a speculation on precedents for Purcell's conservatism, it may be worth noting that William Young, despite his exposure to continental styles during his residence in Munich, shows a similar exceptional fondness for the tonic key in the interior movements of his sonatas (1653).

As we move from baroque to classical styles, the incidence of the *V of vi* cadence decreases markedly, undoubtedly resulting from the increased definition of tonality as a structural element. Thus such examples as may be found in G. M. Monn, Holzbauer, Haydn, Mozart, and Schubert are highly exceptional.[8] Although Vivaldi was included in the baroque list, the notable rarity of connective cadences in his works (as compared with Bach and Handel) is significant of his almost pre-classical handling of problems in form and tonality. Of the one-hundred-fifty instrumental works (mainly concertos) thus far issued in his collected edition, only fourteen employ connective cadences between movements.[9] The fact that four of these are on *V of vi* again confirms the structural importance of this chord.

In view of Beethoven's preoccupation with third relationships in tonal planning both within and between movements, one might expect frequent appearances of the *V of vi* to *I* progression. The present search, however, has failed to uncover a single example of a structurally connective use of this progression in his music. As a sample of Beethoven's attitude, it is instructive to look at the two rondos in *G*, opus 51 no. 2 and opus 129 (*a Capriccio*), both containing middle sections in *E*. There are obvious opportunities for the progression in preparing a return on the dominant of *E*, then going directly to *G*;[10] yet in both cases Beethoven makes a normal dominant preparation on *D*. His consistent avoidance suggests that the descending third progression lacks sufficient directional force to meet his intense requirements for connective chords.

Having established in a general way the locale of the *V of vi* cadences, it remains to discover a rationale. As we have already noted, the effect of these cadences is ambiguous from a tonal point of view. It would seem logical, therefore, to begin by seeking a modal explanation. Is it possible, for example, that in some atavistic way the *V of vi* chord, as a result of its position on the third degree, was regarded as a phrygian final by baroque composers? Such strange survivals are not unknown in music history, particularly in the case of time signatures; but they seem usually to result from force of habit ingrained by a universally accepted convention. Let us survey briefly the extent of phrygian conventions.

Making some preparatory searches in the Renaissance, it is interesting to note that Palestrina and Victoria in third and fourth mode settings of the *Magnificat* employ both full and plagal cadences, with only a small minority of phrygian closes.[11] This general attitude continues when transferred to organ by composers like Scheidt and Pachelbel, whose *Magnificat* versets and fugues in third and fourth modes each include only one phrygian cadence.[12]

It is possible that the variable terminations characteristic of psalmodic practice reduce the composers' feeling for typical mode endings in *Magnificat* verses. Yet in the case of hymns directly based on unvarying phrygian chants such as *Doctor egregie* or *Exsultet*, Palestrina felt no need to use phrygian cadences.[13] Victoria's hymns, on the other hand, more frequently employ the typical third mode close, perhaps because of his generally more literal and obvious use of the plainsong cantus.[14] Or is it because of his general predilection for the color of this cadence? The expressive use of the half-tone progression in many non-phrygian pieces, such as the response, *O vos omnes*,[15] suggests the coloristic explanation. Where the polyphonic setting does not directly employ a cantus, any original connection of the text with a phrygian melody seems to have no influence on Victoria. Thus the well-known responses, *O magnum mysterium* and *Ecce quomodo moritur* [16] (third and fourth mode in plainsong) are set by Victoria with no hint of their phrygian antecedents.

Divergent practices among composers should not surprise us when Glareanus himself, the great codifier of modal theory, gives us no solid precedent for a single characteristic phrygian cadence. His three examples of hypo-phrygian all contain the characteristic descending second in the tenor line, as would be expected. The harmonic effect, however, is by no means consistent, since in the first example the bass approaches the unison with the tenor's final *E* through *C*, giving a more unsettled effect than the regular *A-E* plagal cadence of the second and third examples.[17] The phrygian examples show even more variation: the first two short examples are in two parts, neither containing the half-tone cadences, while the third example contains the *F-E* progression in the bass rather than in the tenor.[18] To increase the confusion Glareanus also cites what he calls a *hyper*-aeolian example containing a cadence similar to the third phrygian example.[19]

Since the main line of tradition does not appear very clear, it is worth while to examine some offshoots. One might think that composers who took the trouble to fight the Glarean tradition by setting up new systems of their own would also take special pains to clarify their thinking on important matters such as cadences. Such is not the case, however, with Claude Le Jeune, who begins his modal numbering system with ionian even while borrowing his very title from Glareanus. Since the modern reprint of his *Dodecacorde* extends only to the third mode (hypo-dorian in his system) we must look to the *Octonaires* (1606), where his fifth and sixth mode pieces (phrygian and hypo-phrygian) show only one typical phrygian cadence [20] as against five plagal cadences. Similarly Charles Guillet, the Belgian organist, employs a new nomenclature (probably stimulated by Zarlino's renumbering of the modes) in which the *E-B* modes are "Lydien" and "sous-Lydien"; but in his two fantasies (1610) illustrating these modes, one cadence is *F-E* with a plagal appoggiatura on the final chord, the second is an ordinary plagal cadence.[21] Most confused of all is Denis Gaultier's *Rhétorique des Dieux*, where the lydian and hypo-lydian are clearly shown as *E* and *B* modes in the accompanying illustrations of Bosse, but Gaultier's "sous-lydien" is transposed for lute purposes to *G* major, with no modal characteristics whatsoever, and "lydien" is omitted entirely from the musical examples.[22]

Since keyboard works tend to be arranged in categories by mode more often than vocal works, the search for a phrygian tradition was concentrated on the former, extending through all of the chief monumental and collected editions, together with various performing editions of works in the seventeenth century. Without dragging the reader through unnecessary statistical detail, with regard to works classified as phrygian or hypo-phrygian, modes three or four, or based on *E* or on evident transpositions,[23] the following conclusions may be drawn: most phrygian pieces end with plagal cadences (*iv/IV* to *i/I*); and while the descending half-tone terminal cadence is reserved for phrygian, it occurs in less than twenty per cent of phrygian pieces. A still smaller percentage end with full cadences. A neat capsule of the situation may be seen in the *Octi-*

Tonium Novum Organicum (1696) of Murschhauser, where all three types of cadences occur in the same series of short phrygian pieces.[24]

It is evident from this brief review of earlier music that the Corelli-Bach-Handel use of phrygian cadences is actually more consistent than anything to be found in nominally phrygian pieces. From this fact two conclusions emerge: first, it seems unlikely that baroque usage is prompted by any survival of modal thinking; second, as a result we may safely consider the phrygian cadence as a connective device, since it was only by a modal interpretation that it could be considered terminal.

We can study the background of the connective cadence in early Baroque by examining the structurally analogous point of interior repeats in dance forms. The dance collections of Franck (1603) and Haussmann (1602–04) show such variety in harmonic schemes that no particular conclusions can be drawn beyond pointing out that descending third relationships are common. In the following examples the letters indicate chords at beginnings and ends of sections rather than stabilized key areas:

F   F : :   c   D : :   B♭   F   Franck, *Pavana* (DdT XVI: 23)

B♭   D : :   g   D : :   B♭   G   Franck, *Gagliarda* (DdT XVI: 30)

g   D : :   B♭   G : :   D   F : :   d   G   Haussmann, *Intrada* (DdT XVI: 138)

By the time of Peurl's *Neue Paduan* (1611), Schein's *Banchetto Musicale* (1617) and Posch's *Musikalische Tafelfreude* (1621), key schemes are already less haphazard, centering more about relative majors and minors and their dominants, with third relationships still much in evidence:

F   F : :   F   A : :   F   F   Peurl, *Intrada* (DTOe XXXVI/2: 15)
                                       Schein, *Padouana* (CE I: 186)

G   G : :   D   D : :   B♭   G   Posch, *Paduana* (DTOe XXXVI/2: 102)

d   D : :   d   A : :   F   D   Posch, *Gagliarda* (DTOe XXXVI/2: 93)

If we follow this situation into later suite composers, it becomes clear that our descending third progression must have seemed entirely usual to baroque ears:

b F♯ : : D b   Froberger, *Sarabande* (DTOe VI/2: 78)

g D : : B♭ g(G)   Chambonnières, *Gigue* (CE 102)
                           Froberger, *Allemande, Courante* (DTOe
                              VI/2: 51-2)
                           Pachelbel, *Courant* (DTB II/1: 82)

g G : : D D : : B♭ G   Jenkins, *Ayre* (WE I: 101-102)

The progression was apparently so normal that even in reverse it was not considered disruptive: [25]

F F : : A G : : C F   Schein, *Gagliarda* (CE I: 187)

e G : : B e   Froberger, *Sarabande* (DTOe VI/2: 70)

a C : : E a   Pachelbel, *Gavott* (DTB II/1: 89)

This whole harmonic climate is conveniently precipitated in the progressions of the *romanesca* ground bass pattern current in early baroque music: [26]

B♭ F g D (: :) B♭ F g (C, E♭) D g(G)

The following works, all containing the descending third relationship between sections or movements, furnish some final links in understanding the development leading up to Corelli:

S. Rossi, *Sonata a 3,* 1642 (OCM 120)
Neri, *Sonata a 4, 1644* (MB no. 98)
Legrenzi, *Sonata La Torriana,* 1655 (MB no. 102)
——, *Sonata a 3* (d minor), 1655 (WIS no. 23)
Rosenmueller, *Lamentationes Jeremiae* (NMA nos. 27-28) [27]
Vitali, *Sonata La Graziani,* 1669 (HAM no. 245)
Legrenzi, *Sonata La Buscha,* 1671 (HAM no. 220)
Furchheim, *Sonata a 5,* 1674 (BCM no. 60)

From the above investigation it is clear that in the practice of baroque composers *V of vi* frequently functions as alternate for the dominant. As an interpretation of this fact we may observe that there is a half-way station in the development between modality and tonality, a point of *bifocal tonality* combining major and relative minor to form a broader but not indefinite harmonic arena. If we bear in mind this concept of dual tonics and dominants, there is no ambiguity in the connective use of *V of vi*: for the baroque ear it is a full-ranking dominant substitute and therefore can form a logical and satisfying link between movements in a variety of tonal relationships. Certain exceptional but significant cases show *V of vi* invading even that most central of dominant functions, the connection of tonic areas. Thus in a sonata of Fux and a concerto of Abaco, consecutive movements in tonic are connected not by *V*, but by *V of vi*.[28]

The idea of bifocal tonality also furnishes an explanation for the curiously migratory nature of much baroque harmony: moving in a dual area considerably larger than any single tonality, it focusses now on major, now on relative minor. Although other third relationships and various exceptions appear from time to time,[29] the major-relative minor axis constitutes the main bifocal framework. In each case the secondary tonality, though partly out of focus, is still very much in view; and only the slightest inflection is required to change the focus. This delicate balance is clearly shown in the *romanesca* harmonies cited above, and in a more advanced form in the following example from Corelli:

Corelli: *Sonata* (CE p. 43)

We certainly cannot consider this example as modal: it has a sense of direction utterly different from the itinerant harmony of the Renaissance. On the other hand, from the point of view of classical tonality it appears inconsistent and disorganized, since beginning and end are in different keys. Such movements are by no means uncommon in middle and even late Baroque.[30] The most famous example is undoubtedly the Bach *Crucifixus* from the *B Minor Mass*, which closes peacefully in *G* after the poignant harmonies of the *E* minor ground bass. It is not necessary to give this modulation a pictorial explanation ("sepultus est"), for as we have seen, it fits easily into an established practice. An extreme extension of this same type of enlarged harmonic thinking may be seen in the very first concerto grosso of Handel, in which the opening movement in *B♭* is followed by two movements in *G* minor.[31]

In understanding these examples, neither the modal nor the classical approach helps, for we are dealing with a middle ground. It is important to stress that this middle ground is not disorganized, but on the contrary, quite highly organized according to its own characteristic patterns of harmonic migration between dual tonal objectives. While we have not reached the directional unity of the classical tonic-dominant relation, a satisfying artistic framework results from the baroque opposition of major and relative minor as peer tonalities.

A final contribution of the bifocal analysis lies in the realm of form. Classical tonal analysis often misconstrues the fundamental motion of baroque music, since it requires frequent modulations to keep abreast of the shifts in harmonic focus. Such modulations cut the music into small pieces, contradicting the clear evidence of broader continuity in bass line, rhythmic flow, and melodic extension. By applying the bifocal principle, the essential harmonic unity of large areas becomes apparent. The harmonic span thus matches the dimension of other musical elements, and we achieve a breadth of view appropriate to the grandeur of the Baroque.

1. See also the *Sonata in E major*, Bach CE IX: 98.
2. Similar patterns may be seen in the concertos for flute, violin, and harpsichord, Bach CE XVII: 252, for two harpsichords in *c* minor, CE XXI/2: 23, and for three harpsichords in *d* minor, CE XXXI/3: 31.
3. Original major key: Handel CE XXVII: 14, 21, 28 (sonatas); CE XXX: 71, 100, 127 and CE XXI: 20, 31, 71 (concertos). Original minor key: Handel CE XXVII: 31, 96, 139 (sonatas only).

4. See also Handel CE XXVII: 17, 24. For a unique example of a movement in subdominant closing on *V of vi*, see Bach, *Brandenburg Concerto no. 6.*

5. Corelli CE 32, 69.

6. Corelli CE 202, 298. Compare also CE 180.

7. Compare Corelli CE 258–259 with Handel CE XXVII: 11, 24, and Corelli CE 324 with Handel CE XXVII: 3, 10.

8. Monn, *Symphonia a Quattro* (DTOe XIX/2:39); Holzbauer, *Sinfonia a 10,* The Periodical no. 29 (DTB VII/2: 129); Haydn, *Symphony No. 103* (introduction); Mozart, *Phantasie fuer eine Orgelwalze,* K. 608; Schubert, *Adagio und Rondo* (piano, violin, viola, cello), 1816.

9. Vivaldi connectives: CE nos. 6, 12, *15,* 21, 22, 33, 36, 74, *78, 80,* 114, 128, 129, 150 (those employing *V of vi* are in italics).

10. A common Haydn procedure: see *Symphony no. 85,* first movement, preparation for recapitulation.

11. Of fifty-two Palestrina settings, only three are phrygian (Palestrina CE ed. Haberl XXVII: 57, 108, 184). Of twenty-two Victoria settings, only two use phrygian cadences (Victoria CE III: 29, 35).

12. Scheidt DdT I: 173; Pachelbel DTOe VIII/2: '48. Three other Pachelbel fugues use modal (D-E) cadences: DTOe VIII/2: 49, 54.

13. Palestrina CE VIII: 63, 98.

14. Victoria CE V: 45, 54, 72.

15. Victoria CE V: 189.

16. Victoria CE I: 11 and CE V: 191.

17. *Glareani Dodecachordon,* tr. P. Bohn, *Publikationen der Gesellschaft fuer Musikforschung* XVI (1888): 215, 221, 227.

18. *Ibid.,* 271, 278.

19. *Ibid.,* 229.

20. MMfR I: 61.

21. MMB IV: 13, 15.

22. Oskar Fleischer, *Denis Gaultier,* VfM II (1886): 136 and two following plates; A. Tessier, *La Rhétorique des Dieux, Publications de la Société française de Musicologie* VI: plates 41, 43; VII: 28.

23. See for example Hassler's *Ricercar* on *A* with one flat, DTB IV/2: 77.

24. DTB XVIII: 85–89.

25. Compare Biber, *Sonata VIII,* DTOe V/2: 71.

26. See settings of the *romanesca* by S. Rossi (1613) and Landi (1620) in Riemann, *Handbuch der Musikgeschichte* II/2: 88–92; Biagio Marini (1620) and Frescobaldi (1637) in HAM nos. 192, 199; Monteverdi CE VII: 152 (1641).

27. The limited scope of the present investigation cannot include vocal music. This single example may serve to remind us that the harmonic phenomena under discussion are not restricted to instrumental forms.

28. DTOe Bd. 85: 10–11; DTB I: 166.

29. See footnotes 4 and 6; Purcell CE V: 13, 68; Abaco DTB I: 102, 156.

30. Corelli CE 20, 53, 180; Purcell CE VII: 17, 72; Handel CE XXVII: 4, 11, 17; Vivaldi CE nos. 5, 33, 49, 50.

31. Handel CE XXI: 3.

DYNAMICS IN SEVENTEENTH- AND EIGHTEENTH-
CENTURY MUSIC

David D. Boyden

THE notes accompanying a recent recording of the complete concertos of Corelli attempt to justify a claim to a historically
"correct" performance by remarking, "Dynamic markings in all
the music of this period were based on the terrace principle; crescendi and diminuendi are unknown, contrasts between forte and
piano and between the large and small string groups constituting
the dynamic variety of the scores."

This opinion is widely held in spite of documentary evidence to
the contrary,[1] and it may be that the idea of terraces as the sole
resource of dynamics has been made plausible by the recent revival of harpsichords and Baroque organs whose mechanism limits
them to terraces rather than gradations of sound. Whatever the
reason, we should discard once and for all the notion that keyboards
enforced their dynamic limitations on the voice and on melodic
instruments for which nuance and gradation of tone was one of the
most natural and characteristic means of expression, at least from
the beginning of the seventeenth century.

The advent of a deliberately expressive style of performance in
the Florentine *Camerata* around 1600 required an extension of the
existing dynamic possibilities. Consequently, nuance of *crescendo*,
diminuendo or both, on single notes or even short phrases, in addition to the existing *forte* and *piano*, was extensively employed by
members of the *Camerata* to bring out the emotional connotation of
the text in music for the solo voice. Caccini's Preface to *Le Nuove
Musiche* (1601) explains various ways of increasing and decreasing
the sound under the general name of *esclamazione*. According to
Della Valle (1640), this practice of the Florentines spread almost

immediately to Rome through Cavalieri. Mazzochi's madrigals of 1638 are a good example of Roman practice, and an especially interesting feature is the use of letters on the score to indicate dynamics, including brief *crescendi* and *diminuendi*, as well as *loud* and *soft*. A less appreciated fact is that Caccini's Preface was known in England through Playford's *Introduction to the Skill of Music* in which it appeared anonymously and in English at least by the 1667 edition (first edition, 1654).

While dynamic nuance appears first as an ornament for the solo voice, the melodic instruments, most of which looked on the voice as a model of expression, rapidly followed suit. Monteverdi indicates a *diminuendo* for the violin in *Il Combattimento* (1624) by writing "questa ultima nota va in arcata morenda," and Fantini's trumpet method (1638) uses the most characteristic of all singing nuance, the *messa di voce* (already exploited by Caccini and Mazzochi), consisting of a *crescendo* to the middle of a note and then *decrescendo* to its end. It is not surprising that from the early seventeenth century certain theorists made a point of differentiating the technique of the different instruments (e.g., in Agazzari's *Del suonare il basso*, 1607), and began to complain about the limitations of the keyboards with respect to dynamic nuance as practiced by the voice and the melodic instruments (see Praetorius *Syntagma Musicum*, II, 68–69).

The new expressive style not only used dynamic nuances but also recognized a greater number of degrees of loudness and softness. Mersenne, for instance, already distinguished eight such degrees by 1636. Passing gradually from one dynamic degree to another is a natural consequence. Mazzochi speaks of the sound dying away to nothing, and his 18th madrigal (1638) closes with a *diminuendo* expressed by *forte — piano — pianissimo*. Similarly Leonhard Lechler (c. 1640) uses the signs p - pp - ppp - pppp for a still subtler effect. The first convincing example of the long *crescendo* as well as the long *diminuendo* occurs in England after the publication of Playford's *Introduction* containing Caccini's Preface. In Matthew Locke's *The Tempest* (1672) an indication on the score says "lowder by degrees," and the "tempest" gathers intensity for nearly nine measures of *crescendo*. The climax of the tempest is marked "violent" in the score, and the end of this piece is marked "soft and slow by degrees."

The extent of the use of *crescendo* and *diminuendo* in seventeenth-century practice is impossible to determine. Documentary evidence points to its existence, particularly in the "new" and in descriptive music, but indications in the scores, such as that just cited, are relatively rare. Dynamic signs are generally limited to the use of *forte* and *piano*, although, as explained below, these terms may have special meanings.

The use of dynamics in the eighteenth century is far easier to measure. Not only are the treatises more explicit but performing indications on the scores themselves become more numerous and specific. The *crescendo* and *diminuendo* are now indicated by signs, which in outline are the same as those used today: for *crescendo*: < ; for *diminuendo*: > ; and for the combination (the *messa di voce*): <> . These signs appear first in Piani's sonatas for violin and continuo, published in Paris in 1712. Significantly, Piani was an Italian violinist of Venetian origin, and these sonatas were the first Italian violin pieces to appear in Paris after Corelli's sonatas. These same signs reappear in the 1744 violin sonatas of Veracini (but the dynamic range of the *messa di voce* sign is extended to mean p - ff - pp), in Geminiani's music (1739) and, among other places, in his *The Art of Playing on the Violin* (1751). Leopold Mozart (1756) defines the terms *crescendo* and *decrescendo* but he does not give graphic signs for them. It is not clear when or where these written-out terms first appear in the scores themselves, although the word *crescendo* occurs very early in explanations of dynamics, for instance in Mazzochi's Preface to his 1638 madrigals.

One may infer that musicians in general felt an increasing need for dynamic nuance toward the end of the seventeenth century, judging by the efforts of instrument makers to fit the keyboard instruments with devices for producing *crescendo* and *diminuendo* (the clavichord being too limited in power to satisfy the needs of ensemble). These experiments culminated in the invention of the pianoforte (1709) — called by Cristofori, its inventor, *Gravicembalo col piano e forte* — and several years later in the addition of the Venetian swell shutter to the organ. In 1711 Scipione Maffei describes the new pianoforte in a lengthy document of considerable importance,[2] a few excerpts of which follow:

It is known to everyone who delights in music that one of the principal means by which the skillful in that art derive the secret of especially delighting those who listen, is the piano and forte in the theme and its response, or in the gradual diminution of tone little by little, and then returning suddenly to the full power of the instrument; which artifice is frequently used and with marvellous effect, in the great concerts of Rome . . .

Now, of this diversity and alteration of tone, in which instruments played with the bow excel, the harpsichord is entirely deprived . . .

[On the pianoforte] the production of greater or less sound depends on the degree of power with which the player presses on the keys, by regulating which, not only the piano and forte are heard, but also the gradations and diversity of power, as in a violoncello . . .

Maffei's evidence is important because it implies that the invention of the pianoforte was stimulated by a desire to emulate the gradations of power of string instruments, and because he specifically mentions such effects with respect to Roman orchestras of the time, presumably referring to Corelli.

Shortly after this, the cycle of imitation from voice to instrument is completed, since at first the violin imitates the voice, the keyboards in turn emulate the strings, and in the early eighteenth century Tosi complains in his singing method (1723) that the voice is trying to imitate instruments in ways that it cannot. The violins, however, still continue to model their tone on the cantabile of the voice, as a number of violin treatises state explicitly.

The early eighteenth century increased its interest in the extended *crescendo* and *diminuendo*, but the methods of expressing these effects are reminiscent of the seventeenth century. One of the earliest pieces for the Cristofori pianoforte, the sonatas of Pistoia (1732) uses the following indications to express a *decrescendo* of six measures: *for. - pia. - piu pia.*[3] This succession of terms is followed by a *forte*, which would produce an effect identical with that described by Maffei. Similar indications occur in the violinists, Vivaldi for example, who uses *p - piu p - pp* for *decrescendo*. C. P. E. Bach's "older" practice in indicating graded dynamics "is the use of successive abbreviations such as ff, f, p, pp or a more widely spaced ff, pp." [4]

At any rate, by the 1740s the long *crescendo* and *diminuendo* came into common vogue, and, as every schoolboy knows, became a stylistic feature of the Mannheim orchestra. According to Burney, the Italian opera composer Jommelli introduced this style of playing into the Ducal court at Stuttgart. As one would expect, individual virtuosi used such effects prior to these orchestras, according to Reichardt's later testimony (1776).

Even the French, who were reluctant to follow the lead of the Italians at least until the second quarter of the eighteenth century, used graded dynamics in exceptional cases (e.g., Rameau's ballet *Zaïs*, 1748). From the middle of the eighteenth century the range of dynamic expression, its gradations, and its signs rapidly increased.

The documentary evidence makes perfectly clear that graded dynamics of some sort were used under certain conditions from at least 1600 in the voice and melodic instruments, and that in the first decade of the eighteenth century the desire for greater dynamic expression on the keyboard led to the invention of the pianoforte and the Venetian swell on the organ. How can this evidence be reconciled with the lack of signs for graded dynamics in the scores especially in the seventeenth century? And more difficult to answer, where (if at all) can graded dynamics be used in scores that indicate explicitly only *piano* and *forte*? If there is an answer, it is probably the old one: our guide must be the notation and the musical context, as explained in contemporary treatises.

There is at least one clear-cut case of notation that indicates in itself dynamic nuance: the long appoggiatura of the eighteenth century, written by "small" (grace) notes. Those who wonder why the note values were not written out as played must seek out Leopold Mozart's explanation, or better for our purpose, that of Tartini in his *Traité des Agremens*.[5] With respect to the following example (Ex. 1a) of a long appoggiatura,

Tartini explains that this "small" note method is used to distinguish differences of expression. If the passage just cited (he says) were written out as two "large" notes, as in Ex. 1b, "it would be necessary to play it [the first 8th note] with more force than the second, and it would require a short trill. But as it is only a small note [as in Ex. 1a], the bow or the voice must commence it softly, augmenting the sound by gradation to half of its value and similarly diminishing it as it comes to rest on the large note to which it is joined.

This great note requires a short trill which makes it heard with more force . . ." Thus, two different notations indicate *per se* two opposed interpretations concerning the dynamics and the ornaments to be inserted.

Extensive nuance suggested only by notation and by musical context is discussed in Leopold Mozart's *Violinschule* (Chapter XII), where a number of passages, such as those involving chromatic alterations, relatively long notes, etc., are explained in relation to their usual dynamic gradations. The long-held note is also traditionally graced with the *messa di voce* (cf. Veracini's 1744 sonatas, and Geminiani). As a matter of fact, the long-held note with its nuance (and where applicable, vibrato) was considered a special violinistic effect, as such passages as the 14th variation of Corelli's *La Follia* suggest.

Quantz wishes the figured-bass player to distinguish degrees of consonance and dissonance in the harmony by corresponding degrees of softness and loudness in the performance, and he furnishes a complete piece so indicated. This information implies that the player must possess a good knowledge of harmony and also that the instrument must be a pianoforte, the clavichord being far too weak for the dynamic range demanded. C. P. E. Bach's *Versuch* contains similar information but he stops far short of Quantz.

The problem of inserting dynamic nuance in music according to notational and musical principles is far more difficult in the seventeenth century. In a few cases, such as long notes, it is likely that nuance was expected as a matter of course, but, for the most part, the insertion of graded dynamics will remain conjectural until more documentary evidence is uncovered, or until present knowledge is utilized in more significant ways. With respect to the latter, one may suggest the possibility that unusual eighteenth-century practices may be traced backward to seventeenth-century origins, now unknown or appreciated only in part.

As a final section of this paper we may examine tentatively one suggestive instance, the autographs of Mozart's ten famous quartets.[6] A study of the dynamic marking in these works is very instructive. The long *crescendo* of a measure or more is most usually written out *crescendo* (or cre sce ndo). The same practice applies to the long *decrescendo*, Mozart's usual term being *calando*, and less often, *decrescendo* (he does not use the term *diminuendo*). The modern graphic signs are infrequent. The short *crescendo* of less than a measure is written *cresc.*, of which there are literally hundreds of instances. How does it happen, then, that in a body of music occupying over 300 pages in modern score that there is but a single short *decresc.* marked? The reason is that Mozart has a *notational* method of indicating the short *decrescendo* by f   p, so that only under the most exceptional circumstances is the word *decresc.* necessary for a short *diminuendo* of less than a measure. That f   p must mean a short *diminuendo* and not *forte* followed by *subito piano* can be inferred from the above, and its intent is clarified in explanations given in Leopold Mozart's *Violinschule* (Chapter XII particularly).

It can be shown, too, that this same notation may have a similar meaning in earlier music, for example in the Mannheim school, and also in Geminiani who gives frequently the sign for *crescendo* but quite infrequently the sign for *diminuendo*.

If one begins to explore the possibilities that under certain conditions *forte* and *piano* are general terms which cover the range from *forte* to *piano*, one arrives at the theoretical possibility of short and long *diminuendo* and *crescendo* merely by the use of *piano* and *forte*. There is some evidence to support this possibility. In the later seventeenth century, Mylius [7] says "with both (*p* and *f*) it is to be noted that one does not go suddenly from *piano* to *forte*, but one should gradually strengthen the voice and again let it decrease so that at the beginning *p* is heard, *f* at the middle, and once again *p* at the close" (i.e., the *messa di voce*).

It is very tempting to apply graded dynamics to certain passages in Corelli's music, the scores and parts of which indicate only *piano*, *forte*, and (rarely) *pianissimo*. For one thing, the known possibilities of nuance in the seventeenth century and the evidence of Mozart, Maffei, and Mylius suggest it. In addition, the original dynamic markings, literally interpreted, seem occasionally to serve no particular musical function; and finally, the fact that the indications of *forte* and *piano* do not always coincide in the ensemble of all the parts — thus destroying, if literally interpreted, certain vital structural elements — argues in such cases for graded, as opposed to terraced, dynamics. On the other hand it is probable that one should not, for structural reasons, apply graded dynamics to genuine echo effects; and one should note that (in Corelli at least) *forte* and *piano* are used for the most part to underline the echo effect in the music.

The opening of Corelli's Sixth Concerto (perhaps composed before 1682; published 1714) will serve as an illustration (Ex. 2) of a "non-echo" passage, other than the above-mentioned long notes,

to which graded dynamics may be experimentally applied. (In Ex. 2, the dynamic indications in the single part shown represent identical indications in all the other parts.) Several dynamic interpretations are possible here: (1) by extending the meaning of Mozart's notation device, the first 3½ measures of the above passage could be taken as a *diminuendo* from the opening *forte* to the following *piano*; (2) in conjunction with Maffei's description ("diminution of tone little by little, and then returning suddenly to the full power of the instrument"), the "Mozart" *diminuendo* might be extended from the opening to the *forte* that follows the *piano*; (3) Maffei's information, taken alone, might be interpreted to mean that the *diminuendo* proper begins at the *piano* and is limited to five notes. It is doubtful if Mylius's information, which describes the *messa di voce*, is applicable to Ex. 2.

In general the first interpretation above would be hard to apply to anything but a short passage of *forte* followed by *piano*, inasmuch as in a long *forte* passage it would be impossible to determine where the *diminuendo* began. This fact in itself may have hastened the adoption of specific terms for *diminuendo*. One might also logically expect that *piano* followed by *forte* indicates *crescendo*. But strangely enough, the contemporary accounts consulted for this paper say nothing to suggest this possibility; and dynamic indications in a succession and in a context that would prompt a *crescendo* interpretation are far fewer than the succession of terms indicating *diminuendo*.

Since f - p may be considered as an abbreviated form of f - p - pp, our interpretation of Ex. 2 is consistent with the diminuendo meaning of the latter. The f - p - pp indication occurs (as far as we know) only once in Corelli's works: the last eleven measures of his Eighth ("Christmas") Concerto are marked f - p - pp - f - p - pp, indicating two long *diminuendi*. The first four of these markings represent exactly the effect described by Maffei.

In his full statement, cited above, Maffei seems to refer to two kinds of dynamic effects: the "echo" and the "diminution" followed by *forte*. The "echos" are self-evident in the music. The other effect, which "is frequently used," is not fully accounted for by the relatively rare indication f - p - pp. Hence it must have been introduced in some cases (1) without dynamic indications, *ad libitum* or in special musical context; or (2) by a graded-dynamic interpretation of such *forte* and *piano* signs as are not used in connection with echo effects.

The discussion above, devoted primarily to graded dynamics, is not meant to imply that terraced dynamics did not exist or were unimportant. Both types of dynamics existed side by side in the same manner and for the same reason as the *stile moderno* and the *stile antico* to whose criteria of expression they roughly corresponded. While documentary evidence clearly establishes the existence of graded dynamics although not their extent or precise use, the scanty markings on the scores themselves seem to suggest only terraced dynamics, thus fostering the erroneous idea that graded dynamics did not exist before 1750. One must always keep in mind that the musical score of that time indicated very little about a number of vital matters such as dynamics: it was merely the starting point for a trained musician imbued with the traditions and conventions of his time and inspired by his own feeling for beauty.

1. Cf. Rosamond E. M. Harding's excellent essay in her *Origins of Musical Time and Expression* (London, 1938), pp. 85–106.

2. Scipione Maffei *Nuova Invenzione d'un Gravecembalo . . .* , article in *Giornale dei Letterati d'Italia*, tom. v, p. 144, Venezia, 1711. Cited in full and translated by E. F. Rimbault, *The Pianoforte* (London, 1860).

3. A facsimile of this piece is printed in Rosamond E. M. Harding's *The Pianoforte* (Cambridge, 1933), facing p. 6.

4. See C. P. E. Bach *Essay . . .* translated and edited by W. J. Mitchell (New York, 1949), p. 162, fn. 31.

5. French edition, 1770. The original Italian edition, *Trattato delle appogiature* was written before 1750. See Lionel de la Laurencie *L'École Française de Violon*, III, 64. Leopold Mozart copied parts of this work of Tartini for his *Violinschule* of 1756.

6. Now in the British Museum. They formed the basis of Alfred Einstein's splendid edition of *The Ten Celebrated String Quartets* (Novello).

7. In Rudimenta musica (1686). I use this quotation with some trepidation, as it may be out of context. I have not seen the original, but quote from Robert Haas *Aufführungspraxis* (1931), p. 143.

NOTES ON THE SIGNIFICANCE OF SEVENTEENTH-

AND EIGHTEENTH-CENTURY

MUSIC CRITICISM

Gordon A. Sutherland

Somewhat as Renaissance men of letters first rediscovered the poetry of the Ancients and subsequently rediscovered and studied classic literary criticism, during the nineteenth century musicians began seriously to explore and revive the music of their past and in the twentieth century have shown signs of growing interest in old music criticism. But this interest is still new enough so that it is necessary for a musician discussing *criticism* with musicians to define and delimit his use of the term. Clearly, it excludes that part of journalistic "criticism" which is merely a factual reporting of events or of the "critic's" unanalyzed reactions to them. It customarily excludes treatises on purely technical matters — the grammar of a language, the minutiae of musical syntax — as such, although these treatises often contain much purely critical material in prefaces, conclusions, or digressions. On the other hand, *criticism* is the proper designation for some of what is often loosely called *music aesthetics*; for much of the latter lacks the impersonality, the detachment, the disinterestedness, and the essentially scientific or philosophical qualities that characterize *aesthetics* as this term is used by psychologists and philosophers. That musicians sometimes call it *aesthetics* rather than *criticism* perhaps stems from their feeling that all criticism must be, as most twentieth-century criticism is, primarily interpretive. Literary men take a broader view of criticism. They include in it not only the qualitative analysis of a specific work of art, but also the more abstract and more systematic criticism which is essentially polemic or didactic. They recognize as criticism not only Coleridge's attempt to deepen and sensitize his readers' experience of certain of Wordsworth's poems, but also Wordsworth's abstract defense of his own principles and methods of making poetry. From this viewpoint, either to call attention to the particular beauties of the rhyme-scheme of a given verse, or to make the abstract pronouncement that verse is not really poetry unless it rhymes, are equally acts of criticism.

Following literary scholars, then, I understand music criticism to be the act of judging abstractly or concretely, *a priori* or *a posteriori*, the goodness or badness, the partial or complete success or failure, of actual or potential musical compositions; and examining the reasons for this success or failure; excluding only those sorts of badness which are mere solecisms.

Contemporary interest in old music criticism inevitably centers in that of the seventeenth and eighteenth centuries. For nineteenth-century criticism is just remote enough to seem dated and too close to seem highly significant; and, at the other extreme, music criticism hardly existed before the sixteenth century. There is incidental and unsystematic criticism in the works of such theorists as Glarean and Zarlino; but the oldest known school of music criticism was that of the Florentine Camerata.

The twentieth-century musician does not find it easy to satisfy his curiosity about seventeenth- and eighteenth-century music criticism. Sources (original, or reliable reprints) of this material are less readily available than are the important medieval treatises on music. And there exists for music criticism no definitive study even remotely comparable to Saintsbury's great *History of Criticism* [1] *and Literary Taste*. The modern reader is thus thrown back upon isolated monographs, and such compressed surveys as those of Goldschmidt, Schäfke, and Serauky. From these fragmentary or compendious studies he is likely to jump to two conclusions: (1) that the old music criticism should *directly* illuminate the music of its time; and (2) that it stands in the same relation to that music as did seventeenth- and eighteenth-century literary criticism to the literature of its age. This essay purposes to demonstrate that these two conclusions are fallacious, and to suggest in general terms how the old criticism should be regarded.

The first of these fallacies grows out of the contemporary assumption, already mentioned, that all criticism must be interpretive

— at least in the sense that major critics reflect the attitudes and opinions of major creative artists of their times. Now even where this assumption proves correct, it is so not because the critic tries to reveal the mind of the creator, but because the creator is willing to be guided by the critic. Boileau did not attempt to reveal Racine to his contemporaries; he laid down rules for Racine to follow. Demonstrably, Racine was compliant. But where the creator — for example, Shakespeare — resists such critical legislation, the study of didactic criticism can be illuminative only indirectly. Most seventeenth- and eighteenth-century critics intended not to interpret but to legislate.

Equally misleading is the assumption that criticism stood in the same relationship to music as to literature. It did not and could not, as a brief historical review will demonstrate.

During most of the Middle Ages and the early Renaissance, literary criticism was dormant. But in the sixteenth century, following the rediscovery of Aristotle's *Poetics*, Italian scholars busied themselves with literary criticism, and by the end of the century had completed the formulation of the basic principles of the school of criticism generally called *neo-classic*. (For reasons that will become self-evident, in this paper we shall need a more precise designation; hereafter I call this school the neo-Aristotelian.) Early in the seventeenth century the intellectual headquarters of neo-Aristotelianism shifted from Italy to France, then the dominant intellectual and cultural force in Europe. Within a short time neo-Aristotelian criticism became, and throughout the seventeenth and the early eighteenth centuries continued to be, a major influence on French letters. Probably it could have become as influential as it did only under the circumstances then prevailing in France. "French" culture and intellectual activity were not so much French as Parisian. Virtually all the great French literary work of the period was done in Paris. And in Paris the men of letters and the cultivated laymen formed a tight little social group whose cultural activities centered about the *salons*. In the *salons*, critical dogmas were debated by critics, creators, and laymen; there these dogmas were so effectively promulgated that Racine expressed his unwillingness to violate "the rules," not for fear of the critics, but for fear of the cultivated audience to which his works must be addressed.[2] The authority that the *salons* enabled the critics to assume was increased by the French

Academy in one of its earliest actions. The first performances of Corneille's *Le Cid* (1636) raised a storm of controversy. Intellectual Paris was divided over the question whether or not it obeyed the critical dogmas supposedly derived from Aristotle. Richelieu instructed the newly-formed (1635) Academy to judge the work and hand down a decision. The resulting "Sentiments of the French Academy on the tragi-comedy, *Le Cid*" (1637), written largely by Chapelaine, attempted to be fair and dispassionate. It found Corneille innocent of some and guilty of other charges leveled against him. The effect in France was to give neo-Aristotelian criticism very nearly the status of national law. Elevated to this eminence in France, the creed quickly spread over most of Europe.

To sum up: from the mid-sixteenth to the mid-eighteenth century, there was in Europe only one school of literary criticism. Its doctrine is reflected in virtually every treatise of any sort on literature. Almost no important man of letters ignored it; even the few who resisted it let it be known, in one way or another, that they did so deliberately and not through ignorance. Didactic criticism could achieve such influence because critics were numerous, prolific, and in almost complete agreement about critical principles; and because they were so situated that they could bring criticism to bear upon the creative artist both directly and by indoctrinating his audience.

Only in Paris could literary criticism so quickly have achieved such effectiveness; but not even Paris produced an equally influential music criticism. For one thing, Parisian musicians were not then generally admitted to the intellectual circles in which they might have been exposed directly to critical pronouncements; for another, the intellectuals did not concern themselves seriously with the criticism of music.[3] Indeed, in all Europe the total volume of music criticism is much smaller than that of literary criticism. Moreover, whether because creative musicians tend more strongly than creative men of letters to content themselves with unanalyzed intuitive reactions, or for whatever reasons, major composers wrote criticism much less often than did major poets and dramatists. Lope de Vega, Milton, Jonson, Dryden, Pope, Corneille, Molière, Racine, and Voltaire all wrote significant literary criticism, but the chief composer-critics before 1750 are Steffani and Rameau. Yet even more important to an understanding of the relationship of criticism to music is the fact that whereas for literature throughout some two hundred years there was just one school of criticism, for music there were three different and conflicting streams or trends of criticism.

One school of music criticism rested upon the Pythagorean concept that number and proportion are the foundation of all phenomena making up what we call "real" physical existence. The doctrine that music was a branch of mathematics was preserved into and through the Middle Ages. But its manifestation in the seventeenth and eighteenth centuries was not, as is sometimes supposed, merely a strange anachronism. Seventeenth-century scientists established the modern scientific method by replacing the medieval and quasi-Aristotelian method of *a priori* speculation and comparative classification with the Pythagorean method of experiment and mathematical measurement. These same scientists applied their mathematical method to all areas open to them for investigation — including music. Through mathematical calculations, Kepler reduced the music of the spheres to musical notation.[4] Such men as Alsted, Descartes, Mersenne, Kircher,[5] Leibniz, and Euler wrote formal treatises on music. Under the stimulation of these minds — in general, the finest minds of their time — some seventeenth- and eighteenth-century musicians turned once again to mathematics as a basis for music criticism. Thus the Pythagorean music criticism of the seventeenth and eighteenth centuries is less a survival than a resurgence of Pythagoreanism — a fact observed by the bitterly anti-Pythagorean Johann Mattheson, but by few since.[6] Among the chief critics of this school were Berardi, Steffani, Printz, Werckmeister, Buttstett, and Mizler. Their basic doctrine is that music is proportion — that is, *form*. On this principle they defended the older polyphonic, modal tradition against the newer homophonic, tonal, and eventually *gallant* style then inundating Europe.

To the Pythagoreans music was form, in the broadest sense of that ambiguous word — as it is to many twentieth-century musicians. To other seventeenth- and eighteenth-century critics (again, as to many musicians of our own day) music, fundamentally, was not form but speech, a sort of language; even, a language able to communicate concepts more often expressed in words. These word-minded critics, whom I call neo-Aristotelians, fall chronologically into two groups — the Florentine Camerata in the late sixteenth and early seventeenth centuries, and a predominantly German group in the first half of the eighteenth century.

Scaliger and other neo-Aristotelian literary critics of sixteenth-century Italy preached that art is the imitation of nature; but that the best way to imitate nature was to imitate "the Ancients," who had understood nature better than any men since classic times. Also, notwithstanding their lip-service to Longinus's doctrine that poetry must move, must transport, they regarded both artistic creation and artistic experience as fundamentally "rational" or cerebral. The Camerata applied this creed to music, with only a few changes of technical terms and slight shifts of emphasis: art is the imitation of nature; but music (understood only as tonal organization) cannot imitate distinctly. Art must move; but one can be moved only by that which his reason clearly understands, and music offers nothing to the understanding. Therefore, as in classic times, we must conceive of music as consisting of word and tone united. Music's noblest part, its soul, is word. Tone — eloquent declamation — merely heightens the power of text. Music without a text, or music (contrapuntal) in which the text cannot be understood, is a body without a soul. The model for music-as-it-should-be is classic Greek drama as it was actually performed.

The Camerata's criticism apparently had little lasting influence. Doubtless it was too extreme ever to have won much sympathy from musicians. Also, in its own time it was still so close to the old contrapuntal practices as to be destructively revolutionary. But a hundred years later circumstances had changed. The facile, homophonic style had spread over Europe; yet there remained those who struggled against it on behalf of the old contrapuntal traditions. And in Germany these conservatives, the cantors, were in charge of musical education. Consequently, early in the eighteenth century there arose a second group of neo-Aristotelian critics — the most important were Heinichen, Scheibe, and Mattheson — who as proponents of the new style attacked the music and the criticism of the Pythagoreans. They took their critical inspiration not from the Camerata but from seventeenth-century French neo-Aristotelian literary criticism. They were less extreme than the Camerata in subordinating music to poetry; that is, they did not transfer Boileau's doctrines to music as faithfully as the Camerata had transferred Scaliger's. And since each critic made his own individual modifications of the literary creed in his effort to apply it without violence to music, the group never achieved a unanimity of agreement comparable to that which prevailed among literary critics. But all had a passion for classifying and legislating; all regarded vocal music as superior to instrumental, because of the added meaning provided by the text; all (to Scaliger's rationalism adding Descartes' equation of the true with the clear-and-distinct, and to this Boileau's equation of the beautiful with the true) held as their musical ideal that which is simple, symmetrical, "natural," restrained, and so clear-and-distinct as to be immediately comprehensible — an ideal summed up in the phrase "edle Einfalt." Like the Camerata, this school was vigorously anti-contrapuntal — this one, however, not merely because polyphony renders the text inaudible, but also because it is not "natural," not nobly simple. To fugues in as many as four voices Mattheson objects [7] that even the trained musician may have to hear one several times before he grasps it fully, while the untrained listener can only be confused by it.[8]

The third stream of music criticism, for which *empirical* is perhaps as good a designation as any, hardly coalesced before the mid-eighteenth century into what may properly be called a school. Yet from the sixteenth and seventeenth centuries there is a fair amount of material which is unquestionably music criticism, but whose only appeal is to experience. "This is recommended because it makes a good effect; that is bad because it spoils the effect." Such non-rationalistic criticism is found in Glarean, Praetorius, Schönsleder, Speer, Christoph Bernhard, and others. Early in the eighteenth century this empirical criticism takes a definite turn and becomes not simply non-rationalistic but actively anti-rationalistic. The first major works of this sort known to me are Johann Beer's *Musical-ische Discurse* (1719) and Malcolm's *Treatise of Musick* (1721). Musically the most important of these empiricists was Rameau — who clothed in rationalistic cliches the anti-rationalistic statements that he published his treatises on theory not to improve composers' practices but merely to bring their understanding abreast of their practice; [9] that in listening to vocal music one must not think about the text, and even must not *think* about the music, but must simply give himself up to an intuitive experience of it.[10] By the middle of the century there had developed a small group of empirical and anti-rationalistic critics centering about Berlin, of whom the most interesting were Caspar Ruetz and Christian Gottfried Krause.

Between the mid-sixteenth century and the mid-eighteenth, then, there was just one school of literary criticism, all but universally accepted; during this same period there were three conflicting streams of music criticism. And since almost all this criticism was either polemic or didactic rather than interpretive, the conflicting schools of music criticism do not throw on the music of their time the same light that literary criticism throws upon the literature. Boileau does tell us more fully than Racine himself what Racine's critical principles were; but who speaks for Bach — the Pythagorean Buttstett, the neo-Aristotelian Scheibe, or the empirical Beer? Even when the composer turns critic, his criticism may be so abstract that it throws little light upon his own compositions. It would be impossible for me to deduce Steffani's musical style from his criticism, or his critical principles from his compositions. In his discussion of Wordsworth's critical doctrines, Coleridge gently points out that a poet's theories may have very little to do with the poems in which he supposes that he embodies them.

All this is not to say that old music criticism is without value for the twentieth-century student. Much of it is interesting for itself, and as part of the history of man's speculation about music. No one with intellectual curiosity can read it without reward. Moreover, the three reasonably well-defined streams of music criticism, and the very fact that there were three, all reveal something of the musical attitudes, expectations, and prejudices of significant numbers of cultivated men of those times — attitudes, expectations and prejudices considerably less uniform than we sometimes suppose, and much like those that we see about us today. Thus extensive reading in the music criticism of the seventeenth and eighteenth centuries, even if it is not directly interpretive, will at least help us to avoid willful and laborious misunderstanding of the music of its time.

1. A misnomer; Saintsbury ignores criticism of music and the visual arts.
2. *Brittanicus*, Première Préface (1670).
3. Most French criticism of opera in this period is essentially literary criticism rather than music criticism. It treated opera not as a musical form, nor as a composite form blending music and literature, but as a literary form with extraneous musical ornament.
4. Johann Kepler, *Harmonices Mundi* (Linz, 1619), Lib. V, Cap. 6.
5. It is true that Mersenne and Kircher are more important to music and less important to modern science and philosophy than Descartes or Leibniz. But all four were philosophers, mathematicians, scientists. It is a mistake to regard any of them as being primarily musicians or music theorists.
6. Johann Mattheson, *Das Forschende Orchestre* (Hamburg, 1721), Th. I, 219.
7. Johann Mattheson, *Critica Musica*, I (Hamburg, 1722), p. 345.

8. The critics of this group borrowed (directly, and through French literary critics) from classic rhetoric. But their discussions of *loci* or *topics* and of *tropes* or *figures* had nothing whatever to do with any convention of musical symbolism or allegory — a convention inevitably complex, and thus foreign to their ideal of naturalness and simplicity. Their borrowings from rhetoric were intended only to aid the composer's "invention" — a faculty which they seemed to see always at the point of exhaustion, and to stimulate which they distilled from rhetorical techniques and devices a code that Mattheson called the *Erfindungslehre*.

9. J. P. Rameau, *Traité de l'harmonie* (Paris, 1722), Préface (n.p.).

10. J. P. Rameau, *Observations sur notre instinct pour la musique* . . . (Paris, 1754), pp. 61–62.

CARROUSEL MUSIC AT THE COURT OF LOUIS XIV

Caldwell Titcomb

During the Middle Ages and the Renaissance, music contributed much to the facets of life — both religious and secular — in the royal courts of Western Europe. In the secular sphere the joust, the tourney, the various kinds of dramatic representations, the cavalcade and many other elements both old and new helped to form what was certainly the grandest, most sumptuous and extravagant spectacle devised by the Baroque mind and probably by any mind: the equestrian ballet, *Rossballett* or *carrousel*.

Such affairs were the particular darlings of the French Bourbon monarchs. The first great carrousel at the French court took place toward the end of the reign of Henry IV at the Hôtel du Petit-Bourbon, near the Louvre, in 1605. After Henry's assassination in 1610, carrousels were lavishly staged under Louis XIII, who reigned till 1643. His marriage was celebrated by a carrousel on April 29, 1612 in the Place Royale (now the Place des Vosges) in Paris. A description lists among the participants "twelve mounted drummers dressed in silver cloth, each having two drums across the saddle-bow, and giving forth some pleasant sounds."[1] Along with these kettledrummers rode trumpeters, their inseparable companions for many centuries.

Why trumpets and kettledrums, you may ask. C. F. le Menestrier, in his *Des ballets anciens et modernes* of 1682, gives us one of the reasons: "It is always to the sound of trumpets and kettledrums that horses are made to dance, because they are accustomed to march and to move to the sound of these instruments."[2] Indeed the trumpet and kettledrum had their most illustrious careers with mounted troops on military campaigns. In fact, so exalted *intaminatis honoribus* was their social and musical prestige that they were reserved and respected as prerogatives, concomitants and attributes of high royalty.

The royal carrousel reached its peak under the Roi Soleil, Louis XIV, who reigned from 1643 until 1715. During this period he opened three *grandes places*. Two of these were the result of military achievements: the Place des Victoires, and the Place des Conquêtes (later renamed the Place Vendôme in honor of one of Louis' great generals, Louis Joseph, Duke of Vendôme). The third was the Place du Carrousel, named from the huge carrousel of 1662 in which the King himself was a major participant. Indeed so huge was this carrousel that it required two full days to run off, the fifth and sixth of June.

This carrousel embraced a great many events of divers sorts. For example, an engraving by Israel Silvestre [3] shows one of the relatively small-scale productions that took place the first day: it is an historical representation of the eighth *canto* of Ariosto's *Orlando furioso*, in which King Louis seated on an ornate carriage, along with some of his cavaliers, including kettledrummers and trumpeters, are depicting Roger and his attendants on Alcina's island.

Tremendously impressive was the great procession of the many participating groups with which the carrousel opened. Of one group we read:

> It was the brigadier-general, preceded by the first aide-de-camp, a kettledrummer, two trumpeters, an equerry and six pages, and by eight led-horses each guided by two ostlers, and by two other kettledrummers, four trumpeters and ten flunkeys. . . .[4]

Some idea of the size of this procession can be gained from the fact that the engravings of it required (besides a title panel) seven panels which, if joined, would stretch over more than twelve and a half feet.[5] And the procession contained, in all, nineteen of these mounted kettledrummers!

This parade was a quasi-international affair, in which, besides the many ordinary groups, there were five chief squadrons, designated by the Latin word *turmae*, that represented horsemen from different nations. The first *turma*, representing Romans, was headed by King Louis himself. The other four represented Persians, Turks, Indians and Americans, and were led by the Duke of Orléans, the Prince of Condé, the Duke of Enghien and the Duke of Guise, respectively.

The procession entered a large amphitheater in front of the Tuileries. There followed a series of spectacles called *pompae* (what a superb choice of word!), starting with the King's Quadrille:

The King's quadrille was the first to be presented. There came a kettledrummer and two trumpeters all covered with gold and silver embroideries, with gold eagles embroidered on the banderoles of their trumpets . . . then came three kettledrummers and eight trumpeters. . . .[6]

The rich decking-out of the kettledrummers and trumpeters that appeared in a later *pompa* was quite fully described:

The head-dress was a turban of silver cloth with blue stripes, and the lining of blue satin embroidered with silver. The feathers were in three rows — black, blue, and white. The vest was of blue satin bordered with black satin and fringed with silver; it was lined with silver cloth. The undervest and the undersleeves were of white satin, striped with gold-embroidered satin. The boots were of blue satin trimmed with black and white lace. The horse-trappings and banderoles were of blue satin, striped with black satin embroidered with gold, and all the crescents were of silver.[7]

Most fortunately for us, François Chauveau engraved a wonderful series of close-up views of some of the kettledrummers and trumpeters of the five *turmae*;[8] from this series, Example 1 shows the fourth, a trumpeter and kettledrummer of the quasi-Indian *turma*. In the face of such magnificent and detailed engravings, more words would be superfluous, nay even inadequate to describe this ultimate in lavish costumes, banderoles, drum "aprons" and caparisons. Even so, we must imagine the added splendor of the many colors.

To round out our idea of this carrousel we must finally consider a massive *pompa* staged by the combined forces of the five *turmae* in the amphitheater. This *pompa* was immortalized in a monumental engraving by Silvestre.[9] King Louis on horseback is at the center of a semicircle. At the left and right are stationed two groups of four kettledrummers alternating with five trumpeters. The counter-clockwise procession around the central square contains several kettledrum and trumpet groups, the kettledrums always in front. In sum, then, there participated all nineteen of the kettledrummers in the entrance parade along with thirty trumpeters.

This Great Carrousel of 1662, this typically Baroque two-day manifestation of the Roi Soleil's disciplined megalomania is certainly, Barnum & Bailey notwithstanding, a strong candidate for "the greatest show on earth."

One of Louis XIV's other pet megalomaniac projects was the enlargement from 1661 on of the palace, gardens and the other myriad components that made up the Royal Estate at Versailles. He kept adding to and increasing the scope and content of the Estate right up until his death. He could not, however, enlarge upon the Carrousel of 1662; but he did continue to stage carrousels. The site was transferred from the Place in Paris to the more spacious grounds at Versailles. A carrousel took place here in 1665; and, of those that followed, the carrousels of 1683 and 1686 were the most important.

The tremendous expense lavished on these carrousels was by no means irresponsible waste; for the music of court and military kettledrums and trumpets was always conceived, and rightly so, with regard for its impact on the eye as well as on the ear. The element of color, of pageantry, of spectacle, of pomp was ever present. Here especially sound and sight were inextricably fused, as should be the case ideally in all music. Igor Stravinsky well realized the crucial importance of the visual aspect in music when he wrote: "I have always abhorred listening to music with eyes closed, without an active participation of the eye. The sight of the action and movement of the different parts of the body which produce it is an essential necessity for grasping it in all its breadth." [10]

This attitude had a great effect on the actual playing technique of the kettledrummers. Indeed almost all illustrations present the player with one or both of his hands flung high in the air (as in Example 1). When Baroque splendor was in full force, ostentation, often to an extreme degree, became a general *sine qua non* for all kettledrummers. In writers of the time we find references to the contortions of the body, the becoming motion of the arms, and the flamboyant movements of the hands which elsewhere would seem ridiculous.

This is all very well, you say, but what did the trumpeters and kettledrummers actually play at the carrousels? The answer to this question is made difficult by the fact that these musicians constituted a privileged ingrown society extremely jealous of its "noble" and "heroic" art and obliged not to divulge information about it to outsiders. One of the results was that for years and years this music

Engraving by François Chauveau   Paris: Louvre

Example 1. Kettledrummer and Trumpeter of the
Indian Squadron in the Great Carrousel of 1662

was generally not written down, and hence could not fall into un-authorized hands. The music and playing technique were passed on by oral tradition from one generation to the next; each appren-tice learned his art by rote from his master, and for the rest of his career played his music from memory. When such was not the case, the musicians improvised pieces by combining and ornament-ing motives and patterns from their large basic repertory. As might be expected, improvisation was a prerequisite of the drummers even more than of the trumpeters.

Fortunately, however, a certain amount of this music did manage to get written down. The most illuminating source for our purposes is the virtually unknown MS 168 in the town library of Versailles. This volume is a collection of seventeenth-century marches, car-rousel pieces and other court music written down in 1705 by André Philidor (one of the famous prolific Philidor musical dynasty), who was a kettledrummer to Louis XIV, librarian of the Royal Music Library at Versailles, and father of the renowned chess champion.

He includes three marches for kettledrums alone,[11] one written by his younger brother Jacques, and two by Claude Babelon, who was Louis' *timbalier des plaisirs* (a kettledrummer who, along with four *trompettes des plaisirs*, stayed near the king for private service at his "pleasure"). The third march has many rhythmic subtleties and is quite a masterpiece for a composition limited to but two notes.

The most curious item in the collection, however, is a four-hand duet for two pairs of kettledrums [12] composed and performed by the Philidor brothers with striking effect at the Versailles carrousel of 1683. One brother had a pair of drums tuned to G and c, while the other's was tuned to e and g. The seventeen *couplets* in the piece contain a good deal of variety and ingenuity, with passages of homorhythm, syncopation, imitation, echoing and *Stimmtausch*. At the carrousel this *tour de faste* was not only a virtuoso *tour de force* but a great *tour de florès* as well.

Taking the corpus of solo kettledrum music *in toto*, one can see that the kettledrummer had an extremely large and varied reper-tory of motives and strokes; and that he gave free rein to his inven-tive abilities, which were, at least in the case of the best players, by no means meager.

The trumpet used with kettledrums in court and military music was of course the natural trumpet. Until the second half of the eighteenth century, almost all trumpets were pitched in D, sometimes with a tone crook to lower the pitch to C. This explains why nearly all Baroque music using trumpets and drums, usually festive in character, is in the key of D; though the trumpet and drum were both treated as transposing instruments and thus written for in C.

The fundamental was virtually worthless, so that the usable notes began with *c*, the second harmonic, and continued up as high as *g'''*, the twenty-fourth harmonic. Each trumpeter, however, was not expected to play the whole series of harmonics; rather he specialized in one portion of the range and played only those parts confined to it.

Most trumpet and drum pieces had from two to six trumpet parts besides the drum part. The commonest medium of performance was three or four trumpet parts with drums; and the trumpet parts were often doubled or tripled at will.

For the carrousel of 1686 Louis commissioned Jean-Baptiste Lully to compose a suite, in which the usual group of four trumpets and drums is augmented by four oboes. Included in the Philidor volume,[13] the charming suite consists of a long prelude followed by a minuet, gigue and gavotte. The gigue twice requires the top trumpeter to play *f♯"*, which was accomplished by readjusting the embouchure and altering the out-of-tune eleventh harmonic upwards instead of the more usual lowering for the regular *f"*. Such notes were used as early as Giròlamo Fantini da Spoleto's *Modo per imperare a sonare di tromba* of 1638 but did not become too frequent until the eighteenth century.

The admission of *f♯"* into the series of usable notes was important, for it meant that the leading-tone of the dominant could now be employed to produce a real internal cadence on the fifth degree. From the point of view of harmony, the restriction of the kettledrums and lowest trumpets to the tonic and dominant meant that the chordal repertory was meager. Yet the *f♯"* added a fourth basic harmony to the three previously possible ones: (1) the tonic in root and six-four position; (2) the dominant (or dominant seventh) in root position; (3) the subdominant in six-four position; and (4) the dominant seventh of the dominant, in its last inversion.

Finally, one other piece in the Philidor volume contains several noteworthy features and is titled *La marche royalle* (see Example

The actual rhythm suggests 3/2 as a more appropriate meter:

Example 2

2).[14] Though put on paper in 1705, it was evidently a much older piece and had been known for a long time, since Philidor added an annotation to the effect that this march was the one played by King David on the harp in front of the Ark of the Covenant! It was undoubtedly played at the carrousels and other festive court functions when the king participated. Although no instruments were specified in the manuscript, the march was obviously for two clarin trumpeters, one bass trumpeter and a kettledrummer.

It will be at once noted that the burden on the two clarinists was equalized by having the two parts cross back and forth throughout the march. The "x" marked over some of the notes in the first clarin part doubtless called for a trill or an appoggiatura. The second clarin part contains the note *b'* four times. Though not in the harmonic series, this note was sometimes written and was produced by playing the note *c''* out of tune through altering the embouchure. Such imperfect notes were required as early as the aforementioned trumpet method of Fantini; but they were rare and occurred almost always in a weak rhythmic position — in this case as unaccented auxiliary tones.

After the two clarin parts were composed, the bottom part for the kettledrums was devised. Then the third part for a bass trumpeter was added, which nearly duplicated the drum part. The psychological influence of the drum part was so strong that the trumpet part was written in the drum range too, and was then meant to be played an octave higher. Even so, a desire for a greater identity between the parts led to the writing of the low C several times in the trumpet part, which notes, when the part was played at the octave, would actually sound in unison with the C-drum.

This composition also illustrates a problem facing the transcriber and editor of old music: rhythm and barring. The piece, although clearly labeled a march and barred in duple meter, has something a bit strange about it. If one looks at the actual notes and penetrates to the real inner rhythmic life of the piece, one will see that a correct barring demands triple meter instead. This is not unique; I know of quite a number of marches of this period that are unequivocally in triple meter (and this does not include 6/8 either).

Throughout its whole history, the music for trumpets and kettledrums has for the most part existed under the severest limitations. And these limitations obtained in the Baroque period despite the unchecked, ostentatious pomp and pageantry in which the trumpet and kettledrum music was immersed, as epitomized by Louis XIV's carrousels. Nevertheless, a great deal of fine music has emerged from this medium; which is but one more illustration of the fact that exceptional works of art may be fathered by the most strict of means as well as the most unbridled. Yet does not the Book of Common Prayer speak of "God . . . whose service is perfect freedom"?

1. Michel Brenet, *Dictionnaire pratique et historique de la musique* (Paris, 1926), p. 441. (This and all following translations are mine — C.T.)
2. P. 239. Cf. also Werner Menke, *Die Geschichte der Bach- und Händel-trompete* (London, 1934), p. 44.
3. Louvre (Paris): Dept. of Chalcography, item #3919.
4. Edmond Neukomm, *Fêtes et spectacles du vieux Paris* (Paris, 1886), p. 99.
5. See Louvre: Dept. of Chalcography, items #3829/1–8.
6. Neukomm, *op. cit.*, pp. 101–102.
7. *Ibid.*, pp. 107–108.
8. Louvre: Dept. of Chalcography, items #3831, 3850, 3866, 3882, 3898.
9. Louvre: Dept. of Chalcography, item #3915 (similar are #3916, 3917). This is also reproduced in octavo size in Louis Hautecoeur, *Le Louvre et les Tuileries de Louis XIV* (Paris/Brussels, 1927), plate 15 opp. p. 88.
10. Igor Stravinsky, *Chroniques de ma vie* (Paris, 1935), p. 157.
11. Versailles MS 168, pp. 112–15.
12. *Ibid.*, pp. 106–10.
13. *Ibid.*, pp. 129–43.
14. *Ibid.*, p. 122.

MOLL DAVIES, FIRST LADY OF ENGLISH OPERA

Henry Leland Clarke

Sometime during the bloody years of the English Civil
War, under obscure circumstances, but probably at Charlton, near
Malmesbury Abbey in Wiltshire, Moll Davies was born. According
to a story long circulated among the cottages in the neighborhood,
her father was a blacksmith and she was a milkmaid.[1] But if Pepys
was correctly informed, she was the natural daughter of one of the
Howards, whose imposing country seat, Charlton House, with a
west front by Inigo Jones, dominates the countryside.

On the authority of the wife of James Pearse, the Duke of York's
surgeon, Pepys reports: "It seems she is a bastard of Colonell Howard, my Lord Berkshire." [2] Now the elder Thomas Howard, first
Earl of Berkshire, was still alive and was certainly no colonel. On
the other hand, his second son, Colonel Thomas Howard, was as
yet no lord. The father was Gentleman of the Bedchamber to
Charles II and had been his boyhood governor for three years, after
being released from the Tower by Parliament as "a man that could
do them no harm anywhere," [3] but there is no record of his being
a military man. Furthermore a man born only a few years after
the defeat of the Spanish Armada would be a little old to be the
father of a girl of the Restoration theater.

Although not actually a lord until the eldest son, Charles, died at
Paris in 1679, Colonel Thomas Howard is clearly intended. If he
was indeed the father of Moll Davies, she was the niece of four early
Restoration dramatists and a connection by marriage of two more.
He had eight brothers, four of whom contributed to the theater of
Charles II: Colonel Henry Howard, who died in 1663; Edward;
Sir Robert, Dryden's roommate, patron, and critic, who became
the influential Auditor of the Exchequer; and James.[4] Roger Boyle,

Earl of Orrery, married his first cousin,[5] and Dryden married his sister — according to a malicious line of Shadwell's, "By Brawny Brothers hector'd into Marriage." [6]

Thus it is not unlikely that Moll was brought up in one of the cottages near Charlton House, possibly with a blacksmith as a foster father, and came up to London under the powerful protection of the brawny brothers, one of whom was presumably her father.

She is first discovered boarding at Sir William Davenant's house along with his three other principal actresses in the Duke of York's Company.[7] One of them, Mary Saunderson, afterwards Mrs. Betterton, has often been called "the first English actress," but she was actually antedated by Thomas Killigrew's actresses in the King's Company.[8]

Even before the Restoration, Mrs. Edward Coleman had appeared as Ianthe in Davenant's *Siege of Rhodes* (1656).[9] But just as historians of the theater deny her the title of first English actress on the grounds that she was an amateur, so we must deny her the title of first lady of English opera on the additional grounds that *The Siege of Rhodes* was not an opera in the full sense of the word. To be sure it was called an opera, but the long passages performed in so-called *stilo recitativo* appear to have been melodramatic declamation to music, rather than genuine lyric drama. Judgment is difficult since all the music has been lost, but essentially the work belongs to the annals of the legitimate stage.

Pretense that *The Siege of Rhodes* was not really a play was dropped when Charles II removed the ban on plays. Having rehearsed the First Part and the Second Part of this work, in 1662 Davenant "Open'd his House with the said Plays, having new Scenes and Decorations, being the first that e're were Introduc'd in England." [10] He assigned the role of Ianthe not to a singer, but to Mary Saunderson, soon to become famous as Mrs. Betterton, tragedienne.

The name of Mrs. Davies first appears as Violinda in *The Stepmother* by Sir Robert Stapylton at the Duke's Theatre, November 1663. In this improbable tale Moll is already acting her typical role of *ingénue* and dancing and singing as Philomel in the incidental masque to the music of Matthew Locke.[11] Her roles during the following year included Aurelia in *The Comical Revenge: or, Love in a Tub* by "gentle George" Etherege,[12] and Anne of Burgundy in *Henry V* as conceived by the Earl of Orrery, presumably her cousin by marriage.[13] She was playing the Queen of Hungaria in the latter's *Mustapha* on April 3, 1665,[14] when Pepys first sat next to "pretty witty Nell" Gwynn.[15]

During the Plague the theaters closed for a year and a half, the Court fled, Dryden retreated to write at his father-in-law's house in Charlton,[16] and countless poor people, perhaps including our young actress, went out into the open fields and literally made their lodging on the cold ground.[17] After the Great Fire of September 1666, the Plague continued to abate, the Court reassembled, and on October 18 Moll's company presented a revival of *Mustapha* at Whitehall.[18] By the end of the year the public theaters were open again.

In 1667 the brief stage career of Moll Davies reached its peak. When she danced a jig dressed as a boy at the end of John Caryl's *English Princess*, Pepys exclaimed, "there is no comparison between Nell's dancing the other day at the King's house in boy's clothes [19] and this, this being infinitely beyond the other." [20] He was similarly pleased with Moll's dancing in shepherd's clothes in a revival of Shirley's *Love Tricks*.[21]

Her most extensive opportunities for acting were in the two plays that Dryden wrote for Davenant. She was Mrs. Millisent in *Sir Martin Mar-all*, but as usual her dancing was the chief box office attraction. The famous dancer, Josias Priest, who invited Purcell to compose *Dido and Aeneas*, was her partner.[22] Dryden's version of *The Tempest*, written in collaboration with Davenant, introduced a character undreamed of by Shakespeare, Hippolito, "one that never saw Woman." The role of this incredibly naïve, love-starved youth seems tailored to suit Moll, already famous for her "breeches parts." The king heard Dryden's prologue, closing with these inviting lines:

> What e're she was before the Play began,
> All you shall see of her is perfect man.
> Or if your fancy will be farther led,
> To find her Woman, it must be abed.[23]

Earlier in 1667 Davenant revived his comedy, *The Rivals*, based on Fletcher's *Two Noble Kinsmen*. Miss Davies, appearing for the

first time as Celania, sang the song for which she is most remembered, "My lodging it is on the cold ground." [24] The scene of this
touching love song must have reminded her of what she had heard
or experienced of those anxious nights passed in the open fields by
the refugees from the Plague.

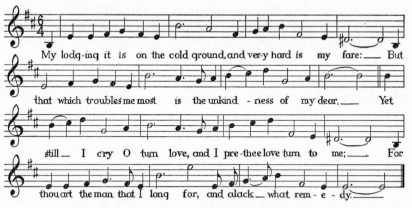

My lodg-ing it is on the cold ground, and ver-y hard is my fare:___ But
that which troubles me most is the unkind - ness of my dear.___ Yet
still___ I cry O turn love, and I pre-thee love turn to me;___ For
thou art the man that I long for, and alack___ what rem - e - dy.___

(Music ascribed to Matthew Locke)

"My lodging it is on the cold ground" remained a favorite with
ballad-singers for generations, but by 1775 the original melody,
with its wistful suggestions of the old modality, had been replaced
by a squarely tonal tune.[25] And in the early nineteenth century this
new tune in turn became the vehicle for entirely different words,
including Thomas Moore's "Believe me if all those endearing young
charms" and, a very few years later, Samuel Gilman's "Fair
Harvard."

Moll sang "My lodging" as "a Shepherdess being Mad for Love"
and, in Downes' much quoted words, "She perform'd that so
Charmingly, that not long after, it Rais'd her from her Bed on the
Cold Ground, to a Bed Royal." [26]

At the other theater, in *All Mistaken* by James Howard, presumably one of Moll's uncles, her rival, Nell Gwynn, mimicked her in
a coarse parody:

> My lodging it is on the cold boards,
> And wonderful hard is my fare,
> But that which troubles me most is
> The fatness of my dear;

Yet still I cry, Oh, melt, love,
And I prithee now melt apace,
For thou art the man I should long for,
If 'twere not for thy grease.[27]

This verse could scarcely have appealed to Charles Sackville, author of "To all you ladies now at land" and future Earl of Dorset, but he was very much attracted by Nelly herself, as she rolled on the floor in an abandoned manner, eluding the grasp of her fat lover. Approaching Nell's "keeper," Charles Hart, Charles Sackville bought her off for himself.[28]

As for Moll, there are really too many explanations of how she became the king's mistress. While Downes lays her success to merit alone, others attribute it to influence. To Bishop Burnet it was all part of a plot by George Villiers, Duke of Buckingham, to weaken the power of his cousin Barbara, Lady Castlemaine, then his majesty's reigning mistress.[29] To Pepys it was the doing of Colonel Howard, her alleged father.[30] Wilson ties the two stories together and calls the colonel and his brother, Sir Robert, "Buckingham's chief aides." [31] But Buckingham and his fellow Jonsonian wits were in the opposite camp from the brawny brothers Howard. Buckingham had attacked Henry, ridiculed Edward, and originally intended Sir Robert for the butt of his *Rehearsal*. He later transferred that attention to Sir Robert's brother-in-law, Dryden, the poet laureate, in the unforgettable character of "Mr. Bayes." [32] At any rate the Howards and Dryden and Buckingham and Moll herself all seem to have worked in the same direction, and her conquest of the king was assured.

Moll had one more stage success, as Gatty in Etherege's *She would if she could*, which opened on February 6, 1668.[33] Pepys recounts that the king was present and that a thousand people were turned away from the pit.

Moll now retired from the public stage, but rejoined her old company when they brought Etherege's comedy to court on May 29.[34] Pepys records that

. . . when she was come to dance her jigg, the Queen would not stay to see it, which people do think was out of displeasure at her being the King's mistress, that she could not bear it. My Lady Castlemaine is, it seems, now mightily out of request, the King coming little to her, and thus she mighty melancholy and discontented.[35]

At a performance of Macbeth on December 21 Pepys observed Lady Castlemaine: "when she saw Moll Davis, she looked like fire; which troubled me."

Charles provided Moll with a comfortable establishment in Suffolk Street, Haymarket, and "a mighty pretty fine coach."[36] Now officially one of the royal mistresses, she differed from the others in many respects. While Nell called the king her "Charles III," Charles Hart and Charles Sackville having preceded him,[37] and while Lady Castlemaine, to even the score with Moll, ran off with the same Charles Hart and later had many assorted lovers,[38] the name of Moll Davies has never been seriously linked with that of any man other than her sovereign.[39] Nor did she, like the others, constantly importune Charles for money and titles for herself and her offspring.

While not as expensive and not nearly as shrill as the others, Moll was far from being tossed aside. Over five years after being recognized as a mistress of the king, she gave birth to the fourteenth and last of the royal bastards, Lady Mary Tudor, on October 16, 1673.[40] Of Charles's four other children born in the 1670's, Gwynn's son Charles was then three and her son James nearly two; Castlemaine's daughter Barbara was fifteen months and Louise de Keroualle's son Charles not much younger.[41] Thus, as a bearer of royal children, Moll got the last word.

And still later she played a leading role in the two most important amateur theatrical productions given at court during the entire reign, John Crowne's *Calisto* (1675) and John Blow's *Venus and Adonis* (c. 1682).

Crowne, who had been a student at Harvard from 1657 to 1660,[42] was commissioned by the Duchess of York to write a masque with prominent parts for her daughters, the Princess Mary, aged thirteen, and the Princess Anne, aged ten. He turned hurriedly to the myth of Calisto and altered it to suit the tender years of the future queens.

Furthermore, just as Dryden had reversed Shakespeare to afford Moll Davies a boy's part in 1667, now in 1675, to give her a matron's part, Crowne reversed the traditional sex of the Thames River. In his preface the author explains:

The principal part of the Prologue being the River, my business was not to consider how the Latin Poets painted it, but how to represent it best and most beautiful on our Stage; not to trouble my head with *hic haec hoc*, to please the Grammarian, but how to have the Part sung best to delight the Court; and the graceful motions and admirable singing of Mrs. Davis, did sufficiently prove the discretion of my choice.[43]

Moll not only personified the Thames, but sang the role of Sylvia, a shepherdess, carrying the usual crook, sporting a green ribbon, and wearing a "fine white straw hat lined with red silk" and faced with cherry taffeta.[44] Dent would like to think that Cambert had something to do with the music of *Calisto*, but his reference applies to Cambert's rehearsing twelve violins during the preceding summer for a different occasion.[45] The statement in Crowne's preface stands, that all the music was by Nicholas Staggins, then Professor of Music at Cambridge.

While sharing the triumph of the two legitimate young princesses in *Calisto*, Madam Davies must have had dreams for the future of her own little daughter. Although not yet two, little Mary received a tribute in print that very year. Richard Flecknoe's latest epigram to Moll included verses "on her pretty daughter," of a sweetness in marked contrast to his usual scurrility.[46]

Madam Davies now moved into one of the stately new piles in St. James's Square erected by Henry Jermyn, Earl of St. Alban's, founder of London's exclusive West End. In a later age members of the Army and Navy Club occupying this site luxuriated in the thought that Nell Gwynn once lived here, but Dasent shows that the true occupant from 1676 to 1687 was the king's other actress, Moll Davies.[47]

In the palatial new residence Lady Mary's mother must have instructed her in the arts of singing, dancing, and charming her admirers. The little lady received a warrant from the king on December 10, 1680, giving her the precedency of the daughter of an earl, with confirmation of the surname of Tudor.[48]

Before she was even in her teens, Lady Mary was presented to the court in an entertainment calculated to display her to even greater advantage than had *Calisto* her princess cousins a few years before. Called "A masque for ye entertainment of the king," [49] *Venus and Adonis* is in fact the first full-fledged English opera.

The music is by John Blow,[50] and the text, if not his own, must have been written by some courtier who had reason to remain anonymous. Venus was by far the most important role, affording

Madam Davies ample opportunity for affective singing and graceful action, but not requiring her to dance. In 1682 — the date of performance according to manuscript indications — [51] she was not as young as in 1667 when all accounts named dancing as her outstanding accomplishment. Most prominent next to Venus was not Adonis, but Cupid, a dancing, singing, and prettily posturing role that the precocious Lady Mary must have carried off to the delight of the entire court.

While it inspired Blow's pupil Purcell in his masterpiece, *Dido and Aeneas*, the work itself was long forgotten. At present, thanks to a recent recording,[52] more ears than ever before are charmed by the beauty of Blow's music, its Restoration wit gradually deepening into authentic Baroque tragedy.

Exactly how the death of Charles II in 1685 affected the fortunes of the mother and daughter is not known. But from the accession of James II to the time of her marriage, Lady Mary received an annual bounty of fifteen hundred pounds, paid for her to Anne, Countess Dowager of Marischall,[53] who may well have been her governess. This cousin of Lady Castlemaine's [54] was entrusted with a thousand pounds "to buy the wedding cloaths of the Lady Mary Tudor." [55] The wedding took place on August 18, 1687, and the bridegroom was Edward Radcliffe, who became the second Earl of Derwentwater on the death of his father in 1696. Before her death in Paris, November 5, 1726, Lady Mary outlived three husbands and her son James, who held a command in the Jacobite army and was beheaded for high treason on Tower Hill in 1716.[56]

Moll herself is last heard of in 1687, when the parochial books still list her as living in St. James's Square.[57] Therefore it has been assumed that she died in the year of her daughter's marriage. But it is possible that the young couple provided other living accommodations for her, where she might have lived quietly on until a later date.

Never attaining anything like the legendary status of "pretty witty Nell," "little Mis Davis" nevertheless has been the subject of a number of stories. She is said to have been fed jalap at supper by Nell to embarrass her relations with the king, to have been catastrophically outwitted at basset by a notorious card sharper, and, dressed as a man, to have defeated a colonel in a duel, the king looking on *incognito*.[58]

Such tales suggest what might have happened. But what we know of Moll Davies and what distinguishes her is this: she was the first *ingénue* on the London stage, the first lady of English opera, the first actress to win the affections of Charles II, and the mother of his youngest and most engaging child.

1. Peter Cunningham, *The Story of Nell Gwyn* (New ed.; London: Navarre Society, 1927), p. 65.

2. *Diary*, January 14, 1668. (Wheatley ed.)

3. G. E. Cokayne, *The Complete Peerage* (2nd ed.; London: St. Catherine Press, 1910–   ), II, 150.

4. *Collins's Peerage of England* (Rev. ed.; London: F. C. and J. Rivington, 1812), III, 162; Montague Summers, *The Playhouse of Pepys* (London: Kegan Paul, Trench, Trubner & Co., 1935), p. 152.

5. John Dryden, *The Dramatic Works*, ed. by Montague Summers (London: Nonesuch Press, 1931), I, xxxvii.

6. *Ibid.*, p. liii, quoting from Thomas Shadwell, *The Satyr to His Muse* (1682).

7. John Downes, *Roscius Anglicanus*, ed. by Montague Summers (London: Fortune Press, 1928), p. 20.

8. Summers, *Playhouse*, pp. 83–86.

9. Edward J. Dent, *Foundations of English Opera* (Cambridge: University Press, 1928), p. 55.

10. Downes, *loc. cit.*

11. *Ibid.*, pp. 26, 188.

12. *Ibid.*, p. 25.

13. John Genest, *Some Account of the English Stage* (Bath: Printed by H. E. Carrington, 1832), I, 53. Mrs. Davies is listed as Anne of Burgundy in the printed play (1668) and appears to have created the role.

14. Downes, *op. cit.*, p. 26, 186.

15. *Diary*, April 3, 1665.

16. James M. Osborn, *John Dryden: Some Biographical Facts and Problems* (New York: Columbia University Press, 1940), p. 185.

17. Cf. Daniel Defoe, *A Journal of the Plague Year*, ed. by E. W. Brayley (Rev. ed.; London: William Tegg, n. d.), pp. 194–95.

18. Evelyn, *Diary*, October 18, 1666.

19. Pepys, *Diary*, March 2, 1667.

20. *Ibid.*, March 7, 1667.

21. *Ibid.*, August 5, 1667.

22. August 15, 1667. (Downes, *op. cit.*, pp. 28, 194–95.)

23. Pepys, *Diary*, November 7, 1667; Dryden, *Dramatic Works*, II, 154. (Note by Summers on p. 148.)

24. Summers, *Playhouse*, p. 156.

25. William Chappell, *Old English Popular Music*, ed. by H. E. Wooldridge (New ed.; London: Chappell & Co., 1893), II, 137–41.

26. Downes, *op. cit.*, pp. 23–24.

27. As quoted by John Harold Wilson, *Nell Gwyn, Royal Mistress* (New York: Pellegrini & Cudahy, 1952), p. 73.

28. *Ibid.*, p. 74.

29. *Burnet's History of My Own Time*, ed. by Osmund Airy (Oxford: Clarendon Press, 1897), I, 474.

30. *Diary*, January 14, 1668.

31. Wilson, *op. cit.*, p. 83.

32. Summers, *Playhouse*, pp. 179–80, 281–82.

33. Downes, *op. cit.,* p. 29.

34. Date given by Eleanore Boswell [Murrie], *The Restoration Court Stage* (Cambridge, Mass.: Harvard University Press, 1932), p. 283.

35. *Diary,* May 31, 1668.

36. Pepys, *Diary,* February 15, 1669.

37. Burnet, *op. cit.,* I, 475.

38. Arthur Irwin Dasent, *The Private Life of Charles the Second* (London: Cassell & Company, 1927), pp. 104–7.

39. Dasent (*op. cit.,* p. 164) discounts the story of "Captain" Alexander Smith in *The Lives of the Most Celebrated Beauties* (1715) that Moll was the wife of a goldsmith at York before coming up to London.

40. Cokayne, *Complete Peerage,* IV, 224.

41. "Bastards of Charles II," *ibid.,* VI, 706.

42. "The first Harvard man who succeeded in making a living by practising a recognized form of literature was the Restoration dramatist John Crowne." (George Parker Winship, *The First Harvard Playwright, A Bibliography of the Restoration Dramatist, John Crowne* [Cambridge, Mass.: Harvard University Press, 1922], pp. 3, 5.)

43. John Crowne, *Calisto: or, The Chaste Nimph, the late Masque at Court, As It Was Frequently Presented There by Several Persons of Great Quality* (London: James Magnes and Richard Bentley, 1675), "To the Reader."

44. From the accounts in the Wardrobe Books in the Public Record Office given by Murrie, *Restoration Court Stage,* p. 326. Mrs. Murrie's book is most detailed in its "Particular Account of the Production of *Calisto.*"

45. Dent, *Foundations,* p. 139. Dent's footnote: "H. Cart de Lafontaine, *The King's Musick*" (without page number) can only be to *The King's Musick,* pp. 273 and 280.

46. Richard Flecknoe, *Euterpe Reviv'd; or, Epigrams Made at Several Times in the Years 1672, 1673, & 1674* (London, 1675), pp. 64–65.

47. Arthur Irwin Dasent, *The History of St. James's Square and the Foundation of the West End of London* (London: Macmillan and Co., 1895), pp. 18, 182–83.

48. Cokayne, *Complete Peerage,* IV, 224.

49. British Museum Additional MS. 22100, f. 123.

50. For an estimate of John Blow, see the present writer's "John Blow: A Tercentenary Survey," *Musical Quarterly,* XXXV (July, 1949), 412–20.

51. British Museum Additional MS. 22100, ff. 150–51 gives "1681/2," apparently the date of this MS. of *Venus and Adonis.*

52. The complete opera, conducted by Anthony Lewis: 12″ LP. Editions de l'Oiseau-Lyre OL-LD 34, reviewed by the present writer, *Musical Quarterly,* XXXVIII (October, 1952), 651–55.

53. *Money Received and Paid for Secret Services of Charles II. and James II.,* ed. by J. Y. Akerman (London: Camden Society, 1851), *passim.*

54. Cokayne, *Complete Peerage,* VIII, 483.

55. *Money Received,* p. 162.

56. Cokayne, *op. cit.,* IV, 224–25.

57. Dasent, *History of St. James's Square,* p. 245.

58. James Granger, *A Biographical History of England* (London: W. Baynes and Son, 1824), III, 220; Dasent, *Private Life,* pp. 170–71; *ibid.,* pp. 169–70.

MUSICAL SYMBOLISM IN THE VOCAL WORKS OF

JOHANN PACHELBEL

Henry Woodward

THE use of symbolic devices is a conspicuous feature of baroque vocal music. From the middle of the sixteenth century composers tend to shape their music in conformity with the meaning of the text, both in its local and in its general aspects. Even Palestrina yields to the charm of word painting in the motets from the *Song of Songs*, and what Zarlino and Cerone teach about the use of appropriate musical patterns reflects what is already common practice — the use of joyful harmonies and lively rhythms for joyful matters, and the converse for mournful ones; devout consonances and slow notes at phrases of deep significance such as "Jesu Christe" or "et incarnatus est." [1] Later composers refine and multiply these natural devices in a thousand different ways.

Musical symbolism thus operates at the level of the general, in the broad expression of mood or "affect," and also at the level of direct imitation of the individual word. It is a simple process to translate the idea of high or low or slow or fast into terms of musical pitch or pace, and the expressive musical gesture, once discovered, is so natural as to be almost inevitable. Morley warns of the need for attention to such details, "for as it will be thought a great absurdity to talk of heaven and point downwards to the earth, so it will be counted a great incongruity if a musician upon the words 'he ascended into heaven' should cause his music to descend, or by the contrary upon the decension should cause his music to ascend." [2] Similarly a number in the text may be represented by a corresponding number of voices or by repetitions of a figure. Or symbolism may function through a derived or associated meaning, as in the suggestion of humility or strength. All these devices of word illustration, which are carried to such sophisticated extremes by the Italian madrigalists, become in the seventeenth century the daily bread of the German church composers.

It is not the purpose of this paper to demonstrate the continuity of the development of symbolical musical language from the six-teenth to the eighteenth century,[3] but rather to observe the prac-tice of a composer of the generation just before Bach. Johann Pachelbel's vocal compositions deserve attention on purely musical grounds, but they also offer much of interest in this connection in a study of the relations of music and text. Whether or not Bach and Handel knew this music, it is characteristic of the music they grew up with, and many passages suggest parallel ones in the later masters. Little relevant to this study is to be found in the chorale cantata and the double chorus motet contained in the volume of Nuremberg church music in the Bavarian Denkmäler,[4] but the twenty-seven choral works preserved in manuscript in the Library of St. Michael's, Tenbury,[5] are rich in examples of symbolism and show throughout a sensitive and poetic treatment of the text. The manuscripts contain five works with German texts (three of them complete psalms), eleven magnificats, ten settings of the *Deus in adjutorium*, and a mass. In expressive quality and sublimity of ex-pression these compositions are worthy forerunners of Bach's cantatas. Their brevity and the *concertato* style point to the sacred concerto of the seventeenth century, while the distinct individuality of the movements and the musical plan as a whole anticipate the cantata proper.

The setting of Psalm 46, *Gott ist unser Zuversicht*, with its un-usually beautiful text, may serve to illustrate some of Pachelbel's procedures. The scheme of the movements is shaped closely to the form of the psalm; the repetition of the music of the seventh move-ment ("Der Herr Zebaoth ist mit uns") at the end, following the repetition in the psalm, strengthens the unity of the work. The in-troductory sonata and the opening chorus establish and confirm the mood of confidence and faith in their use of a strong theme embodying leaps of perfect fifths and fourths and firm stepwise movement. "Stärcke" is underlined by a vigorous sixteenth note figuration.

The following movement, "Darum fürchten wir uns nicht," set

as a soprano solo, illustrates the use of several divergent symbols
contributing to a unified whole. The confident opening phrase, in
A major, is cheerfully and wholly diatonic. "Wenn gleich die Welt
unterginge" continues in the same confident major, but the down-
fall of the world is naturally represented in a long descending scale,
carried down a ninth by the voice, continued in the bass, and again
taken up by the voice (Ex. 1). A somewhat condensed version of

Ex 1

wenn gleich die Welt unter gin - - - ge, unter-gin - - ge

Continuo

the same material serves for an instrumental interlude. "Und die
Berge" is set to a rising figure treated sequentially through three
measures; there is a drop of a fifth at "sinkt," and for "ins Meer"
a two measure wave motion serves; this is repeated, then answered
in a string ritornello.

Thus the natural implications of the individual words are symbolized by appropriate figures, while the unity of the whole is in-
sured by the continued major key, the essentially diatonic motion,
and the use throughout of rhythmic patterns similar to those of the
opening phrase. The music employs the most direct kind of word
painting, the rising and falling figures, and the repetitive wave motion. In the succeeding movement ("Wenn gleich das Meer wütet
und wallet"), a brief chorus of some dramatic power, the wave
motion is given a more intense form, and repeated notes in the
strings embody the *stile concitato*.

Many other interesting illustrations may be found in the same
psalm. In a later bass solo with full string accompaniment, "das
Erdreich müssten verzagen wenn er sich hören lasst," "Erdreich"
naturally calls for low tones, but there is a stroke of genius in the
rolling sixteenth notes at "hören" and the awesome succession of
triads on adjoining scale degrees (Ex. 2). Even more moving, yet
less easy to explain, is the means chosen for the expression of joy
at "Dennoch soll die Stadt Gottes fein lustig bleiben," where the
solo alto reiterates a disarmingly simple figure on "lustig," in B

major (Ex. 3). This idea is developed further at some length, and at the close of the movement a long ritornello for strings sustains the mood of heavenly joy. A characteristic effect of realistic "painting" may be observed in a later verse where "Seid stille" is sung by the bass voice alone and followed by a half measure of silence.

In *Gott sei uns gnädig*, a fine setting of Psalm 67 for voices, strings, five trumpets, and tympani, we may note a familiar Bach-like figuration at "freuen sich und jauchzen" (Ex. 4), and in another place a curious representation of the idea of growth — intertwining thirty-second note patterns in the two violins developing out of a rhythm of slower notes — at "das Land gibt sein Gewächs." "Es danken dir Gott die Völker" is appropriately set for full chorus, heralded by trumpets and drums.

Psalm 150, *Lobet den Herrn*, has often appealed to composers because of its mood of exultation and because of the richness of the musical references. In some settings of the psalm the instruments named are suggested in the voices by the use of characteristic figures, as in Schein's unaccompanied version in the *Cymbalum Sionia* (1615), particularly at "Lobet ihn mit Pauken und Reigen" and

at "mit Saiten und Pfeiffen"; in others some of the named instruments are employed, as in Schütz's *Psalmen Davids* (1619), where trombones, flute, and violins appear where they are mentioned in the text.

Pachelbel's setting of this Psalm is more realistic than symbolical since he uses almost all of the named instruments at the appropriate

times. The first two verses, and the last, expressing the idea of general praise, are set as choruses; then come the succession of middle verses which name the individual instruments of praise. These are treated as a series of solos, with one duet, and each is accompanied by one or more of the appropriate instruments. The first, "Lobet ihn mit Posaunen," is an alto solo, accompanied by the organ and a lively trombone obbligato. The second, "Lobet ihn mit Psalter und Harfe," is a tenor solo accompanied by a harp. The text of the third, in the translation Pachelbel uses, is "Lobet ihn mit Pauken und Trompeten." How the trumpets got in is a mystery, except for the complete naturalness of the phrase, for Luther's translation is "mit Pauken und Reigen," and the older German "in der Baucken und in der Seyten" — perhaps mistaking the Vulgate's "choro" for "chordis"! This verse is set as a vigorous bass solo beginning in sixteenth notes and repeating "mit Pauken" on a tonic dominant figure suggesting tympani. Once the words have been heard the tympani themselves enter, building up the same figure to lead to the entrance of five trumpets, which play a fanfare-like march in two parts, each repeating after a phrase in voice and continuo. "Lobet ihn mit Geigen und Pfeiffen" is set for alto and continuo with an accompaniment of two violins and two flutes. The last of the middle verses introduces the cymbal, "Lobet ihn mit hellen Cimbalen, . . . mit wohlklingenden Cimbalen," in a duet for two sopranos. The voices move chiefly in parallel thirds, but there are occasional brief passages in imitation. The cymbal at first plays repeated quarter notes in a $\frac{3}{2}$ measure, then dotted whole notes which enable its full resonance to develop. There is a concluding ritornello for cymbal and continuo! "Alles was Odem hat" is symbolized by a tutti, all

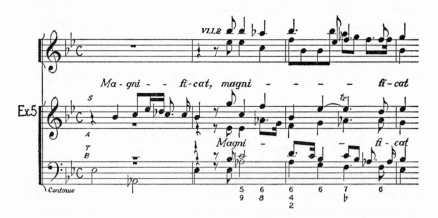

voices and instruments joining together in a homophonic passage. The final "Hallelujah" is a lively fugal movement.

The colorful text of the Magnificat evokes in Pachelbel's settings a number of symbolic devices ranging from the fairly literal to the general. Contrasts in mood between the verses call for definite differences in the general expression of the music — praise, exultation, joy, and blessing alternate with the idea of strength and power, or with pity, fear, or humility. The joyful nature of the canticle is reflected in the choice of the major mode for all eleven of the Magnificats (though of course some of the movements are in minor), while by contrast four of the ten *Deus in adjutorium*'s are in minor. But the opening choruses vary greatly, and the choice of materials and methods seems to be governed by musical considerations. All are nevertheless appropriate to the text, though some begin in a mood of quiet joy, while others partake of jubilant or majestic praise. A few measures from the *Magnificat in E flat* show a combination of restrained melisma and a rich harmonic effect (Ex. 5).

"Quia respexit" is frequently accorded a quiet treatment, often in minor, in keeping with the idea of humility. There is usually a drop in pitch or a suggestion of graceful obeisance to symbolize "humilitatem ancillae suae." A brief excerpt from an F major Magnificat illustrates the tone of a quieter movement, and an unusual harmonic progression at the key word (Ex. 6). "Ecce enim" is

often a solo with an abrupt entrance of the full chorus at "omnes generationes," as in the Bach *Magnificat*.

The manifestation of divine power in "Quia fecit," "Fecit potentiam," and in "Deposuit potentes" is always accorded a vigorous treatment, either in full chords or in sturdy sixteenth note figuration. In the "Deposuit" a descending scale illustrates the operative word, and there is corresponding ascent at "exaltavit" (with a drop at "humiles") — the whole often set as an air for a man's voice. "Fecit potentiam" is frequently a chorus, and at "dispersit superbos" a new idea is introduced — a short figure tossed back and forth in the voices to symbolize the scattering.

Of the quieter movements "Et misericordia ejus" is given a special treatment, divine mercy being suggested in a number of ways, by a change to the minor mode through unusual modulations to a very expressive arioso, by a meditative recitative, or by a melodious song form. "Esurientes" is also treated quietly, and one or two settings make a special point of repeating "inanes" at the close on a figure and in a context which is clearly intended to suggest emptiness (Ex. 7).

The "Gloria Patri," like the opening "Magnificat," may be set in a great variety of ways, but always with a particular emphasis which sets it apart from the rest of the work. The music may be divided into two sections following the natural division of the Latin text, or into four, with each part of the text repeated. However, the composer sometimes chooses to symbolize the Trinity in a three-fold division, repeating the "Gloria" with each member: "Gloria Patri," "Gloria Filio," and "Gloria et Spiritui Sancto." The C *major Magnificat* (Tenbury MS 1311) has an impressive three part "Gloria" for chorus supported by repeated chords in the strings,

each section being introduced by an eight measure brass fanfare. In the double chorus Magnificat (Tenbury MS 1356) the three-fold division also occurs, and there is a further attempt to differentiate between the Father and the Son through a process of diminution in the accompaniment. The whole is over a ground bass (Ex. 8).

In contrast to the Magnificats the *Deus in adjutorium*'s find little in the brief text to stimulate word painting. "Intende" and "festina" generally are set to more rapid notes than the other words as appropriate to a sense of urgency, but otherwise the choice of motives seems to be determined by purely musical considerations, subject to the generally prayerful mood. The "Gloria Patri" often receives a treatment as rich as in the Magnificats. In several works the setting embodies the idea of the Trinity in musical form, and in two of the larger works there is to be found a differentiation between the Persons. In the G minor work (Tenbury MS 1209, No. 8) the Three Persons are praised separately, the Father by two sopranos representing (one may suppose) the celestial hosts, the Son by the tenor, and the Holy Spirit by the mystical alto and bass. In the final tutti all voices and instruments join in the praise of the One God.

One of the *Deus* settings employs a complete repetition of the music of the opening chorus, adjusted to the different text, to symbolize "Sicut erat in principio." A similar procedure may be found in one of the C major Magnificats. It will be remembered that Bach also recalls the opening motive, though in only a partial repetition, in his *Magnificat* in a literal suggestion of "as it was in the beginning."

A few further passages may be cited, these from the single Mass found among Pachelbel's works. Here the treatment is fairly conservative, and more in the spirit of sixteenth-century church music. "Et incarnatus est" receives the emphasis of sustained harmonies, appropriate to the mystery of the Incarnation; the contrast between "coeli" and "terrae" is made clear; "Osanna in excelsis" finds a rising figure, and "Benedictus" a gentle descending one, with embellishing violins in a contrary moving figure. "Miserere" is set in the "Gloria in excelsis" to a chromatic motive rare in Pachelbel's vocal works but traditional in the period, and in the "Agnus Dei" to an expressive skip of a diminished fourth. Number symbolism is represented by the use of a single voice at "et in unum," and at "tu solus altissimus" by a solo voice in a very high register.

We have perhaps seen enough in these examples to understand in some measure Pachelbel's use of musical symbolism. A true appreciation of the composer's insight can only come from a thorough acquaintance with the music itself, for the study of isolated passages gives undue prominence to special cases. Pachelbel, along with many of his predecessors and contemporaries, found pleasure and artistic appropriateness in forming his music — from motives to whole movements and works — in close sympathy with the meaning of the text. The surface symbols are easiest to see and comment upon, but in the totality of any one piece these aspects are subordinated to the expression of a deeper meaning, and fundamentally to the use of the composition in divine worship.

1. Relevant passages from the *Istituzioni armoniche* (1558) and *El melopeo y maestro* (1613) may be found in Strunck's *Source Readings in Music History*, pp. 256 and 267.

2. Thomas Morley, *A Plaine and Easie Introduction to Practicall Musicke* (1597). I have used R. Alec Harman's edition (New York, 1952), p. 291.

3. Compare Pirro's *L'Esthétique de Jean-Sébastien Bach* (1907) and Bukofzer's "Allegory in Baroque Music," in the *Journal of the Warburg Institute*, 3:1–21 (1939–40).

4. *DTB* VI, 1: 93ff.

5. See *The Catalogue of Manuscripts in the Library of St. Michael's College, Tenbury*, Edmund H. Fellowes, compiler. Paris, Éditions de L'Ouseau Lyre, 1934. Also Henry Woodward, *A Study of the Tenbury Manuscripts of Johann Pachelbel*, Harvard Dissertation, 1952, and an organ-vocal score of Pachelbel's *Magnificat in C (Tenbury MS 1311)*, Boston, C. C. Birchard & Co., 1952.

Since the time this essay was written Hans Heinrich Eggebrecht has published a valuable article, "Johann Pachelbel als Vokalkomponist," in *Archiv für Musikwissenschaft*, 11:120–45 (1954), surveying the known vocal works and including an up-to-date index of them.

THE RITORNELLO FORMS IN BACH'S CATECHISM

CHORALE PRELUDES

Robert S. Tangeman

THE structure of Bach's extended chorale preludes presents fascinating problems in formal analysis in several directions. Many of these long preludes are written as fugal compositions in which all the devices of imitative counterpoint such as diminution, augmentation, melodic inversion, invertible counterpoint, etc., are employed. Opposed to this general type one finds that many of the most attractive extended preludes are built in a way which seems more or less an invention of Bach's own ingenuity. At the risk of ambiguity, because the term is used loosely in several differing connotations, the term *ritornello* form may be applied to a majority of those extended chorale preludes of Bach which do not belong to the fugal categories of musical construction.

The ritornello chorale prelude form seems to have been overlooked by such later masters of the organ chorale as Brahms and Reger. Coming as they did after the great Bach renaissance of the nineteenth century, they seem to have followed Bach's fugal forms almost exclusively in writing their own chorale preludes.

* * *

Ritornello forms are found universally in two important types of late Baroque composition: in vocal music they appear in most arias, whether or not they be of the *da capo* variety; in instrumental music the ritornello forms appear as the underlying framework for the first movements of concertos, whether or not these be of the *concerto grosso* or *solo* variety. But ritornello forms also appear in late Baroque sonata movements, in preludes, in such vocal ensembles as the duet, in choral movements and in vocal compositions based on the Lutheran chorale melodies.

These ritornello movements are usually extended compositions involving considerable dramatic contrast between the individual sections which comprise the movement. The psychological effect produced differs entirely from that of a fugal composition for the listener's attention is not invoked in the same way. In fugue each detail is of great importance and the total effect is of an organic whole whose parts are related to each other in the greatest intimacy. The ritornello forms (they are so varied that it seems advisable to use the plural in speaking generally) emphasize contrast and diversity in building a dynamic whole whose parts are intended to complement each other. In fugue the melodic unit and even its subdivisions (subject, head of the subject, codetta, counter-subject, etc.) are of basic importance. In the ritornello forms the harmonic unit or phrase unit is what matters. In fugue one often has the feeling that no important cadences punctuate the flow of imitative polyphony until the final one comes to conclude the "musical debate." In many ritornello forms important cadences occur constantly serving to mark off the sections from each other and to give the ear an opportunity to grasp fully the contrasting character of the ensuing section. At the end of an entire ritornello composition we usually can recognize that we have merely restated the first large section and we now realize why it was given such a definite cadence on its original appearance at the start of the work.

In explaining the usual design of an instrumental movement in ritornello form it is customary to draw a comparison with simple rondo form. It is usually stated that what the two designs have in common is a sectional arrangement which may be diagramed: A B A C A. It is then said that in a ritornello movement A need not, in fact will not, return in the tonic key on its second appearance as it invariably does in a simple rondo.

Such a simplification is dangerously misleading for the inexperienced student although certain celebrated ritornello pieces do fall into this general scheme. The *Prelude in E Flat* which opens *Part III* of the *Clavierübung* is a case in point. Usually, however, there are more than five sections in ritornello movements of this length by Bach. The Preludes for any of the so-called *English Suites* excepting No. 1, or the first movement of the *Concerto in the Italian Style*, would illustrate these more complex types in the field of keyboard music.

In the late Baroque *da capo* aria where the singer must usually work with a poetic text divided into two sections with a concluding return of the first section (A B A), it is often stated that the ritornello is presented by the orchestra alone before the entry of the voice, also between sections and at the conclusion.

Ritornello (orchestra)   A (voice)   R   B   R   A   R
    (1)   (2)   (3) (4) (5) (6) (7)

The three final sections (5–7) constitute the *da capo* and are not written out.

This generalization does not seem as misleading as the previous one cited above. It is important to note that the number of sections in an aria may be increased by dividing A into sub-sections in which the orchestra and singer alternate; this may also occur in B.

The plan may be abbreviated if the text justifies such treatment into a design such as the following:

R (orchestra)   A (voice)   R   A   R
 (1)   (2)   (3) (4) (5)

Bach wrote a ritornello aria of this type as No. 8, *Deposuit*, in his *Magnificat*, for he was setting a single line of prose text from St. Luke.

Without wishing to confuse the reader it must be pointed out that in spite of what has been said above regarding the element of dramatic contrast, in certain ritornello forms there is little important contrast in the thematic material between the various sections comprising the whole. In the *Deposuit* aria, for example, contrast is found only in opposing the orchestra and the solo tenor voice, or in color, also in varying the harmonic direction of the five large sections. The opening orchestral ritornello serves as a thematic storehouse for the entire movement yet it is repeated exactly only in the final section. In a sense then this ritornello aria is closely akin to a free variation form.

                    Ritornello (1) Theme
                    Section A (2) Variation I (from F sharp minor to A)
(abbreviated)   Ritornello (3) Variation II (in A major)
                    Section A (4) Variation III (from A to F sharp minor)
                    Ritornello (5) Theme

The significant feature of this aria, in the writer's view, is not the source of the melodic material or the harmonic progressions, which are all stated or implied in the opening ritornello, but the strong cadence placement at five points in the movement making of the whole an organic sectional form.

*   *   *

In inventing the ritornello chorale prelude form, Bach seems to have kept certain principles clearly in mind. Individually these compositions present great diversity of detail but two general conditions may be observed in all of them:

(1) The first phrase of the chorale melody is not stated until the *ritornello* theme or theme group has been heard. The *ritornello* will be a significant, arresting opening passage of striking individuality. These passages vary considerably in length, content, texture and phraseological independence but they will be recognizable as structural units serving as thematic sources for the entire movement. Frequently they are of an active rhythmic character contrasting with the slow moving chorale cantus. The melodic material in a given ritornello may be derived from the chorale melody of the composition or it may be freely conceived.

(2) The entire chorale melody is heard, usually in one and the same voice or voices, during the composition but the phrases are separated by extended interludes based on the opening ritornello passage. During the statement of the chorale phrases the voices not so engaged are working out ritornello materials.

*   *   *

How fascinating to observe Bach's achievement in adapting the fundamental principles of the aria and concerto forms to the organ chorale prelude! In the aria one of the main points of interest is the contrast between the large *ripieno* group of players and the small *concertino* group or the *solo* performer. In all cases there is a rondo-like alternation of large against small group or soloist, beginning and ending with the larger musical group. In the ritornello chorale prelude the separate chorale phrases replace the small instrumental body or soloist in a similar rondo-like structure. In order to stand out from the ensemble the chorale melody is usually slower moving than the other parts, is usually more simple and direct in melody and rhythm, and, of course, may have its own color due to the possibilities of organ registration. In inventing this form by adapting the ritornello principle to the organ chorale Bach achieved a structure permitting length and still *sustaining interest* without the exacting requirements of fugue.

Perhaps the clearest example of the ritornello technique in the chorale preludes under consideration is found in No. 20 *Jesus Christus unser Heiland*. The chorale melody has only four phrases. These phrases are assigned to the pedal and are spread out widely throughout the 118 measures of the composition. The ritornello itself consists of 17 bars of animated two part writing in a highly imitative texture. There are three important ideas in this ritornello:

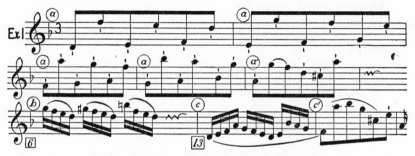

No. 20 — Jesus Christus unser Heiland

Figures a, a' and b (bars 1–6) seem, at first hearing, to constitute an amusing fugue subject quite unforgetable because of the long sequence on figure a. Bars 7–12 offer a real answer in the left hand manual with no deviation from strict fugal convention until the codetta-like figure b is stated. The soprano has meanwhile devoted itself to sixteenth note figures which are partially sequential. The whole right hand manual part here might well be understood as a counter-subject. At measure 13 the soprano states figure c. This is imitated in canon at the lower octave one bar later by the bass. This five bar canonic phrase might serve as an episode in a two voice fugue. At bar 18 Phrase I of the chorale appears in the pedal while the soprano makes a "false" entry of the fugue subject in the tonic key accompanied by the counter-subject in the bass. After one further measure the "true" entry appears in the bass while the soprano adopts a syncopated version of figure a. This bass entry eventually turns out to be free as it extends the original subject by four measures in order to accompany Phrase I of the chorale to its end.

At about this point we realize that bars 1–7 constitute a very special type of fugal ritornello. We see that what appeared to be a fugue subject will be treated in a most elastic way according to the requirements of the cantus firmus. We begin to suspect that the various figures in the subject, the counter-subject and the canonic episode will be used in "unfugal" ways to complete a large ritornello design.

The large sections of the piece are:

		Measures	Length of section
(1)	Opening fugal ritornello	1– 17	17
(2)	Phrase I of the chorale	18– 29	12
(3)	Interlude I (ritornello material)	18– 46 (overlap)	18
(4)	Phrase II	47– 56	12
(5)	Interlude II	59– 72	14
(6)	Phrase III	73– 82	10
(7)	Interlude III	83– 98	16
(8)	Phrase IV	99–114	16
(9)	Ritornello (subject only)	112–118 (overlap)	7

These nine sections merge into one another freely because the two voices not concerned with the cantus use the opening ritornello material constantly and do not discriminate in any way between interludes and chorale phrases. In this way the composition has a somewhat fugal quality due to the avoidance of sectionalizing cadences. However the unfugal aspect of a three part texture in which one voice has no relation whatsoever to the other two absolutely wedded voices is the significant feature of the style. The timing of events is also characteristic of the ritornello forms for before the one independent, slow moving voice has appeared we have encountered all the melodic material the other voices will use in the entire movement. At the close of the piece Bach evidently felt it sufficient to state only the opening subject of the ritornello and does so in the bass voice in measures 112–118.

Certain details of workmanship call for special attention. Beginning with Phrase II of the chorale in measure 47, figure a is used frequently in retrograde form:

No. 20 — Jesus Christus unser Heiland — Measure 47 f.

This puckish turn of events is soon followed by the appearance in the left hand manual of the inverted retrograde form of the same figure:

No. 20 — Jesus Christus unser Heiland — Measure 51 f.

There is also the more conventional treatment of figure a by melodic inversion in the right hand manual beginning with bar 59, at the opening of Interlude III.

The four forms of motive a (direct, inverted, retrograde and inverted retrograde) appear in the remainder of the composition. Figures a' and b are not usually dealt with in this way but do appear in altered forms from time to time. Much of the writing in this piece is as freely imaginative as that in Bach's longer fugue episodes.

* * *

Composers in search of fresh forms in which to place cantus firmus materials will find stimulation and inspiration in knowing the ritornello chorale preludes of Bach. Organists and ministers of music will find these extended compositions to be magnificent sermons in the tonal language in which theology and musical ingenuity combine to produce works of sublime eloquence, interest and beauty. Let none of us forget the inscription with which the humble Leipzig cantor was wont to conclude his scores: SOLI DEO GLORIA.

DOMENICO SCARLATTI'S CHORAL MUSIC

Ralph Kirkpatrick

Mᴏsᴛ of Domenico Scarlatti's surviving choral music appears to date from the early part of his life, particularly from the period of his tenure as *maestro di cappella* at the Vatican (1715–1719) [1] and of his service at the Portuguese Court (c. 1720–1729). None of the music which he composed in his early youth (1701–1705) for the functions of the viceregal chapel in Naples appears to have survived. In that latter part of his life (1729–1757) which he spent in Spain, he seems to have devoted himself almost exclusively to keyboard music. (The only definitely known non-keyboard work of this period is the A major *Salve Regina* for soprano and strings, reputedly his last work.)

The choral music which Domenico Scarlatti and his contemporaries composed for papal and royal chapels was seldom designed for large bodies of performers. The regular forces of the Cappella Giulia in Domenico's time consisted of sixteen to eighteen singers. Those of his later patron João V of Portugal, who maintained some of the most extravagant church music in Europe, included only about twice as many. Walther (*Musicalisches Lexicon*, 1732) lists the Portuguese royal chapel under Domenico's direction as consisting of thirty or forty singers and about as many instrumentalists. The royal chapel in Madrid, with which, however, Domenico never seems to have been closely associated, had fifteen singers, three organists, and thirty-five instrumentalists in 1756.

Only on special occasions, particularly outdoor performances, were these forces augmented. The archives of the Cappella Giulia record the engagement for certain high feast days of supernumerary singers and the use of additional choirs.

Much of this choral music was sung by solo voices, or, in the ordinary functions, by seldom more than four voices to a part. The sopranos and altos were of course *castrati*.

Of the music which Domenico composed for the Vatican and for the Portuguese Court, remarkably little has survived. The archives of the Cappella Giulia include two *Miserere's* (one of them Domenico's only known musical autograph) and a simple four-part setting of the hymn *Iste Confessor* (probably designed for the outdoor processional that took place on the occasion of the translation of the body of St. Leo on April 11, 1715). The great *Stabat Mater* for double five-part chorus and continuo probably dates also from this period.

The church music which Domenico composed for Rome and Lisbon lies, like that of his father and many Latin contemporaries, between the two extremes of simple four-part chordal writing with organ accompaniment, and the neo-Palestrina polyphony of so-called *a cappella* style. Both styles, whether accompanied or not, are clearly under the domination of *basso continuo* harmony.

Extremely competent, brilliant in sound, but undistinguishable from a mass of equally competent contemporary church music are those examples of Domenico's straight *basso continuo* style such as the four-part setting of the *Iste Confessor* for the Cappella Giulia, and the C major *Te Deum* now in the archives of the See of Lisbon. This latter, like the surviving examples of Domenico's secular choral writing (the *Contesa delle Stagioni*, performed in Lisbon on September 6, 1720), bases its principal effectiveness on the opposition in broad and simple harmonies, with continuo accompaniment, of a *concertino* of solo voices and a *ripieno* which for the most part seldom augments the actual partwriting, but doubles the four voices of the solo group.

None of Domenico's surviving church music, except the A major *Salve Regina* (for solo voice), has instrumental accompaniment other than organ continuo. Even in Domenico's secular vocal ensemble music, the *concertante* style of the instrumental accompaniment is but rudimentary. (The opening and closing choruses of the surviving part of the *Contesa delle Stagioni* are accompanied, with instrumental interludes, by strings and two trumpets.) Only in solo arias and in the Vienna solo cantatas with strings are there florid instrumental parts.

Closer to the *a cappella* style are such pieces as the two settings of the *Miserere*, which have no indication of continuo, and which alternate rhythmically simple chordal writing with strands of incipient polyphony consisting of occasional outstanding phrases of independent melodic interest, or of fragmentary imitative entrances of parts. The harmonic vocabulary of these pieces is wilfully restrained, with limited and utterly orthodox use of dissonance, and narrow modulatory range. They give no indication whatever that they are by the same composer who was later to develop the most strikingly original harmonic style of his century.

A genuine example of neo-polyphony, in obvious even if *basso-continuo*-ridden homage to Palestrina, is the four-part *a cappella* Mass in G minor, copied out in 1754 in one of the part-books of the royal chapel in Madrid. (The same volume contains a Mass by Victoria.) This Mass of Domenico's might very probably have been written in Rome. I have not been able to ascertain whether it is identical with one reputedly preserved in the archives of the Basilica Liberiana (Santa Maria Maggiore). The Madrid Mass is a monument of neo-polyphonic competence, severe and restrained even in its espressivo passages. All of its vocal lines are good, if not always strikingly distinguished. Its outstanding characteristic is its unfailing rhythmic interest, not only in the construction of the separate vocal phrases, but in the ensemble of the parts. Here one understands the basis which such an *a cappella* discipline furnished Domenico Scarlatti for the inexhaustible rhythmic variety of his harpsichord sonatas, and for his frequent and striking independence from any tyranny of the bar line. One understands the origin of the rhythmic interrelationships that lend to his two-part keyboard writing a polyphony characteristic of a much greater ensemble of parts. Here too, in the rigorous and restrained conduct of his vocal parts, one understands the solidity of the basis from which Domenico departs in hitherto unprecedented audacities of keyboard partwriting.

That Domenico owed this discipline to the influence of his father and of certain of his father's contemporaries with whom he was associated is made perfectly clear, not only by their own music, but by their frequent expressions of verbal homage to the counterpoint of an earlier day. Francesco Gasparini speaks with reverence of Frescobaldi in the preface to his *L'Armonico Pratico al Cimbalo*, and Bernardo Pasquini set down the following effusion at the end of a volume of motets by Palestrina that he copied out in 1090. "Whoever pretends to be a musician, or organist, and does not taste the nectar, who does not drink the milk of these divine compositions of Palestrina, is without doubt, and always will be, a miserable wretch. Sentiment of Bernardo Pasquini, pitiful ignoramus."

Domenico himself in later life, on the occasion of putting into score two hymns of the Netherlands composer Pierre du Hotz, points out somewhat ironically that "many modern theatrical composers may observe and profit (if indeed they will) by the true fashion and the true laws of writing counterpoint, a thing I observe in few today, and yet which I hear praised."

To us, despite these verbal protests of allegiance, the actual musical homage of Domenico and Alessandro Scarlatti to the age of Palestrina often seems pale enough indeed. It often inspires in us no greater special interest than much of the painting of eighteenth-century churches as compared with the works of the early and high Renaissance. Yet, like much of the painting, this music was frequently better suited to its age and to its function than would have been a series of outstanding and obtrusive masterpieces.

Of Domenico Scarlatti's compositions in this style, few can command our interest independently of their relationship to the composer of the keyboard sonatas. The one *a cappella* piece of his (fortunately published) which along with the A major *Salve Regina* can command attention for its own sake, is the *Stabat Mater*. It is Domenico's only really outstanding choral work. It has a considerably broader tonal scheme than his other church pieces, and the setting of the words abounds in eloquent melodic declamations and striking turns of harmony. Particularly expressive are Domenico's settings of such words as "moriendo," and his setting of the word "inflammatus" in every way foreshadows the fire and intensity of his harpsichord writing.

1. Source references for the factual statements of this essay may be found in my *Domenico Scarlatti* (Princeton University Press, 1953), along with a catalogue of Domenico's known vocal music, and documentation concerning his activities as chapelmaster.

SOME WORKS FALSELY ASCRIBED TO
FRIEDEMANN BACH

George Benson Weston

Two Minuets by J. W. Hässler. Erfurt, 1782.

Hässler's Minuets ascribed by Hompesch to W. F.
Bach. Leipsig, circa 1886.

Reproduced from the title page of J. W. Hässler's
Sechs leichte Sonaten. Erfurt, 1786.

Nºs 3, 4 & 5, of

REVIVALS,

Consisting of Pieces hitherto only existing in Manuscript or which have been long out of print. Selected from the Works of Eminent Masters.

Edited by

J. W. DAVISON.

Nº 3. SONATA in C MAJOR. *Price* 5/-
4. SONATA in E MINOR. — 5/-
5. SONATA in E FLAT MAJOR. 5/-

FOR THE

Piano-Forte,

Composed by

WILHELM FRIEDEMANN BACH.

Ent. Sta. Hall.　　　　　　　　　　　Nº 5. Price 5/-

LONDON:
DUNCAN DAVISON & Cº.
244. REGENT STREET, CORNER OF LITTLE ARGYLL ST.

"REVIVALS". Nº 1. consists of W. FRIEDEMANN BACH'S Grand Fantasia in E & A minor & major. 6/-
Dº ... 2 .... Dº ...... Dramatic Fantasia in C major 6/-

Reproduced from the title page of J. W.
Davison's *Revivals*.

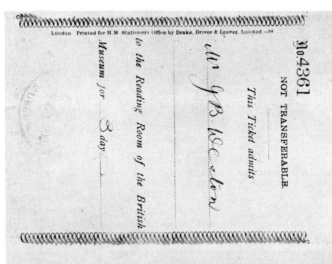

London Printed for H.M Stationery Office by Drake, Driver & Leaver, Limited.—58

№ 4361

NOT TRANSFERABLE.

This Ticket admits

Mr G.B. Weston

to the Reading Room of the British Museum for 3 day

Permission to use the Reading-Room and Students' Room in the Department of MSS. will be withdrawn from any person who shall write or make marks on any part of a Printed Book, Manuscript, or Map belonging to the Museum.

Readers are not, under any circumstances, to take a Book, Manuscript, or Map out of the Reading Room or Students' Room.

Before leaving either Room, Readers are particularly requested to return MSS. to an attendant at the receiving counter, and to reclaim the Tickets, READERS BEING RESPONSIBLE FOR THE MSS. SO LONG AS THE TICKETS REMAIN UNCANCELLED

Collection and Number of MS. wanted.

Additional 23 929

(Date) May 29, 1900   G.B. Weston   (Signature).

Please to restore each Volume of the Catalogue to its place, as soon as done with.

W B & L (87ss)—1435E—20000-7-99

SOME WORKS FALSELY ASCRIBED TO

FRIEDEMANN BACH

George Benson Weston

It was some time during the winter of 1911–12 that I learned that the Organ Concerto in D-minor, published by Peters in 1844 as a work of J. S. Bach's oldest son Wilhelm Friedemann (1710–1784), had been shown to be an arrangement by his father of a Concerto Grosso (no. 11 of Opus 3) by Vivaldi. Having discovered years before, in 1900, that a quantity of keyboard music published in Germany and England as Friedemann Bach's was spurious, I decided to call attention to this, and wrote in German a short article dealing with these publications.[1] I had expected to include a discussion of this matter in a new study of this much-misunderstood and most gifted of the sons of J. S. Bach, but an opportunity to examine the fundamental material in the then Royal Prussian Library in Berlin never occurred. In this article I limited myself to giving the bare facts regarding the true sources of the works fraudulently ascribed to Friedemann, without mentioning that this was my own discovery.

It has been suggested to me that a short account of how this came about might not be wholly without interest.

I had become interested in Friedemann early in 1898 at Harvard, through the notice of him in the first edition of Grove's Dictionary — inaccurate, as were all the earlier encyclopaedia accounts of him. Ironically, the only work under his name at that time in the Harvard College Library was the Peters edition four-hand piano arrangement of the J. S. Bach-Vivaldi organ concerto. This work — now frequently played both in Siloti's orchestral version and in J. S. Bach's organ arrangement — impressed me so deeply that, looking about, I came upon the volume of sonatas, fantasias and smaller pieces edited for the Steingräber edition by Hugo Riemann, as well as his unfortunately pedantic and hard-to-read arrangements for two pianos of five harpsichord-and-string concertos, and early two-harpsichord sonata — which latter had been edited about 1862 by Brahms (anonymously) for Rieter-Biedermann, and included, by the error of Count Waldersee, in the monumental edition of J. S. Bach's works as by him. But however impractical Riemann's concerto-arrangements were, they were based on manuscripts — some autograph — of genuine Friedemann works, and appealed to me so strongly that I resolved during a forthcoming stay in Europe to secure as many full scores of them, — and of other significant works of his, — as I could.

My first opportunity came in Vienna in the autumn of 1898. The librarian of the renowned Bibliothek der Gesellschaft der Musikfreunde, the eminent musicologist Dr. Eusebius Mandyczewski, received the young American kindly, though with some surprise that a trans-Atlantic music-lover should have developed an interest in Friedemann Bach. The chief Friedemann items in the collection were eighteenth-century manuscripts of his largest-scale instrumental work, the concerto in E-flat major for two harpsichords, strings, horns, trumpets and drums; and two copies of the cantata: "Lasset uns ablegen die Werke der Finsternis und anlegen die Waffen des Lichts" ("Let us put off the works of darkness and put on the armor of light") (Romans, XIII, 12), one of which had belonged to his younger brother Carl Philipp Emanuel (1714–1788), and bore notes by the latter of performances he gave in his Hamburg church in 1772 and 1779.

As during this Vienna stay I was primarily interested in the concerto, I asked Dr. Mandyczewski for permission to have a copy of it made, which was readily granted. Those were the days before photostats. I could not stay in Vienna long enough to make the copy myself, but Dr. Mandyczewski recommended one Wilhelm Kupfer, whom Brahms had often employed, who put together, from the separate parts of the manuscript, a very satisfactory full score, which was forwarded to me in Florence. Here I turned for a time from music to the study of early Italian literature in the University and libraries, and did not take up further study of

Friedemann until the following summer in Switzerland. Here I secured from Dresden a copy of the E-minor concerto for harpsichord and strings from the manuscript in the Royal Library. This is a work not only of great originality and intrinsic worth, but one of the few to which he gave the date (1767), and the only one of which he gave his own critical estimate — "das sehr practicable Concert," he calls it in the dedication to a Saxon princess.

After a renewed stay in Florence I returned late in 1899 to Vienna for work at the University, and in odd moments copied the separate parts of this score, which were soon used for a performance as a piano quintet in a private circle. On that occasion one of the violin parts was taken by the later distinguished conductor Artur Bodanzky, at that time a member of the Vienna Philharmonic orchestra. He was so much impressed with the work that he borrowed the parts to play with another group.

During occasional visits to the Musikfreunde library I became acquainted with a young musicologist, Hugo Botstiber — the author later of a history of the Overture — whom Dr. Mandyczewski had engaged to bring the catalogue of the library up to date. One day he asked me if I knew the review by Robert Eitner — in one of the 1886 numbers of his "Monatshefte für Musikgeschichte" — of the then recent publication of a number of keyboard pieces by Friedemann Bach. From this chance question stemmed my investigation of these pieces, resulting in proving them spurious. I read Eitner's severe review of these works, in which he did not shrink from suggesting that John Sebastian's predilection for Friedemann was due to parental indulgence — and sent for them. After an impatiently endured delay they arrived; and even a hasty glance revealed that nobody familiar with Friedemann's style could imagine them as genuine works of this master. But how to prove this? I seemed to have reached a dead end.

A few weeks later, however, by an improbable stroke of good fortune, the clue came into my hands. On the left-hand arcaded side of the Vienna opera house was the shop of the music publisher and dealer Albert Gutmann. One of his salesmen occasionally arranged piles of music for me to look over. Dropping in one day, I began on a pile of sheet music. Most of it was of little interest to me; but suddenly my eye was caught by a Breitkopf & Härtel re-issue of a "Grosse Gigue in D-moll" by Johann Wilhelm Hässler. I had never heard of this composer before; but the pages I examined seemed strangely similar in style to those of the so-called Friedemann pieces reviewed by Eitner. I looked up Hässler; found he was a nephew and pupil of the organist Kittl, one of the last pupils of J. S. Bach, and had lived 1749–1822. (Jahn gives an anecdote about him in connection with Mozart.) I inquired for works of Hässler at the Musikfreunde library, but they had none. However, reaching London shortly after, I went to the British Museum and found the distinguished William Barclay Squire in charge of the music division of the library. On explaining my reasons for wishing to examine works of Hässler, he courteously sent an assistant, who shortly returned wheeling a kind of tea-wagon loaded with a sizable collection of volumes published in the 70's and 80's of the eighteenth century containing sonatas and miscellaneous pieces — printed, not engraved — by the prolific Hässler, who, incidentally, besides composing sonatas, was a manufacturer of caps in Erfurt.

I spent most of that day — May 29, 1900, according to the library permit which I kept as a souvenir — studying these volumes and can vividly recall the youthful glow of satisfaction with which I found every one of the pieces reviewed by Eitner as Friedemann Bach's in these volumes of Hässler.

Fortunately there was no difficulty in finding the source of these spurious publications, as Eitner had indicated it as a manuscript of the library of the Cologne Conservatory. In fact they had been prepared for publication by one of the piano teachers of the Conservatory, Professor N. J. Hompesch. Stopping accordingly at Cologne on the way back to Switzerland, I had the good fortune to find Professor Hompesch, a charming little old gentleman with a white goatee, at the Conservatory. On my inquiring for the manuscript, he obligingly brought it. It was in four sections, in a late eighteenth- or early nineteenth-century hand, and inscribed with the name of Wilhelm Friedemann Bach. Needless to say, I took my leave of Professor Hompesch without mentioning the Hässler volumes.

There is little to add, except that later I found that the same Cologne manuscript had been used, long before Hompesch's time, by J. W. Davison, for many years music critic of the London Times, for a series of some half-dozen sonatas and fantasias which he issued in London under the name of *Revivals,* and labeled as Friedemann Bach's. The Arabella Goddard mentioned in the Grove article as playing these works in her recitals was Davison's wife, who lived until some years ago, almost a centenarian.

1. George B. Weston, "Fälschlich Wilhelm Friedemann Bach zugeschriebene Kompositionen," *Zeitschrift der Internationalen Musikgesellschaft,* Jg. XII, Heft 7 (1912), 240–41.

A NEGLECTED WORK IN BEETHOVEN'S CHORAL

MUSIC: THE FUNERAL CANTATA

Elliot Forbes

As a member of the Harvard Glee Club, I first came into direct contact with Beethoven's Missa Solemnis. And I well remember that the only way for the conductor to generate endurance in the singers was to apply a good deal of humor to the task. The results of this policy were so fruitful that the preparation of Beethoven's choral music became a grand challenge, with each installment keenly anticipated no matter what physical exertions the composer were to demand. The more I get to know Beethoven the more I appreciate the extent of this feat in rehearsal technique.

This memory led me to a consideration of Beethoven's choral output and to the question of how many of these works are significant musically; how many make anything like the demands on the voice of any one section of the Missa Solemnis. As the following chronological list of Beethoven's choral music shows, the quantity of pieces is larger than is generally realised; yet the quality varies greatly, so that over half are of historical rather then musical interest. But, the exceptional pieces, of which I am going to speak of one in detail, well warrant the survey of the literature as a whole. An asterisk indicates a work written for a certain number of "Singstimme" rather than "Chorstimme," which, although probably sung by one on a part originally, can be performed by a chorus.

1. Cantata on the Death of Joseph II for soloists, chorus and orchestra (Text: Severin A. Averdonk), composed 1790.
2. Cantata on the Elevation of Leopold II to the Imperial Dignity for soloists, chorus and orchestra (Averdonk?), composed 1790
3. Oratorio: *Christus am Ölberg* for 3 solo voices, chorus and orchestra, Op. 85 (Franz X. Huber), composed 1801–02.

4. *Opferlied* for 3 solo voices, chorus and small orchestra (Matthisson), version 3, first sketched in about 1802.

With orchestral accompaniment, from *Leonore*, Op. 72a (Sonnleithner), composed 1803–06:

5. Aria with chorus: *Ha! welch'ein Augenblick!* (No. 8)
6. Chorus of prisoners: *O welche Lust!* (No. 12)
7. Final chorus; *Zur Rache* (No. 18)

8. Mass in C for 4 solo voices, chorus and orchestra, Op. 86, composed in 1807.
9. Fantasy for pianoforte with accompaniment of orchestra and chorus, Op. 80 (author unknown: Kuffner? Treitschke?), composed 1808.

With orchestral accompaniment, from *Die Ruinen von Athen*, Op. 113 (Kotzebue), composed in 1811:

10. Chorus: *Tochter der mächtigen Zeus* (No. 1)
11. March with chorus: *Schmückt die Altäre* (No. 6)
12. Chorus: *Wir tragen empfängliche Herzen* (No. 7)
13. Chorus: *Heil unserm König! Heil!* (No. 8)

With orchestral accompaniment, from *König Stephan*, Op. 117 (Kotzebue), composed in 1811:

14. Men's chorus: *Ruhend von seinen Thaten* (No. 1)
15. Men's chorus: *Auf dunkelm Irrweg* (No. 2)
16. Women's chorus: *Wo die Unschuld Blumen streute* (No. 4)
17. Chorus: *Eine neue strahlende Sonne* (No. 6)
18. Sacred march and melodrama with chorus: *Heil unserm Könige!* (No. 8)
19. Final chorus: *Heil! Heil! Heil unsern Enkeln!* (No. 9)

20. Closing chorus: *Germania's Wiedergeburt* for bass solo, chorus and orchestra, from *Gute Nachricht* (Treitschke), composed in 1814.

With orchestral accompaniment, from *Fidelio*, Op. 72b (Sonnleithner-Treitschke), composed in 1814:
(Aria with chorus: *Ha! welch'ein Augenblick!* (No. 7))
(Chorus of prisoners: *O welche Lust!* (No. 10))
21. Final chorus: *Heil! Heil! Heil sei dem Tag* (No. 16)

22. *Un lieto Brindisi**, cantata campestre for 4 voices with piano accompaniment (Bondi), composed in 1814.
23. Elegischer Gesang* for 4 voices with string quartet accompaniment, Op. 118, composed in 1814.

24. *Chor auf die verbündeten Fürsten* for chorus and orchestra (Bernard), composed in 1814.
25. Cantata: *Der glorreiche Augenblick* for 4 solo voices, chorus and orchestra, Op. 136 (Weissenbach), also set to *Preis der Tonkunst* (Rochlitz), composed in 1814.
26. *Abschiedgesang** for 3 men's voices (Von Seyfried), composed in 1814.
27. *Kriegerchor* for men's voices for *Leonore Prohaska* (Dunckner), composed in 1814 (–15).
28. *Meeresstille und glückliche Fahrt** for 4 voices with orchestral accompaniment, Op. 112 (Goethe), composed in 1814–15.
29. Closing chorus: *Es ist vollbracht* for bass solo, chorus and orchestra from *Die Ehrenpforten* (Trietschke), composed in 1815.
30. *Lobkowitz-Cantate* for a solo, 3-part chorus and piano accompaniment, composed in 1816.
31. *Gesang der Mönche* for 3 men's voices (Schiller), composed in 1817.
32. Missa Solemnis for 4 solo voices, chorus and orchestra, Op. 123, composed from 1818 to 1823.
33. *Hochzeitslied** for 4 voices and piano, composed in 1819. According to Oldman's article, Music and Letters, *17*(1936)328, this is version no. 1.

With orchestral accompaniment from *Die Weihe des Hauses* (Meisl), composed in 1822.

34. March with chorus: *Schmückt die Altäre*, Op. 114 (extension of No. 6 from Die Ruinen von Athen)
35. Chorus: *Wo sich die Pulse*

36. *Bundeslied* for 2 solo voices and 3-part chorus with 6-part wind accompaniment, Op. 122 (Goethe), composed in 1822? [1]
37. Finale to Symphony No. 9 for 4 solo voices, chorus and orchestra, Op. 125 (Schiller), composed in 1822–24.
38. *Opferlied* for soprano solo, chorus and orchestra, Op. 121b (Matthisson), composed in 1823–24? Version 4. See article by Herbst, Neues Beethoven-Jahrbuch V(1933)137.

He who would search further for choral music by Beethoven can find choral sections in the following folk-song arrangements from Series 24 of the collected works: No. 257, Scottish songs, #1,13,22: No. 258, Irish songs, #8; No. 259, 12 different folk-songs, #1,9,11; No. 262, Irish songs, #8. Finally there are works for a solo and chorus in unison: *Kriegslied der Oesterreicher* (Friedelberg), 1797; *Der freie Mann* (Pfeffel), 1797; and *Hochzeitslied*, version 2, 1819.

This summary shows that aside from the choral sections of larger dramatic works, Beethoven's choral writing falls into five main periods in his life: in 1790 with the emperor cantatas, in 1801–2 with *Christus am Ölberg*, in 1807–8 when he wrote his choral fantasy and the Mass in C, in 1814–15 when he wrote many occasional pieces, and in 1822–23 with the Missa Solemnis and the finale to the ninth symphony. Only in these last two works does the composer make great demands of the voices both in range and endurance. Yet since these two works dwarf all other contenders in musical content, his reputation as a choral writer naturally rests on them. Working backwards, almost all the compositions of the 1814 era are surface pieces for surface occasions, either political or social. There are exceptions like the *Elegischer Gesang* that go deeper, in which Beethoven seemed to feel really moved by the occasion as he created. The two big works of 1801 and 1807 represent sincere attempts to use the chorus in larger forms; the Mass in C is certainly a neglected work but one feels that the oratorio is an echo of more inspired works in that form by Haydn. The first period, however, presents the most fascinating contrast. Here are two cantatas composed at the age of nineteen years; the first clearly inspired, the second written more out of duty and with the lack of any personal interest on Beethoven's part for the subject of his text.

Thus, I would like to dwell on the Funeral cantata as a work and its relation to the nearby Elevation cantata; for here, it seems to me, exists that which is found in none of the later works: namely, significant musical content in a larger vocal form without the extremes in demands upon the voice that are made once Beethoven is inspired again. Here, rather, to an astonishing degree considering that it is a first attempt in the medium,[2] one experiences that serenity through a knowing treatment of choral parts that after Haydn one does not expect to find until Mendelssohn and Brahms.

The history of the work may be recalled briefly. When Emperor Joseph II died on February 20, 1790, all Bonn mourned the death of their Elector's older brother. The Lesegesellschaft planned a memorial service for which the speaker, Prof. Schneider, asked for some music to be composed. Beethoven accepted and planned a work for soli, chorus and orchestra on a text by Severin Anton Averdonk. But two days before the meeting on March 19th, the minutes of the society record "for several reasons the projected cantata will not be performed." Two explanations have been advanced: that the work was not ready in time and that the wind parts were too difficult. This will be considered further. The composer borrowed an idea and also a complete melody from this work for his Leonore-Fidelio. The alternation of strings piano with winds forte in the 4 introductory measures makes the sound effect at the start of the prison scene in the opera; one is also struck by the resemblance in accent and melodic figure between the passage in eighth notes at the start of page 2 in the cantata with the passage in sixteenth notes at the bottom of page 173 (collected works edition). Secondly, the melodic essence of the soprano aria in F is extracted from the cantata (again played first by the oboe and in the key of F) to introduce the most moving section of the second act finale, page 258. As in the early work the 1805 Fidelio starts with soprano alone who is joined by the other voices; but in the Fidelio of 1814 the section is shortened and perhaps improved by the avoidance of the cantata's exact repetition of melodic line. These borrowings show both that Beethoven cared for this work and that he had the manuscript presumably until at least 1805 when he was at work on the opera. The next known fact is that the manuscripts of both cantatas were advertised in 1813 in the auction catalogue of a Baron de Beine. From here they passed through the hands of Johann N. Hummel, the Leipzig dealers List and Francke, and Armin Friedmann before being secured by the State Private Library in Vienna. Eduard Hanslick's account of their discovery in the Neue Freie Presse in May 13, 1884 was followed by a first performance of the Funeral cantata in Vienna in November of the same year. They were first published in the supplement to the collected works, Series 25, in 1887.

The first performance in Bonn on June 29, 1885 leads back to the question of its failure to be performed there 95 years earlier. The contention that the wind parts were too difficult is substantiated by both Wegeler and Simrock in accounts of the attempt to perform the work in Mergentheim in the fall of 1791. Simrock as a hornplayer in the orchestra is certainly a reliable source; and the fact that he has not referred to this difficulty as having already been present in March, 1790 shows that it is more likely that the originally scheduled performance did not take place because the piece was not ready. At any rate it is worth quoting from his letter to Schindler to show how adamant Beethoven was even when barely twenty-one about the performance of his works. He writes, "In Mergentheim I only remember that he wrote a cantata there which we did rehearse several times but did not perform in court. We had all manner of protests over the difficult places before us, and he asserted, each player must be able to perform his part correctly; we proved that we couldn't simply because all the figures were completely unusual, therein lay the difficulty." The account goes on to relate how conductor Ries dared not risk a performance. In examining the score it is hard to believe that the obstacle could have been the figures as much as the problem of ensemble. Surely wind players at the end of the eighteenth century had worked out a way with the keys then available to play three consecutive chromatics in a slow tempo as well as the predominately diatonic parts throughout, and this leaves only the combination of the two as on pages 4–5 and 50 which as figures could be called at all unusual. In contrast the problems of ensemble such as the syncopated accompaniment to counterpoint in the strings (on pages 23–24) or the dotted rhythms (on pages 4–6, 50–52) seem more plausible reasons for giving the conductor pause.

It is not clear whether it was on Haydn's first visit to Bonn at Christmas time, 1790 or on his second in July, 1792 that Beethoven laid one of these cantatas before the older master, received encouragement to continue to study, and possibly first conceived the idea of going to Vienna to learn from Haydn himself. If the earlier date, then Simrock's "In Mergentheim . . . he wrote a cantata" could be referring to revisions worked out from suggestions of his future teacher. But it is logical to think that Beethoven chose the Funeral cantata because of its superior musical content, a fact which he obviously appreciated in as much as he borrowed from it. As Hanslick expressed it in the Neue Freie Presse, the Leopold cantata is of interest merely as it contributes to our knowledge of young Beethoven while the Funeral cantata stands as a significant historical monument in our time due to the combination of Joseph II and Beethoven in an art-work. Clearly the composer felt deeply only about the latter, whom he may even have seen in 1787 at Vienna.

As for the texts, presumably both by Averdonk, it may be said that in the Joseph cantata the music manages to reach down to the basic emotions underneath the Klopstockian bombast, whereas in the Leopold cantata it fails to do so. Schiedermair has pointed out in his book, *Der junge Beethoven*, that both works in the recitatives and arias show the results of the composer's intimate contact with Italian and French opera so well cultivated at that time in Bonn. Yet the striking thing is the sense of original power in the one, completely lacking in the other, which transcends in so many places the influence of a Neefe or a Holzbauer to show the kind of expression which one associates with Beethoven ten years later.

The work is divided into 4 main sections with a concluding section which restates the material of the first section. The first, a chorus with solos starts in c minor and ends in E♭; the second, a recitative and aria is for bass with a modulation to D major for the start of the main section; the third is a soprano aria in F which is repeated by the chorus; the fourth is a recitative and aria for soprano in E♭; and the concluding section differs from the first only in that the last part is slightly extended and ends in the home key of c minor. The stamp of original musical thought is apparent in the first five measures as the sound of c minor, then c in a diminished seventh fails to proceed to the dominant. The significance of this frustration becomes clearer as the introductory motive is reused (page 2, top) with chorus; the strings now alternate with winds and voices singing "Todt!" As the tempo changes from Largo to Larghetto, the dominant is passed through in the form of a diminished seventh harmony; and the sense of loss and grief continues as the music steers toward g minor and then E♭. The setting of "meinet es wieder" (page 4) will serve as the second example of how Beethoven breaks through the surface meaning of the text to its deeper emotion. Here against a full string background the high winds piano alternate with the voices forte; the second chromatic descent is confirmed by the top line of the chorus. The resultant deceptive cadence sounds, it must be said, a little crude due to successive fifths F-C, G♭-D♭ in the bass, tenor and soprano. Yet in general the instinct is sure, and the manipulation of text to fit the logical flow of musical thought is masterly. Such climaxes as the statement in octaves for "Joseph der Grosse" (page 5) completely satisfy the needs of variety, continuity, and appropriateness to the meaning of the text.

Textually, the second section has two ideas: first, a monster arose to threaten the earth, fanaticism; second, then came Joseph to crush it under foot. It is interesting that the first idea caught the imagination of the composer in a recitative, presto the power of which lies in the instrumental counterpoint, all built out of two rhythmic ideas first expressed by the second violin in measures 3 and 4 respectively. A closer look shows that the eighth note in measure 3 has already been established by the figure in the basses. In contrast the second idea produces an aria which Schiedermair rightly calls an imitation of Mozart. True originality returns in the third section for soprano and chorus. The last 20 measures confirm the earlier statement that in this work (which is illustrating the fruits for man of Joseph's victory) exists some of the choral magic of Mendelssohn and Brahms. For instance, the second descent of the first sopranos from high G (page 35) produces a reaction in the slow descent of the basses. This is answered by three increasingly drawn out descents from high F, which are echoed the last two times by the tenors in contrary motion. The other three parts by their relative passivity bring out these very lines. One has to wait to find again such gratifying treatment of voices.

I find myself in disagreement with Mayer-Reinach (Die Musik VI_{iv} (1906–07),330) concerning the next soprano aria. In a performance of this work in Kiel, June, 1906, the author thought so little of the piece that he made a cut from the end of the recitative to the final chorus. There is no problem in the recitative; it is a beautiful setting for the idea of Joseph's peaceful sleep, a natural return to the original idea of death and a sense of loss. But the text of the aria with its affectation is admittedly hard to swallow: Joseph is a martyr who could not break a stem of a rose without wounding himself. The wonder is that Beethoven even here could penetrate through to the basic emotion: the contrast of a life in pain with a death in peace. But the melody succeeds in expressing these two ideas by a diatonic start answered by a predominantly chromatic sequel (page 40), which results in a melodic sweep the length of which is rare in Beethoven. The final three-note descents in chromatics for the flute, a reminder of the "weinet es wieder" passage, is the affectation of the text raised to a higher plane. In short, despite operatic mannerisms like the two firmatas (pages 42, 45), the music has real sincerity and charm.

Starting with the idea of death, the poem has led logically back to death, and one must admire Beethoven's decision to repeat the musical material with which the cantata started and to enlarge it into an ending which in the minor is even more expressive of the emotion inherent in the event commemorated.

Unlike the Leopold cantata, a competent work but without any remarkable musical ideas, it is hard to see why the Funeral cantata has not been performed more often. Mayer-Reinach back in 1906 believed that it was because no one any longer could feel akin to the topic of a Kaiser grappling with fanaticism. Both he and H. E. Krehbiel (in 1920 for a performance by the Beethoven Association) had the idea of a paraphrase "to rid it of its local application and some of its bombast and make its sentiment applicable to any heroic emancipator." I would like to plead for more performances but with the original text. First of all, it is not certain that a new text would be a real improvement as literature over Averdonk; second, the text as it stands and the subject that it represents are what inspired Beethoven to write as he did. Such a work of art is well served by a performance in its original form.

In this paper I have tried to review Beethoven's choral works in toto and to show that among these lies a neglected work of significant musical value. As Brahms said, "It is Beethoven through and through. Even if there were no name on the title-page none other than that of Beethoven could be conjectured."

1. Beethoven made another setting of the text to the melody of the 4th movement of Opus 20 for tenor and baritone solo and three-part chorus. This setting is given in *Die Musik*, XVIII$_{vi}$ [1926].
2. One can discount I think the legend of the Cressener cantata.

PART FIVE
The Twentieth Century

HINDEMITH'S "FRAU MUSICA": THE VERSIONS OF 1928 AND 1943 COMPARED

William Austin

Not for the concert hall," we are informed in the preface, but rather "for those who like to sing and play for their own pleasure," Hindemith made a setting of Luther's poem in praise of music, "Frau Musica," using solo voices of medium range, chorus in one or two parts, and whatever instruments might be at hand. This little work first appeared in 1928, when the slogans *Gebrauchsmusik* and *Gesellschaftsmusik* were new and exciting; it is one of the most memorable works to which these slogans can be applied. In 1945 it was published in America [1] with a happy English version of the text by W. Strunk, jr., and Harvey Officer, and with some inconspicuous changes in the music. Indeed, on the title page of the American edition we may read in small print "revised by the composer," and again on the first page of music, in parentheses, "revised 1943," but there is no mention of the revision in the composer's prefatory note. We may surmise that Hindemith cares more for this work than for some that have been republished in America without revision. On the other hand we can be confident that he takes "Frau Musica" more lightly than his cycle of songs, "Das Marienleben," of 1922, for in this case he has prefaced his revision, 1948, with an eight-page essay, full of profound remarks on details of the work and on general principles of composition.

Although the revision of "Frau Musica" might easily go unnoticed, it is a topic worth some attention. Many of "those who like to sing and play for their own pleasure" are curious about how composers work, and when a composer has provided two versions of a piece that serious amateurs can sing and play and know from the inside, they should seize the opportunity to compare the two and observe his progress. Moreover, students of composition and musical history as well may find this comparison profitable, and convenient because of the small dimensions of the work.

Certain elements of the original version are preserved intact: all the vocal lines throughout, and even the number of measures of rests for the voices; in part I the new accompaniment resembles the old only in texture; in part II (pastorale-musette) the bass-line and most of the obbligato duet that accompanies the solo soprano are unchanged; in part III the texture, most of the rhythm, and many notes remain; in part IV (a purely instrumental trio) only the fugal texture and the main subject; in the concluding duet and chorus, everything.

Hindemith has added a few details of notation that were absent from the original: metronome values for the tempi, and a ritard at the end of part I. He has not removed any other marks.

The most drastic change is in the instrumental trio, part IV, and this is a good place to begin a careful scrutiny. The change affects the whole structure of the piece. This can best be described by means of a schematic outline:

	1928 VERSION			1943 VERSION	
measure	melodic material	tonal points of departure	measure	melodic material	tonal points of departure
110	x $^{1st voice}$	a	110	x ^{1}	a
			116	x ^{2}	d
117	x $^{2nd voice}$	c			
			123	x ^{3}	a
127	x $^{3rd voice}$	g			
			129	y ^{1}	a
133	y ^{1}	a			
			134	y $^{1 \& 3}$	d
			138	x $^{2 \& 1}$ varied	c#
142	cadence	d	142	x $^{1 \& 3}$ varied	g
143	z ^{1}	d			
146	z ^{2}	f#			
			148	y ^{2}	d♭
149	z ^{3}	e			
152	z ^{1}	e	152	y ^{1}	g

	1928 VERSION			1943 VERSION	
measure	melodic material	tonal points of departure	measure	melodic material	tonal points of departure
155	z^3	d			
156	z^2	f#	156	y^1	d^b
160	lighter texture		160	cadence dotted rhythm	g
			165	x^2	a
168	z^1	g			
			170	x^3	g
171	y^1	e^b			
			173	x^1	a
178	y^3	b		sequence	
182	x^2	a	182	y^1	e
			187	y^3	a
190	y^2 dimin. transition to duet	c		cresc. transition to duet	

Here, evidently, Hindemith has undertaken a new act of composition. We might say, using the terms he has used in his Norton lectures,[2] either that he must have had a new "vision" of the piece as a whole, in which his original "idea" — "inspiration" — *"Einfall"* — appeared more fully developed; or else, if the two versions are based on the same vision, that his ability to realize his vision must have improved immensely. For there can be no doubt of the relative merits of the two.

The new piece is more *economical* and *concentrated* than the old: the third bit of melody, "z," is dispensed with — no loss, because its rhythm was similar to that of "x" and "y" and its profile less distinctive. The new piece is more *ingenious* and *cumulative*: the main subject is treated in stretto, measures 138–146, 165–175. It is more *coherent*: modulations are restricted so as to confirm the main tonality, *a*, yet there is as agreeable a variety as before. And it is more *confident* and *conclusive*: the biggest contrast, measures 160–164, leads to recapitulation of main material instead of to continuation of subordinate material. All these changes can surely be recognized as improvements, even from a study of the outline above, without a hearing of the two versions. Hearing them leads at least

one listener to an immediate feeling of the new concentration, cu-
mulation, coherence, and confidence; the careful study and the
hearing reinforce each other, and the hearing, so reinforced, justifies the study. What could demonstrate more neatly the growth of
Hindemith's craft? and what could show better the interplay of
craft, idea, and vision in his work than this instance of a completely
new composition on the themes of an old one, precisely equal to
the old one in duration and vastly more powerful in effect?

From this point on, our discussion proceeds backward through
the work, from the trio, part IV, just considered, through parts III
and II to the beginning.

In part III the changes are relatively slight. An obbligato part for
viola becomes a real melody instead of a quasi-ostinato. Purely
accompanying parts are merely adjusted at a few points to fit.

In part II also the changes are slight, but here they are puzzling.
The obbligato violins in this movement have a theme featuring the
alternation of major and minor thirds; in the revision these thirds
are shifted so that the major one appears where the minor did
before, and vice versa. No change in the melodic or harmonic sense
of the music is apparent to this writer; the change seems whimsical.

In part I again the revision is radical. Free contrapuntal lines in
the new version give more support to the vocal melody than the
original accompaniment gave, and at the same time they have more
true independence as melodies, and more sustained drive through
the phrases. A *fugato* instrumental interlude, measures 14–24, is
altogether reconstructed, so as to build up a climax with stretti,
measures 23–27, sequences, 18–22 and 23–26, and diminution of
the subject, 27; whereas in the original version this interlude
thinned out from a dense beginning. The cadence ending this interlude is approached with more diatonic motion and less extreme
reining in of rhythmic momentum than in the original version. In
measures 30–41, for the accompaniment of a vocal duet, there is a
delightful touch: unobtrusive diminutions of the subject replace
mere scale passages. The coda of the movement is much improved
by transferring the final entry of the subject to the bass — something for him to look forward to during his four-measure pedal-
point, instead of three more measures of pedal to count — and thus
incidentally relieving the top voice of a rather bombastic re-
dundancy.

With respect to chord-structures and voice-leading, both versions are remote from the common practice of what Hindemith calls "traditional harmony." Both have the characteristic sounds of empty octaves and fifths at beginnings and ends of phrases, although in part I these sounds appear more consistently in the new version. Both versions are replete with seconds and sevenths maintaining harmonic tension between the cadences, and in both the tritone is conspicuously less frequent than it is in most music by Strauss or Schoenberg or Stravinsky. To say more than this about Hindemith's chords is difficult; it would be almost impossible without reference to his own principles of harmony, as expounded in *The Craft of Musical Composition*.[3]

This book was completed during the years that elapsed between the original composition of "Frau Musica" and the revision. It provides several concepts that we need to complete an analysis. A juxtaposition of the two versions of measures 1–14 is provided here (p. 270) as a convenient basis for applying these concepts.

First let us observe that the new bass-line has a broader sweep than the old, with more prominent stepwise progressions, making more prominent the counterpoint of bass and main melody, which Hindemith refers to as "the two-voice framework." The new bass also increases the interest of this framework with a descent to new depths, and maintains interest up to the full cadence in measure 14 instead of relaxing prematurely on a pedal-point. The two inner voices (not shown above) likewise reflect a broader, surer conception of the whole texture and its movement. The polyphonic independence of voices in both versions makes it hard to tell which notes are chord-tones and which are not (Hindemith's theory leaves room for the several alternative analyses that his music invites.[4]) The harmonic roots indicated here, by small notes on the bass staves, are simply those most prominent to one listener's ear. They show that in the new version root-progressions hardly ever parallel the main melody, as they occasionally did in the old version; that the progression of roots has become somewhat slower; that the strong progression by fourth appears more frequently than before, and the weak progression by third less frequently; and that the tonic note is more emphasized by recurrence and by a balance of other notes closely related to it, especially in the approaches to cadences at measures 8 and 14. Further, the analysis suggests that

Example 1

Hindemith has exercised his newly won control over what he calls "the fluctuations of harmonic tension." The numeral II shows where chords including a tritone appear, and III indicates chords without tritone but with seconds or sevenths as essential constituents. (All other chords in this passage belong to Hindemith's Type I, with every dissonant interval attributable to a non-chord-tone.) In the revised version, it can be seen that the rich chords are placed more effectively to enhance the drive of each phrase toward its cadence, whereas in the original version similar chords seem to appear at random.

The detailed account of roots and harmonic fluctuation in this analysis is somewhat doubtful, as acknowledged above, because of the difficulty of distinguishing chord-tones from non-chord-tones. The same reason warrants some skepticism about the importance of these theoretical elements in Hindemith's style. But even if his theory of roots and fluctuation is ultimately rejected, it still may have helped the composer achieve his evident mature mastery of the kind of polyphony he discovered as a young man, and it may help us appreciate this mastery.

But "those who like to sing and play for their own pleasure" have probably satisfied their curiosity by now, and professional students of harmony may be left to pursue the analysis as far as they like, in privacy, but not without testing the actual sounds and their coherence in a complete performance.

Either version of "Frau Musica" amply rewards its performers and listeners. The new version better than the old, and the two together better than either alone should long assist amateurs to rise "from the somewhat shameful role of mere consumers of music to a role of sympathetic understanding." [5]

1. New York, Associated Music Publishers, copyright 1928, 1945. Permission to quote from the score is gratefully acknowledged. The original publisher was Schott, Mainz.

2. *A Composer's World*, Cambridge, Harvard University Press, 1952, pp. 58–63.

3. Originally *Unterweisung im Tonsatz*, Mainz, 1937–39; the translation of volume 1 by Arthur Mendel was published in New York in 1942 and that of volume 2 by Otto Ortmann in 1941.

4. Vol. 1, p. 174.

5. From Hindemith's statement of the intent of his work in the preface to *Das Marienleben*, p. x. Another eloquent appeal to amateurs may be found in *A Composer's World*, pp. 215–18.

THOUGHTS ON THE CHORDAL CONCEPT

Walter Piston

How often in listening to music the thought comes to mind, "What an interesting and evocative chord! I must examine it to see what it is." And how often is the intention frustrated through our inability to explain musical materials as employed by composers. Putting aside the important and difficult consideration of association, musical or otherwise, as a common source of interest and suggestiveness in musical sounds, let us look into what we may presume to call the purely musical aspects of the question.

Let us say the chord that attracted us proves to be this:

Some would say it is no chord, but what is a chord? A chord is something everyone knows, but none can define in a way to cover all cases. The definition in the Harvard Dictionary of Music is as good as any: "the simultaneous occurrence of several tones, usually three or more," which of course means that we may put any tones whatever together and make a chord. This definition is hardly helpful, even though perfectly true. For some theorist is sure to introduce utter confusion with a blithe observation that one or more of these tones may be non-harmonic, that they are not members of the chord with which they happen to be sounding.

The suggestion will be made that chords are formed by the superposition of intervals of a third, and to determine the chord in question we must first arrange the tones so that they appear as a vertical series of thirds. It is within memory that this seemed a sound assumption, because it could be borne out in its application to most music. But in the twentieth century we have seen, not only in the music of our own time, but in the music we have come to know of earlier periods, that other intervals may be used in the construction of chords.

Some of the forms arrived at by rearranging our chord in a series of like intervals are as follows:

Ex.2
thirds

● = omitted factors

fourths

seconds

The other intervals give less distinct forms, since they are multiples or inversions of these three. But the list can be indefinitely extended if we consider the possibility that the composer might have employed an arbitrary or irregular series of intervals to build his chord, e.g., alternating fourths with thirds, or adopting a sequence of major, minor, and augmented intervals. Furthermore, the chord could be of synthetic origin, resulting from the not unconventional process of combining two chords. For example, it is not impossible to imagine the chord, as it stands in Ex. 1, to be, in G minor, dominant ninth above with Neapolitan sixth below. The last word in the harmonic combination of intervals was thought to be the experimental *Mutterakkord*, composed of all the intervals that exist within the octave, until the discovery of the completely invertible *Grossmutterakkord*. It is unnecessary to recall that the principle of omitted factors, even roots, is accepted in conventional harmonic theory.

Composers are notoriously careless about accuracy of notation, and the enharmonic reading of one or more notes of the chord should not be overlooked as a possibility. Perhaps the chord we are considering ought to have been written in one of these ways:

Doubtless most readers will object that these combinations have the appearance of musical nonsense, and that, anyway, the notation can be judged only by seeing the next chord and observing the progression of the voices. The objection is reasonable, even if it does bring up the question of the existence of musical sense, of whether or not it is possible to write musical nonsense.

The musical meaning of tones is an inescapable fact. It is, however, not at all certain that the logic we perceive in the behavior of tones is of physical or acoustic origin. The progression of a dominant seventh to its tonic is understood by everyone, even when played on the most out-of-tune piano imaginable. The analogy with spoken and written language is close. Successions and combinations of tones, like those of letters and syllables, take on meaning through usage, and that meaning is understood by all those who participate in the usage.

This is illustrated in the principle of chromatic alteration of notes of a chord. We feel that by chromatic alteration a note is given a melodic tendency, and we sense a musical logic when that tendency is respected and affirmed. The first chord in Ex. 3 is seen to have musical meaning in the following progression:

Another way to interpret the chord, so as to reconcile its apparent lack of sense with our notions of musical meaning preconditioned by usage, is to find that one or more tones are non-harmonic. In this case, there being no antecedent tones, the type of non-harmonic tone will be the appoggiatura. Now the unresolved appoggiatura is not unknown to conventional harmonic theory (e.g., the dominant thirteenth chord in nineteenth-century practice). We are prepared to accept the unresolved appoggiatura in lieu of its note of resolution. Here, then, are some hypothetical implications of our chord:

When four appoggiaturas are presumed, as in the last of the above solutions, we are led to an explanation of the chord in Ex. 1 as the dominant seventh of A-flat, an explanation that may be called "advanced."

The label, "non-harmonic tone," is one of the least happy in the jargon of musical theory. It is the more unfortunate in view of the often repeated advice to the student, "chords are made by moving voices." The effects known as non-harmonic tones are perhaps the most striking and distinctive features of the melodic lines of which they are a part, and their purely melodic character should be appreciated.

In Ex. 5, chords created by the presence of unresolved appoggiaturas are made intelligible by means of assumed resolutions. It is submitted that the chords possessed the same orientations, at least potentially, previous to their clarification. The particular orientation may be known only to the composer, but if the chord were used in that musical sense often enough to establish a usage, it would be regarded as a normal item in our harmonic vocabulary.

The appoggiatura is a decorative melodic tone of strong rhythmic stress. The numerous other types of "non-harmonic" tone are rhythmically weak. Their identity would become apparent if we learned their melodic antecedents. As a matter of fact, we are being most presumptuous in attempting to describe melodic qualities without the evidence of at least a phrase of music. But we are able to say that the "simultaneous occurrence of several tones," creating a chord, is often an instance of the coincidence of melodic tones not selected from components of a predetermined vertical series of intervals. On the contrary, it is frequently just this coincidence of melodies that makes the chord.

This contrapuntal origin of chords has always attracted composers. What was at first an effect caused by the chance meeting of melodic tones becomes a vertical sonority to be employed harmonically, because it has appealed to the taste and imagination of the composer. Its subsequent status, as far as usage is concerned, is unpredictable.

There are other influences upon the composer's choice of tones. One of these is his selection of scales from which to make his melodies. It is here that usage asserts itself in most exaggerated fashion, for we find it next to impossible to hear music without interpreting everything by reference to the major-minor system. Yet the church modes and the modes existing in folk music are familiar forms, imparting tonal meaning to melodic tones quite other than that we sense in major-minor. The instinct for relating music to a tonal center, the feeling for tonality, seems to be so strong that it insists on clouding our understanding of music using any but major-minor scales.

Known modes are not the only scales that could have formed the basis of the harmony. The invention of artificial scales is virtually without limit. Some composers have envisaged a chromatic mode, in which the twelve notes in an octave are of equal tonal status, not by any means to be understood as containing chromatic alterations of a major scale. The music composed on this principle may be intended to be atonal, or a tonal center may be suggested by root progressions and other devices.

Passing from the artificial scale to the more or less complete harmonic system is a logical step. It is a step, however, that takes us far from the musical usage to which we have referred above. In our hypothetical explanations of a chord, we have invoked usage in order to find in the chord a musical sense. The criteria derived from usage seem now to have reached the point where they are of little or no use. Among the artificial systems developed in the twentieth century, the most important is the twelve-tone system of Arnold Schoenberg. How shall we describe our chord if it is discovered in a twelve-tone texture?

Ex.6

Explanations like those given in Ex. 5 can have little point here. They have no more relevance than has the discovery of a diminished seventh chord in Schoenberg's Third Quartet.

We have the right to judge unfamiliar music against the background of conventional usage, and to find in it musical meaning in so far as it appears to have a relationship to what we feel to be musical sense. But we must realize that usage is a powerful force against the introduction of new sounds in music, and that intelligent appraisal or analysis cannot be made without consideration of the composer's intent. Knowledge of the composer's intent may be hard to achieve, even it may have to be simple conjecture, but the attempt must be made, by study of the man's origins and environment, and his other musical works. The task of the analyst, rather shall we say of the musicologist, is the two-fold one of clarifying the personal usage of the composer as far as it can be known, as well as summarizing the effect on the listener in terms of accepted musical sense.

The reader will have recognized our chord as occurring in the Well-tempered Clavier, volume one, fugue no. 12, measure 28.

PROBLEMS OF CHORAL TEXTURE IN THE TWENTIETH CENTURY

Harold C. Schmidt

A SURVEY of the major choral contributions of the twentieth century indicates that some harmonic and contrapuntal procedures are well-suited to choral composition while others pose obstacles which may be surmounted, but finally offer no substantial proof for their validity in choral music performance practice.

The first fifty years of the twentieth century have produced a singularly large amount of choral music, indicating a most sympathetic response to the need for choral music of all kinds. There has been a conscious effort to supply a literature for an average community or college singing group, or a highly trained professional choral group. Not all of this literature avoids the grave danger of isolating choral practice so that it runs a risk of remaining a medium of performance with a set of technical procedures riveted to those of the past.

Moderate departures from traditional choral practice appeared with "King David" (1921–24), "Oedipus Rex" (1924), "La Cena" (1927), and Janacek's "Festival Mass" (1928). To keep pace with the new harmonic thinking of the twenties, speedy relief was needed from the nineteenth-century melodic patterns, heavy harmonic and contrapuntal masses, wearisome dynamics varying from ppp. to fff., tedious mass choral and orchestral sonorities and complex structures. These textures were replaced by a new-found interest in baroque and classic concepts of musical composition which appeared in the late twenties and early thirties.

The followers of Gregorian ideas in choral composition appeared in considerable numbers. Some conservative contemporary choral composers, particularly in shorter works, used a tonal vocabulary emphasizing pseudo-modal harmonies supporting yards of plain song or imitations of the same. Fortunately, in recent years, there has been a swinging away from such "stock-in-trade" items: what might be referred to as Kyrie Eleison and Stabat Mater infections. These mannerisms had their place, but their vitality as ideas was short-lived. The "Hymn of Jesus" by Gustav Holst, written in 1919, is a case in point. As imaginative as the choral color is in such a passage as "To you who gaze, a lamp am I," these passages are too few, and the work suffers from a limited harmonic and contrapuntal vocabulary. Quotations from plain song establish an archaic flavor, but definitely date the work. The same is true of the "Psalmus Hungaricus" by Kodaly (1924), and the "Requiem" by Pizetti (1923).

Short choral works following the general pattern of the six-teenth-century *a cappella* tradition have been overdone. Some contemporary composers have relied too often on a borrowed chordal vocabulary at the expense of rhythmical and metrical organization and a strategic use of dissonance. These writers were guilty of much the same faults as the nineteenth-century *a cappella* idealists who viewed the sixteenth century with aesthetic concepts entirely false to the period. Renaissance choral music is something more than a few chordal progressions written to create an atmosphere of sanctity and mystery.

While mannerisms may occur in any period, some of those used between 1920 and 1930 served only as a temporary stimulus to choral writing. It is only in recent years and through conscious effort that a happy balance has been achieved between the idiomatic choral expression of the past and twentieth-century harmonic thought. The desire to experiment with new colors and more demanding contrasts of harmonic and contrapuntal texture, plus a certain propensity for virtuosity, have changed past modes of choral writing. The problem facing us today is well expressed by T. S. Eliot: "To conform [to tradition] merely would be for the new work not to conform at all; and would not be new, and therefore would not be a work of art. We do not say that the new is more valuable because it fits in, but its fitting in is a test of its value." [1] In applying this "test of value" we must penetrate beyond the acknowledged problems of vocal range, virtuosity, color, or projection of a text to the fundamental question of the extent and the adjustment of dissonance to effective choral writing. This problem affects every facet of choral style determining whether it invites or repels performer and listener. It is in the reconciling of past choral tradition with present harmonic practice that Eliot's concept of "fitting in" becomes a true test of value.

I

The first part of the discussion relating to the extent and adjustment of dissonance to choral writing will consider dodecaphonic technique in relation to the chorus. In any successful composition, and particularly in choral music due to textual problems, the element of contrast is vital. Contrast may be accomplished by such various means as an alternation of harmonic and contrapuntal textures, changes of pace, the profile of one idea or section with another, different levels of dynamic intensity, special tricks of choral timbre, or some dramatic way in which the text is high-lighted.

In dodecaphonic composition the principles involved are constant rhythmic elaboration and manipulation of the tone row series. There is a lack of feeling for tonal centers as we know them, and a fanatic avoidance of the principle of doublings. In operation the tonal progression is one of continuous dissonance varying in degree and amount. A vital element, contrast, is lost. Rhythmical ingenuity cannot replace the need for an adequate and conscious feeling of tonal stability. As Roger Sessions has pointed out:

The real point is that the "chord" as a valid concept, as an entity, has in this type of progression, once more ceased to exist, much as it may be said not to have existed in the pretonal technique. What prevails is a certain sonorous quality which results from . . . the interplay of voices which maintain a certain constancy of tonal dissonance among themselves.[2]

It is this "constancy of tonal dissonance" which more than any other factor distresses the singer. In any listening experience the ear must coordinate what it hears; sustaining a dissonant tension over a long span lessens the possibility of coordinating and interpreting progressions.

The following example from the "Männerchor" by Schönberg, Op. 35, No. 3 (1930), illustrates dodecaphonic technique applied to choral writing.[3]

Within this five measure phrase, the series is presented in the second bass part. This is a singable line and, for the most part, is possible without undue concern to the singer. When this part is put into context with the other parts, there are too many successive moments of conflict. The cadence at the *fermata* is not one conducive to any true sense of rest or tonal stability. From the point of view of dynamics and tessitura, nothing short of instrumental technique is demanded.

An example by Anton Webern from "Das Augenlicht" (1935) [4] demonstrates incredible problems of intonation, unnatural vocal leaps and awkward voice leading. Although there is a feeling for the shaping of individual phrases, periods and sections, the *modus operandi* of the twelve-tone technique stifles the choral texture. As sounds apart from words, the parts are better adapted to an instrumental medium.

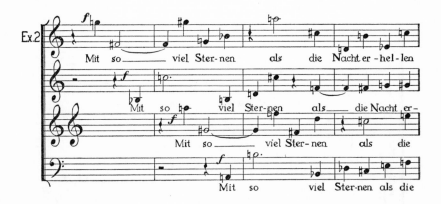

These composers make no attempt to give a satisfactory answer to the extent and adjustment of the problem of dissonance to choral writing. Whether or not one can reduce works like those of Schönberg or Webern, so rich in rhythmical ideas, to a fundamental chordal skeleton is not of much assistance to singers who must negotiate difficult intervals with rhythmic and tonal precision. Thematic and rhythmic richness — the products of an inventive and systematically organized mind — have created choral difficulties which are incredible. The successful application of dodecaphonic concepts, unless tempered judiciously for singers, reaches a point equivalent to the "sonic sound barrier" where choral safety is jeopardized.

Luigi Dallapiccola is a more conservative follower of the dodecaphonic school who has made compromises in handling the problem of dissonance, especially in the three "Canti di Prigioni" published in 1939, 1940, 1941. The example from the "Preghiera di Maria Stuarda" [5] demonstrates the extent to which atonal problems have been relaxed making it possible for the chorus to absorb the total sonority problem satisfactorily. While the contrapuntal and harmonic texture is thick, there is a reasonableness about the voice leading that is feasible and highly effective. The chorus has a strong feeling for a point of arrival in the handling of vertical and horizontal structure which is a compromise necessary to insure successful choral texture when more than average dissonance is in operation.

II

Another approach to the adjustment of dissonance to choral writing may be seen in the later style of Paul Hindemith. Whereas the break with tradition is a fundamental premise of the dodecaphonic composer, Hindemith establishes his system of composition on diatonic practice of the past with modifications. His is the firm hand of a disciplinarian, one who knows where he is going and how to get there. Aaron Copland in a chapter devoted to "Tradition and Innovation in Recent European Music," put it as follows:

His writings have made perfectly clear the doctrine that he applies to his own composition, and in his finest pieces, it is a marvel to behold these same doctrines filled out with inspired music. The Hindemithian theories will always have vast appeal to those minds that feel comfortable only with a closely reasoned and systematic approach to any problem.[6]

Whatever merits the dodecaphonic composers may have in the contemporary musical scene, there is no indication that choral writing is regarded by them apart from instrumental writing. On the other hand, Hindemith is sensitive to vocal writing and constantly speaks of musical composition from the singers' point of view.

The "Five Chansons," the "Six Chansons," "Apparebit Repentina Dies," and "A Requiem" are the result of well-clarified theoretical principles put into action. In Hindemith's procedure, the sound of chords built on intervals of the second, fourth, fifth and seventh, "add strength and tension," and when used with thirds and sixths, produce a basic concept that "tensions and relaxations must alternate." It is obvious that Hindemith is certain of the quality of sound he desires and that he moves with precision and assurance in the handling of horizontal and vertical problems.

The first illustration is the opening of the "Death Carol" from a Requiem "For those We Love." [7] The center of gravity in the first phrase, the F in the alto part, acts as a constant center, away from which the other voices move step-wise at the interval of a second and skip of a fourth until the phrase reaches its highest point of tension on the word "soothing"; the lowest degree of tension or relaxation occurs on the word "death." In such degree progressions *crescendo* and *diminuendo* go hand in hand, and occur because of the music itself. The same principles are in operation on the phrase "Undulate round the world, serenely, arriving," at which point the soft quality inherent in the text is brought out by a cadence progression based on the skip of a third (bass E flat to B natural). This feeling of softness is possible because of the chordal context Hindemith has systematically worked out in terms of melodic degree-progression and harmonic degree-progression in relation to cadences.

In "The Doe," number one of the "Six Chansons" (measures 9–11), the principle of harmonic fluctuation is illustrated. Moving away from a unison C sharp, the parts pass through a more dissonant texture and are finally relaxed on the C sharp major chord in measure eleven. The tension between the soprano and tenor parts, and alto and bass is not extreme; by a careful consideration of step progression each part is guided satisfactorily toward the final cadence.

Compared to the Schönberg methodology, Hindemith never puts the choral texture at a disadvantage by having complex tonal and rhythmic forces working against each other simultaneously. Whatever "dissonantal tension" results, one is aware that Hindemith articulates dissonant passages by well-spaced releases of harmonic and contrapuntal texture, thereby enabling the chorus to feel and experience a more than reasonable degree of performance safety.

III

One of the most effective choral textures in use today is that of Francis Poulenc, who has contributed a large amount of choral music, mostly sacred, to the contemporary scene. It is a typically French idiom with antecedents reaching back to Leonin of the Notre Dame School and to composers of the Burgundian Group in the fifteenth century.

A marked feature of his choral texture is emphasis upon triadic structure. Poulenc does not indulge in dissonant counterpoint or polytonal choral writing for its own sake. His harmonic idiom is clearly major and minor usage with a few modifications. In the example [8] all four measures take G minor as a tonal center. The first two measures are clearly triadic, while the second two measures, by adding notes such as F sharp against F natural, create the kind of dissonant usage which is typical for Poulenc. This texture, not the outgrowth of contrapuntal movement, comes from the desire to get color by means of block chord effects.

The Mass in G Major is an excellent example of how plain song melodic structure may be used without being banal. In the opening of the Kyrie a sustained pedal note G, against an F sharp which ornaments the pedal, is a device recalling the texture in *organum purum*. A constantly shifting metrical structure with a rich palette of choral color, the result of unique placement of voices, shows that Poulenc in his writing moves with the skill of a prestidigitator.

In the absence of contrapuntal writing, the usual *sine qua non* in a choral work of any proportions, Poulenc avoids tediousness of harmonic writing by a subtle handling of individual voice parts. Sections are broken down into *coro concertato* versus *coro ripieno* scoring. For example, in the Gloria, four *solo* voices per part are used on "tibi propter magnam" (piano), *tutti* on "gloriam tuam" (mezzo-forte). In the Kyrie Poulenc requires three tenors to sing *falsetto* in a very high *tessitura* passage. Such meticulous considerations for timbre are not customary in contemporary choral writing. No problems of dissonance act as a barrier to successful performance in his choral music.

IV.

The Mass (1948) by Stravinsky is a significant step in successful contemporary choral writing. The antiquarian interest in this work as in the Cantata on Anonymous fifteenth- and sixteenth-century Texts (1952), does not rely upon modal clichés of the early twentieth century or misconceptions of renaissance choral style. Pre-sixteenth-century choral writing and contrapuntal devices are adeptly worked into the Mass. The harmonic vocabulary involves a use of chords built from seconds, fourths, fifths and sevenths which occur as the result of a contrapuntal treatment of the vocal lines. Numerous passages in the Credo point to E minor or F sharp minor with a note added a second, fourth, fifth or a seventh away from the root of the triad in the instrumental accompaniment. In the Kyrie and Agnus Dei sections a repeated instrumental figure, like a *ritornello*, establishes a tonal center away from which the chorus may move with a feeling of security. This method of repeating melodic material around a given tonal center is one way of unifying a moderately dissonant over-all texture. Stravinsky has struck a felicitous equilibrium between vertical and horizontal forces. A highly economical kind of tonal structure is attained with maximum expressiveness from all musical factors.

A remarkable quality of this work, in contrast to Poulenc, is its freedom from dynamic markings. At a first glance the performer might consider Stravinsky negligent, but experience with the chordal texture soon shows that dynamics go hand in hand with the harmonic and contrapuntal texture. Vocal movement up or down, the increase or lessening of dissonant tension, and the extraordinary rhythmical and metrical organization of phrases make for a chorally-minded texture like that of the renaissance.

An example from the *Agnus Dei* [9] illustrates the extent to which Stravinsky uses dissonance and how carefully he handles it when there is no instrumental support. Singers reading these choral parts are guided by a feeling for interval structure rather than chordal structure as in Poulenc. In most cases one part finds a point of agreement with another member of the same chord either through a unison, third, perfect fifth or octave. In short, the ear perceives tonal relationships in a moderately dissonant texture and the voice

moves with a sense of safety. There is an immaculate feeling about the texture which is like that of Josquin and his predecessors. Undoubtedly, any chorus which has "cut its teeth on *The Messiah*" will not feel comfortable in such a passage.

There are many other contemporary uses of dissonance ranging from controlled to bizarre. Other composers who control the problem of a dissonant choral texture include Benjamin Britten who, resting on the shoulders of the English choral tradition, in his "Spring Symphony" goes beyond the folk song pattern; likewise, Darius Milhaud, who in his "Cantique du Rhône," uses a post-Ravelian texture, dissonance with the sparkle of a good French champagne.

Several contemporary composers have used a dissonant texture for color effects and raise problems unrelated to linear writing. In a recent composition, "In Certainty of Song" (1951) by Wallingford Riegger, there appears a use of tone clusters with the text "so may we find some meagre light." Over a long span, writing of this kind lacks clarity of line and is apt to become monotonous. Frequently the choral texture of contemporary works involves dissonant, exotic or primitive influences. "Cinq Réchants" (1949) by Olivier Messaien, written for twelve voices, three to a part, employs Hindu *ragas* and chords with eight to twelve different notes sounding at one time: rhythmic and melodic demands incredible for the singer. As a chamber choral cantata it is virtuoso in character and carries out the same ideas as Roussel did in "Padmavati" and Caplet in "Le Miroir de Jésus Christ." Villa-Lobos in "Chorôs No. 10" and "Nonetto" uses a dissonant percussive texture which suggests African tribal music and the rhythmic and metrical organization of "Sacre."

In 1953 there is no lack of variety in the choice of choral textures. Pseudo-Gregorian texture with parallel fourths and fifths has disappeared; the "extremists" are showing admirable restraint; a middle group is pointing out the way. This group, by careful exploration, has found vital new sources of successful choral writing. Machault, Perotinus, Leoninus, Dufay and Josquin are serving as points of departure in contemporary choral practice. In the middle group are many contemporary composers who solve the problem of the extent and adjustment of dissonance to choral texture with a keen regard for the particular problems of choral writing. By

turning in this direction the best harmonic and contrapuntal practice of today will be "fitting in" to an ideal choral framework with
meaning for this century.

1. "Tradition and the Individual Talent," *Selected Essays,* Faber and Faber, 1932.
2. Sessions, Roger; *Harmonic Practice,* p. 400, Harcourt Brace and Co., New York, 1951.
3. Quoted by kind permission of Associated Music Publishers, New York, N. Y.
4. Quoted by kind permission of Associated Music Publishers, New York, N. Y.
5. Quoted by kind permission of S. A. Carisch, Editori, Milano, Italia.
6. Copland, Aaron; *Music and Imagination,* p. 66, Harvard University Press, Cambridge, 1952.
7. Quoted by kind permission of Associated Music Publishers, New York, N. Y.
8. Quoted by kind permission of Salabert Inc., New York, N. Y.
9. Quoted by kind permission of Boosey and Hawkes, New York, N. Y.

OPERA IS NOT WHAT IT SHOULD BE

Robert E. Middleton

Aᴛ ᴛʜᴇ theater the spectator must participate in the drama; at the opera house he must participate not only in the drama but also in the music. Opera is a co-existence of drama and music. Without a susceptibility to both, this co-existence can only be misjudged or disliked. The artificiality of the co-existence must be assumed and accepted, or enjoyment is impossible. Aside from the singing telegram, we do not communicate with each other melodically. Acceptance should not be difficult. Just as the theater makes us more verbal and intellectual than we normally are, so the opera makes us more musical.

Assuming that this two-dimensional participation in drama and music is worth while, what is required to make it complete? In simplest terms, music is the ordering of sounds which have no specific meaning into situations which have no specific meaning. Drama is the ordering of sounds which have a specific meaning into situations which have a specific meaning. The former is ambiguous; the latter is specific. Co-existing with the word, music takes on a specific emotional quality it does not possess naturally. The word, however, remains specific no matter what the music.

The spectator can never participate in the drama to a full extent unless he understands the specific meaning of the words. He can never understand the specific meaning of the words if they are in another language, unless he knows this language as well as his own. While translation is seldom questioned in the theater, in opera it is not accepted without controversy. The obstacle of language is placed in the way of a full participation in the dramatic element of opera. The incomplete participation which results leads to artificialities in opera production, hinders the acceptance of opera, and fails to provide the stimulation for the composition of new operas.

It is not necessary to argue the case for opera in English. But the arguments against translation are based on assumptions about opera which are not necessarily true. These assumptions determine what opera is. Each age must align them in its own fashion, for they affect both opera production and opera composition. Translation into English, or any other language, does not imply any change of viewpoint concerning the alignment. But improper viewpoint can result in artificialities which need not be, artificialities which are obstacles in the way of maximum participation in *both* music and drama.

Unless there is a change of attitude concerning these assumptions, opera cannot be what it should be, but will remain as it has been. If the assumptions, on which the argument against opera in English is based, are acepted as true, opera can have no contemporary vitality. If these assumptions are considered false, contemporary opera can become a powerful musical force.

There are three types of reaction against translation. The first maintains that understanding of the word is unnecessary; the second that understanding of the word is impossible; the third that understanding of the word is "undesirable because."

The school of thought which maintains that understanding of the word is unnecessary has two arguments. The first argument states that a study of the printed libretto in English translation is enough to outline the plot events for the listener. With some assistance from the action, the music can tell the rest. The second argument states that opera can be enjoyed for the music alone. Both are based on assumptions concerning what music can do, why words are set to music, what singing is, and what acting can do.

What music can do. The assumption that music can portray emotions is false. Music without words is emotional only to the extent that the listener puts in his own emotional meaning. Music is exciting, calm, melancholy; it can portray a state of excitement, calmness, melancholy. But it is incapable of expressing the specific degree of or the reason for these states. It is only when sounds without specific meaning co-exist with sounds with specific meaning (or words) that emotional exactness in music can be obtained.

The music does not give emotional significance to the words; the words give emotional significance to the music. Music without words can be intellectually satisfying, but can only be emotionally ambiguous. Opera exists when there is a conviction that the emotional exactness which results from the co-existence of words and music is desirable. This conviction demands that the listener is neither timid nor embarrassed when faced with the specific emotion. The word must be understood, or opera is only an excuse for vocalism.

Why words are set to music. Words are set to music because singing is the only natural and specifically expressive musical medium. Words are set to music because of the meaning they contain, and for the stronger emotional significance which the musical sounds will therefore possess. The assumption that words are set to music as an excuse for vocalism is false, for vocalism in itself is flat and meaningless. Vocal sonority without words has never been successful because the potential power of the word is conspicuous by its absence. The word must be understood or singing is meaningless.

What singing is. It follows, therefore, that singing is not primarily a tonal or sonorous art. Singing is nothing more or less than projection of the word at pitch levels different from those of speech, and the extension of certain sounds in the words. Both are artificialities added to speech so that it may become musical. But since the artificialities of pitch and extension are ambiguous and have no real significance in themselves, the word is the most important factor in singing. The assumption that singing is primarily a tonal art is false.

What acting is. The belief that acting can give the music its true significance has led to ridiculous staging in opera. Acting can show action, but is very limited in its ability to portray emotional states with any exactness. The "expressive face" is not so expressive as one has been led to believe. The emotional significance is dependent on the word that goes with it, before it, or after it. Even the silent films required explanatory dialogue. Acting consists of proper projection of the word, degrees of intensity in this projection, natural movement, and timing. Opera singing need be no more or no less. The assumption that acting can be emotionally significant without full projection of the word is false. Opera is not ballet.

Action must substitute for acting when the word is not understood, or when the word is nonsense.

The second school of thought maintains that understanding of the word is impossible. This argument states that the mechanics of singing are such that the words cannot be understood no matter what the language. This school points to the ensemble and the chorus as being particularly vulnerable in this respect. The assumption here has to do with the true function of singing.

What singing can do. Singing is the most intimate of all musical media since it is the most specifically emotional. It has been pointed out previously that singing is not a succession of beautiful sounds. It is the most chamber music of all chamber music, and was never meant for a large hall. The attention to sonority itself indicates a loss of concentration on the words. When volume to fill a large hall and sound above a large orchestra is an added burden, the projection of the words becomes a tertiary consideration. Opera was never meant for large halls, large orchestras, and large ensembles. The most important factor in singing — projection of the word — is hindered by size and complexity. As long as these are expected, the "grand style" of singing will be a necessity, or more electrical amplification must be utilized. The assumption that the "grand style" of singing is true vocal art is false.

Opera must be put where it belongs — in a small theater, and must use a chamber ensemble as accompaniment. Real acting, real emotional correctness, and real participation on the part of the spectator are impossible otherwise. This means that the grand operas of the nineteenth century must be reduced in size, glorious as they may be. If these operas cannot be successful with such a new orientation, they should be taken off the boards. Their presence hinders the creation of vital opera today.

When intelligibility has been sacrificed to volume, a true technique for singing pianissimo is impractical. Loudness relaxes concentration; softness sharpens it. The smaller the degree of volume, the better the comprehension. Without a pianissimo technique, ensembles *are* unintelligible. If ensembles are performed with greater variety of degrees in volume among the various voices, the words will be understood. It is only the style of singing in use which makes ensembles unintelligible.

The chorus is one of the prime artificialities in opera, and has no place there at all. The chorus in Greek drama was artificial. The theater has long ago either done away with it or substituted for it. In opera it is only an excuse for sonority and spectacle. Yet even the chorus, if cut in size, could be intelligible.

The final consideration about singing does not have to do with mechanics, but with responsibility. As opera became more complex, the tacit assumption grew that the music is most important. As a result, the musical responsibility in opera descended from the stage to the conductor in the orchestra pit. This is aesthetically false. The dramatic and musical force should be controlled from the stage by the singer. The singer has avoided this responsibility, and the psychological loss has been detrimental. This responsibility must be onstage. The attention of the spectator will then be focused on one spot — the exact spot where the co-existence of music and word is realized.

The third school of thought maintains that understanding of the word is "undesirable because." There are five arguments, but two of them are exceptionally weak. No one will deny that subtleties of the original libretto may be lost in translation. But if the subtleties are not understood in the first place, what does it matter if a million are lost. That understanding of the words is undesirable because the literary merit of the libretto is questionable seems a very negative criticism. It is the fault of the translator if improvements are not made to adjust the libretto to present-day standards. Making the libretto more literary is difficult but not impossible. Even the repetitiousness of opera libretti can be altered effectively. Both these arguments hinge upon the success or failure of the translator, and depend upon the assumption that the word is an excuse for writing music. This assumption has already been dealt with in previous paragraphs.

The three remaining arguments are important ones:

1. Compared with other languages, English is not essentially apt for musical setting.
2. In translation, words other than those originally intended must be fitted with the music, therefore the music is altered in emotional intent and technical arrangement.

3. The original language determines the musical style, therefore the juxtaposition of another language with the original musical style is disturbing.

The assumptions behind these three arguments are assumptions about the influence of words on music.

The influence of the particular language on the emotional intent of the music. Composers do not set words to music because the words are sonorous. Words are used for the specific expressive and emotional possibilities they can contain and not for any sound effects they have. For this reason no language is any more fit for musical setting than any other. For this same reason no language is more fit for listening to than one's own. Music without words can portray an emotional state. The specific degree of this emotional state is clarified by the specific word. Music which portrays a state of excitement can portray any one of a variety of degrees of excitement — the excitement of love, the return of a loved one after a long absence, inheriting a fortune. Music which portrays a state of tension can be used for any number of emotional situations differing in degree of tension. The same music will in no way appear false to the state of emotion, but will take on the different degree from the impact of the words. The basic states of emotion are not monopolized by any particular language. Music is arranged to portray the state of emotion which the specific words imply. Translation need have no effect on the basic emotional situation.

The specific degree cannot be a part of the musical arrangement, for music by itself is ambiguous; the specific degree is clarified in the listener's mind by the presence of words. The specific degree is often changed in translation, but does not make any intrinsic change in the emotional state itself. The particular word in the particular language requires no special setting beyond portrayal of the basic emotional state. Words other than those intended, as long as they do not disregard the original state of emotion, do not alter the original emotional intent of the music.

The influence of the particular language on the technical arrangement of the music. It cannot be denied that translation requires certain changes in the technical arrangement of the music. Words will need placement at different pitch levels than originally intended, and the rhythm of the vocal line will need adjustment.

These two aspects are only superficial, however. One has only to look at Schubert songs, wherein two or more verses have been set to the same melody, to see that rhythmic adjustments were not considered distortions of the vocal line and that the pitch level of words is not as important as assumed. These changes can be made in translation without destroying the original emotional intent of the music at all.

Once it is understood that the words can be altered considerably when it comes to the specific degree of the emotional state, a greater range of words becomes available to the translator. The original balance between pure melody and proper prosody will be easier to maintain; the necessary adjustments will be few. The emotional intent of the music determines the technical arrangement more than any factors in the particular language. It would be a mistake for a composer to assume that rhythmic and pitch considerations connected with his language should determine the technical arrangement of his music, for these considerations may be completely alien to the emotional state which should be portrayed. The words imply and determine the state of emotion, but have only a superficial influence on the technical arrangement needed for musical portrayal of this state.

The influence of language on musical style. The particular language itself influences the emotional intent of the music, determines superficially a part of the musical arrangement, but has no effect on the musical style. Composers make or adopt musical styles. Certain languages are associated with certain musical styles because composers wrote in that language. The assumption that language *influences* musical style is false. The differences between a Bach Cantata or a Handel Oratorio are in no way connected with German and English. They are associated with those languages by specific knowledge of the style of the composers. There is no real musical or dramatic reason why the juxtaposition of English with music normally associated with another language should be disturbing. It is a question of habit on the part of some, special knowledge on the part of a few, and snobbery on the part of the majority. The advantages of translation far outweigh this disturbance.

A composer, however, must not assume that language influences musical style. A composer invents or adopts a style which is natural to him. He can combine any language with this style. If he writes enough operas which hold the attention of a public, and which are not replicas of past works, *his style* will be associated thereafter with *whatever language he has used.*

In conclusion let these negatives be put into a positive form. Certainly the viewpoint which these positives sustain will necessitate an entirely new approach to the production of the operas of the past, an approach which some will regard as mutilation. Opera is a perishable product, but no more perishable than the theater. The theory that the printed score is inviolate is a detrimental one. Each age must either revitalize the art of the past or put it into a museum. The printed score of an opera should be in a library, but not on the stage. If the past is on the stage there can be no present.

The following must be accepted as truths if opera is to become a musical force in the present:

1. Words give music its emotional significance.
2. Singing is the only natural and specifically expressive musical medium.
3. The production of sonority and volume is not the function of singing.
4. Singing is chamber music and has no place in a large auditorium.
5. The responsibility for the dramatic and musical force must come from the stage.
6. Acting is entirely dependent upon the word.
7. No langauge is any more fit for musical setting than any other.
8. The particular language does not influence the emotional intent or technical arrangement of the music.
9. The particular language does not influence musical style.

Opera based on these assumptions can result in a co-existence of music and drama which insures the maximum participation of the spectator in both elements. Acceptance of these can do away with all the obstacles of opera except the single artificiality of the co-existence itself. In addition, acceptance can make possible a strong argument in favor of this co-existence. When contemporary opera succeeds in illustrating to the listener the greater emotional variety resulting from the combination of words and music — variety which instrumental music does not naturally possess — he will be equipped to read more emotional significance into instrumental music. The success of the latter depends on the former. Once this balance is recognized, opera is appreciated for inherent values, not condemned for artificialities that need not be there.

MUSIC VIA TELEVISION

Norma Bertolami Sapp

TELEVISION producers are not sure what the role of music is on television, other than its traditional one of assisting in some spectacle. Musicians, and particularly music educators, are even less sure. They are apt to be suspicious of the medium and view it as merely one more step away from the live experience, one more bar between the direct communication which is the deepest and truest experience. The purpose of this short paper is to explore some of the ways music and television can be reconciled for entertainment and education.

Opera and ballet are the two most appropriate forms for music via television. They are relatively expensive to produce but not exorbitantly so. Every composer looks to television for the perfect outlet for a new kind of musical theater; but first there are all the financial and commercial hazards to be faced. Network sponsorship of opera is a possibility, based on the traditional sponsorship of the symphony orchestra series or, in some cases, maintenance of symphony orchestras. Opera over radio has been commercially sponsored for many years with a regular following of millions of listeners. We are speaking of two related but basically different things: *television* opera and *televised* opera. The opera or series of operas which is written for television, with the full range of technical possibilities in mind, can be a significant new form, accomplishing what the film industry has never been able to do. The televised opera which is part of a regular production offering of a major opera company is a great advance over radio opera to be sure, but it is still a hybrid in which sets, acting, and time schemes belong to a foreign medium.

The way to accomplish the equally desirable ends of generating a stream of new operas composed and conceived for the medium and of bringing the antiquities to television is to establish a Theater which would produce an opera twice a week or so throughout a nine month season, subcontracting for singers and costumes but maintaining a production staff of stage managers, conductors, and orchestra. Each opera would be restaged with the new medium in mind at each step. Such a theater would not be in competition with regular opera companies but actually would serve to educate a new public and advertise traditional opera.

Ballet is perhaps most ideal for television entertainment. The problems of restaging or readapting which beset the opera are almost negligible here. There is no question about it: a composer planning a ballet has an excellent chance of seeing it and hearing it on television. The principal danger is the same, however, as in opera — that too many pressures will combine to depress the level of work, i.e., limited budgets, timetables, mass audiences, or amateur production.

To return for a moment to opera, it will be extremely interesting to see what form the new tradition of television opera takes. There may be elements of the revue, of the musical comedy, the night club skit, the burlesque act, the film short subject, the radio half hour play — all these very characteristic minor forms may play as important a role in shaping the tradition as the longer, more impressive, and more oppressive standard operatic literature. One of the aspects which is almost sure to emerge is the short time scheme. Operas of a half hour or at most an hour will be the rule. Short operas based on fairy tales, exploiting the national traditions or mythology of many countries, are likely to be a fundamental type, since they should include the two principal ingredients of fantasy and violence. So far the most successful opera has been "Amahl and the Night Visitors," a piece of delicate fantasy which is apt to be the "Christmas Carol" of the Television world.

Televising of concert music is quite another question. Here the premise that a symphony orchestra and its conductor are fascinating to watch runs into the hard fact that a concert is a communal experience of a quite special sort, in which the visual effect of the orchestra is not half so important as the undercurrent of group communication and the reality of the sound in an acoustically vibrant hall. Looking at an orchestra is exciting once or twice, and if you happen to be a student of orchestration it is always stimulating. When the second oboe starts to act and the conductor begins to "emote" for the cameras, then the quality of the event is inevitably bound to suffer. In other words, televising a symphony orchestra concert involves much more than a mere technical production problem of obtaining variety in camera angles and focal lengths, in balancing "solo" and "group" views. It is a fundamental question, pivoting around the very meaning of a concert. The inescapable compulsion to dramatize through the conductor is only less revolting than the pandering which could take place to a highly emotional guest soloist.

One grim prospect is the thought that is sure to occur to some enterprising television producer of permitting the music to be accompanied by "free association patterns" in the manner of Walt Disney's "Fantasia." One shudders at the thought of what could happen during the Beethoven Third Symphony; a whole panoply of Napoleonic lore could be unslung. If a concert *has* to be televised or is of such extraordinary interest that it should be, the most important thing to create is the mood and atmosphere of the audience and the tone of the concert hall. The pre-concert tuning period, entrances and exits of performers, arrival of latecomers, the glow on the faces of the musicians after a good concert — these are much more important than etched lines on the conductor's face.

Related closely to this is the matter of an audience's privacy. A violation of this privacy, an intrusion on the communication channels between orchestra and concertgoer is unthinkable. Not only are many people ridiculous looking when lost in the transports of a piece they love, but they are also sleepy on occasion. The right to nap through a boring piece is inalienable; to infringe it is to breach one of the last citadels of private action.

It is doubtful if a televised series of symphony concerts is either desirable or valuable. A much more ideal medium is Frequency Modulation radio. There are some ways that the violations of privacy mentioned above can be minimized. For instance, a camera might be placed in a position exactly like that of one of the audience so that the visual experience of the audience is shared with television viewers. In such a case it is to be hoped that a producer does not impishly decide to take a position behind a pillar; this experience, a frequent enough one, would seem to be one that television might spare us. An occasional concert of special interest, either because of the presence of a distinguished guest or because of unusual music or a massing of forces, might be a great entertainment experience; a continuous series could be catastrophic.

Much more plausible and more appropriate to the medium is the rehearsal of a symphony orchestra, not the *rehearsed* rehearsal but a genuine one without any audience at all. Broadcasts of rehearsals lack all the elements which telecasted rehearsals would have: the shirtsleeves, baleful glares, unseemly explosions and aggressive informality. This would be in the category of "candid television" and would involve close production supervision and editorial moderation.

In fact a series of programs revolving around the stages of putting music together, examined in an almost clinical way, would have high entertainment *and* educational value. To trace through a choral work from first contact to partial mastery to final rehearsals or to show the evolution of a chamber music performance as two players work out the details of a new work is to get at the roots of music-making. All the grinding together and the tempering of personal ideas and all the slowly cumulative excitement of discovering a new piece would be dramatized.

One of the most interesting of this type of program is the televised composer's workshop. Three or four composers gather together to discuss recent works, informally and frankly. The music is played several times and laid on the operating table for humane dissection. If the session could be done without formality and awkwardness with a completely spontaneous series of reactions and comments, it would be enormously instructive and provocative.

A second type of program of this same general class is the discussion of a single piece of music, preferably a solo work, by a number of performers who have studied it and who are anxious to compare ideas on it. If the work were, let us say, the Schumann *Papillons* and the performers three pianists with markedly differing views on its interpretation, the specific problems of phrasing, pedaling and tempo would be only less interesting than the general problems of playing all Schumann and all Romantic piano music. Obviously, a series of such programs concerned with significant works would be of great interest; a permanent moderator, himself a performer, would probably be essential for continuity.

It seemed wise to pause for these two more precise examples of musical programs in order to make a graceful transition to educational television, for it is in the general area of educational television that music can play a more critical role. As in educational radio broadcasting, the mission of educational television is not specific, vocational, or technical but broad, liberalizing, and synthetic. While it is possible to postulate an audience which is literate and eager to be more so, it is not always wise to restrict the offerings to this particular group. Gilbert Seldes points out [1] that *audiences are created* when good material is supplied, that an imaginative program builds an audience. The televised concert, perhaps the televised opera, and special programs of the type already mentioned, may certainly be a prime part of any television station's programming, but explicit education is also a function of such stations, although perhaps less so on television than on radio.

The historical survey course at an introductory level is the basic music course for television. Particularly is this true if the course assumes no prior knowledge about music. Such a course, the more elaborate the better, has the inherent dramatic as well as the broad educational properties which suit it well for the medium. In breadth of design, in the personal expression of deep underlaying beliefs about the functions of music, in the very rhythm of constantly changing topics and personalities, it is less troubled than other courses in its program to program continuity. While it is true that a series of lectures about individual composers or some selected period of history could be treated in much the same way, it would be a mistake to substitute a series of televised lectures for a real course designed for television, with the advantages and disadvantages of the medium clearly in mind in all the planning and execution stages of the venture.

And yet, from a practical point of view there is a great obstacle in the way of realizing this objective: the simply incredible amount of time it will require to organize and produce it on a high scholarly level. The need for cross-checking extends not only to the spoken word but also to the seen thing, the diagram and the picture. Timing is of the highest importance. Such an ideal course is much more than a mere photographing of a lecture, even though the lecture be a lively one with much variety and change of pace. To be most telling, the history of music course should bring in material cutting across forms of art — particularly the graphic forms. In the evocation of an era, films, slides, paintings, all may be germane. Probably, therefore, the idea will be only approached with the inevitable compromises along the way. As long as they are compromises of tangential things, reluctant discarding of some complicated apparatus, the compromises do not matter so much. For, in the final analysis, no amount of machinery is going to ennoble an impoverished set of ideas, weakly marshalled.

Does instruction in music theory offer any promising scope in television? Yes, it is both more practical and more necessary than the basic history course or special history courses. The most useful disciplines are courses in instrumentation, the history of musical instruments, or orchestration. One course combining elements of all three is best. The rich field of musical instruments is endlessly fascinating, not only to the music student but to all people with a mechanical turn of mind. In this one instance the music historian or theorist has some of the trappings which many television producers think are necessary to proper programs. We need not envy the chemist with his banks of tubes, foaming flasks and colored bottles of reagents; we have the *tromba marina*, the Russian bassoon, and the *cornetto* to bring an exotic aura to the course. In practical instrumentation, a lecture can be illustrated by demonstration on the spot and recorded excerpts from the literature. The ability of the camera to draw in close to the mechanism, to get on top of the parts usually obscured by the performer's hands is a distinct advantage over the ordinary class demonstration. Since, in any case, a certain amount of physics plays a role in orchestration, this might require even more apparatus! Orchestration itself will be as difficult over television as it is in class, but there will be the one major difference: that recorded music will be much less inappropriate. An orchestration course could reach a wide audience and serve as a continuously useful adjunct to radio programs of serious music as well as to courses in music history.

Harmony and counterpoint are of less general interest and lack the visual attractiveness of orchestration. The lecture on harmony is of dubious value; on counterpoint it is rather beside the point. In the realm of harmonic analysis the course would have more obvious relevance in the medium of television, although if one *had* to give a course on harmony or counterpoint one possible way to improve it would be to revive the dialogue style, the *magister-discipulus* relationship. Informal conversation (carefully organized in structure, but not in diction) could create a warm and creative atmosphere, would serve to repeat important ideas in a natural, unforced way.

A small chorus, to perform music being analyzed, is a part of a harmony or theory course; this is much more satisfactory than the piano which is useful enough in illustrating technical points but less effective when treating voice leading. In contrapuntal analysis, good performances of the work under consideration, which would ordinarily be done by a class functioning as a chorus, add immeasurably to the vitality of the course. A great many of the essentials of counterpoint can be grasped through analysis and performance alone. It is clear enough, however, that the major (and almost insuperable) problem in harmony and counterpoint is that no one can learn either without putting notes to paper and receiving close criticism of these trials. Analysis of form or for that matter analysis of anything has the natural adaptability of a high proportion of charts and tables or diagrams, all of which fit easily into the medium, but there is not a great deal specifically suggested by the medium to alter present pedagogical methods in the teaching of theory. The difference between televising classroom work and preparing educational programs for television production have already been stressed.

Advanced courses — seminars and conference groups of graduate students — are of relatively little general appeal; and the need for private, unruffled communication is so great that under no circumstances should televising ever be permitted. The delicate balances of such groups of scholars are easily enough upset without the added hazards of a probing camera. This does not exclude the occasional prepared *colloquium* made particularly for television and more or less outside regular class functions.

So far, the approach to music via television has been from the consideration of types of instruction now being offered, and a few points about the "quotient of adaptability" to television. Another way of investigating the whole subject is to summarize some of the obvious gains or advantages of television. One point that should be made once and repeated concerns the reminder that serious education whether by radio, television or in actual classrooms depends on excellent teaching and vital personalities. No amount of machinery or effect can alter this humble limitation. If the accent in this paper is on methods and techniques, it is only because the premise is, of course, that there is a problem of adaptation and of understanding a new and quite taxing medium a little more. Poor teachers will be even poorer on television; charlatans and frauds will remain what they are, no matter how many tricks they evolve.

What are some of the advantages of the medium for teaching, not advantages over classroom or private instruction but positive features which suggest that preparing courses for television involves more than merely tidying up. *Television can save time.* It necessarily requires that, whatever special effects or special props are used, they must be worked into the course hour or half-hour automatically, i.e., so that time is not lost in changing position or waiting for slide machines to be focussed properly. Ideally, all the *extrania* incidental to teaching can be regulated more efficiently than they can be in classrooms. *Television can dramatize.* No matter how skillful a lecturer is, there is always an occasion when he wishes to point up or highlight something and finds that he lacks the apparatus to do it forcefully. The sudden change of illumination, the sharply focussed spotlight, the rapid change of focal length lens, or the double image effects which are routine in television productions have a legitimate place in dramatizing major points. *Television unifies a lecture-recital.* As the apparatus of the large lecture increases — the lecturer surrounded by a battery of push buttons, platoons of assistants, public address systems, intermixtures of piano music and recordings — so does the disunity of the event. What television can do is reduce all this to one plane, so to speak. All the sound is electronically reproduced and all the images are transmitted through lenses. Under normal and optimum reception conditions, sound and image merge into a unified, albeit two dimensional, effect. There is no need, it is hoped, to make it clear that, unity or no, the impact of a television lecture does not begin to compare with the vitality of a great lecturer, in a proper hall, with an attentive audience. *Television brings the university into the community.* Not only does it bring instruction but it helps to break down false ideas about who teachers are and how they talk and act. By bringing out the tone and the ideals of a university faculty, it serves a valuable public relations function. In no period is it as necessary to assert the interest of university in community affairs and the willingness of its faculty to serve.

While admittedly this last point is a general one, applicable to music as it is to all fields, the musician, who is teacher, performer, composer, historian, and any mixture of these, is particularly well suited to representing the university. The great dangers to music from television concern the infringement of the group experience of the concert, the substitution of system and method for substance and scholarship, and an emphasis on personalities rather than on materials. Over-dramatic handling, not the reverse, is a clear pitfall. The advantages of music via television stem from the opportunities to unify the presentation of courses to a mass audience and to bring music-making in various stages out of the purely professional areas. A corollary danger associated with the coming of television is the menace to educational and quasi-educational Frequency Modulation radio broadcasting of good music.

In conclusion, music via television creates more problems than opportunities at the moment; there is no agreement as to how important a part serious music and serious music education will play in commercial or in educational television. In five years the subject will be ready for research, for statistics and for remedial action. Now the patterns are yet to be fixed, and the ideas await implementation.

1. "Radio, TV, and the Common Man," *The Saturday Review*, August 29, 1953, p. 12.

THE RECORD REVIEW: CONTENT AND PURPOSE

Allen Sapp

THE best reviews of recordings discuss music, criticize performance, and evaluate many technical features. They meet the
highest standards of literary criticism and, like a perceptive book
review, may range far or focus sharply. In a sense, the type of
review now appearing in critical journals specifically aimed at the
professional musicologist or music librarian is a model. The highest
degree of musical literacy can be presumed; references to the music
can be precise, technical; and all the scholarly apparatus of the
critical essay is appropriate. The recordings to be reviewed are
carefully selected. Often only important or particularly noteworthy recordings are reviewed. Since the reviews are usually
written by specialists who speak authoritatively in their field, there
is a unique opportunity for giving aid and comfort to the harassed
faculty record committee or record librarian. The seriously limiting
factors on the usefulness of these reviews are: a high degree of
selectivity of recordings and a conspicuous absence of information
about the engineering characteristics of individual records.

Recorded sound, facsimile sound, is becoming the sound which
we know best. This is deplorable. There is no particular point in
comparing live and recorded sound. Recording equipment, no
matter how expensive, elaborate or complex, always distorts; and
reproducing equipment distorts even more. Listening to recorded
music is an experience inferior in every respect to hearing music
actually being performed. However, the fact is that records are a
part of every college and university library. The problems of en-
larging it and meeting current requirements in course instruction
become more complicated each month. The number of new recording companies, the broader and deeper coverage of the literature of music, and a bewildering variety of technical improvements

designed to make distortion less irritating all suggest a need for more comprehensive and informative record reviews.

What does a complete review include? It examines the music. The work or works are identified and placed in context. This is an extremely important stage in the record review of an unfamiliar piece, where matters of performance practice, medium, and edition may all come to bear. All the usual bibliographical methods for establishing the text actually recorded are appropriate. Essentially then, a record review made on the basis of what is on the record alone is insufficient, even though the record may be very attractive in a number of ways — tasteful performance and fine sound quality. Perhaps this is an elementary point; it is surely a fundamental one. In the case of so many of the recent *Long Playing* recordings of works composed prior to 1750, text emendations and alterations are frequent and often open to question. Whenever a text is a composite or a collated version made by one of the performers, it ought to be compared with manuscript sources or published editions.

Data about the composer may be important. This will depend obviously on the work, the specific recording, and the composer. Certainly, the brief critical essay on a composer being represented for the first time on recordings is always relevant, as is background on major composers which correlates more or less with the music. The formula for this has already been established in the program notes of the leading Symphony Orchestras, in particular the consistently informative and scholarly notes of the Boston Symphony Orchestra, written by John N. Burke.

After establishing a version of the music actually recorded and providing a factual background for it, the reviewer evaluates it. The pretense, or rather the fraud, of "objective" criticism is no more valid here than it is in any other essay. It is this phase of the record review which is least consequential at present. There seems to be reluctance to "criticize" — and perhaps the very phrase *record review* shows up the point. To "review" is not to "criticize" in many an instance. There is a reporting function in the record review, to be sure, and the lists of new recordings which many periodicals include (in addition to articles) are useful up to a point. The record review in which music is discussed exclusively in terms of collated bio-bibliographical information misses the mark. An opinion must be rendered, an honest judgment on the recording,

not an accolade for meritorious service in bringing a forgotten
work to life, not a flip dismissal of it on a pearly epigram. We should
be able to form some estimate of the reviewer's real critical ability,
as distinct from his scholarly thoroughness. The faceless, grimly
impartial essay which tells us nothing of the man behind is no accomplishment; it is a failure.

Writing of the music leads to the performance. If the recording
is one of several performances available, comparisons are invariably
illuminating. If it is the only one — or the first one in a series, the
need for careful appraisal is clearly redoubled. As the number of
historical recordings grows, closer attention to performance is
warranted. Among other points to be considered here are:

(1) Is the recording what it purports to be?

(2) If it is what it purports to be, is it musically and historically
reliable?

(3) In which particulars is there variation from accurate or conventional performance?

Authenticity is definitely not restricted to educational series such
as the *Anthologie Sonore* or *Music of the Orient*. Baroque music
in particular is recorded in an amazingly large spectrum of performance attitudes. Consider the versions of the Bach *Second
Brandenburg Concerto*, for instance. Variations in instrumentation,
in ornamentation, and in rhythmic interpretation are quite discon-
certing. The review must point out performance practice which
is obviously out of style or inaccurate. If the work is an arrangement (frankly so or not) it is important to mention other recorded
versions which are in original scorings. On the other hand, the
historical recording is not the only acceptable one by any means.
Many such a performance is inelastic, rhythmically mechanical,
technically deficient, downright boring. In comparing recordings
of a Corelli *Concerto Grosso* a review should single out the versions in which harpsichord plays the keyboard part as being closer
to contemporary practice than the versions which omit it altogether
or use piano. There might be all sorts of deficiencies in performance
which could cancel out these "historical advantages." Many a con-
scientious and worthy effort is aborted by leaving the impression,
through mediocre or sloppy performance, that the music is, in fact,
dull or pedestrian.

Just as the record review has many points in common with the concert bulletin of a Symphony Orchestra or the program notes of a chamber music series, so it resembles a review of a concert, particularly in its concern with musicality as distinguished from authenticity. The record reviewer has the obvious advantage of being able to vary the conditions under which he listens to a performance. He can space out hearings so that a factor like fatigue is neutralized as far as possible. Everyone who has done reviewing knows how important what came before a performance is, what a difference it can make in the net impression. Seen in the perspective of a day or a week of dreary recitals and unimaginative programs, a concert performance may loom up all out of proportion. A recording freezes the notes, but the *moment* of music is when you listen to it. A decision about performance almost always involves comparisons — with other recorded versions and with live performances or even broadcast versions. Sometimes a performer has made several recordings of the same work. One very irritating habit of some record reviewers, after making some diluted pronouncement ("competent," "musicianly," "adequate," "commendable"), is to wax rhapsodic about some recording first issued in 1927 and long since unobtainable, except through the antique avenues of record commerce. This mixture of snobbery and sticky nostalgia serves very little purpose and helps perpetuate the cult of record collecting, which has so frequently nothing to do with music at all.

The music, the performance, and finally the engineering are the three principal points for review. It can safely be said that the man who is qualified to judge music and performance is rarely competent to speak of engineering and *vice versa*. However, to ignore the engineering aspect completely or to minimize it unduly is to fail as much as if no reference is made to the music. At the beginning of the review, preferably in some conventionalized way apart from the main body, it is important to specify what equipment is being used to study the recording. Most professional reviewers have elaborate sound-reproducing apparatus and know something about the technical specifications of the various units which make it up. There is a jargon, far from conventionalized, highly imprecise and exasperating, which may eventually become standard usage for describing "record surface." At the present time it is not particularly valuable except in cases where a major engineering defect is being examined. Despite the lack of a generally useful vocabulary or glossary of terms, engineering evaluation is too critical to be omitted or slighted. There is a basic problem of describing sound. To do it in terms of graphs or formulas is little help. To become poetic may be possible if one is poetically endowed. All musicians resent strongly the tendencies of some "high-fidelity" fanatics who submerge music and performance, musicianship and the creative imagination in a nomenclature both controversial and faddistic; and yet, a recording which is distorted or sonically irritating is a poor pedagogic tool. If it is "dead" or reverberant or shrill, it may be as useless as any shocking misrepresentation of the score.

There are some things a record reviewer can do to cope with the admittedly paradoxical problem of treating engineering:

(1) He can familiarize himself with the "kind of sound ideal" a manufacturer has chosen. Each recording company has adopted a different set of compromises in the continuing search for what is most practical and what is most true. The matter goes beyond curves on paper or needles fluctuating on delicate gauges. Choice, preference, and suppression enter into the final version of the "recording sound ideal." Over a period of time this tends to be consistent within medium and is capable of description in one way or another. Naturally, this fact is apt to lead a reviewer to certain prejudices, but, basically, prejudices of the same sort as those connected with performers, to be weighted the same way.

(2) He can weigh in the influence of the *place* of recording and in some cases the *manner* of recording. While most large orchestras record in their permanent concert halls, some do not or are forced to use inferior halls in the first place. Some of the idiosyncrasies of halls affect recordings. It is often difficult to find out just where recordings of chamber ensembles have actually been made. It occasionally helps to explain why a recording is lustreless. The *manner* of recording is more important. A relatively large number of recent *Long Playing* records are pressings made from tape-recorded broadcasts. A few are from actual concert performances. In either case the recording may suffer — from extraneous noise, from unsatisfactory microphone placement, from inferior audio modulation transmission.

(3) He should consider a great variety of other mechanical

points which do not call for any particular special orientation or background. Most of these arise from technical problems stemming from tape recording and more specifically from the editing of tapes:

(a) When American equipment is used abroad, motor speed is apt to be affected by differences in voltage and phase of current. When tapes are replayed on machines in this country differences in motor speed may cause a pressing in the wrong key. In some cases the difference is as much as a half-tone. When this initial defect is compounded by a turntable which is rotating at the wrong speed, the deviation from true performance may be critical.

(b) Most recordings involve splicings of several tapes and may involve much more complicated editing procedures such as using a section of one tape for part of a movement and a section of a second for the rest. An increasingly high number of recordings are actually composites of many performances. Poor editing results in pitch fluctuation, omission of portions of the music, repetition of music, or severe dynamic distortion. This latter defect is apt to occur if two machines are not exactly equalized in recording level. A careful processing engineer will compensate, but there may be a fraction of a moment in which there is a sharp change in volume.

(c) Tape recorders which are improperly serviced or are below high quality can seriously distort the tone of some difficult to record instruments such as oboe or piano. These distortions ("wow" or "flutter") spring from variability of tape speed and irregularity of contact of tape with recording heads. Of course, very few of the larger manufacturers permit release of recordings in which tape flutter is perceptible, but an amazingly high percentage of piano recordings reaches the commercial market in an unsatisfactory condition.

(d) Record turns or breaks which come in the middle of phrases are no longer tolerable. This is now purely an editorial process, not an insuperable part of the recording itself. *Long Playing* records have made this less and less of a real problem but all the more reason for eliminating it completely.

(e) *Long Playing* records are usually divided up in bands, indicating different pieces or movements of a whole work. When this is not done it often leads to confusion and wasted time. It is hard enough to find isolated parts of a work on *LP* records; without bands it is practically impossible to use them for classroom teaching or lecture purposes.

Records are usually accompanied by some sort of brochure or pamphlet, ranging from embarrassing effusions to learned essays of some brilliance. Format, quality, style vary widely. There has been a marked and welcome improvement in their tone with the recent turning to less familiar music. It is not uncommon for the complete text of an opera in the original language and a good translation to be included. In many historical recordings facsimiles of the music are provided. Song texts, as important as opera texts, often lack good translations. How much a record review should take this material into account will vary with the work, but it is always appropriate to correct gross blunders of fact or clear typographical errors which distort meaning. The more ambitious and pretentious they are, the more they deserve mention — commendation or correction. While it is the responsibility of record manufacturers to make the brochures increasingly useful, the record review can help by keeping up a vigilant campaign against slovenly, inaccurate, frothy or heavily biased material.

So far in this survey of the record review the focus has been on content: the music, the performance, and the engineering of each recording under consideration. There is no reason why reviews of records should not be as witty, as incisive, as pleasurable as the thoughtful book review. Reviewers of records seem strangely confined, limited in their outlook and their perspective. It is partially because of medium itself, partly because of extremes in prospective audience, partly because of a lack of tradition in the essay form, and — in great part — because of the antipathy to records which many musicians still have. However, the record review is now respectable, even if extraordinarily inconsistent in style, form, and tone. Some of the *purposes* of the record review are not clearly defined, although the reporting function is the one universally accepted.

Teacher, scholar, or librarian (often one and the same person) need dependable reviews of new recordings. This is not the place to discuss the role of records in music education, but it is clear that a library of disk and tape recordings can play a growing role in stimulating interest in music and make more vivid courses in the history and theory of music (particularly orchestration). The record is *sui generis* less important than the making of music. For whatever uses the record has in course instruction — as an adjunct to lectures, as the basic material for "listening hours," or as the raw material of detailed analysis in smaller gatherings — good reviews can help point the way. At present there is no consistently reliable guide to new recordings. A library official is handicapped in taking care of all aspects of his collection, although there are admittedly some areas which are covered very well indeed.

The general public need record reviews. By favoring works outside the standard repertory and by insisting on good taste and faultless processing the review can help bring music to more people — particularly those whose interests are intellectual but not specifically musical as yet. In this role, the review is in itself education or should be. A well written critique of new recordings can be the door leading to a whole treasure of music. Since the fare offered by manufacturers continues to be less and less anchored to the dreary conventional literature, the public which buys records or listens to them over good music radio stations need essays which stimulate and inform. In a very real sense the good review is adult education and, like all branches of that poor relation, can be conducted on an inspiringly high level or an appallingly low one.

For the retailer, the direct marketer of records, informed reviews are most helpful. He is nurtured on the publicity pap of his wholesalers, baffled by the Middle Ages, often in no position to pass judgment on the merchandise he is selling. Even if it was commercially inexpedient for him to follow the advice of the review, at least he would know a little more about what he was trading in. Since the retailer is a man in a good position to influence the large public through personal contact, he might just as well be leading it to new music, more accurate performances, more exciting discoveries. The thirty or so smaller manufacturers with no sales organizations, limited advertising budgets are in a disadvantageous position *vis à vis* the major ones in "educating" the retailer. While a catalog of current monthly issues cumulated is extremely useful, it only emphasizes the need for more comprehensive reviews. Everyone always complains about the unsatisfactory and frustrating service given by most record stores; here is a way of improving it.

Record companies have the prick of competition to goad them to better workmanship and more distinguished recordings, and this pressure will always be the major spur to improvement. An alert review can force manufacturers to maintain high standards. As a watchdog on the industry so to speak there are any number of useful things to be accomplished:

(1) By steady pressure a review can promote the reissue of

valuable records which are "out of print." There are any number
of pioneer recordings made in the early 1930's of modern works
(The *Gurrelieder* or the Roy Harris *Symphony 1933*) or of memorable performances of better known works (The Rachmaninoff-
Kreisler *Duo Sonata* of Schubert or the Gieseking *Ondine* of Ravel)
which should be reissued.

(2) A review can insist that the literature accompanying records
be useful and attractive. There is a need for a code to operate
throughout the industry, and a review could establish and police
such a code.

(3) A review should agitate for the recording of works as yet
unrecorded or available in substandard versions.

(4) A review can bring to the attention of a large public a fine
performer who is beginning a career or who has not concertized
in the United States. While there is hardly any performer whose
fame rests exclusively on recordings, there are many who have
prepared the way by recordings (Artur Schnable and Paul Badura-
Skoda, for example). Many European performers are known to
American audiences only through recordings — Mogens Wöldike,
Heinrich Schlusnuss, David Oistrakh, Herbert Haefner, Monique
Haas, or Elizabeth Schwarzkopf. A review should be quick to distinguish, alert to praise a fine performer, and it should furnish
information about such performers.

(5) A review can publicize the worth-while projects of recording companies, particularly the enterprises which are obviously
courageous such as the Haydn Society's plans for recording all the
works of Haydn or the Columbia Records plan for a regular series
of contemporary American works.

(6) A review is a check on uncontrolled and confusing advertising. It can present opinions and facts about much-trumpeted
technical advances.

An independent record review militant, literate, and urbane has
a place in review sections of daily and Sunday newspapers, of large-
circulation general magazines, of literary magazines with small but
often vocal subscription lists, and of musical journals of greater and
lesser scholarship. While the *Record Review* sections of publications like the *Musical Quarterly* or *Notes* accomplish superbly
their limited objective — the assessment of new recordings of ex-

traordinary interest in a scholarly fashion — they do not provide the completeness of coverage which custodians of University collections need, and they have relatively little effect on the producers of recordings.

It was tempting to explore the record review as it is rather than as it might well be. The causes of poor reviews are many, and it might be worth while to summarize some of them. Many of the underlying reasons have already emerged, implicitly at least. Common to many particular causes is lack of agreement about the uses of records in education. Here, attitudes range from complete dismissal of records as sinister and monstrous distortions to whole hearted embrace of them as the quickest, easiest and most effective way to reach the largest number. These underlying attitudes affect the tone and assumptions of reviews. Nothing is really more tiresome than ill-concealed irony or contempt about facsimile sound, a *given* condition.

In a somewhat similar sense the review aimed at the collector shows almost as much lack of common agreement about the uses of records. *Collector* is not used in any particular, derogatory sense. Many collectors are constantly being reinfected by close contact with concert music or by the making of music. With the collectors who are collectors of records rather than of first editions or autographs or figurines, the snobbery is apt to be worst. The market is of names. The focus is on the antique, a dismal preciousness. Reviews aimed in this direction flounder in this stew, setting a tone which is occasionally elegant but seldom illuminating. The pontifications of these oracular cultists are hardly worth condemning.

The review written for the general audience makes frequently the classic error of writing down. No special knowledge is presumed; but just enough technical material is strewn through the essay to impress and authenticate. Sarcasm and waspish wit are the usual substitute for considered judgment. Behind all this may be a sketchy musical training coupled with an underestimation of the public's interest in and capacity to understand music. It recalls the familiar story of music appreciation geared too low, cluttered with systems and methods, weak on substance.

While it has already been stated that the scholarly review is a model, even here there are unsatisfactory features. Too often the music itself is criticized with little relation to the sounds on a recording. It is fine to commend a recording of an obscure work or a special one, but if it is poorly performed and badly engineered it can easily do more harm than good. It is by no means enough that a manufacturer has released a historical recording. Brilliant recordings of "historical" works can be commercially successful. The hazardous ones are those made by musicians whose voices are thin and whose musicianship is thinner. It is curious that record reviews have a prevailingly kind and tolerant tone while book reviews continue in the tradition of scalpel, acid-bath, and direct mortar fire. More venom in record reviews and less in book reviews might be beneficial.

Since the record review is a form handled by professional critics, scholars, musical amateurs with an interest in sound recording, composers — in short a wide variety of persons with differing contacts with the "Worlds of Music," it is apt to remain an orphan in the literary-musico world. It has been the hope of this short and extremely general survey by speculating on what the review needed to do, by defining some of its minimum goals and primary missions, that those who are most able to improve it will take more of an interest in the form. There is much that better reviews can accomplish. Now respectable, with a broad range of purposes ample and worthy, what the record reviews need most is a higher tone and a richer style, a more inclusive approach. This writer's conclusion after reading several hundred of them has been a sharp awareness that very few writers think of the review as much more than a minor chore. At present it is indeed a minor, ambiguous form, but it is not impossible to look forward to a slim volume of collected record reviews, which would be revealing about music as a whole. The trend is definitely up; there is far to go.

CHURCH MUSIC

Lowell P. Beveridge

"A work of genius is a work not to be obtained by the Invo-
cation of Memory and her Syren Daughters, but by devout
prayer to that Eternal Spirit who can enrich with all utterance and knowledge and send out his seraphim with the
hallowed fire of his altar to touch and purify the lips of
whom he pleases." JOHN MILTON

THOSE who are concerned with cultural problems must consider the foundations upon which culture is built. No culture can develop or endure without a foundation in faith. Western culture by
definition is Christian and unless the depths of Christian faith are
drawn upon there is little promise of achieving creative heights.

There is evidence in contemporary literature of renewed concern for the relationship between culture and faith but there is little
agreement about primary assumptions. It is difficult to find a common starting point in the midst of conflicting presuppositions about
the nature of man and the universe. The humanist disagrees with
the theist: the idealist with the naturalist. Indifference toward
metaphysics and epistemology is widespread.

The point of view adopted here will be that an understanding of
the nature of Church Music is possible only through commit-
ment to the faith of the Church, that only from within the community of Christian believers can the needs and hopes of this
community be fully known. The problem of Church Music is a
theological problem.

The inadequacy of Church Music today is the result of a loss of
faith. It may be a mistake to insist that music is a necessary component of Christian worship as it often is a distraction and frequently, as an aid to worship, ineffective. In a recent report issued

by authority of the Archbishops of Canterbury and York the statement is made that music is by no means essential to worship. The report is favorable toward music but stands firmly on the ground that it is non-essential. The starting point is not music but the Church and the message that has been entrusted to it.

The fact of a divided Church is no excuse for evading the issue. The Church never has been perfect and never will be perfect within the limits of human history. Likewise, to say that Church Music can be saved from bankruptcy by purely human means or that it is beyond hope of repair is heretical.

One of the great historic facts about Christianity is its ability to transform and infuse new life into cultural forms through the power of faith. When a civilization loses this faith it surrenders the creative power derived from it.

What is Church Music, or rather, what is Christian Church Music? Neither tradition nor esthetics offers a satisfactory answer. No definition based upon abstract theories or individual taste can do full justice to the breadth and depth of a universal concept such as is needed.

Each of the terms "Church" and "Music" needs explanation. In this context "Church" is not the equivalent of "religious," "sacred," "ecclesiastical" or "liturgical": it is more comprehensive than any of these and contains them all.

"Church" does not mean a building, a congregation or an institution: it means the total aggregation of all Christian people from its inception to the end of history. Its membership consists of all baptized people. The Church is "catholic." This is the greatest conception of society ever expressed in human language. No distinctions are intended: the Church is open to all mankind on the basis of decision. It offers man a solution for his problems: it is realistic and not utopian.

"Catholic" is an ambiguous word: as a description of taste it is unitive, as a description of the Church it is divisive. Its proper meaning is "universal." When used with Church it means a universal society, a great community, containing and supporting the lives, thoughts and enterprises of all its members.

Church Music is not merely the music of worship: it is the music of the whole Christian Folk. Evidence of this concept is to be found in the theological literature of all eras. Church music should be the matrix, the reservoir from which all music is derived. Church music can be great only when it is supported by a great conception of the Church.

Webster defines music as any art over which the muses presided. This definition reflects the classical conception of a musician as a cultured gentleman but fails to do justice to other strains in our musical heritage. Deeply embedded in our cultural subconsciousness are the scientific and ethical ideas of Pythagoras, Aristoxenus, Plato and Aristotle. We can ill afford to ignore the brilliant galaxy of thinkers and writers who established the foundation of our modern culture, ranging from the Church Fathers through Boethius, Isidore, Augustine, Aquinas, and countless others. No definition can ever be completely satisfactory. Schumann described music as a poor orphan whose parents nobody knows but allowed that the mystery of her origin probably accounted for her beauty.

Regardless of the origin and nature of music it is a striking fact that music in western culture differs radically from that of all other cultures. The reason for this cannot be deduced from the music but from the forces which shaped it.

Western culture is built upon the double foundation of Hebrew and Greek elements which were brought together and given new meaning by Christianity. Greek thought was primarily man-centered: Hebrew thought, God-centered. Greek thought was non-historical: Hebrew thought, historical. Western culture developed under the influence of these opposing ideas giving it a unique character. These two points of view are ultimately irreconcilable but Christianity succeeded in maintaining the tension and used it creatively in producing a culture with distinctive characteristics.

Cultural forms are determined by conceptions of man and the universe which are most widely accepted at a given point in history. An exact timetable would be hard to make. Scholasticism controlled the development of medieval music, humanistic thought shaped the music of the renaissance, a return to the essential teachings of Biblical revelation shaped the music of the Reformation, deistic theology greatly influenced the musical products of the eighteenth century, etc.

Musical scholarship has rediscovered the music of past ages but has done little to explain it. No amount of factual information, however reliable, can explain music: music is not self-explanatory. No fact of history can be explained as such: all history is subject to a theory of historical interpretation.

Preoccupation with history is indicative of a lack of faith in the future. Interest in history is essential for establishing a solid foundation but the abstract facts of history give little indication of hope for the future. Reverence for the past is good but when it inhibits the cultural drive into the future it is barren.

Our culture is static from another point of view. We are specimen-minded. Art works are valued intrinsically rather than extrinsically. Art works are valued commercially rather than spiritually. This is understandable but uncreative.

The breach between musical theory and practice is unfortunate. This radical split is rooted in the fundamental difference between Hebrew practice and Greek theory. This is not a purely musical idea. It is derived from the difference between the Greek belief in the immortality of the soul and the Hebrew belief in the survival of the total personality.

The antagonism between theory and practice was articulated by Boethius and his disciples and forms a part of our inheritance. The quadrivium of the medieval university was built on this foundation and this radical split was driven deeper by the acceptance of a Cartesian metaphysic as the academic norm. This attitude is expressed in the statement by Charles Burney that "it seems as if theory and practice were ever to be at strife, for the man of science, who never hears music, and the musician, who never reads books, must be equally averse to each other, and unlikely to be brought to a right understanding."

Eighteenth and nineteenth century philosophers made the final breach between theory and practice, between ethics and esthetics. This was a recognition of the final liberation of music as an independent art but at an exorbitant price.

The concept of music as an integral component of poetry, drama and ceremonial is foreign to our culture. This is the concept upon which western music was originally based but was abandoned with the emergence of music as an independent art. None of the attempts to restore this original unity have been successful. It is a vain hope that the power of Greek drama and poetry or of the Psalms can ever be restored.

St. Paul is often quoted in defense of Christian music but is seldom understood. A thorough understanding of New Testament references might prove embarrassing to defenders of current musical practices in the Church. These references to music are ambiguous and open to various interpretations. There is reason to believe that "music" and "singing" as used in the New Testament have no modern equivalents.

St. Paul admonished the Corinthian Church to sing both with the spirit and the understanding. In so doing he was not laying down a law of esthetics but one of decency and order in the Christian assembly. All vocal utterance was to be for edification as opposed to the emotional and meaningless confusion which had been reported to him and which he intended to suppress.

One of the most conspicuous gaps in modern literature about music is in the field of Biblical exegesis and of ideas about music in the writings of early and medieval theologians.

Any suggestion of an immediate practical solution would be contrary to the spirit of this presentation. There can be no solution at all until the problem is more widely recognized as primarily theological and ultimately Christological. Church music can regain its former power and relevance only through submission to the "Word" and the Christian Gospel. Christian music must help to express fundamental Christian teachings and must enable the Christian folk to participate actively, sincerely and wholeheartedly. Such music would reflect the universality and timelessness of the Christian message. It would employ elements of contemporary culture without being bound by them: it would transform and revitalize these elements. It would appeal to people of all classes and conditions. Above all else it would express the joy, the strength and the hope of the message entrusted to the Christian Church.

CHURCH MUSIC

Willard L. Sperry

Young men going into the ministry are usually given, before they leave a theological school, various rules to guide them in the practice of their profession. Many of these rules are matters of prudence rather than principle. One of them advises the minister not to intermeddle with the music; leave the music committee, the organist and the choirmaster to their own devices. On the whole, this is sound advice and most of us follow it. But, even though few of us ministers have any technical musical training, many of us enjoy and profit by the music of the church and are entitled, as is any member of the congregation, to our own reaction to it. This is doubly true of the man who has spent the whole of a long professional lifetime in the ministry. On this basis I am hazarding a few reflections — confessedly those of a layman rather than a professional — upon what is in fact a very complex problem.

A church service ought to impart the impression of an overall unity. It ought not to be an assembly of theological and aesthetic odds and ends. To put it in no more positive terms, the music ought not to be a violent contrast to the Bible lessons, the prayers and the sermon. If the minister and the choirmaster are good personal friends, the former can tell the latter early in the week what the general idea of the service for the following Sunday is to be, and then the choirmaster can make his choices accordingly. Both together can thus avoid the suggestion of entire indifference to each other.

I remember, from years ago, a first service of morning prayers at the beginning of a college year. It was a lovely late September day. We were all of us cheerful, resolute in our purposes and hopeful for the immediate future. I had prepared a little talk to fit the

occasion and our instinctive mood. But the choir sang in Latin a
Miserere from the Mass as a theme song for the service. The music
was undoubtedly beautiful, and that presumably was the reason for
its selection. Perhaps our musicians believed that our proud human
nature needed to be chastened, but I have to admit that the cheerful
little talk I had proposed was considerably handicapped by the
austere penitential anthem which preceded it. So, a minister in one
of the large Boston churches told me that on a given Sunday he
preached a rousing temperance sermon. When he had finished, the
quartet sang "Crossing the bar." The discrepancy brought a smile
on the faces of his people. In short, it ought to be possible, without
too flagrant intermeddling either way, to avoid striking incon-
gruities of this sort.

Any mature musician will have an instinctive feeling for what
is recognized as church music, for such music presupposes the
general idea of religion. Religion has been described, rather than
defined, as an attempt to live in two worlds at the same time. One
of these worlds is the here-and-now world of hard facts; the other
is the world of our ideals. For Plato and his followers this is the
real world. Religion is an attempt to live in both these worlds at
the same time; that of the facts and that of the ideals. It is easy
enough to live wholly in one of these worlds; it is hard to live in
both at once, indeed that attempt is seldom realized. But it is a
misuse of words to take it for granted, as most persons do, that the
world of hard facts is the real world. Therefore every great religion
involves an awareness of something other than that of which we
are immediately aware here and now. Indeed one of our best modern theologians, Rudolf Otto, speaks of God as "The Wholly
Other." Whoever and whatever God may be at the same time that
he is indwelling in this world, he also stands apart from this world,
in contrast to it. If, by too great preoccupation with this world, a
religion loses its intimation of otherness, its distinction as a religion
is impaired. The affairs of this world are commonly spoken of as
secular; the concerns of the "other world" are called sacred. This
other world need not be heaven hereafter; it may be the quality
of a life lived here and now at a higher level than that of every-day
secularity.

Therefore, however antiquated its style may be, we get in the
King James Bible a hint of the nature of religion which is to a cer-

tain extent sacrificed in any translation which turns to the current vernacular. The Bible ought to be made intelligible, many of its verbal archaisms should be brought up to date. But the process ought not to be carried so far that the initial impression of sacredness is subtly sacrificed to that of secularity. In all these matters we are faced with a paradox which can seldom be resolved. Indeed the tension between sacredness and secularity is itself the core of the religious consciousness. I suppose that something of this sort is implied in the answer which an intelligent doctor once gave me in answer to my question, "Why do you come to church?" He said, "I don't know; I only know that it is for something I don't get the other six days of the week." He wanted, and was right in wanting, some felt otherness to correct or supplement the wholly secular techniques of his professional practice.

One can only say of church music, therefore, that it ought not to be too like the music of the secular world. It will gain by contrast to that music. Very few of us Protestants can understand, much less use confidently, the plain song of the Roman Church. It is so far away from "this world" with which we are familiar, that it fails to touch us. But none of us is wholly immune to the mysterious intimation of otherness as we overhear the singing of the Mass in some great Catholic cathedral. Not that the taste of the Roman Church in these matters is impeccable. I once found myself in the parish church in St. Germain, just outside Paris, penned in a side chapel while a funeral was being conducted in the main church. During the prayers which the priest was saying in private, the silence was given over to a cello soloist who, with an organ accompaniment, played Delilah's song to Samson, "My heart at thy sweet voice," from the opera. Musicians tell me that structurally, that song is the perfect example of secular music; its connotations are not merely sensuous, they are unashamedly sensual. That cello solo lingers on in memory as the most inappropriate bit of "church music" I have ever heard. It had nothing to do with the otherwise high seriousness of a Requiem Mass.

We can understand the necessary intimation of a sacred otherness in the Bach chorales, which are being used more and more frequently in our Protestant worship. They tend to be dragged in tempo, and ought to be sung more boldly than is our custom. But we feel them to belong in church, rather than in the concert hall or on the operatic stage. "Now thank we all our God" is ideal church music. The average congregation can sing it, and usually does so with zest. So, also, the simple tunes to which the Scotch metrical Psalms are sung. In many ways, from the standpoint of corporate congregational worship, our Protestant hymnals have little to compare with the singing of these Psalms in a Scotch service. The members of the congregation are not inhibited in their share in the singing by the false modesty which chills so many church-goers in most of our churches.

Whether in anthems or hymns there is usually a problem of the degree of affinity between the words and the music. Musicians naturally, and perhaps quite properly, have a greater interest in the music itself than in the words. This prior interest sometimes commits a congregation to words about which it may have grave reservations. It is much the fashion in most college chapels today to make constant use of material from the Roman Mass. Very few members, even of an academic congregation, are alert enough clas-sicists to be able, as it were, to catch and translate a Latin text on the wing. Moreover, the use of Latin is a rather radical departure from the Protestant principle that a service of worship should be in the vernacular. The contrast between such anthems and the rest of the service destroys the cultural unity of the service. Familiar as I have become with these Latin anthems I have never become wholly reconciled to them. The late Dr. Johnston Ross was a visiting preacher at the Harvard Chapel some years ago. The choir chanced to sing a Latin anthem to the Virgin. Dr. Ross served notice on us that if we ever did that again when he was with us he would never come back. The words theologically offended his Scotch Presby-terianism. Perhaps Protestants are oversensitive at such a point; perhaps they are religiously mistaken in denying veneration to the "eternal feminine" in the person of the mother of Christ. But be that as it may, nothing is gained in church music by seeming to commit a congregation to propositions to which they cannot consent or against which they have a hereditary aversion. Their animus may be irrational and indefensible, but for the purpose of public worship nothing is gained by rousing it. I doubt whether the beauty of any music is, in itself, a warrant for the use of words which cannot, of themselves, be said in good faith. Thus the familiar apologia for the use of the Athanasian Creed, that it was written as a hymn and meant to be sung, is a rather sophisticated apologia for its liturgical use.

Has the tune antedated the hymn or the hymn the tune? On the whole, the hymn seems to have had priority. In many instances, and those among the best in the hymnal, the words were written as poetry, quite independent of music. Whittier, whose hymns are among the most beautiful in our books, probably never expected, much less intended, his verse to be set to music. Such a usage falls outside the silent meeting to which he was accustomed. It would be hard to leave out "Dear Lord and Father of mankind" from a modern hymnal. But the traditional tune with which most of us associate it has had to be declared out of bounds in most modern hymnals. The arbitrary remarriage of the words to a Bach tune is not very convincing.

That instance may serve as an example of the changes which an improved musical taste have forced on many of our more recent editors of hymnals. The church music of the last century, whether as anthems or hymns, was undoubtedly too sentimental. It reflected the romantic mood of the century, but in so doing it drifted in the direction of a rather saccharine quality. Professor George Foot Moore used to talk about "the vanilla-flavored hymns of Barnby." Such tunes, in an exaggerated form, were the stock in trade of the gospel hymns used in revival meetings. It has been a hard task to get some of these tunes removed from our hymnals. Vanilla flavor is stubborn and longlived. Only a certain amount of actual discipline, however unwelcome at the first, can prove to us the musical superiority of more austere tunes.

In his *Religious Consciousness* the late Professor James Bissett Pratt had two chapters on Subjective and Objective Religion. Every musician, like every minister, should know them. As in the case of the contrast between this-worldliness and other-worldliness we have here a paradox which is never resolved. The world within and the world without can never be totally divorced, but they are seldom resolved in a single experience.

The religion of the nineteenth century, as one phase of the romantic movement, was predominantly interested in the subjective approach to religion. So much was this so that psychology has become for American Protestants the most important theological discipline. But Professor Pratt points out that, while psychology has thrown great light upon the happenings in the mind and the emotions which we associate with religion, its deliberate indifference to the outer world which supposedly warrants these inner experiences has undoubtedly imperiled our assurance as to their validity.

Not only so, but Professor Pratt goes on to say that we get what is commonly called more "religious help" from the objective warrants for religion than from its subjective interpretation. The yearnings to be "purer yet and purer" and to rise "higher yet and higher" are no guarantee of their realization. Those aspirations are rather like the attempt to lift yourself by your own boot straps. You need the leverage of some outside reality. The way to become purer and to rise higher is to put yourself in touch with some high and pure reality apart from yourself. Religious experience can never be vacated of its subjective reference and thus become wholly impersonal, but if we wish to become purer and higher, the best way to do so is to think about God or fasten the mind's eye on Christ. In so doing we do not change ourselves, but we are changed "into the same image." Therefore, objective anthems and hymns, in contrast to those which are subjective, are more effective. "Our God, our help in ages past" is, both in its words and in its tune, ideal in this connection. This thesis is capable of indefinite expansion and illustration. See your Pratt and select your anthems and hymns accordingly.

SCHOLAR-MUSICIAN AS TEACHER

David Stone

During the past hundred years colleges and universities throughout the United States have increased and expanded their musical offerings until today these institutions not only include music as a part of the curriculum in general education and culture but undertake as well to train professional performers, composers, scholars and teachers in all branches of music.

Although the teaching of music at the college level will constitute a large portion of this discussion, it will be necessary to take a broad and all-inclusive point of view if the continuity and total picture of the training of both professional student and amateur are to be considered. One need not be greatly concerned with private instruction by the instrumental or voice teacher whose work is carried on in a more or less traditional fashion. However, the situation is quite different with respect to college teachers of theory, history and general background courses who find it necessary in their classes to deal with students from both the sociological and professional points of view. If the teacher is to contribute anything to the general student, he must be a truly educated individual possessing qualities of mind and character which will enable him to make music an inspiring aesthetic experience for this type of student. On the other hand, in order to meet the challenge of the student embarking upon a professional career, this same teacher must be skilled in all the phases of musicianship which relate to the technical courses which he teaches.

If one accepts this premiss, it then goes without saying that teachers in the aforementioned areas of music should be both scholars and thorough musicians, bearing in mind that to be scholarly one need not be a writer of great books and that to be musicianly one need not be a virtuoso performer. In addition, teachers must be educators. They must know not only what they teach and how they teach, but also why they teach. It is with respect to this last point that many of the scholars and professional musicians to be found on faculties of colleges and universities throughout the country fail miserably in the role of teacher. How is one to deal with the heterogeneous group of students with which one finds himself confronted in college classes? Even to begin to answer this question we must draw upon every possible resource.

The art of teaching, like creative art, encompasses the whole of human life. Just as an empty mind is incapable of producing a work of art, so the teacher who is insensitive to the drama of life and who lacks understanding of the human values which hold an inextricable place in teaching, will fail in his task. There is no implication here that scholarly research or complete devotion to the cultivation of a special talent is an unworthy pursuit in its own right; but individuals preoccupied with these pursuits ought never to teach unless they are willing to assume the responsibility of acquiring the breadth, mastery of pedagogics and human understanding essential to the successful guidance of their students. There are too many who give no more thought to the intrinsic problems and principles of teaching than do the students whom they are turning loose to carry on in their footsteps. The fact remains that most graduates in music today are forced to turn to teaching in order to earn a livelihood, and so teachers and curricula should be dedicated to the cultivation of scholarly and musicianly traits and an understanding of our aesthetic responsibility to the profession and to society as a whole.

It is obvious that the function of the music teacher should be twofold: as a scholar and musician it is his duty to serve the cause of music in the most effective way possible; as a scholar and teacher it is his duty to serve humanity through the medium of music as a guide and sympathetic stimulant. This means that the music teacher in order to be successful in his task must possess a well-integrated personality which will in turn permit satisfactory social adjustment. It would then be possible for him to interest himself objectively in music education of all types and at all levels, and there would be no place for the cleavages which exist today between teachers of our various professional ranks, cleavages which are the result of misunderstanding, prejudice, narrowmindedness and conceit. The influence of all this is disastrous, for whether teachers be classified as professional musicians, musicologists or music educators, cleavages lead them to work against each other rather than with each other and for the good of the student.

Let us give our attention to a specific situation which illustrates very well the problem implied in the preceding statements, namely the unwillingness of many college teachers to interest themselves in the role of the public schools in preparing students for advanced study in music. This is a most serious failing, because it is one which is so far-reaching in its effect and bearing upon music study at the college level. All too often the college teacher assumes the attitude that it is beneath his dignity to concern himself with what he feels to be the feeble and inadequate musical endeavor of the public schools. No sincere teacher should adopt such an attitude, and any teacher who does, entirely misses the issue. Whereas it is true that the quality of contributions made by the schools varies greatly according to locality, it is inadvisable and quite unfair for college teachers to pass judgment if they have deliberately maintained a state of ignorance with respect to the problem involved. The wisest course, especially in the case of areas where public schools may fall short of desirable achievement, would be to refrain from wasting time in faultfinding and to set oneself immediately to the task of teaching students and removing deficiencies before it is altogether too late. How can we afford to remain aloof from a problem which is so important to our own work?

If more college teachers were to establish a relationship with the public schools based upon coöperation and sincerity of purpose in which the musical education of the student is the principal objective, then students at all levels of instruction would be more apt to receive that which they rightly deserve. We are entirely too prone to demand arbitrarily that students, when they reach us in college, meet us on our own ground, without taking the trouble to determine whether or not this is a wise or possible point of view. Often this ruins any chance of achieving continuity in the student's musical development. Psychologically this approach is faulty, but it is quite typical of the teacher who is preoccupied with "self" and who is insincere in assuming the obligation to make the welfare of the student his main objective. It might be wiser to ascertain first the student's weaknesses and strengths, taking into account the nature of his preparation, the extent of his innate talent and the tenor of his psychological and emotional make-up. Then, one might begin a building process in which the student is served through the establishment of a series of relationships between him and the art of music and in which he becomes ever increasingly sensitized to the beauties of great music.

The scholar-musician as teacher can and should exert a tremendous impact upon students in the melee of the present world of learning. Those who have been fortunate enough to have passed through the hands of true scholar-musicians who were also great teachers have perhaps caught something of their spirit and inspirational quality. Scholar-musician teachers never forget to enjoy teaching, and they never forget to enjoy music. They are living models of intellectual and artistic endeavor who have sought through lofty purpose to set forth the highest standards and ideals. Let it be hoped that by virtue of the chain of life this experience will live eternally, transmitted through mind and heart from teacher to student, safeguarding the music of the future and enriching the cultural life of all people.

ON HISTORICAL AUTHENTICITY IN THE
PERFORMANCE OF OLD MUSIC

Donald Jay Grout

Lᴇᴛ us begin by setting down some truisms: An ideal performance is one that perfectly realizes the composer's intentions.
A performance may fall short of the ideal because of technical
insufficiency, ignorance of the composer's intentions, lack of imagination in execution, or from any combination of these, since in
practice technique, knowledge, and imagination are interdependent.

For any performance not supervised by the composer himself,
knowledge of his intentions is obtained from two sources: the written notes and a tradition. "Tradition" is here used to mean all the
customs of musical performance that were in effect in the composer's time but that are not indicated in the notation. If the stream
of tradition continues to flow through several generations it is
gradually modified and eventually transformed to a point where
it can no longer be called tradition of the composer's time. This is
what happened to Gregorian Chant after the end of the Middle
Ages; an early stage of a like process of transformation may be seen
in present-day performances of Handel's *Messiah*. In addition to or
instead of being transformed a tradition may perish, as happens
when owing to a change of taste the music of an earlier style ceases
to be performed.

The fullness of a notation is likely to vary inversely with the
strength of the original impulse that gave birth to a style. Thus
Gregorian Chant up to about the eighth century apparently was
transmitted chiefly if not entirely by oral tradition. The earliest
notation by means of neumes was, as the word suggests, only a reminder to the singers of something already learned. It was not

until after the eleventh century that a precise pitch notation came into use. A precise notation for the rhythm of the Chant was never developed, with the consequence that it has become necessary within the last hundred years to reconstruct, with much labor and some uncertainty, a lost tradition of performance. A similar story could be told with regard to other forms of music that were written down before an unambiguous notation for rhythm had been invented, such as the melodies of the Troubadours and other monophonic types of medieval composition, as well as some of the older examples of polyphony in modal notation. Even in the period since a relatively clear notation for the two essentials of pitch and rhythm has been achieved, there are still many matters for which tradition is the only guide. Thus, in the vocal music preserved from the period 1250 to 1550 the notation seldom tells whether or to what extent instruments were associated with or substituted for voices in performance; again, the notation of music until well into the eighteenth century as a rule gives little or no indication of the melodic embellishments and cadenzas the performer was expected to add; figured bass is another example of an incomplete notation depending on knowledge of a tradition for its realization; the use of the pedal in nineteenth-century piano music is matter of taste and tradition rather than of notation; the details of a performance of improvised jazz in the twentieth century are by definition unnotated and in any event impossible to set down on paper. Fortunately, for this as for all music from the twentieth century onward there will be phonograph recordings to help preserve the knowledge of performance practice; would that present-day historians and conductors had some such aid for the music of Leonin, Machault, Josquin, or Handel!

It is characteristic of our time that we are intent on performing a great deal of "old" music, which may be defined as music that we possess only in notation, not in direct tradition. In the early days of the fashion for reviving old music, people did not bother about the original tradition, but simply assumed that the practice of their own nineteenth century was the universal rule and proceeded to apply it accordingly. Thus there were Zelter's performances of Bach, and Wagner's of Palestrina. Such days of innocence are over. Historical Musicology, like Original Sin, has given everybody a bad conscience: we worry about historical authenticity in the performance of old music, which is to say that we fear lest we interpret the notation in accordance with the wrong tradition.

Underlying all striving for historical accuracy in the performance of old music are three tacit assumptions which we propose to call in question, and which we shall therefore state in interrogative form.

(1) How definite was the tradition? Was there one authoritative, "correct" way of performing this music in the composer's day, or did he allow for considerable latitude in certain respects, including possibly some matters that we now are accustomed to regard as not properly within the discretion of the performer? The whole question of instruments vs. voices in the period 1250–1550 lies in this indefinite realm: we have no reason to conclude, for example, that because a motet of Josquin was performed with a certain ensemble of singers and players under the composer's direction, he would have regarded it as in any way contrary to his intention if the same piece were performed elsewhere or at a different time with a different ensemble. It is simply that the composer's intention on this point did not include a specific combination of voices or instruments. This holds true, more or less, for all Medieval and Renaissance music, vocal and instrumental, sacred and secular. Perhaps the closest familiar analogy would be that of a modern composer writing for the organ: he may have a particular instrument in mind, but anticipating that the piece will be played on other organs that differ in an infinite number of ways from his own, he wisely refrains from indicating an exact registration or even sometimes from indicating any registration at all. Similar but even greater freedom is left to the performer in the matter of unnotated melodic embellishments and cadenzas in the music of the sixteenth to the eighteenth centuries, and in the realization of figured basses. It may be advanced as a general principle that where a precise notation exists but a composer does not avail himself of it there is a presumption that he does not intend uniformity in execution. The problem with regard to most old music, then, is not to determine a single fixed, invariable practice but rather to determine the limits within which the several aspects of performance might have fluctuated without leading to results that the composers would have found unacceptable.

(2) Whatever the tradition was, can we rediscover it? We are

perhaps prone to be over-sanguine in this regard because of recent salient successes in the two fields of Gregorian Chant and the music of Bach. Yet even for these our knowledge is not complete. No one can fail to acknowledge the tremendous debt of gratitude that both the Catholic Church and the whole musical world owe to the devoted labors of Dom Pothier, Dom André Mocquereau, and their colleagues at Solesmes for the restoration of Gregorian Chant; but there is by no means universal agreement that the present official interpretation of Gregorian rhythm is wholly correct historically or that the last word has yet been said on the subject. With respect to Bach there can be no doubt that we now have at our disposal an immense quantity of exact knowledge about ornaments, dynamics, tone-color, balance in ensembles, and the musical aesthetic of the eighteenth century; but many of the details are still uncertain, and there are other points about which we are still ignorant. If our knowledge is imperfect in those two fields of old music to which the most work has been devoted and in which the results of such work have been most assiduously applied to modern performance, it may readily be imagined how much less well informed we are about the vast areas of old music that have hitherto been less intensively studied from the viewpoint of performance practice. The extent of our ignorance may be suggested by asking at random a few questions which, in the present state of music-historical knowledge cannot be decisively answered: What kind of a tone did a well schooled singer of the thirteenth century aim to produce? How did a choirmaster in the first half of the sixteenth century instruct his singers to fit the syllables of the words to the notes of the music when, as was usually the case, the choirbook or partbook did not clearly indicate the text underlaying? How much did Palestrina make use of crescendo and diminuendo? Were the different texts of a polytextual Gothic motet actually sung simultaneously? What was the interpretation of the long melismas with interspersed rests, so often found on the first syllable of fourteenth-century madrigals? What chords were played over the bass notes of Monteverdi's *Orfeo*? At what tempo did Lully conduct the opening movements of his overtures? How widespread was the practice of the "secret chromatic art" in the sixteenth century? What is the significance of the "chiavette" in the sixteenth and seventeenth centuries? These are not merely academic questions.

Unless they are answered we cannot be sure of perfectly authentic performances of the music to which they relate. But it is doubtful whether some of them, at any rate, will ever be answered.

(3) Suppose, however, that we do find out the tradition: can we apply it? Have we now the resources, instrumental and vocal, that were at the disposal of the composer? Take for example the organ music of the sixteenth and seventeenth centuries, all of which was written for instruments tuned in some variety of the mean-tone system. Anyone who has heard the works of Sweelinck or Scheidt played on an organ like the one in the Museum at Haarlem, which can reproduce the intervals (particularly the thirds) as these composers heard them, realizes with something of a shock how serious a distortion is wrought in this music by playing it on an instrument tuned to the tempered scale. Yet it is a distortion we must endure if we are to hear the music at all, since specially tuned organs are not generally accessible. In the same way we must accept the sound of women's voices in many vocal ensemble lines that we know were written for boy sopranos or male altos, and in much vocal solo music that we know was written for castrati — departures from the composers' intentions roughly comparable to the substitution of clarinets for oboi da caccia in Bach. The whole matter of obsolete instruments is a formidable problem in the performance of old music: there is not even an approximate modern equivalent for the tone of the cornetto, for example, and no very close equivalent for the vielle. Again, there are obsolete techniques: few if any modern singers can execute the *trillo* of Caccini, which was not a trill but a rapid reiteration of one note in the manner of a string tremolo; some of the cadenzas sung by the great eighteenth-century castrato Farinelli have been preserved in notation, but where is one to find a singer now who could cope with them?

There is no need to multiply instances further. It is evident that a completely authentic modern performance of old music is, at least in the overwhelming majority of cases, an impossibility. Attempts at such performances succeed only by virtue of compromise, reckoning not on certainties but on probabilities, taking into account the variable factors of the original tradition, confessing but when necessary disregarding the imperfect state of our knowledge, and ignoring the anachronisms that result from the unavailability of the correct media or the disappearance of older techniques.

One is tempted at this point to speculate as to whether we have any business to be performing old music at all. If one of the composers of this music could by some miracle be brought to life in the twentieth century to be quizzed about the methods of performance in his own times, his first reaction would certainly be one of astonishment at our interest in such matters. Have we no living tradition of music, that we must be seeking to revive a dead one? The question might be embarrassing. Musical archaism [1] may be a symptom of a disintegrating civilization, or it may be (as music historians would prefer to think) the sign of a laudable desire to apprehend and use the past for the sake of the present. One is not likely to "withdraw" into the music of an earlier time in quite the same way that he can withdraw into a past period of painting, architecture, sculpture, literature, or philosophy, for the fundamental reason that a piece of music is not made to be gazed upon, read through, or contemplated, but to be sounded — which involves activity, and of a very strenuous and exacting sort, in the present. As long as one is aiming at the *performance* of old music, the movement of withdrawal into the past is by hypothesis completed and justified by an opposite movement of return into the present. Musical archaism can begin only after the music of the past has been realized in sound and thus become a possible object of passive contemplation. The typical musical archaist or escapist of the twentieth century is the person whose principal musical "activity" consists in going to concerts and listening to phonograph records instead of making music himself.

If perfect historical authenticity in the performance of old music is unattainable, what value has the ideal?

Some of the best modern historical writing about music has been stimulated by the desire to rediscover a lost tradition in order to use it in performance: examples are the work of Dom Mocquereau on the rhythm of Gregorian Chant, of Arnold on the realization of thoroughbass, and Aldrich on the ornaments of seventeenth- and eighteenth-century music. The ideal of authenticity, even when only imperfectly realized, leads to performances of old music that are on the whole more satisfactory than those by interpreters who are still naïve or unpersuaded about historical styles: one may compare Busoni's Bach with the Bach of Ralph Kirkpatrick, or Muench's with Arthur Mendel's. The only danger in the ideal would seem to be that it could mislead one into regarding knowledge of the past as a substitute for imagination in the present, rather than as food for it.

1. Cf. Toynbee, Arnold J., *A Study of History* (London, etc., 1935–1939. 6 vols.), Vol. VI, pp. 59 ff; Vol. III, pp. 248 ff.

PART SIX

A Bibliography

A BIBLIOGRAPHY OF

ARCHIBALD THOMPSON DAVISON'S WORKS

J. M. Coopersmith

Thus we salute thee with our early song,
And welcome thee, and wish thee long.
(JOHN MILTON, *Song on a May Morning*)

Books, Lectures, and Periodical Articles

[Address delivered at the annual meeting of the Harvard University Glee Club, Cambridge, May 15, 1934] *The Boston Transcript*, May 16. Boston, 1934.

Bach and Handel, the consummation of the baroque in music. Cambridge, Harvard University Press, 1951. ANOTHER ED.: London, Oxford University Press, 1951.

Bach as a choral composer [Lecture, Cornell University, Ithaca, Mar. 1, 1950, with illustrations by the Sage Chapel Choir]   Ms.

Choral conducting. Cambridge, Harvard University Press, 1940. 6TH PRINTING: 1950.

Choral technique; a recording of 4 rehearsals [Phonodisc]   Harvard Film Service M–1000 — M–1005. 1940. [6 s. 12 in. 78 rpm.]

Church music [Lowell Institute Lectures, Boston, 1940–41]   Ms.

Church music and choir training [Lowell Institute Lectures, Boston, 1934–35]   Ms.

"Church music and reality." *Music Teachers National Association. Proceedings* [*1948*] 42d series, pp. 98–117. Pittsburgh, 1950.

Church music, illusion and reality. Cambridge, Harvard University Press, 1952. ANOTHER ED.: London, Oxford University Press, 1952.

Conditions affecting the selection of service music [Lecture, American Guild of Organists, Boston, June 22, 1932. Cf. *The Dia-*

pason (Chicago) June 1, 1932, p. 34 and July 1, 1932, pp. 2–3]   Ms.

The Development of choral music [Lowell Institute Lectures, Boston, 1916–17, 1923–24]   Ms.

The Development of music in New England, 1800–1952 [Lecture, Bowdoin College, Brunswick, Maine, April 1952. Cf. Harvard University. Dept. of Music. *Annual report, 1951–52*]   Ms.

The Folk-songs of the British Isles [Lowell Institute Lectures, Boston, 1926–27]   Ms.

The Folk-songs of France, Italy, Germany, and Russia [Lowell Institute Lectures, Boston, 1927–28]   Ms.

Friedlaender, Max, 1852–1934. *Choral exercises, founded on Stockhausen's method. 2d ed. Translated by A. T. Davison.* Leipzig, C. F. Peters [1911]

"Gifts of music." *Harvard Alumni Bulletin*, Apr. 17, pp. [872]–873. Cambridge, 1936.

"Good music for community singing." *Playground*, v. 16, pp. 455–57, 498–99 (Jan.) New York, 1923.

"Händel, Georg Friedrich. *Messiah, an oratorio. Edited from the original sources by J. M. Coopersmith.* New York, Carl Fischer, 1947" [Review] *Notes*, 2d series, v. 5, p. 122 (Dec.)   Washington, Music Library Association, 1947.

The Harmonic contributions of Claude Debussy [Thesis, PH.D., Harvard University, 1908]   Ms.

"The humanistic approach to music." *Music Teachers National Association. Proceedings* [*1949*] 43d series, pp. 67–79. Pittsburgh, 1951.

"Introductory remarks." In: Symposium on Music Criticism, *Harvard University*, 1947. *Music and criticism, a symposium*, p. [3]–7. Cambridge, Harvard University Press, 1948.

"Joseph Lee and music." *Recreation*, v. 31, p. 558 (Dec.)   New York, 1937.

[Leaflets issued in connection with the lectures on folk-song, Lowell Institute, 1927–28. Boston, 1927–28]

[Lectures, Stanford University, Stanford, Calif.: *English folk-song*, Jan. 23, 1951; *Choral music of the 20th century*, Jan. 26, 1951; *Pre-university music education*, Jan. 27, 1951. Ms. Cf. Marguerite Slater, "Music on the peninsula," *Opera and concert*, v. 16, p. 39 (Jan.) p. 38–39 (Mar.)   San Francisco, 1951]

"Mayo Adams Shattuck." *Harvard Glee Club Foundation Bulletin*, no. 7, p. [1]–2 (Apr.) Cambridge, 1953.

"Music." In: *The Choice of a field of concentration*, pp. 17–18. Cambridge, The Committee on Choice of Electives [and] The Harvard Crimson [1925?]   Reprinted 1927. Another ed. of the 1927 reprint was published as a supplement to the *Harvard Alumni Bulletin*, May 23, pp. 34–35 (Cambridge, 1929). Later editions (1929 and 1934) were published by The Committee on Choice of Electives.

"Music deficiencies among average college students; abstract of an address." *The Musical courier*, v. 101, p. 38 (Dec. 13) p. 38 (Dec. 20)   New York, 1930.

Music education in America. What is wrong with it? What shall we do about it? New York, Harper, 1926.

[On the study of music]   *Harvard Crimson*, Apr. 30. Cambridge, 1923.

The Place of music in worship [Gates Lecture, Grinnell College, Grinnell, Iowa, Nov. 16, 1948. CONTENTS. — Church music: its nature and traditions. — The technical substance of church music. — Church music and reality. — The music of humility and confidence. — An ideal for church music]   Ms.

"Popular music." *Playground*, v. 15, pp. 192–96 (June)   New York, 1921.

Protestant church music in America. Boston, Unitarian Laymen's League [1920]   2D ED.: [1921?]

Protestant church music in America. Boston, E. C. Schirmer Music Co. [ᶜ1933]   4TH PRINTING: 1948.

"Ralph Vaughan Williams; an appreciation." *Harvard Glee Club Foundation Bulletin*, no. 5, pp. 2–3 (Mar. 20)   Cambridge, 1952.

"Religion and music." *Harvard Alumni Bulletin*, Jan. 13, pp. 413–15. Cambridge, 1927.

Report on music at Wells College, Nov. 13–18, inclusive, 1932. [Aurora, N. Y.?] Privately printed [193–]

"Singing good music" [Letter] *Harvard Alumni Bulletin*, Jan. 2, pp. 257–58. Cambridge, 1919.

"Style in church music." *The Methodist review*, v. 108, pp. 358–69 (May-June) New York, 1925.

"Style in church music; an address delivered to the students of the Seminary." *The Princeton Seminary Bulletin*, v. 18, no. 1, pp. 11–17 (May) Princeton, 1924.

The Technique of choral composition. Cambridge, Harvard University Press, 1945. 3D PRINTING: 1951.

Words and music; a lecture delivered by Archibald T. Davison in the Whittall Pavilion of the Library of Congress, December 10, 1953. Washington, Library of Congress, 1954. [Louis Charles Elson Memorial Lecture]

Compositions

The Counterfeiter; comic opera in two acts. Book and lyrics by Clarence P. Whorf, '05. Additional lyrics by James V. Dignowity, '06. Music by Archibald T. Davison, Jr., '06, Frank Grey, '06. Presented by the Pi Eta Society, 1905, Winchester, April 14, Worcester, April 15, Cambridge, April 26 and 28, Boston, April 29, afternoon and evening. [Cambridge] Bennet, ᶜ1905. [Piano-vocal score (65 pp.) The song, "We're engaged," is headed: "Words by H. F. Hurlbut, Jr. Music by Joseph S. Chipman."]

The Girl and the chauffeur; a musical comedy in two acts. Book and lyrics by James Dignowity, Jr., '06. Music by Archibald T. Davison, Jr., '06. Presented by the Pi Eta Society of Harvard University, Malden, April 16, Boston, Tremont Theatre, April 17, Cambridge, April 23 and 26, Lowell, April 24. [Cambridge] Pi Eta Society, ᶜ1906. [Piano-vocal score (88 pp.)]

The Gondoliers; concert waltzes [*for orchestra*. Ms., 191–?]   Cf. *Boston Symphony Orchestra Programmes, 1917–1918*, p. 1392.

Hero and Leander; a symphonic poem. [Ms., 1908?]   First performance by the Boston Symphony Orchestra at Sanders Theater, Cambridge, Mass., April 23, 1908. [Score (71 pp.) Harvard University, Widener Library: 90.742.2F]

Romance [*for orchestra*. Ms., 191–?]   Cf. *Boston Symphony Orchestra Programmes, 1917–1918*, p. 1392.

Tragic overture. [Ms., 191–?] "Composed during the summer of 1914 and revised from time to time." First performance by the Boston Symphony Orchestra, April 26, 1918; cf. its *Programmes, 1917–1918*, pp. 1391–1392.

Will o' the wisp; a comic opera in two acts. Book and lyrics by Douglas P. Cook, '05. Music by Archibald T. Davison, Jr., '06, Frank H. Grey, '06, Harry R. Pratt, '06. Presented by the Pi Eta Society, 1904, Lowell, April 18, Winchester, April 19, Boston, April 21, Cambridge April 26–27. [Cambridge, Pi Eta Society] ^c1904. [Piano-vocal score (80 pp.)   At end: "White-Smith Press, Boston."]

Editions and Arrangements of Music: Collections

A Book of songs with piano accompaniment for unison and part singing. For grades IV, V, and VI. Compiled and edited for use in school and home by Archibald T. Davison, Thomas Whitney Surette, and Augustus D. Zanzig. Boston, E. C. Schirmer, ^c1924 (Concord series, no. 14)

—— *Students' ed.* Boston, E. C. Schirmer, ^c1924 (Concord series, no. 4) [Words and melodies only]

The Church organist's golden treasury, edited by Carl F. Pfatteicher and Archibald T. Davison. Philadelphia, O. Ditson; Press, distributors, ^c1949–51 [3 v.]

The Concord anthem book; forty anthems for the use of mixed voice choirs in Protestant churches, compiled and edited by Archibald T. Davison & Henry Wilder Foote. Boston, E. C. Schirmer, ^c1925 (Concord series, no. 13)

The Concord junior song and chorus book. (Boys and girls)   For unison and part singing, with piano acc., for grades VII, VIII, and IX. For use in school or home. Compiled and edited by Archibald T. Davison, Thomas Whitney Surette, and Augustus D. Zanzig. Teachers' ed. Boston, E. C. Schirmer, ^c1928 (Concord series, no. 15)

—— *Students' ed.* Boston, E. C. Schirmer, ^c1928 (Concord series, no. 16) [Words and voice parts only]

Concord song book for women's voices, unison, two-, three-, and four-part. For use by colleges, schools, and choral societies. Compiled and edited by Archibald T. Davison and Thomas Whit-

ney Surette. [Complete ed. with piano accompaniment] Boston, E. C. Schirmer, ^c1935 (Concord series, no. 17)

—— *Vocal ed.* Boston, E. C. Schirmer, ^c1935 (Concord series, no. 18) [Words and voice parts only]

Fifty songs for rote singing to be used in the first three elementary grades of the Boston public schools. Compiled and edited by Archibald T. Davison and Thomas W. Surette. Boston, Published by the School Committee of the City of Boston, ^c1915.

—— *Book of words.* Boston, Published by the School Committee of the City of Boston, ^c1915.

Fifty rote songs for grades I, II, and III. Collected and edited by Archibald T. Davison and Thomas Whitney Surette. Boston, Boston Music Co., 1915 (Boston school music series, no. 1A)

The Harvard song book. 5th ed., rev. [Edited by Archibald T. Davison] Cambridge, Harvard Glee Club, 1922.

Harvard University Glee Club collection of part songs for men's voices. Arranged by Archibald T. Davison. Boston, E. C. Schirmer, ^c1922–38 (Concord series, no. 50, 100, 1000, 1050, 1100, 1400) [6 v.]

The Harvard University hymn book. [Edited by Edward Caldwell Moore and Archibald Thompson Davison] Cambridge, Harvard University Press, 1926. 2D IMPRESSION: 1931.

Historical anthology of music, by Archibald T. Davison and Willi Apel. Cambridge, Harvard University Press, 1946–50. CONTENTS. — [v. 1] Oriental, medieval, and Renaissance music. — [v. 2] Baroque, rococo, and pre-classical music.

—— *Rev. ed.* Cambridge, Harvard University Press, 1949. CONTENTS. — [v. 1] Oriental, medieval, and Renaissance music.

The Home and community song book. Compiled and edited by A. T. Davison and Thomas Whitney Surette. Boston, Boston Music Co., ^c1919 (The Concord series of educational music and books on musical pedagogy, no. 2) ANOTHER ED.: Boston, E. C. Schirmer, ^c1921 (The Concord series of music and books on the teaching of music, no. 2)

The Home and community song book, by Thomas W. Surette and Archibald T. Davison; sponsored by Better Homes in America, inc. & National Recreation Ass'n. Complete ed.: words, melodies & pianoforte accompaniment. Boston, E. C. Schirmer, ᶜ1931 (Concord series, no. 2, revised and enlarged)

—— *Vocal ed.: words and voice parts only.* Boston, E. C. Schirmer, ᶜ1931 (Concord series, no. 19)

140 folk-songs for school and home. Rote songs for grades I, II, and III. Compiled and edited for use in school or home by Archibald T. Davison and Thomas Whitney Surette. [*Complete ed. with piano*] *New and rev. ed.* Boston, E. C. Schirmer, ᶜ1921 (Concord series, no. 7) ANOTHER ISSUE: Boston, E. C. Schirmer, ᶜ1948.

—— *Vocal ed.: words and voice parts only.* Boston, E. C. Schirmer, ᶜ1948 (Concord series, no. 3)

140 folk-tunes with piano accompaniment. Rote songs for grades 1, 2, 3. Compiled and edited for use in school and home by A. T. Davison and T. W. Surette. Boston, Boston Music Co., ᶜ1920 (Concord series of educational music and books on musical pedagogy, no. 7)

140 folk-tunes. Rote songs, grades I, II, and III, for school & home. Compiled and edited by Archibald T. Davison & Thomas Whitney Surette. New and revised ed. Boston, E. C. Schirmer, ᶜ1922 (Concord series, no. 3) [Unaccompanied]

Rote songs for grades I, II, and III. Compiled and edited by Archibald T. Davison and Thomas W. Surette, members of the Advisory Committee on Music. [Boston] Published by the School Committee of the City of Boston, ᶜ1917 (Boston public school series)

—— *Book of words.* [Boston] Published by the School Committee of the City of Boston, ᶜ1917.

Rote songs for grades 1, 2, and 3. Compiled and edited by A. T. Davison and T. W. Surette. Boston, E. C. Schirmer, ᶜ1920 (Concord series, no. 3)

The Second Concord anthem book; forty anthems for the use of mixed choirs in Protestant churches. Compiled and edited by Archibald T. Davison and Henry Wilder Foote. Boston, E. C. Schirmer, ᶜ1936 (Concord series, no. 1200)

Songs and exercises for grade four. Compiled and edited by Archibald T. Davison and Thomas Whitney Surette, members of the Advisory Committee on Music. [Boston] Published by the School Committee of the City of Boston, ᶜ1916 (Boston school music series) [with piano accompaniment]

Songs of freedom. Compiled, arranged, and edited by Archibald T. Davison , Katherine K. Davis, [and] Frederic W. Kempf. Boston, Houghton Mifflin Co., ᶜ1942. ANOTHER ED.: Boston, E. C. Schirmer, ᶜ1949 (Concord series, no. 621)

Editions and Arrangements of Music: Separate Works

Abbreviations:

For each work, unless otherwise stated, the source of title is the caption on the first page of music, the size is 26 cm., the text is English, the medium is chorus, a piano or organ reduction for rehearsal purposes is included, and the number within parentheses following the date of imprint is the publisher's series or order number.

A	— alto
acc.	— accompaniment
arr.	— arrangement
B	— bass
Bar.	— baritone
CAB	— reprinted in *The Concord anthem book*
ECS	— Boston, E. C. Schirmer
HUGCC	— reprinted in the *Harvard University Glee Club Collection*, vol.
S	— soprano
SCAB	— reprinted in *The Second Concord anthem book*
T	— tenor

ALLEGRI, GREGORIO, 1582–1652. *Miserere. [Abridged] Arr. by A. T. D.* ECS ᶜ1922 (Concord series, 27 and HUGCC 1: TTBB; Latin text)

ANERIO, FELICE, 1560–1614. *Christus factus est. Arr. by A. T. D.* ECS ᶜ1930 (Concord series, 922 and HUGCC 4: TTBB; Latin text)

Les Anges dans nos campagnes. Angels o'er the fields were flying. Old French carol. Arr. by A. T. D. ECS ᶜ1930 (Concord series, 926 and HUGCC 4: TTBB; English and French text) ANOTHER ARR.: ECS ᶜ1931 (Concord series, 844: SSA; English text)

ARCADELT, JACOB, *c.* 1514–*c.* 1562. Spurious and doubtful works. *Hear my prayer, O God (Ave Maria) Edited by A. T. D.* ECS ᶜ1925 (371 and CAB: SATB)

ARENSKIĬ, ANTONIĬ STEPANOVICH, 1861–1906. *The crystal brook. Arr. by A. T. D.* ECS ᶜ1924 (Concord series, 52 and HUGCC 1: TTBB, with violoncello)

—— *The mystic stars. Arr. by A. T. D.* ECS ᶜ1924 (Concord series, 51 and HUGCC 1: TTBB, with violoncello)

—— *O God, we pray. Edited by A. T. D.* ECS ᶜ1925 (1126 and CAB: SATB)

At father's door; Russian folk-song. Arr. by A. T. D. ECS ᶜ1924 (Concord series, 73 and HUGCC 2: TTBB, with piano)

ATTWOOD, THOMAS, 1765–1838. *Teach me, O Lord. Edited by A. T. D.* ECS ᶜ1925 (372 and CAB: SATB, with organ)

—— *Turn Thee, again, O Lord. Edited by A. T. D.* ECS ᶜ1936 (1721 and SCAB: SATB, with organ)

BACH, JOHANN SEBASTIAN, 1685–1750. *Break forth, O beauteous, heav'nly light, from the Christmas oratorio. Arr. by A. T. D.* ECS ᶜ1924 (Concord series, 53 and HUGCC 1: TTBB, with organ) ANOTHER ARR.: *Edited by A. T. D.* ECS ᶜ1925 (302 and CAB: SATB) ANOTHER ARR.: *Arr. by A. T. D.* ECS ᶜ1928 (803: SSAA, with piano)

—— *Come, Thou, oh, come! Four-part chorale. Arr. by A. T. D.* ECS ᶜ1922 (Concord series, 28 and HUGCC 1: TTBB)

—— *Crucifixus, from Mass in B minor. Arr. by A. T. D.* ECS ᶜ1924 (Concord series, 54 and HUGCC 1: TTBB, with piano; Latin text)

—— *Cum Sancto Spiritu, from Mass in B minor. Arr. by A. T. D.* ECS ᶜ1924 (Concord series, 55 and HUGCC 1: TTBB, with piano; Latin text)

—— *God, my King, Thy might confessing; choral. Edited by A. T. D.* ECS ᶜ1925 (368 and CAB: SATB)

—— *Grant me true courage, Lord; choral. Edited by A. T. D.* ECS ᶜ1925 (313 and CAB: SATB, with keyboard acc.)

—— *Grant us to do with zeal; four-part chorale. Arr. by A. T. D.* ECS ᶜ1922 (Concord series, 29 and HUGCC 1: TTBB, with piano)

—— *Jesu, joy of man's desiring; choral from the cantata, Herz und Mund und That und Leben. Arr. by A. T. D.* ECS ᶜ1927

(Concord series, 96 and HUGCC 3: TTBB, with piano, 3 hands, or flute and piano)

—— *My spirit, be joyful. Wie will ich mich freuen. From Cantata no. 146. Acc. by A. T. D.* ECS ^c1931 (Concord series, 938 and HUGCC 5: TB, with piano, 4 hands; English and German text)

—— *Now let every tongue adore Thee; four-part chorale from the cantata, Sleepers awake. Arr. by A. T. D.* ECS ^c1922 (Concord series, 30 and HUGCC 1: TTBB, with piano)

—— *O Lord, Thou hast formed my every part. Edited by A. T. D.* ECS ^c1925 (369 and CAB: SATB)

—— *To God on high be glory. Jesu, nun sei gepreiset. Edited, and the organ part arr., by A. T. D.* ECS ^c1936 (1684 and SCAB: SATB, with organ) ANOTHER ARR.: *To Thee alone be glory; choral from Cantata no. 41, Jesu, nun sei gepreiset. Arr. by A. T. D.* ECS ^c1936 (Concord series, 961 and HUGCC 6: TTBB, with piano, 4 hands)

BEETHOVEN, LUDWIG VAN, 1770–1827. *Hallelujah chorus, from Mount of Olives. Arr. by A. T. D.* ECS ^c1924 (Concord series, 56 and HUGCC 1: TTBB, with piano)

—— *O triumph, all ye ransom'd, from the Mount of Olives. Arr. by A. T. D.* ECS ^c1926 (Concord series, 87 and HUGCC 2: S solo, TTBB, with piano)

Bonnie Dundee; Scotch folk-song. Arr. by A. T. D. ECS ^c1928 (Concord series, 909 and HUGCC 3: TTBB, with piano, 4 hands)

BORTNÎANSKIĬ, DMITRIĬ STEPANOVICH, 1751–1825. *Lo, a voice to heaven sounding; Cherubic hymn. Arr. by Piotr Ilyitch Tchaikovsky. Edited by A. T. D.* ECS ^c1925 (1102 and CAB: SATB)

BRAHMS, JOHANNES, 1833–1897. *How lovely is Thy dwelling place. [From Ein deutsches Requiem] Edited, and the organ part arr., by A. T. D.* ECS ^c1936 (1713 and SCAB: SATB, with organ)

—— *Four love songs. Arr. by A. T. D.* ECS ^c1924 (Concord series, 58 and HUGCC 2: TTBB, with piano, 4 hands. CONTENTS: Was once a pretty tiny birdie, op. 52, no. 6. — In wood embowered, 'neath azure skies, op. 52, no. 9. — No, there is no bearing with those spiteful neighbors, op. 52, no. 11. — Secret nook in shady spot, op. 65, no. 8)

——*I hear a harp, op. 17, no. 1. Arr. by A. T. D.* ECS ᶜ1924 (Concord series, 57 and HUGCC 2: TTBB, with horn and harp or piano)

——*O God, Creator of mankind. Ach lieber Herre Jesu Christ. Edited by A. T. D.* ECS ᶜ1936 (1717 and SCAB: SATB) ANOTHER ARR.: ECS ᶜ1936 (921: TTBB)

——*O Jesus, tender Shepherd, hear; German folk-song. Harmonized by Johannes Brahms. Arr. by A. T. D.* ECS ᶜ1930 (Concord series, 921 and HUGCC 4: TTBB)

——*Six love songs. Arr. by A. T. D.* ECS ᶜ1924 (Concord series, 59 and HUGCC 2: TTBB, with piano, 4 hands. CONTENTS: A tremor's in the branches, op. 52, no. 18. — Nightingale, thy sweetest song, op. 52, no. 15. — Bird in air will stray afar, op. 52, no. 13 [TT, with 2 pianos] — From yon hills the torrent speeds, op. 65, no. 7. — Locksmith, ho! a hundred padlocks, op. 52, no. 12. — Now, ye Muses, be hushed, op. 65, no. 14)

——*Songs from Ossian's Fingal. Arr. by A. T. D.* ECS ᶜ1924 (Concord series, 60 and HUGCC 2: TTBB, with 2 horns and harp or piano)

——*Suabian folk-song. Harmonized by Johannes Brahms. Arr. by A. T. D.* ECS ᶜ1922 (Concord series, 31 and HUGCC 1: TTBB)

——*The trysting place. Der Gang zum Liebchen. Op. 31, no. 3. Arr. by A. T. D.* ECS ᶜ1930 (Concord series, 928 and HUGCC 4: TTBB, with piano; English and German text)

Brennan on the moor; English folk-song. Arr. by A. T. D. ECS ᶜ1937 (Concord series, 955 and HUGCC 6: T solo, TTBB, with piano)

Bring a torch, Jeanette, Isabelle; old French carol, attributed to Saboly. Arr. by A. T. D. ECS ᶜ1926 (Concord series, 97 and HUGCC 3: TTBB) ANOTHER ARR.: ECS ᶜ1927 (Radcliffe choral music, 838: SSAA)

BYRD WILLIAM, 1542 or 3–1623. *Ave verum; four-part motet. Arr. by A. T. D.* ECS ᶜ1930 (Concord series, 919 and HUGCC 4: TTBB; Latin text)

——*I will not leave you comfortless. Arr. by A. T. D.* ECS ᶜ1935 (Concord series, 951 and HUGCC 6: TTBB)

——*Iustorum animae. The souls of the righteous.* Arr. by A. T. D. ECS ᶜ1926 (Concord series, 90 and HUGCC 3: TTBB: English and Latin text)

The Caisson song; old army song. Piano acc. by A. T. D. ECS ᶜ1946 (2242: Solo voice, SATB, with piano)

The Campbells are coming; Scotch air. Arr. by A. T. D. ECS ᶜ1930 (Concord series, 923 and HUGCC 4: TTBB, with piano, 4 hands)

CARISSIMI, GIOVANNI GIACOMO, d. 1674. *Plorate, filii Israel.* Arr. by A. T. D. ECS ᶜ1922 (Concord series, 32 and HUGCC 1: TTBB, with piano or organ; Latin text)

CHAĬKOVSKIĬ, PETR IL'ICH, 1840–1893. *How blest are they.* Edited by A. T. D. ECS ᶜ1925 (1138 and CAB: SSAATTBB)

——*O Thou, from whom all blessings come.* Edited by A. T. D. ECS ᶜ1925 (1139 and CAB: SATB)

CHESNOKOV, PAVEL GRIGOR'EVICH, 1877–   *Cherubic hymn.* Arr. by A. T. D. ECS ᶜ1925 (Concord series, 77 and HUGCC 2: TTBB)

——*Salvation belongeth to our God.* Arr. by A. T. D. ECS ᶜ1935 (Concord series, 947 and HUGCC 6: TTBB)

——*Thou life of life.* Edited by A. T. D. ECS ᶜ1936 (1720: SSAATTBB)

CLÉMENT, JACQUES, 16th cent. *Adoramus te.* Edited by A. T. D. ECS ᶜ1935 (Concord series, 948 and HUGCC 6: TTBB; Latin text)

CORNELIUS, PETER, 1824–1874. *Salamaleikum, from the Barber of Bagdad.* Arr. by A. T. D. ECS ᶜ1922 (Concord series, 33 and HUGCC 1: Bar. solo, TTBB, with piano)

Cradle-song of the shepherds. Wiegenlied der Hirten. Arr. by A. T. D. ECS ᶜ1936 (1728: SATB)

Crudele Irene. O heartless maiden. Italian folk-song. Arr. by A. T. D. ECS ᶜ1938 (Concord series, 956 and HUGCC 6: TTBB, with piano, 4 hands; English and Italian text)

CUI, CÉSAR ANTONOVICH, 1835–1918. *Nocturne.* Arr. by A. T. D. ECS ᶜ1926 (Concord series, 95 and HUGCC 3: TTBB)

——*Spread your wings. Arr. by A. T. D.* ECS ᶜ1922 (Concord series, 21 and HUGCC 1: S or T solo, TTBB)

DARCIEUX, FRANCISQUE, 1880–   *Christians, hark! Noël of the Bressan waits. Harmonized by Francisque Darcieux. Arr. by A. T. D.* ECS ᶜ1925 (Concord series, 89 and HUGCC 3: TTBB, with piano) ANOTHER ARR.: *Harmonized by A. T. D. Arr. by H. W. K. Acc. by Francisque Darcieux.* ECS ᶜ1930 (1027: SA, with piano)

DECIUS, NIKOLAUS, *d.* 1541, supposed composer. *To God on high; four-part choral. Arr. by A. T. D.* ECS ᶜ1924 (Concord series, 61 and HUGCC 2: TTBB) ANOTHER ARR.: *To God on high be thanks and praise; choral. Edited by A. T. D.* ECS ᶜ1925 (1127 and CAB: SATB, with keyboard acc.)

DEPRÈS, JOSQUIN, *d.* 1521. *Ave, verum Corpus Christi; motet. Arr. by A. T. D.* ECS ᶜ1922 (Concord series, 34 and HUGCC 1: TTBB; Latin text)

DOWLAND, JOHN, 1563–1626. *Come again, sweet love. Arr. by A. T. D.* ECS ᶜ1923 (Concord series, 35 and HUGCC 1: TTBB)

DURANTE, FRANCESCO, 1684–1755. *Misericordias Domini; eight-part motet. Arr. by A. T. D.* ECS ᶜ1936 (Concord series, 941 and HUGCC 5: TTBB (Chorus I) TTBB (Chorus II) Latin text)

DVOŘÁK, ANTONÍN, 1841–1904. *An anthem of praise (Praise Jehovah: Psalm 149) Abridged. Edited, and the organ part arr., by A. T. D.* ECS ᶜ1936 (1701 and SCAB: SATB, with organ)

——*Around us hear the sounds of even. Arr. by A. T. D.* ECS ᶜ1923 (Concord series, 36 and HUGCC 1: TTBB)

FARRANT, RICHARD, *fl.* 1564–1580. *Lord, for Thy tender mercies' sake. Edited by A. T. D.* ECS ᶜ1925 (374 and CAB: SATB)

Fireflies; Russian folk-song. Arr. by A. T. D. Acc. by G. W. W. ECS ᶜ1924 (Concord series, 73 and HUGCC 2: TTBB, with piano)

The Foggy dew; English folk-song. Arr. by A. T. D. ECS ᶜ1935 (Concord series, 952 and HUGCC 6: T solo, TTBB, with piano)

The Foggy dew; Irish folk-song. Arr. by A. T. D. ECS ᶜ1925 (Concord series, 83 and HUGCC 2: T solo, TTBB)

FORD, THOMAS, 1580 (*c.*)–1648. *Almighty God, Who hast me brought. Edited by A. T. D.* ECS ᶜ1936 (1709 and SCAB: SATB)

——Since first I saw your face. Arr. by A. T. D. ECS ^c1921
(1111: SATB)

FRANCK, CÉSAR AUGUSTE, 1822–1890. *Chorus of camel-drivers.
Chœur des chameliers. From Rebecca. Arr. by A. T. D.* ECS ^c1924
(Concord series, 63 and HUGCC 2: TTBB, with piano)

——Far o'er the bay. Arr. by A. T. D. ECS ^c1924 (Concord
series, 64 and HUGCC 2: S solo, TTBB, with piano)

*——They are ever blessed, from The Beatitudes. Abridged.
Edited by A. T. D.* ECS ^c1936 (1729: SATB, with organ)

FRANCK, MELCHIOR, d. 1639. *Father, Thy holy spirit send. Jesu,
dein Seel'. Edited by A. T. D.* ECS ^c1936 (1687 and SCAB: SATB)

GABRIELI, GIOVANNI, 1557–1612. *Jubilate Deo. Arr. by A. T. D.*
ECS ^c1930 (Concord series, 934 and HUGCC 4: TTBB; Latin
text)

The Galway piper; Irish folk-song. Arr. by A. T. D. ECS ^c1926
(Concord series, 99 and HUGCC 3: TTBB, with piano) ANOTHER
ARR.: *The Galway piper; Irish folk-song* ("*The rakes of Mallow*")
Arr. by H. Clough-Leighter. Acc. by A. T. D. ECS ^c1928 (358:
SATB, with piano)

GESIUS, BARTHOLOMÄUS, d. 1613. *We walk the earth as pilgrims.
Ich bin ein Gast auf Erden. Edited by A. T. D.* ECS ^c1936 (1722
and SCAB: SATB)

GIBBONS, ORLANDO, 1583–1625. *Almighty and everlasting God.
Edited by A. T. D.* ECS ^c1936 (1686 and SCAB: SATB)

—— O Lord, increase my faith. Edited by A. T. D. ECS ^c1925
(375 and CAB: SATB)

GLUCK, CHRISTOPH WILLIBALD, *Ritter* VON, 1714–1787. *Two
choruses from Orpheus. Arr. by A. T. D.* ECS ^c1928 (Concord
series, 911 and HUGCC 3: TTBB, with piano. CONTENTS: If
here, where all is dark and silent [with T solo] — Ballet [piano
solo] — From the realm of souls departed)

GOSS, *Sir* JOHN, 1800–1880. *I heard a voice from heaven. Edited
by A. T. D.* ECS ^c1936 (1705 and SCAB: SATB)

—— O Saviour of the world. Edited by A. T. D. ECS ^c1936
(1719 and SCAB: SATB)

GOUNOD, CHARLES FRANÇOIS, 1818–1893. *Chorus of Bacchantes, from Philémon et Baucis. Arr. by A. T. D.* ECS ᶜ1923 (Concord series, 37 and HUGCC 1: TTBB, with piano)

GRAZIOLI, GIOVANNI BATTISTA IGNAZIO, 1746–c. 1820. *God be with thee! Pange lingua. Edited by A. T. D.* ECS ᶜ1936 (1704 and SCAB)

GRECHANINOV, ALEKSANDR TIKHONOVICH, 1864–   *Adore almighty God; Cherubim song. Edited by A. T. D.* ECS ᶜ1936 (1694 and SCAB: SSAATTBB)

—— *Autumn. Arr. by A. T. D.* ECS ᶜ1925 (Concord series, 66 and HUGCC 2: TTBB)

—— *Sun and moon. Arr. by A. T. D.* ECS ᶜ1926 (Concord series, 94 and HUGCC 3: TTBB)

GRÉTRY, ANDRÉ ERNEST MODESTE, 1741–1813. *The watch is passing. La garde passe. From Les deux avares. Piano acc. by Boaz Piller. Edited by A. T. D.* ECS ᶜ1924 (Concord series, 67 and HUGCC 2: TTBB, with piano; English and French text)

HÄNDEL, GEORG FRIEDRICH, 1685–1759. *Father of heaven, from Judas Maccabæus. Edited, and the organ part arr., by A. T. D.* ECS ᶜ1936 (1710 and SCAB: SATB, with organ)

—— *Hallelujah! [From Saul] Edited, and the organ part arr., by A. T. D.* ECS ᶜ1936 (1698 and SCAB: SATB, with organ)

—— *Hallelujah, Amen, from Judas Maccabæus. Arr. by A. T. D.* ECS ᶜ1923 (Concord series, 38 and HUGCC 1: TTBB, with piano)   ANOTHER ARR.: *Edited by A. T. D.* ECS ᶜ1925 (304 and CAB: SATB, with organ)

—— *How beautiful are the feet of him, from the Messiah. Edited by A. T. D.* ECS ᶜ1925 (1129 and CAB: SATB, with organ) ANOTHER ARR.: *Arr. by A. T. D.* ECS ᶜ1927 (Concord series, 912 and HUGCC 4: TTBB, with organ)

—— *How excellent Thy name, O Lord. Abridged. Edited, and the organ part arr., by A. T. D.* ECS ᶜ1936 (1699 and SCAB: SATB, with organ)

—— *Let all their celestial concerts all unite, from Samson. Arr. by A. T. D.* ECS ᶜ1923 (Concord series, 39 and HUGCC 1: TTBB, with piano)

—— *Their bodies are buried in peace.* [*From The ways of Zion do mourn, Funeral anthem for Queen Caroline*] Edited, and the organ part arr., by A. T. D. ECS ᶜ1936 (1706 and SCAB: SATB, with organ)

—— *Then round about the starry throne, from Samson.* Edited, and the organ part arr., by A. T. D. ECS ᶜ1936 (1702 and SCAB: SATB, with organ)

—— *When His loud voice in thunder spoke, from Jephtha. Arr.* by A. T. D. Acc. by L. P. B. ECS ᶜ1930 (Concord series, 937 and HUGCC 5: TTBB, with piano, 4 hands)

—— *Your voices raise, from the sixth Chandos anthem. Arr. by* A. T. D. ECS ᶜ1925 (Concord series, 86 and HUGCC 2: TTBB, with piano)

HÄNDEL, GEORG FRIEDRICH, 1685–1759. Spurious and doubtful works. *In Thee, O Lord, have I trusted. In Te Domine.* Edited by A. T. D. ECS ᶜ1925, ᶜ1952 (1130 and CAB: SATB, with organ)

—— Spurious and doubtful works. *Thanks be to Thee. Acc. by* A. T. D. ECS ᶜ1935 (Concord series, 959 and HUGCC 6: men's or women's unison chorus, with organ) ANOTHER ARR.: ECS ᶜ1935 (Concord series, 960, HUGCC 6: men's or women's unison chorus, with piano)

HANDL, JACOB, *known as* GALLUS, 1550–1591. *Alleluia! today is Christ risen. Arr.* by A. T. D. ECS ᶜ1930 (Concord series, 931 and HUGCC 4: TTBB (Chorus I) TTBB (Chorus II) ANOTHER ARR.: *Alleluia! we sing with joy. Words* by H. W. F. Edited, and the organ part arr., by A. T. D. ECS ᶜ1936 (1692 and SCAB: SATB (Chorus I) SATB (Chorus II) with organ)

Has sorrow thy young days shaded; Irish folk-song. Arr. by A. T. D. ECS ᶜ1922 (Concord series, 23 and HUGCC 1: T solo, TTBB)

HASSLER, HANS LEO, 1564–1612. *Cantate Domino. Arr.* by A. T. D. ECS ᶜ1924 (Concord series, 68 and HUGCC 2: TTBB; Latin text)

HAYDN, JOSEPH, 1732–1809. *Lo, my Shepherd's hand divine; adapted from the Mass in G major.* Edited, and the organ part arr., by A. T. D. ECS ᶜ1936 (1715 and SCAB: SATB, with organ)

HAYDN, MICHAEL, 1737–1806. *Dark was the earth with clouds. Tenebræ factæ sunt. Edited by A. T. D.* ECS ᶜ1936 (1691 and SCAB: SATB)

HENSCHEL, *Sir* GEORG, 1850–1934. *Morning hymn. Arr. by A. T. D.* ECS ᶜ1923 (Concord series, 40 and HUGCC 1: TTBB)

Hunting song. Canto di caccia. Italian folk-song. Arr. by A. T. D. ECS ᶜ1930 (Concord series, 929 and HUGCC 4: TTBB (unison) with piano, 4 hands; English and Italian text) ANOTHER ED.: *The serenaders. Canto di caccia. Italian folk-song. Arr. by A. T. D.* ECS ᶜ1930 (Concord series, 569)

In dulci jubilo; ancient German carol. Arr. by A. T. D. ECS ᶜ1922 (Concord series, 25 and HUGCC 1: TTBB) ANOTHER ARR.: ECS ᶜ1929 (818: SSAA)

J'entends le moulin; French-Canadian folk-song. Arr. by A. T. D. ECS ᶜ1930 (Concord series, 925 and HUGCC 4: TB, with piano, 4 hands; French text)

JÜNGST, HUGO RICHARD, 1853–1923. *While by our sleeping flock we lay; the song of the shepherds. Arr. by Hugo Jüngst. Edited by A. T. D.* ECS ᶜ1936 (1685 and SCAB: SATB)

KASTAL'SKIĬ, ALEKSANDR DMITRIEVICH, 1856–1926. *All blessed, all holy, Lord God. Edited by A. T. D.* ECS ᶜ1936 (1707 and SCAB: SSAATTBB)

Là-bas, sur ces montagnes; French-Canadian folk-song. Arr. by A. T. D. ECS ᶜ1930 (Concord series, 925 and HUGCC 4: T solo, TTBB; French text)

LASSUS, ORLAND DE, d. 1594. *Adoremus te. Edited by A. T. D.* ECS ᶜ1935 (Concord series, 953 and HUGCC 6: TTT; Latin text)

—— *Echo-song (Antiphonal) Arr. by A. T. D.* ECS ᶜ1924 (Concord series, 69 and HUGCC 2: TTBB (Chorus 1) TTBB (Chorus II))

—— *Good-day, dear heart. Bonjour, mon cœur. Arr. by A. T. D.* ECS ᶜ1926 (Concord series, 92 and HUGCC 3: TTBB; English and French text)

—— *Inimici autem. Edited by A. T. D.* ECS ᶜ1935 (Concord series, 954 and HUGCC 6: TTBB; Latin text) ANOTHER ARR.: *Lord, to Thee we turn. Inimici autem. Edited by A. T. D.* ECS ᶜ1936 (1688 and SCAB: SATB)

—— *Matona, lovely maiden. Arr. by A. T. D.* ECS ᶜ1922 (Concord series, 26 and HUGCC 1: TTBB)

LEISRING, VOLCKMAR, *d.* 1637. *O filii et filiæ. Edited by A. T. D.* ECS ᶜ1923 (Concord series, 41 and HUGCC 1: TTBB (Chorus 1) TTBB (Chorus 11) Latin text)   ANOTHER ARR.: *Ye sons and daughters of the King. O filii et filiæ. Edited by A. T. D.* ECS ᶜ1925 (379 and CAB: SATB (Chorus 1) TTBB (Chorus 11)

LOTTI, ANTONIO, *d.* 1740. *Crucifixus. Arr. by A. T. D.* ECS ᶜ1923 (Concord series, 42 and HUGCC 2: TTBB; Latin text)

—— *Mighty Lord, Thy faithfulness abideth ever. Kyrie eleison. Edited by A. T. D.* ECS ᶜ1936 (1716 and SCAB: SAT)

—— *Now with hands to God uplifted. Ecce panis angelorum. Edited by A. T. D.* ECS ᶜ1936 (1696 and SCAB: SATB)

—— *Vere languores nostros. Edited by A. T. D.* ECS ᶜ1924 (Concord series, 70 and HUGCC 2: TTB; Latin text)   ANOTHER ARR.: *Surely he hath borne our griefs. Adapted by A. T. D.* ECS ᶜ1925 (1124 and CAB: SAATB)

MARENZIO, LUCA, *d.* 1599. *Spring returns; four-part madrigal. Arr. by A. T. D.* ECS ᶜ1933 (Concord series, 940 and HUGCC 5: TTBB)

Men of Harlech! Welsh folk-song. Arr. by A. T. D. ECS ᶜ1933 (Concord series, 943 and HUGCC 5: TTBB, with piano)

The Miracle of Saint Nicholas. Le miracle de Saint Nicolas. Old French carol. Arr. by A. T. D. Acc. by G. W. W. ECS ᶜ1924 (Concord series, 81 and HUGCC 2: T and Bar. solos, TTBB, with piano and organ; English and French text)   ANOTHER ARR.: ECS ᶜ1925 (311: A and T solos, SATB, with piano)

MENDELSSOHN-BARTHOLDY, FELIX, 1809–1847. *Behold a star from Jacob shining, from Christus. Edited, and the organ part arr., by A. T. D.* ECS ᶜ1936 (1683 and SCAB: SATB, with organ)

—— *Happy and blest are they, from St. Paul. Edited by A. T. D.* ECS ᶜ1925 (1133 and CAB: SATB, with organ)

—— *How lovely are the messengers, from St. Paul. Edited by A. T. D. Organ acc. by H. Clough-Leighter.* ECS ᶜ1925 (1134 and CAB: SATB, with organ)

The Monks' march; Welsh folk-song. Arr. by A. T. D. ECS ᶜ1933 (Concord series, 943 and HUGCC 5: TTBB, with piano)

MONTEVERDI, CLAUDIO, 1567–1643. *Ohimè! ohimè! Four-part madrigal. Arr. by A. T. D.* ECS ᶜ1928 (Concord series, 913 and HUGCC 4: TTBB; Italian text)

MORALES, CRISTÓBAL, 1500 (*c.*)–1553. *Me ye have bereaved; four-part motet. Arr. by A. T. D.* ECS ᶜ1933 (Concord series, 942 and HUGCC 5: TTBB)

MORLEY, THOMAS, 1557–1603? *April is in my mistress' face; four-part madrigal. Arr. by A. T. D.* ECS ᶜ1933 (Concord series, 939 and HUGCC 5: TTBB)

—— *Dainty, fine, sweet nymph. Arr. by A. T. D.* ECS ᶜ1923 (Concord series, 43 and HUGCC 1: TTBB)

—— *Fire, fire, my heart; four-part madrigal. Arr. by A. T. D.* ECS ᶜ1924 (Concord series, 71 and HUGCC 2: TTBB)

—— *My bonny lass. Arr. by A. T. D.* ECS ᶜ1922 (Concord series, 20 and HUGCC 1: TTBB)

—— *Now is the month of Maying. Arr. by A. T. D.* ECS ᶜ1922 (Concord series, 22 and HUGCC 1: TTBB)

—— *Shoot, false love, I care not. Arr. by A. T. D.* ECS ᶜ1930 (Concord series, 920 and HUGCC 4: TTBB)

MOZART, JOHANN CHRYSOSTOM WOLFGANG AMADEUS, 1756–1791. *Mighty Spirit, all transcending. Ave verum Corpus. Edited by A. T. D.* ECS ᶜ1936 (1695 and SCAB: SATB)

NANINO, GIOVANNI MARIA, 1545 (*c.*)–1607. *Diffusa est gratia. Arr. by A. T. D.* ECS ᶜ1935 (Concord series, 949 and HUGCC 6: TTBB; Latin text) ANOTHER ARR.: *Grant unto us Thy blessing. Diffusa est gratia. Edited by A. T. D.* ECS ᶜ1936 (1711 and SCAB: SATB)

Oh, why camest thou before me; Welsh folk-song. Arr. by A. T. D. ECS ᶜ1933 (Concord series, 943 and HUGCC 5: TTBB)

PALESTRINA, GIOVANNI PIERLUIGI DA, 1525?–1594. *Adoremus te (Antiphonal) Edited by A. T. D.* ECS ᶜ1922 (Concord series, 44 and HUGCC 1: TTBB; Latin text) ANOTHER ARR.: *Alleluia, Lord God! Adoremus te (Antiphonal) Edited by A. T. D.* ECS ᶜ1925 (307 and CAB: SATB (Chorus 1) SATB (Chorus 11))

—— *Adoremus te, Christe. Edited by A. T. D.* ECS ᶜ1935 (Concord series, 950 and HUGCC 6: TTBB; Latin text)

——*Ecce, quomodo moritur. Arr. by A. T. D.* ECS ᶜ1923
(Concord series, 45 and HUGCC 1: TTBB; Latin text)

——*Holy, loving Father. Dei Mater alma. Edited by A. T. D.*
ECS ᶜ1936 (1712 and SCAB: SATB)

——*Improperia (Antiphonal) Arr. by A. T. D.* ECS ᶜ1923
(Concord series, 46 and HUGCC 1: TTBB (Chorus 1) TTBB
(Chorus 11) Latin text)

——*O holy Father, infinite in mercy. O bone Jesu. Edited by
A. T. D.* ECS ᶜ1925 (1137 and CAB: SATB)

——*Tenebræ factæ sunt. Arr. by A. T. D.* ECS ᶜ1924 (Concord
series, 72 and HUGCC 2: TTBB; Latin text)

——*Thou all transcendent Deity. Jesu, Rex admirabilis. Edited
by A. T. D.* ECS ᶜ1936 (1697 and SCAB: SATB)

PAXTON, STEPHEN, 1735–1787. *How sweet, how fresh this vernal
day. Arr. by A. T. D.* ECS ᶜ1930 (Concord series, 924 and HUGCC
4: TTBB)

The Pedlar; Russian folk-song. Arr. by A. T. D. ECS ᶜ1937
(Concord series, 957 and HUGCC 6: T͡TB͡B, with piano, 4 hands)

PERGOLESI, GIOVANNI BATTISTA, 1710–1736. *Glory to God in
the highest. Arr. by A. T. D.* ECS ᶜ1923 (Concord series, 47 and
HUGCC 1: TTBB, with piano or organ)

PILLOIS, JACQUES, 1877–   *Flowering orchards. Tr. from the
original French of Louis Tiercelin by Amy Clare Griffin. Arr. for
men's voices by Archibald T. Davison.* [Boston] C. C. Birchard,
ᶜ1933 (931: TTBB)

PRAETORIUS, MICHAEL, 1571–1621. *Lo, how a rose e'er blooming.
Arr. by A. T. D.* ECS ᶜ1922 (Concord series, 24 and HUGCC 1:
TTBB)

*Prayer of Thanksgiving; Netherlands folk-song. [Edited by
A. T. D.]* ECS ᶜ1925 (306 and CAB: Unison voices with SATB
ending, with organ) ANOTHER ARR.: ECS ᶜ1925 (1033: Unison
voices with SSAA ending, with organ)

PURCELL, HENRY, 1658 or 9–1695. *Glory and worship are before
Him. [Abridged] Edited by A. T. D.* ECS ᶜ1925 (1108 and CAB:
SATB, with organ)

—— *Let my prayer come up into Thy presence* (*Psalm 141: 2*) *Arr. and adapted by Sir Frederick Bridge. Edited by A. T. D.* ECS ᶜ1925 (1109 and CAB: SSATB, with organ)

—— *O give thanks unto the Lord* (*Psalm 106: 1, 4, 48*) *Abridged. Edited, and the organ part arr., by A. T. D.* ECS ᶜ1936 (1700 and SCAB: SATB, with organ)

—— *O sing unto the Lord.* [*Abridged*] *Edited by A. T. D.* ECS ᶜ1925 (1103 and CAB: SATB, with organ)

—— *Rejoice in the Lord alway.* [*Abridged*] *Edited by A. T. D.* ECS ᶜ1925 (1101 and CAB: SATB, with organ)

—— *Remember not, Lord, our offences. Edited by A. T. D.* ECS ᶜ1936 (1609 and SCAB: SSATB, with organ)

—— *Thou knowest, Lord. Edited by A. T. D.* ECS ᶜ1925 (376 and CAB: SATB, with organ)

—— *With drooping wings, ye cupids come, from Dido and Aeneas. Arr. by A. T. D.* ECS ᶜ1925 (Concord series, 85 and HUGCC 2: TTBB)

RACHMANINOFF, SERGEI, 1873–1943. *Triumph! Thanksgiving. Edited by A. T. D.* ECS ᶜ1925 (309 and CAB: SATTB, with organ)

Rantin', rovin' Robin; Scotch folk-song. Arr. by A. T. D. ECS ᶜ1926 (Concord series, 84 and HUGCC 2: Bar. solo, TTBB, with piano) ANOTHER ARR. ECS ᶜ1932 (1198: A or Bar. solo, SATB, with piano)

Reapers' song; Bohemian folk-song. Arr. by A. T. D. ECS ᶜ1927 (Concord series, 905 and HUGCC 3: TTBB, with piano, 4 hands)

RIMSKIĬ-KORSAKOV, NIKOLAĬ ANDREEVICH, 1844–1908. *Choruses from Sadko. Arr. by A. T. D.* ECS ᶜ1930 (Concord series, 935 and HUGCC 5: TTBB, with piano, 4 hands; French text)

RUBINSTEIN, ANTON, 1829–1894. *Three pictures, from The tower of Babel. Arr. by A. T. D.* ECS ᶜ1923 (Concord series, 48 and HUGCC 1: TTBB, with piano)

SCHUBERT, FRANZ PETER, 1797–1828. *Credo, from Mass in A flat. Arr. by A. T. D.* ECS ᶜ1930 (Concord series, 933 and HUGCC 4: TTBB, with piano; Latin text)

SCHÜTZ, HEINRICH, 1585–1672. *Since Christ his head in sorrow bowed, from The seven last words. Edited by A. T. D.* ECS ᶜ1936 (1690 and SCAB: SATTB)

—— *Since Christ our Lord was crucified. Arr. by A. T. D.* ECS ᶜ1926 (Concord series, 88 and HUGCC 3: TTBB)

SHVEDOV, KONSTANTIN NIKOLAEVICH, 1886– *With heart uplifted. Arr. by A. T. D.* ECS ᶜ1924 (Concord series, 74 and HUGCC 2: TTBB)

Song of the life-boat men; Russian folk-song. Arr. by A. T. D. ECS ᶜ1924 (Concord series, 73 and HUGCC 2: Bar. solo, TTBB, with piano)

Spanish ladies; English folk-song. Arr. by A. T. D. ECS ᶜ1937 (Concord series, 958 and HUGCC 6: TTBB, with piano, 4 hands)

SULLIVAN, *Sir* ARTHUR SEYMOUR, 1842–1900. *Choruses from The Mikado. Arr. by A. T. D.* ECS ᶜ1936 (Concord series, 946 and HUGCC 5: TTBB, with piano, 4 hands)

—— *Choruses from Pinafore. Arr. by A. T. D.* ECS ᶜ1933 (Concord series, 944 and HUGCC 5: TTBB, with piano, 4 hands)

—— *Choruses from Princess Ida. Arr. by A. T. D.* ECS ᶜ1937 (Concord series, 962–963 and HUGCC 6: TTBB, with piano, 4 hands)

—— *Choruses from Ruddigore. Arr. by A. T. D.* ECS ᶜ1933 (Concord series, 945 and HUGCC 5: TTBB, with piano, 4 hands)

—— *Choruses from The yeomen of the guard. Arr. by A. T. D.* ECS ᶜ1929 (Concord series, 918 and HUGCC 4: TTBB, with piano) ANOTHER ARR.: *Piano acc. by A. T. D.* ECS ᶜ1931 (1181: SATTBB, with piano)

— *Echo. Arr. by A. T. D.* ECS ᶜ1924 (Concord series, 75 and HUGCC 2: TTBB)

—— *Finale from The gondoliers. Arr. by A. T. D. Acc. by G. W. W.* ECS ᶜ1925 (Concord series, 82 and HUGCC 2: TTBB, with piano, 4 hands. CONTENTS: Dance a cachuca. — Fandango. — Bolero)

—— *Four choruses from Patience. Arr. by A. T. D.* ECS ᶜ1928 (Concord series, 914 and HUGCC 4: TTBB, with piano, 4 hands.

CONTENTS: The magnet and the churn. — Oh list, while we a love confess. — When I go out of door. — After much debate internal) ANOTHER ARR.: *Piano acc. by A. T. D.* ECS ^c1931 (1182: SATB, with piano, 4 hands)

—— *Turn Thy face from my sins (Psalm 51: 10, 11)* Edited by *A. T. D.* ECS ^c1925 (377 and CAB: STAB, with organ)

SWELINCK, JAN PIETERESZ., 1562–1621. *Arise, O ye servants of God. Arr. by A. T. D.* ECS ^c1924 (Concord series, 76 and HUGCC 2: TTTBBB)

TALLIS, THOMAS, 1505 (*c.*)–1585. *All people that on earth do dwell. Edited by A. T. D.* ECS ^c1936 (1708 and SCAB: SATB)

——*O Lord, give Thy Holy Spirit. Edited by A. T. D.* ECS ^c1936 (1718 and SCAB: SATB)

Tell me, fair one. Dimmi, o bella. Italian folk-song. Arr. by A. T. D. ECS ^c1930 (Concord series, 929 and HUGCC 4: T solo, TTBB; English and Italian text)

Thou lovest me so dearly. Tu mi vuoi tanto bene. Italian folk-song. Arr. by A. T. D. ECS ^c1930 (Concord series, 929 and HUGCC 4: TTBB, with piano; English and Italian text)

Thy wisdom, Lord, all thought transcendeth (Divine praise: Kol slaven)   Traditional Russian melody. Arr. by A. T. D. ECS ^c1936 (1703 and SCAB: SATB, with organ)

Touro-louro-louro! Burgundian air. Arr. by A. T. D. ECS ^c1931 (Concord series, 932 and HUGCC 4: TTBB; English and French Provençal text)

Les Trois filles d'un prince; French-Canadian folk-song. Arr. by A. T. D. ECS ^c1930 (Concord series, 925 and HUGCC 4: T solo, TTBB, with piano; French text)

Turn ye to me; Scotch folk-song. Arr. by A. T. D. ECS ^c1935 (1513: SSA, with piano)   ANOTHER ARR.: ECS ^c1927 (Concord series, 908 and HUGCC 3: T solo, TTBB, with piano)

VIADANA, LODOVICO GROSSI DA, 1564 (*c.*)–1645. *O sacrum convivium. Edited by A. T. D.* ECS ^c1924 (Concord series, 78 and HUGCC 2: TTBB; Latin text)

VICTORIA, TOMÁS LUIS DA, 1540 (*c.*)–1611. *Jesu dulcis. Arr. by*

A. T. D. ECS ᶜ1924 (Concord series, 79 and HUGCC 2: TTBB; Latin text)   ANOTHER ARR.: *O Thou joy of loving hearts. Jesu dulcis memoria. Edited by A. T. D.* ECS ᶜ1925 (1125 and CAB: SATB)

——*O vos omnes. Arr. by A. T. D.* ECS ᶜ1928 (Concord series, 915 and HUGCC 4: TTBB; Latin text)

VULPIUS, MELCHIOR, 1560 (*c*.)–1615. *An Easter hallelujah. Arr. by A. T. D.* ECS ᶜ1928 (Concord series, 98 and HUGCC 3: TTBB (Chorus I) TTBB (Chorus II))

——*Now God be praised in heav'n above. Gelobt sei Gott. Edited by A. T. D.* ECS ᶜ1936 (1693 and SCAB: SATB)

WAGNER, RICHARD, 1813–1883. *Chorus and finale from The Mastersingers of Nuremberg. Arr. by A. T. D.* ECS ᶜ1928 (Concord series, 917 and HUGCC 4: TTBB, with piano, 4 hands)

WEELKES, THOMAS, 1575 (*c*.)–1623. *Hark! all ye lovely saints above. Arr. by A. T. D.* ECS ᶜ1928 (Concord series, 916 and HUGCC 4: TTBB)

——*The nightingale. Arr. by A. T. D.* ECS ᶜ1923 (Concord series, 49 and HUGCC 1: TTB)

WESLEY, SAMUEL SEBASTIAN, 1810–1876. *Lead me, Lord, in Thy righteousness. Edited by A. T. D.* ECS ᶜ1925 (378 and CAB: SATB, with organ)

WILBYE, JOHN, 1574–1638. *Adieu, sweet Amarillis; four-part madrigal. Arr. by A. T. D.* ECS ᶜ1924 (Concord series, 80 and HUGCC 2: TTBB)

Ye watchers and ye holy ones; 17th-century German melody. Arr. by A. T. D. ECS ᶜ1924 (Concord series, 65 and HUGCC 2: TTBB, with piano and organ)   ANOTHER ARR.: *Ye watchers and holy ones. Lasst uns erfreuen herzlich sehr. 17th-century German melody. Arr. by A. T. D.* ECS ᶜ1928 (389: SATB, with piano and organ; English and German text)   ANOTHER ARR.: *Ye watchers and holy ones. 17th-century German melody, from Geistliche Kirchengesang, Cologne, 1623. Arr. by A. T. D.* ECS ᶜ1931 (1780: SATB, with piano)